ASIAN CAPITALISM
REGULATION OF COM. _ . . . . ION:
TOWARDS A REGULATORY GEOGRAPHY
OF GLOBAL COMPETITION LAW

Asian Capitalism and the Regulation of Competition explores the implications Asian forms of capitalism and their regulation of competition have for the emerging global competition law regime. Expert contributors from a variety of backgrounds explore the topic through the lenses of formal law, soft law, and transnational regulation, and make extensive comparisons with Euro-American and global models. Case studies include Japan, China, and Vietnam, and thematic studies include examinations of competition law's relationship with other regulatory terrains such as public law, market culture, regulatory geography, and transnational production networks.

MICHAEL W. DOWDLE is an Assistant Professor at the National University of Singapore Faculty of Law, and a Visiting Professorial Fellow at the Asia-Pacific Business Regulation Group of the Department of Business Law at Monash University.

JOHN GILLESPIE is the Director of the Asia-Pacific Business Regulation Group at Monash University. His research and teaching interests include Asian comparative law, law and development theory, and regulatory theory.

IMELDA MAHER is the Sutherland Professor of European Law at the School of Law, University of Dublin. She has published extensively on competition law, where her distinctive contribution is to analyse competition law from a law and governance perspective.

ASIAN CAPITALISM AND THE REGULATION OF COMPETITION

Towards a Regulatory Geography of Global Competition Law

Edited by

MICHAEL W. DOWDLE,

JOHN GILLESPIE,

and

IMELDA MAHER

CAMBRIDGE UNIVERSITY PRESS

CAMBRIDGE
UNIVERSITY PRESS

University Printing House, Cambridge CB2 8BS, United Kingdom

One Liberty Plaza, 20th Floor, New York, NY 10006, USA

477 Williamstown Road, Port Melbourne, VIC 3207, Australia

314-321, 3rd Floor, Plot 3, Splendor Forum, Jasola District Centre, New Delhi - 110025, India

79 Anson Road, #06-04/06, Singapore 079906

Cambridge University Press is part of the University of Cambridge.

It furthers the University's mission by disseminating knowledge in the pursuit of education, learning and research at the highest international levels of excellence.

www.cambridge.org
Information on this title: www.cambridge.org/9781108738224

© Cambridge University Press 2013

First published 2013
First paperback edition 2019

A catalogue record for this publication is available from the British Library

Library of Congress Cataloging in Publication data
Asian capitalism and the regulation of competition : towards a regulatory geography of global competition law / Edited by Michael W. Dowdle, John Gillespie, and Imelda Maher.
pages   cm
Includes bibliographical references and index.
ISBN 978-1-107-02742-8 (Hardback)
1. Antitrust law–Asia.   2. Capitalism–Asia.   3. Restraint of trade–Asia.
I. Dowdle, Michael W., editor.   II. Gillespie, John, editor.   III. Maher, Imelda, editor.
KM758.A85 2013
343.507´21–dc23
2012047169

ISBN 978-1-107-02742-8 Hardback
ISBN 978-1-108-73822-4 Paperback

CONTENTS

v

TABLES

FIGURES

CONTRIBUTORS

FREDERIC C. DEYO is Professor of Sociology and Director of Graduate Studies in the Sociology Department of Binghamton University (State University of New York at Binghamton).

MICHAEL W. DOWDLE is an Assistant Professor at the National University of Singapore Faculty of Law, and Visiting Professorial Fellow at the Asia-Pacific Business Regulation Group in the Department of Business Law at Monash University.

DAVID J. GERBER is Distinguished Professor of Law and Co-Director of the Program in International and Comparative Law at the Illinois Institute of Technology (IIT) Chicago-Kent College of Law.

JOHN S. GILLESPIE is a Professor and Director of the Asia-Pacific Business Regulation Group in the Department of Business Law at Monash University.

BOB JESSOP is Distinguished Professor in the Department of Sociology and Co-Director of the Cultural Political Economy Research Centre, Lancaster University.

IMELDA MAHER is Sutherland Professor in European Law at the School of Law, University College Dublin.

TONY PROSSER is Professor of Public Law at the University of Bristol Law School and Visiting Professor at the College of Europe, Bruges.

NGAI-LING SUM is a Senior Lecturer in the Department of Politics, Philosophy and Religion and Co-Director of the Cultural Political Economy Research Centre, Lancaster University.

SIMON VANDE WALLE is a JSPS Research Fellow at the University of Tokyo Graduate Schools for Law and Politics.

HENRY WAI-CHUNG YEUNG is Professor of Economic Geography at the National University of Singapore.

WENTONG ZHENG is an Assistant Professor at the University of Florida Levin College of Law.

ACKNOWLEDGEMENTS

The subject of this book was not born of our own imagination. We stole it.

In spring 2008, Michael Dowdle ran a graduate seminar on 'Asian Regulation' at Sciences Po in Paris. As with many graduate seminars, or at least the better ones, he was as much student as facilitator, meandering his way through an idea that he was never completely certain was really a topic worth the name. All that changed when he received a term paper from one of the students in that seminar, Soojin Nam. Working out of the variety of capitalisms literature, and tying it together with John Haley's work on Japanese competition law and regulation and Kanishka Jayasuryia's work on Asian styles of law, she offered an extremely compelling demonstration that the best and most fruitful lens for exploring for an Asian regulation would likely be found in its regulation of market competition – that is, competition law. In this case, the student ended up teaching the teacher, as the good ones often do.

Since he works primarily in public law regulation, Dowdle could not go about stealing Nam's idea immediately. But opportunity came knocking in summer 2009, when the Asia-Pacific Business Regulation Group (APBRG) of what is now the Department of Business Law at Monash University, where he was at the time a Visiting Professorial Fellow, offered him a sizeable grant to organize an international workshop on some aspect of Asian regulation. He immediately recalled Nam's paper, and recognized this as a unique chance to explore her thesis further. Monash agreed, and he and the director of the APBRG, Professor John Gillespie, set about organizing the workshop.

The first issue that needed to be decided was where to hold the workshop. For this, Dowdle and Gillespie decided to approach Professor Imelda Maher at the Law School of University College Dublin (UCD). Competition law at UCD is not only renowned throughout Europe, but its pronouncedly comparative focus meshed particularly well with the unique expertise of the APBRG in the diverse practices of business regulation found in the Asian region. UCD agreed to host the workshop under the auspices of its newly formed Centre for Regulation and Governance, and also agreed to provide additional funding.

The workshop, entitled 'The Regulation of Competition: The Case of Asian Capitalism', ran from 30 September to 2 October 2010. A nice write-up, complete with photo, can be found at www.ucd.ie/reggov/newsevents/body,71121,en.html. In addition to the contributors to this volume, other participants in that workshop included Dr Michele Ford of the Department of Indonesian Studies at the University of Sydney, Dr Niamh Hardiman of the UCD School of Politics and International Relations, Professor David Levi-Faur of the Department of Political Science at the Hebrew University of Jerusalem, Professor Ian McEwin of the Faculty of Law at the National University of Singapore, and Professor Colin Scott of the UCD School of Law. Soojin Nam – then completing her JD at the Harvard Law School, now an associate at Axinn, Veltrop & Harkrider LLP in New York – also participated and, in addition, served as the workshop's rapporteur.

The workshop would not have been a success were it not for the support and contributions of a number of others. These include the then dean of the UDC Law School, Professor John Jackson, research assistants John Biggins, Marek Martyniszyn, Yichen Yang, Justyna Cudo, and especially Dan Hayden, through whose immense competence Imelda secured considerable competitive advantage (as is only appropriate for a workshop dealing with capitalism). On the administrative side, the talents of Angela Ennis and Sinead Hennessy proved invaluable. We are also very grateful to the National University of Ireland – especially its registrar, Dr Attracta Halpin, and its staff – for allowing us to hold the workshop in its wonderful Merrion Square house.

In March 2012 the APBRG held a follow-up seminar on the findings of the workshop, whose participants have greatly helped us to understand the possibilities and implications of the studies we had collected. Particularly deserving of mention in this regard are Professor Brandon Sweeney of the Department of Business Law at Monash (also a member of the APBRG group) and Professor Walter Stoffel of the Department of International Law and Company Law at the University of Fribourg and a former president of the Swiss Competition Commission.

Finally, we would like to express our deepest appreciation to Philippa Youngman and her editorial team at Cambridge University Press. Being able to work with her on this project was an unqualified privilege, and the book is inestimably better thanks to her efforts.

Funding from both the Asia-Pacific Business Regulation Group and the UCD School of Law is again gratefully acknowledged.

* * *

Chapter 7, 'State capitalism and the regulation of competition in China', by Wentong Zheng, was adapted from his 'Transplanting Antitrust in China: Economic Transition, Market Structure, and State Control', as published in the *University of Pennsylvania Journal of International Law*, vol. 32 (2010): 643–721.

Chapter 12, 'Addressing the development deficit of competition policy: the role of economic networks', by Frederic C. Deyo, was adapted from Chapter 11 of his book, *Reforming Asian Labor Systems*, published by Cornell University Press in 2012. We are grateful to Cornell University Press for permission to publish this adaptation.

Michael W. Dowdle, Singapore
John Gillespie, Melbourne
Imelda Maher, Dublin

~

Introduction and overview

MICHAEL W. DOWDLE, JOHN GILLESPIE,
AND IMELDA MAHER

This is a rather unorthodox treatment of global competition law and Asian competition law. We do not explore for the micro-economic ideal type of global competition law, nor do we survey the convergences with and deviations from this ideal type to be found throughout the countries of Asia. For this we would recommend, for a start, David Gerber's *Global Competition Law*[1] and R. Ian McEwin's *Competition Law in Southeast Asia*.[2]

(Of course, there is no 'global competition law' in the positive law sense of the term. Here, following David Gerber, global competition law refers to and is identified by that projected point of convergence to which many argue that domestic competition law is or should be evolving. See Chapter 1, pp. 21–4.)

Rather, this is an exploration, not of the possible unities of global competition law, but of its possible diversities. It is founded on a proposition that global competition law is best seen as encompassed not in a single ideal type, but in a multiplicity of ideal types – in the wide diversity of roles and functionalities that markets and market competition actually have in human society. Peter Hall and David Soskice have shown us that there are many capitalisms, not just one.[3] This being the case, the same would hold true for capitalism's way of structuring and regulating market competition. The future of global competition law does not lie in a particular 'sovereignty' but in pluralism.

---

[1] David J. Gerber, *Global Competition Law: Law, Markets and Globalization* (Oxford University Press, 2010).

[2] R. Ian McEwin, *Competition Law in Southeast Asia* (Cambridge University Press, forthcoming).

[3] Peter A. Hall and David Soskice. 'An Introduction to Varieties of Capitalism', in Peter A. Hall and David Soskice (eds.), *Varieties of Capitalism: The Institutional Foundations of Comparative Advantage* (Oxford University Press, 2001), pp. 1–70.

For centuries, pluralism was a defining feature of the East and Southeast Asian legal world. It remains woven deeply into many regulatory systems there. As we shall see, it is reflected in Asian capitalism in the same way that the varieties of capitalism found in the North Atlantic reflect the different ways that national legal systems there regulate corporate governance. And it is reflected in the diversity of models that Asian countries use to regulate competition. In this sense, we examine this Asian diversity, this Asian regulation of competition, in order to find insights into our own condition.

This volume is divided into five parts. The first part maps out the various ideas, concepts, and concerns that frame this volume's investigation. The second part then looks more specifically at issues surrounding the core concept relevant to our investigation, that of competition. The next two parts then explore how the regulation of competition in Asia plays out against this more global concept. Part III looks at competition regulation in the representative Asian countries of Japan, China, and Vietnam. And Part IV then looks at particular cross-cutting experiences in Asian competition regulation, namely the special problems of peripheral environments and issues of public law and regulatory independence. Finally, Part V looks at Asian competition from an evolutionary, dynamic perspective, exploring patterns of change and possible evolutionary trajectories, both internally and from the perspective of a global competition law.

Part I sets out the issues and conceptual frameworks that will inform our investigation. In Chapter 1, Michael Dowdle introduces us to the particular topics and issues that this volume seeks to explore. As discussed above, this volume explores the relationship between Asian capitalism and its way of regulating competition (its 'competition law') and the global movement towards a global competition law. In order to conduct such an exploration, we need first to understand what is Asia in the context of Asian capitalism, what are the defining features of Asian capitalism, and why Asian capitalism's particular regulation of competition provides an especially promising lens for interrogating the emerging transnational movement towards a global competition law. This is the focus of Chapter 1.

Chapter 1 also explains the concept and phenomenon of what this volume terms 'regulatory geography', which brings the legal-theoretical construct of 'global competition law' into communication with the economic-geographical construct of 'Asian capitalism'. The idea of regulatory geography stems from a recognition that asymmetries in spatial distributions of economic and cultural capacities, as detailed for example in the disciplines of economic geography and cultural geography, generate corresponding spatial asymmetries in regulatory needs and capacities. Dowdle shows how this means that global competition law, as it is presently conceived, is not uniformly viable across geographic space in the way that it assumes itself to be. He then applies this resulting regulatory geography of competition law to 'Asian capitalism', generating in the process a speculative and preliminary 'mapping' of Asian competition regulation that details possible spatial patternings of diversities in regulatory issues and needs, which include diversities that are internal to Asian capitalism itself, and diversities that might distinguish Asian capitalism as a whole from North Atlantic varieties of capitalism.

Whereas Dowdle looks at how global competition law is likely to impact Asia, David Gerber, in Chapter 2, examines how Asia is likely to affect global competition law. As he describes, at its heart global competition law is a project of global convergence in national competition law regimes. Gerber explores what effect Asian experience with competition, much of it very recent, might have on this desired dynamic of convergence. When viewed from the perspective of formal law, Asia's recent experiences do appear convergent in the way in which global competition law projects. But, as he shows, underneath this formal surface lies a fair number of historical, economic, and social dynamics that render some of this apparent convergence illusory. Ultimately, he concludes that in order for this convergence to proceed, global competition law will probably have to evolve so as to better accommodate at least some of the challenges and issues of Asian capitalism, just as Asian capitalism is evolving so as to accommodate the agenda of global competition law.

The volume will return to re-examine the issues and hypotheses raised in this first part in its final chapter, but before doing so, these hypotheses and the value of the analytic frameworks that gave rise to them need to be interrogated through the lens of actual practice. This is done through the studies that make up the remaining four parts of the volume.

Part II looks at the political economic dynamics that structure, inform, and constrain the regulatory aspirations of global competition law. Imelda Maher first examines the institutional structure and foci of that law, focusing in particular on the networked structure that it is adopting on a more global level, and the agencification that it is adopting at the national level. These two institutional developments derive from the same phenomenon, a desire to isolate competition regulation from politics. Domestically, this isolation is promoted through the use of independent regulatory agencies. Globally, it is promoted through the establishment of regulatory networks that allow these agencies to communicate and co-ordinate with each other directly, without having to pass through formal state-to-state protocols that are designed for the pursuit of global politics. Maher concludes by showing how this effort to separate competition from politics has proved to be problematic even in the contexts of the North Atlantic states, where the institutionalization of this separation has been most robustly explored and pursued. This separation and its problematics will be further explored specifically in the context of Asia by Tony Prosser in Chapter 10.

In Chapter 4, Ngai-Ling Sum uses a cultural political economy approach to explore the evolving ideological frameworks that global competition law uses to drive its convergences. Here, the story becomes more complicated, as the international community has over the years been forced to adopt a number of different justifications for the global adoption of particular laws and structures for regulating competition. Originally, this ideology focused on the global good of free trade. But with the collapse of the Doha Round of international trade negotiations among the membership of the World Trade Organization (WTO), it evolved into an ideological focus on economic development. More recently, the global competition community seems to have given up the search for an ideological underpinning, and has instead turned simply to presenting itself as an expert in economic regulation, whose regulatory prescriptions, proffered primarily in the particular formularies known as 'best practices', are recommended simply on the basis of the advocating agency's claim to have superior knowledge of the issue.

Bob Jessop's chapter that follows helps to explain the ideological instability detailed by Sum. Jessop shows us that underneath and concealed by the unified conceptual front presented by global competition law is an extraordinarily complex melange of competing and often contradictory concerns, interests, goals, and understandings. Jessop shows how market competition actually encompasses and is shaped by a huge diversity of often competing social, political, and economic dynamics, and that neither competition law nor the orthodox, neoliberal understanding from which it derives – of what it is and how it is that market competition contributes to social welfare – get anywhere close to adequately capturing these dynamics, and often ends up blinding itself to crucial contradictions within its particular world view – such as the internal tension between competition and 'competitiveness', or between competition and innovation. Jessop concludes that, given this complexity, standard Weberian conceptions of regulation may not be up to the task, and that competition regulation may require more heterarchical forms of regulation, sometimes known as meta-governance. The volume returns to this issue in its concluding chapter.

In Parts III and IV we look at how competition regulation actually plays out in various countries and with regard to particular issues in Asia. Part III focuses on particular countries. These include Japan, a representative core economy (as per Dowdle's mapping in Chapter 1), China, Asia's principal intermediate economy, and Vietnam, a more peripheral economy. These will be followed, in Part IV, by chapters looking specifically at how Asian competition regulation manifests itself in economically peripheral environments, and at the interplay in numerous Asian countries between politics and competition policy, as particularly expressed in the notion of regulatory independence.

In Chapter 6, in his investigation of Japanese engagement with competition regulation, Simon Vande Walle documents Japan's well-recognized ambivalence towards North Atlantic – and particularly American – models. Basically, he finds that, when the economy is doing well, Japan tends to embrace a more managed form of competition that is in conflict with standard global competition law understandings of how competition should be regulated (and towards what ends). But when the economy stagnates, as it has done particularly over the past two decades, Japan has tended to find the orthodox, North Atlantic regulatory perspective from which global competition law derives more attractive. In demonstrating this, he shows that conventional portrayals of Japan's economic-regulatory experiences as either confirming or disproving the universal applicability of the neoliberal presumptions that inform global competition law are too simplistic. Japan both embraces and rejects this model in different ways and at different times.

In Chapter 7, Wentong Zheng introduces us to China's competition regulation regime. China's efforts to regulate competition through law (as opposed to simply through the party-state bureaucracy) is of relatively recent vintage, and it remains to be seen how many of its positive, legislative articulations will play out in practice. Like that of Japan, China's approach to competition regulation is distinctly fragmented. But whereas Japan's fragmentation articulates itself temporally, through cyclical changes in legislative approach, China's fragmentation is coeval, articulating itself in the framing legislation itself. It is a fragmentation in which different sectors of the economy are subject, sometimes formally, sometimes informally, to different competition regulatory regimes, and in which enforcement of this regime is also fragmented across numerous regulatory authorities (none really independent in the sense of an independent regulatory agency).

Finally, Chapter 8, by John Gillespie, explores competition regulation in Vietnam, a more archetypically peripheral Asian environment. Here we also find a fragmented regulatory environment, one fragmented coevally as in China. But in contrast to that of China, in which the fragmentation is partly formalized in the law, Vietnam's formal competition law runs primarily according to global models. Vietnam's fragmentation is largely informal, and corresponds with fault lines that separate the informal legal structures associated with social class. This has a number of important implications for competition regulation. It shows, consistent with the observations of Bob Jessop, that market competition can be regulated by numerous regulatory regimes, both informal and formal, social and legal.

In the next chapter Dowdle explores some further regulatory implications of this particular kind of fragmentation. That chapter, Chapter 9, opens Part IV, and looks at the special problems that the orthodox model of competition poses to peripheral economic environments in Asia. Using China's recent problem with melamine milk adulteration as an example, it shows that adulteration was more than anything else the product of neoliberal market competition as it operates within the context of a peripheral regulatory environment. More specifically, it was due to the fact that neoliberal forms of market competition – and in particular its demand that market regulation be institutionally segregated from non-economic, social regulation – require complementary regulatory conditions and capacities that generally are not present in or available to peripheral economic environments. Without such conditions and capacities, the neoliberal model can become socially dysfunctional, as was the case with melamine milk adulteration.

Following on from this, Chapter 10, by Tony Prosser, examines how competition regulation interacts with politics in various countries throughout the region. As described in Imelda Maher's chapter, the orthodox model prescribes that market competition be regulated through independent regulatory agencies, so as to effectuate the segregation of economic regulation from social regulation critiqued in Chapter 9. Consistent with themes introduced to us by Bob Jessop, Prosser shows that the reality is much more complicated than this model portrays, even in the North Atlantic economies it is often claimed to be channelling.

Turning to Asian articulations of this relationship, he finds that whereas the orthodox model prefers juridical negotiation of the conflict between economic and social goals, Asian countries in general seem to prefer to conduct such negotiations through the political system. He suggests that one of the possible causes of this difference is that, in contrast to competition law in North Atlantic countries, in Asia competition law and regulation come more in the form of legal transplants (often adopted under pressure from transnational actors). Such transplantations are themselves ultimately political decisions, and this gives a distinctly political colour to the transplanted competition law, something not found in the competition laws of most North Atlantic countries. Since competition law is more innately political in Asia, it naturally favours political as opposed to juridical forms of regulatory negotiation. And this argues against an independent regulatory agency model of regulation.

Finally, Part V explores Asian capitalism and its attendant regulation of competition from a more dynamic, evolutionary perspective. It opens with a chapter by Henry Yeung that explores the evolving nature of Asia's distinctively disaggregated production processes – that is, production chains. He shows that these processes are becoming more inter-linked, resulting in an evolution from production chains to 'production networks'. One of the major consequences of this evolution is that it is freeing Asian capitalism from its traditional dependence on the 'develop-mental state'. In Chapter 12, Frederic Deyo then looks at the implications of this evolution for Asian approaches to competition and competitive-ness. Looking in particular at a specific kind of industrial park, one that first emerged in Taiwan and South Korea, he identifies a new, social-regulatory side to Asian efforts to promote competitiveness. This Asian form of the industrial park goes far beyond its North Atlantic counter-part in providing not simply infrastructural attractions to residential firms but also a wide variety of social services both to firms and directly to the employees of these firms, such as skills upgrading and networking and referral services. (Interestingly, however, Deyo's analysis also suggests that this linkage tends to break down the further one extends into the periphery: both China and Thailand have attempted to establish these kinds of industrial park, but with much less success in using them to address the social side of their participating firms.) In sum, in Asia, as state-centric production chains morph into stateless production networks, the competitive-regulatory model of the developmental state seems to be morphing into a post-developmental state model in which the state plays more of a supporting role focusing on the development of infrastructure and factor endowments while leaving the more strategic aspects of development policy to the private firm networks described by Yeung in his chapter.

But what does this mean for competition regulation, and for the future of global competition law? This is the subject of the final chapter, which engages in a synoptic review of the other chapters in this volume to extrapolate what, collectively, they might imply both for the future of Asian capitalism and, more significantly, for the future of global competition law. It argues that, collectively, the chapters of this volume do indeed suggest a distinctly Asian approach to competition, but that its distinguishing features are not those that are most commonly attached to purportedly 'Asian' styles of regulation as described by the preliminary mapping set out in the first chapter of this volume. Instead, what really distinguishes Asian capitalism, and its regulation of competition, is its distinctly pluralist structure – a kind of pluralism that corresponds to the legal pluralism that Michael Barry Hooker has famously identified as a long-standing distinguishing feature of Southeast Asian legal systems in particular. In contrast to the varieties of capitalism discussed by Hall and Soskice[4], Asian capitalism does not evince a single form of capitalism that dominates the full reach of national social, economic, and legal space, in the way that liberal market economies and co-ordinated market economies tend to do throughout the North Atlantic. Rather, Asian states tend to evince multiple capitalisms operating simultaneously within a single national space. The regulation of these capitalisms is similarly pluralist, involving multiple models of competition regulation.

This should not, however, strike us as particularly deviant. As a number of the chapters in this volume make clear (perhaps most particularly Dowdle's Chapter 1 and Jessop's Chapter 5), capitalism and competition are much more variegated – to use Jessop's term – than orthodox models and theories acknowledge. The real question that needs to be asked is not 'why is Asian capitalism pluralist?', but 'why are North Atlantic capitalisms monocratic?'. This, too, will be addressed in the final chapter, which concludes by suggesting that, ultimately, global competition law will itself have to be pluralist, and that Asia's particularly pluralist style of regulating competition law might have something important to tell us in this regard.

---

[4] Hall and Soskice, 'Introduction'.

PART I

Asia, Asian capitalism, and global competition
law: conceptual mappings

1

The regulatory geography of market competition in Asia (and beyond): a preliminary mapping

MICHAEL W. DOWDLE

I. Introduction

This volume is ultimately a study of the primarily unexplored relationship between geography and law. It derives from Peter Hall and David Soskice's germinal work on varieties of capitalism. In their work, Soskice and Hall identify at least two kinds of capitalist economic organization, what they called 'liberal market economies (LME)' and 'co-ordinated market economies (CME)'.[1] Working off this insight, Gunther Teubner and Mark Roe have since shown how different varieties of capitalism encourage or facilitate different regulatory strategies for addressing particular social issues. For example, Teubner demonstrated how judges in CMEs and those in LMEs will adopt different methodologies for determining what constitutes 'good faith' performance of contractual obligations.[2] Roe demonstrated how corporate governance in CMEs assumes a role somewhat different from that exercised by it in LMEs.[3]

To this, this chapter adds the insights of economic geography, resulting in something that it – and this volume – calls 'regulatory geography'. Hall and Soskice do not locate a geographic component for their particular understanding of the varieties of capitalism, although there is a certain correspondence between CMEs and continental Europe on the one hand and LMEs and the anglophone world on the other. Economic geography, by contrast, suggests that varieties of capitalism could be more affected by

---

[1] See Peter A. Hall and David Soskice, 'An Introduction to Varieties of Capitalism', in Peter A. Hall and David W. Soskice (eds.), *Varieties of Capitalism: The Institutional Foundations of Comparative Advantage* (Oxford University Press, 2001), pp. 1–70.
[2] Gunther Teubner, 'Legal Irritants: How Unifying Law Ends up in New Divergences', in Hall and Soskice (eds.), *Varieties of Capitalism*, pp. 417–41.
[3] Mark J. Roe, 'Political Preconditions to Separating Ownership from Corporate Control', *Stanford Law Review*, 53 (2000): 539–606.

geography than Hall and Soskice's particular analysis – whose focus is limited to North Atlantic economies – might otherwise suggest.

By contrast, Fernand Braudel's magisterial study of the economic geography of Europe c. 1400–1900[4] suggests that geography can influence capitalist variety in at least two ways. One is via a global-regional dimension that, building on Hall and Soskice's own linkage of LMEs with Anglo geographies and CMEs with continental Europe, implies that other economic regions of the world – what Braudel famously termed 'économie-monde' in the original French, and which he translated as 'world-economy' (the hyphen is important) in the later, English version of his work[5] – may also exhibit their own distinct varieties of capitalism. The other way in which geography affects capitalism is through intra-regional complementaries in comparative advantage, which corresponds to internal core–peripheral ordering that Braudel famously identified as a defining component of an économie-monde.[6]

Extrapolating from the work of Teubner and Roe discussed above, this would suggest that there is likely to be a geographic component to economic regulation as well. And, similarly, this component would likely have two dimensions: a regional dimension, wherein different regions of the world may have different regulatory needs and capabilities stemming from their different varieties of capitalism, and an intra-regional dimension, wherein the core and peripheral areas within a particular region may also have different regulatory needs and capabilities.

Asian capitalism provides a particularly promising platform for this exploration – for two reasons. Of all the possible alternatives to the Anglo-European economies that are the subject of Hall and Soskice's study, that of Asia is probably that which is most thoroughly studied and theorized as a distinct economic model.[7] Also, as a regional economy, it is

---

[4] Fernand Braudel, *Civilization and Capitalism, 15th–18th Century*, Vol. 3, *The Perspective of the World* (Berkeley: University of California Press, 1992).

[5] Ibid., pp. 21–2.

[6] See generally ibid., pp. 21–44. See also Johann Heinrich von Thünen, *Von Thunen's Isolated State: An English Edition of Der Isolierte Staat*, ed. Peter Hall (Oxford: Pergamon, 1966 [1826]).

[7] See, e.g., Marco Orru, Nicole Woolsey Biggart, and Gary G. Hamilton (eds.), *The Economic Organization of East Asian Capitalism* (London: Sage, 1996); Frederic C. Deyo, Richard F. Doner, and Eric Hershberg (eds.), *Economic Governance and the Challenge of Flexibility in East Asia* (Lanham, MD: Rowman & Littlefield, 2001); Bob Jessop and Ngai-Ling Sum, *Beyond the Regulation Approach: Putting Capitalist Economies in their Place* (Cheltenham: Edward Elgar, 2006), pp. 152–209; Michael Carney, Eric Gedajlovic, and Xiaohua Yang (eds.), special issue, 'Varieties of Asian Capitalism: Indigenization and Internationalization', *Asia*

particularly well defined in terms of its core and peripheral areas and of their relationship.[8] We shall explore both of these features in more detail in the next section to this chapter.

In the context of Asian capitalism, this volume focuses in particular on the regulation of market competition – that is, competition law. Hall and Soskice, of course, use the lens of corporate governance in their original exploration of different varieties of capitalism. But competition would actually seem to offer a more promising platform, at least for investigation into Asia. First, as noted in many of the chapters in this study (see, e.g., Gerber, Ch. 2, p. 45; Maher, Ch. 3, pp. 56, 78; Prosser, Ch. 10, p. 228; cf. Sum, Ch. 4), there is a pronounced doctrinal and theoretical agreement among both North Atlantic competition lawyers and North Atlantic institutional economists about the role that competition plays in capitalist economies.[9] This we might call the 'orthodox' theory of competition – what is also referred to in other chapters in this volume as the 'neoliberal' theory – and it is also distinctly universal and scientific in its claims about what competition contributes to capitalism and social good. It is the focal point to which many see the world's national competition law systems converging, a focal point that is captured in the idea of a 'global competition law'.[10] Since this orthodox competition theory, and the regulatory norms that derive from this theory, are very much the product of distinctly Anglo-European (and more particularly than that, of distinctly American) experiences with capitalism, this makes possible Asian deviations in both the practice and structure of Asian capitalism particularly easy to observe.[11] Competition also provides a very useful lens for exploring the difference between core and

Pacific Journal of Management, 26 (2009): 361–609; Michael Carney, Eric Gedajlovic and Xiaohua Yang, 'Varieties of Asian Capitalism: Toward an Institutional Theory of Asian Enterprise', *Asia Pacific Journal of Management*, 26 (2009): 361–80.

[8] See, e.g., Deyo et al., *Economic Governance*.

[9] See Imelda Maher, 'Regulating Competition', in Christine Parker et al. (eds.), *Regulating Law* (Oxford University Press, 2004), pp. 187–206; David J. Gerber, 'Convergence in the Treatment of Dominant Firm Conduct: The United States, the European Union, and the Institutional Embeddedness of Economics', *Antitrust Law Journal*, 76 (2010): 951–73; David J. Gerber, *Global Competition: Law, Markets and Globalization* (Oxford University Press, 2010), pp. vii–viii. Cf. Dani Rodrik, 'Goodbye Washington Consensus, Hello Washington Confusion? A Review of the World Bank's Economic Growth in the 1990s: Learning from a Decade of Reform', *Journal of Economic Literature*, 44 (2006): 973–87.

[10] Gerber, *Global Competition*, pp. 273–92.

[11] See, e.g., Chalmers A. Johnson, *MITI and the Japanese Miracle: The Growth of Industrial Policy, 1925–1975* (Stanford University Press, 1982); Frank K. Upham, 'Privatized Regulation: Japanese Regulatory Style in Comparative Perspective', *Fordham International Law Journal*, 20 (1996): 396–511. Cf. Dan W. Puchniak, Harald Baum, and Michael

peripheral subregions within a particular regional economy (*économie-monde*), since, as noted above, that diversity can be explained in large part by asymmetries in comparative advantage, which is a competitive phenomenon.

The rest of this opening chapter flushes out the conceptual terms of hypothesis, in the process detailing the particular phenomenon of 'regulatory geography' that is the key to understanding this relationship. The next section explains what this volume means by 'Asian capitalism'. Briefly put, Asian capitalism refers to a particular kind of transnational capitalist-industrial organization that both spans and links most of the countries in East and Southeast Asia. As mentioned above, it comprises both a common set of economic practices and an internal architecture involving the interdependent interrelation between core and peripheral subregions. Section 3 will then recount the orthodox understandings of what it is that market competition contributes to capitalism, and how it should therefore be regulated. It will also explore the limits to this understanding – how it is founded on particular assumptions about the nature of capitalism which, while well founded in the context of the advanced, industrial, North Atlantic economies from which it derives, cannot be presumed to be universal, and which, where they are not present, can cause orthodox competition regulation – the primary referent for global competition law – to become dysfunctional.

Section 4 will then offer some preliminary observations on how the limits of the orthodox competition model might play out within the geographical context of Asian capitalism. This is the correlation that we are calling regulatory geography. Its observations are tentative and largely hypothetical, and indeed they largely correspond with alleged particular patterns of conformity and resistance that are already well-rehearsed in the literature. But they are nevertheless useful for laying out an analytic framework through which we can structure our subsequent exploration in the succeeding chapters to this volume.

II.   Mapping 'Asian capitalism'

The continent of Asia encompasses a very big space. It includes a large diversity of languages, religions, identities, and histories – 'cultures', if you will. Many regard it as an artificial construct, a European invention that serves primarily to identify what it means to be European (or, in more

Ewing-Chow (eds.), *The Derivative Action in Asia: A Comparative and Functional Approach* (Cambridge University Press, 2012).

modern parlance, 'Western').[12] As used in the term 'Asian capitalism', however, 'Asia' has a somewhat narrower geographical reference than when used in continental geography. It refers more specifically to the countries of East and Southeast Asia.[13] This vision of 'Asia' roughly encompasses the countries of ASEAN +3, and most particularly from among these Indonesia, Malaysia, Singapore, Thailand, Vietnam, China (which, insofar as Asian capitalism is concerned, includes Hong Kong and Taiwan), Japan, and South Korea. But, of course, this particular narrowing does not by itself address the principal concern described above. Even within this smaller collection of states there exists a large diversity of languages, religions, histories, and identities – that is, 'cultures'. What makes this region any less arbitrary than the larger Eurocentric continental definition of 'Asia' critiqued above?

One answer can be found in Fernand Braudel's germinal notion of an *économie-monde* – 'world-economy' – referenced in the introduction to this chapter. An *économie-monde* is a transnational, regional economic entity that is given coherence by the presence of an overarching economic-industrial system that binds the territories together in a unique pattern of economic interdependency. The unique interdependences that define this system (and its regional boundaries) are in the form of reciprocal comparative advantages, in which different subregions – countries – focus on fulfilling different parts of the overarching economic-industrial system. This gives the *économie-monde* a particular spatial architecture, in the form of a spatial continuum in which a centralized economic core gradually diffusts into a remote economic periphery.[14] We do not need to adhere to Braudel's particular vision of modernity, or to his Marxist influences, in order to appreciate his evocative description of this particular economic architecture:

> The centre or core contains everything that is most advanced and diversified. The next zone possesses only some of these benefits, although it has some share in them: it is the 'runner-up' zone. The huge periphery, with its scattered population, represents on the contrary backwardness, archaism, and exploitation by others.[15]

---

[12] See, e.g., Teemu Ruskola, 'Where Is Asia? When Is Asia? Theorizing Comparative Law and International Law', *UC Davis Law Review*, 44 (2011): 879–96; Edward W. Said, *Orientalism* (New York: Penguin Books, 1979), p. 3.

[13] See, e.g., Carney et al., 'Varieties of Asian Capitalism'.

[14] Braudel, *Civilization and Capitalism*, vol. 3, pp. 21–44.

[15] Ibid., p. 39. See also Herman Schwartz, 'Dependency or Institutions? Economic Geography, Causal Mechanisms, and Logic in the Understanding of Development', *Studies in Comparative International Development*, 42 (2007): 115–35.

Expanding on this, we can identify with somewhat more particularity how, within a particular *économie-monde*, more peripheral economies tend to differ from more core economies (remembering, of course, that progression from core to periphery is graduated, not absolute). Core economies tend to be more wealthy, more consumption oriented, have comparative advantage in product (design-based) competition, and be more stable and more rationalized.[16] Peripheral economies have fewer factor endowments, which means that they have less intrinsic (non-tradable) wealth. They tend to enjoy a comparative advantage in labour and production costs, and therefore tend to compete in price competitive rather than design competitive markets. They tend to be export oriented, making them more production oriented and less consumption oriented.[17] They tend to be more volatile and more fragmented.[18] And they tend not to maintain the rigid distinction between public and private resources and public and private responsibilities that are common to the more advanced industrial economies of the North Atlantic.[19]

By these general criteria, we can generally locate the core economies of the Asian *économie-monde* in Japan, South Korea, and Taiwan. Singapore and Hong Kong also have core-like features, but the fact that they are small (albeit wealthy) entrepôt economies limits the degree to which they might structure the other, more peripheral economies in the region. At the other end of the spectrum, Indonesia and north and western China are strongly peripheral, as are Vietnam and Thailand, albeit perhaps less so. Malaysia and eastern China may be regarded as intermediate – displaying some qualities of peripheral economies and some of

---

[16] Cf. Max Weber, *Economy and Society: An Outline of Interpretive Sociology*, ed. Guenther Roth and Claus Wittich, trans. Ephraim Fischoff et al. (Berkeley: University of California Press, 1978 [1922]), vol. 1, pp. 164–6.

[17] See generally Schwartz, 'Dependency or Institutions?'.

[18] See generally Paul Krugman, 'Increasing Returns and Economic Geography', *Journal of Political Economy*, 99 (1991): 483–99; Paul Krugman and Anthony Venables, 'Globalization and the Inequality of Nations', *Quarterly Journal of Economics*, 110 (1995): 857–80; Schwartz, 'Dependency or Institutions?'; Braudel, *Civilization and Capitalism*, vol. 3, p. 39; von Thünen, *Von Thunen's Isolated State*.

[19] See Abhijit V. Banerjee and Esther Duflo, *Poor Economics: A Radical Rethinking of the Way to Fight Global Poverty* (New York: Public Affairs, 2011); Alice Sindzingre, 'The Concept of Neopatrimonialism: Divergences and Convergences with Development Economics', paper presented at the GIGA (German Institute of Global and Area Studies) workshop 'Neopatrimonialism in Various World Regions', Hamburg, 23 August, 2010). Cf. Albert Hirschman, *The Passions and the Interests* (Princeton University Press, 1977).

more core economies.[20] But this is a very rough mapping, and it will vary from industry to industry. For example, in Chapter 8 (p. 184), John Gillespie describes a particular production network focusing on copper wire production, in which South Korean firms serve as upstream suppliers to more downstream Vietnamese manufacturers, reversing the more general core–peripheral gradient between these countries.

But the 'Asian capitalism' of an Asian *économie-monde* is not identified solely by the presence of a core–periphery gradient. As demonstrated by Braudel, the core–peripheral ordering of an *économie-monde* results from the presence of a particular economic technology, one that is distinctly locatable in the core, but which ties together the larger regions into a coherent economic whole. Insofar as Asian capitalism is concerned, that technology is the disaggregation of production into production chains (or more recently into production networks – see generally Yeung, Ch. 11).[21] This emerged out of Japanese industrial practices developed in the 1960s. During that time, economic instability caused Toyota, and later other Japanese automobile manufacturers, to emphasize flexibility and adaptability in production and design instead of focusing on rigidly exploiting economies of scale. As part of this evolution, leading firms began to focus their attention on developing more flexible assembly routines, more design-sensitive marketing operations, and more market-responsive designing capacities. At the same time, they contracted out those aspects of production – such as the production of standardized component parts – that were not particularly design-sensitive and did not require flexibility in responsiveness to changes in customer demand – to outside firms.[22]

What drove the disaggregation of production, which would later become so characteristic of Asian capitalism, was the different economic and production logics that attended to these two kinds of production. Design flexibility requires very responsive marketing that can rapidly identify evolving changes in consumer demand. It requires operational redundancy and task flexibility so as to promote experimentation, innovation, and productive adaptation. This results in relatively expensive and knowledge-intensive production processes, costs for which must be

---

[20] This mapping is consistent with the presentations found in Deyo et al., *Economic Governance and the Challenge of Flexibility in East Asia.*

[21] See also Deyo et al., *Economic Governance.*

[22] See generally Michael J. Piore and Charles F. Sabel, *The Second Industrial Divide: Possibilities for Prosperity* (New York: Basic Books, 1984).

recuperated by more monopolistic pricing of design-sensitive, product competition. Producers of more design-standardized items, by contrast, cannot engage in product competition. They must concentrate much more on reducing production costs, which they do by removing the expensive redundancy and knowledge-intensive production processes that facilitate design flexibilization.[23]

By the beginning of the 1990s, core Japanese firms were increasingly contracting out standardized production to firms in other parts of Asia – primarily China, Thailand, and Malaysia. This is because the lower labour costs of these subregions allowed firms in these countries to produce standardized components at significantly lower costs than could be done by standardized-production-oriented firms in Japan. Hence was born the transnational production chain, a disaggregated form of production in which certain spaces (countries) specialize in the more design-standardized aspects of product production while other spaces specialize in the more design-sensitive aspects.[24]

These production chains are the sinews that give Asian capitalism its regional economic coherence across the core–periphery spectrum (for a peripheral example see Gillespie, Ch. 8, pp. 184, 187–8). They are the sinews that make the advanced industrial, perhaps even post-industrial, economies of Japan, South Korea, and Taiwan critically interdependent with the less developed economies of Thailand, Vietnam, and Malaysia. It is they that give Asian capitalism a distinct spatial shape and coherence – a shape and coherence that does not depend on commonalities of culture, language, history, or identity.[25]

These production chains also help visibilize the core–peripheral architecture of the Asian *économie-monde*. The more design-standardized end of production chains, upstream component manufacture, tends to be located in the more peripheral regions of Asia, because these regions enjoy a comparative advantage in low-cost production, due primarily to lower labour costs (the principal factor of production costs in design-standardized production). By contrast, Asia's more core economic regions enjoy an absolute advantage (vis-à-vis the Asian periphery) in

---

[23] See generally ibid.; Deyo et al., *Economic Governance*.

[24] Mitsuyo Ando and Fukunari Kimura, 'The Formation of International Production and Distribution Networks in East Asia', in Takatoshi Ito and Andrew K. Rose (eds.), *International Trade in East Asia* (University of Chicago Press, 2005), pp. 177–216; Deyo et al., *Economic Governance*.

[25] Ando and Kimura, 'Formation of International Production'; also Carney et al., 'Varieties of Asian Capitalism'.

high-tech and other design sensitive aspects of production. Here is the downstream terminus of these production chains – where the 'lead firms' that construct and maintain these production chains through the contracting out of design-standardized parts of production are located (see also Yeung, Ch. 11).[26]

Another distinct, structural feature of Asian capitalism is that its core economies tend to be export oriented (for a description of why Asian capitalism might have evolved in that direction see Vande Walle, Ch. 6, p. 127).[27] This is in sharp contrast with the capitalisms of the North Atlantic, whose cores have historically been and continue to be consumption oriented. Indeed, it is the consumption-oriented economies of the North Atlantic core that are the major source of market demand for the exports of the Asian core. (As noted above, peripheral economies everywhere tend to be export oriented, and Asian peripheries are not distinguishable from their North Atlantic counterparts in this regard.)

Production chains and export orientation are the technologies that give the Asian regional economy its distinct economic structure. But there are other features commonly associated with Asian capitalism that are more cultural in nature, and that are sometimes thought to give Asian capitalism a distinctive cultural aspect that spans core-periphery diversities. Principal among these is that of the developmental state (see also Gerber, Ch. 2, pp. 41–3).[28] The states of the Asian économie-monde are seen as having been particularly active in trying to plan and shape economic development through strategic planning. This has involved, for example, directing state resources towards the development of particular chosen industries and/or particular chosen firms (i.e. 'national champions'); and otherwise restricting competition (both domestic and foreign) within these industries and/or among firms so as to allow them time to mature into *internationally* competitive entities. This is in contrast to the practice of most of the economies of the North Atlantic, which has been to act as neutral referees and have 'the market' rather than the state drive economic development.

---

[26] Deyo et al., *Economic Governance*.
[27] See Jessop and Sum, *Beyond the Regulation Approach*, pp. 152–76.
[28] See Adrian Leftwitch, 'Bringing Politics Back In: Towards a Model of the Developmental State', *Journal of Development Studies*, 31 (1995): 400–27; Meredith Woo-Cumings (ed.), *The Developmental State* (Ithaca, NY: Cornell University Press, 1999); see also Johnson, *MITI and the Japanese Miracle.*

Asian capitalism is also sometimes associated with a distinct preference for informal and relational forms of economic ordering and regulation,[29] as contrasted with the more juridified forms that feature more
prominently in Anglo-European forms of capitalism (perhaps more so in
LMEs than in CMEs[30]). This is the world of what is sometimes called
relational capitalism or network capitalism. Asia's relational capitalism is
seen as manifesting along two dimensions. One is in the interactions
between private firms (see especially Gillespie, Ch. 8; Yeung, Ch. 11).
Production chains are an example of this, since these chains tend to be
held together not through arm's-length contractual obligations but
through ongoing, informal long-running social relationships. Another
example is the distinctive intra-regional, ethnically based trading and
financial networks that have emerged out of many centuries of Chinese
diasporas and that continue to play a significant role in many of the more
peripheral economies of the Asian *économie-monde*.[31] And of course,
perhaps the most well-publicized example of this private relational capitalism is the conglomerates known as *keiretsu* in Japan and *chaebol* in
South Korea. As described by both Simon Vande Walle in Chapter 6 and
Tony Prosser in Chapter 10, these conglomerates use private forms of
informal ordering to develop private industrial policies that in North
Atlantic economies would be created by public, juridified institutions.[32]

The other dimension of Asia's relational capitalism, one that is more
controversial as far as Anglo-European observers are concerned,
involves the relationship between private firms and their public
regulators. As with firm–firm relationships, many see Asian capitalism
as evincing a preference for informal forms of public regulation.[33]
Perhaps the defining example of this is the Japanese practice of
'administrative guidance', in which public regulators in Japan – most
famously MITI (the Ministry of International Trade and Industry) – use
relational promises or assistance and support in other matters to secure

---

[29] See especially Peter Evans, *Embedded Autonomy: States and Industrial Transformation*
(Princeton University Press, 1995).
[30] Cf. Roe, 'Political Preconditions'.
[31] Gordon C. K. Cheung, 'The Significance of the Overseas Chinese in East Asia', in Mark
Beeson and Richard Stubbs (eds.), *Routledge Handbook of Asian Regionalism* (London:
Routledge, 2012), pp. 77–89.
[32] See, e.g., Upham, 'Privatized Regulation'.
[33] Kanishka Jayasuriya, 'Introduction: A Framework for the Analysis of Legal Institutions in
East Asia', in Kanishka Jayasuriya (ed.), *Law, Capitalism and Power in Asia: The Rule of
Law and Legal Institutions* (London: Routledge, 1999), pp. 1–27.

compliance with informal industrial policies that are not articulated or authorized in law – what John Haley has evocatively termed 'authority without power'.[34] (See also Vande Walle, Ch. 6, p. 130.) Particularly in the more peripheral regions of Asia, this component of network capitalism has often been disparaged by Anglo-European observers as 'crony capitalism' – a cosy relationship between government and capital in which government officials give preferential treatment to the economic elite at a cost to the larger social good. Other studies suggest, however, that the dynamics of relational capitalism are much more complex than is captured by this particular, pejorative epithet[35] (see, e.g., Gillespie, Ch. 8, pp. 177–80, 191).

This chapter will later offer some preliminary suggestions about how the distinct emphases and technological and geographic structure of Asian capitalism could be shaping the way in which market competition manifests itself and is regulated, both formally and informally, in the region. But it might help first to review what and how market competition is said to contribute to a economy – that is, the orthodox (neoliberal) theory of market competition that drives the globalization of competition law. This is the subject of the next section of this chapter.

III.   The orthodox understanding of competition law: rationale and limitations

A.   The rationale for competition law[36]

Even at the global level, there is a surprising level of agreement about the theoretical foundations that should inform global distinctions of competition law and regulation (see also Sum, Ch. 4). Perhaps no other area of law enjoys such an unchallenged theoretical underpinning. This is not to suggest that there are not disagreements within the field over

---

[34] See especially John O. Haley, *Authority without Power: Law and the Japanese Paradox* (Oxford University Press, 1992).

[35] See, e.g., Surajit Mazumdar, 'Crony Capitalism: Caricature or Category?', MPRA Paper No. 19626, Munich, February 2008, available at http://mpra.ub.uni-muenchen.de/19626/. Cf. Joel S. Kahn and Francesco Formosa, 'The Problem of "Crony Capitalism": Modernity and the Encounter with the Perverse', *Thesis Eleven*, 69 (2002): 47–66; Jeffrey Fear, 'Cartels and Competition: Neither Markets nor Hierarchies', HBS Working Papers, 07-011 (Harvard Business School, 2007), available at www.hbs.edu/research/pdf/07-011. pdf.

[36] For a good overview of the orthodox rationale for competition law, as described in this section, see Tony Prosser, *The Limits of Competition Law: Markets and Public Services* (Oxford University Press, 2005), pp. 17–20.

theoretical questions: economic libertarians, such as those associated with the Chicago school, are less distrustful of monopolies and cartels than more orthodox theory; German ordoliberals pay more attention to the democratic implications of market competition than does more orthodox theorizing, which tends to focus narrowly on efficiency. But at the end of the day, the general theoretical justifications for competition law stand relatively uncontested from within the field, even as they find more considerable opposition outside that field (see generally Maher, Ch. 3; Sum, Ch. 4; cf. Jessop, Ch. 5).[37]

As noted above, this chapter will refer to the standard theoretical model of economic competition that serves as the template for global discourses on competition and competition law (i.e. 'global competition law'[38]) as the 'orthodox model' of competition. At the heart of this orthodox model is the pursuit of what is commonly referred to as 'consumer sovereignty'.[39] Consumer sovereignty is a condition in which consumers enjoy autonomous access to the widest possible variety of goods and services. Many, particularly ordoliberals, also see this as an important underpinning of democracy: since all citizens are consumers, maximizing consumer options and choices with regard to their material welfare is said to provide a firmer foundation for democratic participation.[40]

Competition promotes consumer sovereignty in two ways. One way is by promoting what is called consumer welfare.[41] This is done by allocating the surplus value of production – the difference between the value of the inputs that are used to create the good and the value of the good itself – to the consumer, resulting in and maximizing what is commonly called 'consumer surplus'.[42] Competition does this by pushing prices down to the

---

[37] See also Maher, 'Regulating Competition'; Gerber, 'Convergence in the Treatment of Dominant Firm Conduct'.

[38] Briefly put, the notion of a 'global competition law' describes a normative projected point of convergence in the evolution of a domestic competition law system. See Gerber, *Global Competition*, pp. 273–92.

[39] See also Neil W. Averitt and Robert H. Lande, 'Consumer Sovereignty: A Unified Theory of Antitrust and Consumer Protection Law', *Antitrust Law Journal*, 65 (1997): 713–56.

[40] See generally Giuliano Amato, *Antitrust and the Bounds of Power: The Dilemma of Liberal Democracy in the History of the Market* (Oxford: Hart Publishing, 1997). On ordoliberalism see David J. Gerber, *Law and Competition in Twentieth Century Europe: Protecting Prometheus* (Oxford: Clarendon Press, 1998), pp. 232–65.

[41] See K. J. Cseres, 'The Controversies of the Consumer Welfare Standard', *Competition Law Review*, 3 (2007): 121–73.

[42] The idea of consumer surplus was first developed by Alfred Marshall. See Alfred Marshall, *Principles of Economics*, 8th edn (New York: Macmillan, 1922).

cost of production (or more precisely, to the 'price of production', as described by Jessop in Ch. 5, p. 100). Under conditions of competition, producers can only secure customers by offering goods at their lowest possible price – that is, that of the cost of securing the inputs necessary to produce the good. This promotes consumer welfare by ensuring that the wealth that is generated by production accrues to the consumer, allowing her to maximize her own material resources and the welfare these resources are able to provide.

Competition also promotes consumer sovereignty by increasing consumer choice. In competitive markets, producers can compete in one of two ways. One, as discussed above, is by offering lower prices. The other is by identifying and addressing unmet areas of consumer demand. This kind of competition, called product competition as distinguished from price competition, increases the range and variety of goods available to consumers.

In addition to promoting consumer sovereignty, competition is also said to promote economic growth and development.[43] This is perhaps its principal selling point as far as efforts to globalize competition law are concerned (see also Sum, Ch. 4). Competition is said to promote economic growth and development by ensuring the efficient distribution of limited resources. There are at least two dimensions to this efficiency: productive efficiency (also referred to as 'technical efficiency' or 'X-efficiency'), which refers to a market's ability to maximize output from a given level of input (in practical terms, this means producing goods at their lowest possible cost), and allocative efficiency, which refers to a market's ability to allocate limited resources so as to maximize aggregate social welfare, or 'utility'.[44] Competition promotes productive efficiency by giving evolutionary advantage to firms who use resources more efficiently: more efficient use of resources results in lower production costs, which results in a lower product price, which results in more sales, which allows the producer to better survive in competition for sales and revenue with less efficient users. It promotes allocative efficiency by ensuring that more efficient users of particular resources will enjoy greater access to those resources due to the greater revenue stream they can generate from these resources via the dynamics of productive

---

[43] See, e.g., Eleanor M. Fox and Abel M. Mateus (eds.), *Economic Development: The Critical Role of Competition Law and Policy* (Cheltenham: Edward Elgar, 2011).

[44] See generally Robert H. Bork, *The Antitrust Paradox*, 2nd edn (New York: Free Press, 1993), pp. 91–106. See also Prosser, *Limits of Competition Law*, pp. 18–20.

efficiency. By generating continual pressures to improve productive efficiency, competition ensures that the economy will both generate increasing product from its resource supply and at the same time expand its resource supply in ways that promote an ever-expanding cycle of domestic production and consumption – that is, economic growth.

(Competition law is also sometimes said to promote dynamic efficiency – which refers to capacity to engage in design innovation.[45] But this claim is somewhat controversial.[46])

B.   The limits of competition law

The orthodox model of competition that underlies global competition law derives primarily if not exclusively from the experiences of the advanced industrial economies of the North Atlantic, most particularly that of the United States.[47] Embedded within it are certain presumptions about the nature of an economy, presumptions that are for the most part unproblematic in the context of North Atlantic forms of capitalism, but which are by no means universal. The problematic nature of these presumptions as universal features of economic life is often overlooked – if not ignored – by the orthodox model. They are rarely if ever considered in developmental efforts to globalize competition law, for example. But they are well recognized outside the limited confines of the competition law community. (See also Gerber, Ch. 2.)

In particular, the orthodox model presumes an economy (i) in which consumers and producers occupy the same socio-political space; (ii) that is relatively stable; (iii) that is and should be governed principally by price competition rather than some other form of competition; (iv) in which the delivery of the goods and services associated with citizenship can be adequately provided for by the public sector; and (v) in which competitive firms are able to achieve minimally efficient economies of scale. But many economic spaces deviate from one or more of these presumptions. And where they do, the posited relationship between economic competition and social good that drives the orthodox model

---

[45] See also Prosser, *Limits of Competition Law*, pp. 18–20.

[46] See, e.g., Cosmo Graham and Fiona Smith (eds.), *Competition, Regulation and the New Economy* (Oxford: Hart Publishing, 2004).

[47] See Gerber, *Global Competition*, p. viii.

becomes problematic – as we shall see as we examine each of these presumptions in turn.

1.   Export-oriented (and otherwise production-oriented) economies[48]

As noted above, the social utility of the orthodox model stems primarily from its capacity to ensure that the surplus value of production accrues to consumers. Since consumers represent a more inclusive class of society than producers, this is presumed to promote social welfare and democratic participation.[49] But this assumes that the consumers of the goods being produced are in the same socio-political space as the producers – that is, that the economy as a whole is consumption oriented.

This is largely true for the advanced industrial economies of the North Atlantic. But, as we saw above, it is often not true for more peripheral economies and even for the more core industrial economies of Asia. These economies tend to be export oriented. Their production is dedicated to producing goods that will be consumed by citizens in other countries (or to consumers in other economic regions – see, e.g., Dowdle, Ch. 9). Where this is the case, then the emphasis of competition law on consumer sovereignty and consumer welfare becomes dysfunctional. Instead of promoting the social welfare and democratic strength of citizens in the producing country, it works to promote the social welfare and democratic robustness of citizens in an outside country.

Note that this is particularly problematic in the case of peripheral countries: poorer, peripheral economies tend to depend much more on exporting their produced goods to wealthy consumption-oriented economies. Here, a robust competition regime will have the effect of aggravating global inequalities. But the same often applies within national economies. Even within nations, national economic space tends to disaggregate itself into poorer, generally rural, export-oriented regions and wealthier, generally urban, consumption-oriented regions. For this reason, market competition can promote inequality within a country as well as between countries, which can be a particular problem for national cohesion in poorer countries in which economic fragmentation and class conflict tend to be more virulent. (All this is further explored by Dowdle in Ch. 9.)

---

[48] See also James Q. Whitman, 'Consumerism versus Producerism: A Study in Comparative Law', *Yale Law Journal*, 117 (2007): 340–406.

[49] See also Amato, *Antitrust and the Bounds of Power*, pp. 2–3.

2. Volatile economies

One of the more overlooked limitations of the orthodox model of competition is that it presumes an economic environment that is relatively stable. In economies that are more volatile or dynamic, on the other hand, the orthodox model threatens to become dysfunctional. (See also Jessop, Ch. 5, pp. 103–5.)

Recall that competition law works by pushing price down to the cost of production. This forces producers to operate at razor-thin profit margins. So long as an economy is relative stable, as has been the case with American capitalism in particular since the turn of the twentieth century, this is not so problematic.[50] But in more volatile economies, where there is significant fluctuation in such things as market demand, availability of production inputs, currency value, and availability of finance,[51] these razor-thin profit margins can render producer firms, and even whole industries, particularly vulnerable. These firms simply lack the wealth reserves to weather short-term economic disruptions. Under such conditions, even relatively minor changes in economic conditions – such as a sudden tightening of credit, or a decrease in consumer spending power, or the sudden appearance of a new technology in a competing firm – can be sufficient to bring an end to a firm that would otherwise be viable under conditions of stability.[52]

All this, in turn, further aggravates the economic and social volatility of the poor peripheral economy.[53] Because producers are also employers, this volatility can destabilize the labour environment, which destabilizes the social welfare of workers.[54] The constant churning of

---

[50] Cf. Piore and Sabel, *The Second Industrial Divide*, pp. 49–54.

[51] Joshua Aizenman and Brian Pinto (eds.), *Managing Economic Volatility and Crises: A Practitioner's Guide* (Cambridge University Press, 2005).

[52] See James Crotty, 'Core Industries, Coercive Competition and the Structural Contradiction of Global Neoliberalism', in Nicholas Phelps and Philip Raines (eds.), *The New Competition for Inward Investment: Companies, Institutions and Territorial Development* (Cheltenham: Edward Elgar, 2003), pp. 17–18; Giorgio Monti, 'Article 82 EC and New Economy Markets', in Graham and Smith, *Competition, Regulation and the New Economy*, pp. 22–3. See also Philip A. Anderson and Michael L. Tushman, 'Managing Through Cycles of Technological Change', *Research Technology Management*, 34 (3) (1991): 26–31.

[53] See, e.g., Rabah Arezki and Markus Brückner, 'Food Prices and Political Instability', IMF Institute: IMF Working Paper, WP-11-62 (March 2011).

[54] See Thomas Laursen and Sandeep Mahajan, 'Volatility, Income Distribution, and Poverty', in Aizenman and Pinto, *Managing Economic Volatility*, pp. 101–35.

firms can upend industrial stability and discourage industrial-level innovation and upgrading.[55] It inhibits firms, and the industry as a whole, from developing more robust knowledge bases and agglomeration networks, and thus their ability to become more competitive internationally. Firm stability promotes employment stability, and employment stability is frequently a critical component of a country's social welfare and social security structure. In industries with large start-up costs and small returns to economies of scale, firm volatility can further prevent the realization of minimally efficient economies of scale (see below).

3.   Product competition and knowledge-based economies

When the orthodox model talks about 'competition', it is talking about price competition.[56] On the other hand, it is blind to, and in subtle ways structurally antagonistic towards, product competition – competition in which firms compete, not by offering products at the lowest price, but by offering products that feature the best designs (cf. Jessop, Ch. 5, pp. 103–5). Product competition differs in economic effect from price competition in a number of ways. Most significantly as far as the orthodox competition model is concerned, it allocates the surplus value of production to the producer rather than to the consumer – the ability to sell based on a unique design rather than on its price effectively grants the producer a competitive monopoly, and thus allows monopoly pricing, which maximizes producer surplus at the expense of consumer surplus.

Product competition's monopolistic features and its corresponding assignment of surplus value to producers rather than consumers contradicts the fundamental tenets of the orthodox model of competition regulation.[57] But as described by Joseph Schumpeter, product competition is actually a critical component of an economy's ability to adapt and upgrade – to respond dynamically to and even exploit changes in its larger market environment:

---

[55] Crotty, 'Core Industries', p. 18.

[56] Cf. Joseph A. Schumpeter, *Capitalism, Socialism, and Democracy* 3rd edn (New York: Harper & Row, 1975), pp. 84–5.

[57] Ibid., pp. 82–5. See also K. Sridhar Moorthy, 'Product and Price Competition in a Duopoly', *Marketing Science*, 7 (1988): 141–68; J. Gregory Sidak and David Teece, 'Favouring Dynamic Competition over Static Competition in Antitrust Law', in R. Ian McEwin (ed.), *Intellectual Property, Competition Law and Economics in Asia* (Oxford: Hart Publishing, 2011), pp. 53–94.

> In capitalist reality as distinguished from its textbook picture, it is not
> [price] competition which counts but the competition from the new
> commodity, the new technology, the new source of supply, the new type
> of organization (the largest scale unit of control, for instance) – competi-
> tion which commands a decisive cost or quality advantage and which
> strikes not at the margin of the profits and outputs of the existing firms
> but at their foundations and their very lives. This kind of competition is
> much more effective than the other as a bombardment is in comparison
> with forcing a door, and so much more important that it becomes a
> matter of comparative indifference whether competition in the ordinary
> [static] sense functions more or less promptly; the powerful lever that in
> the long run expands output and brings down prices is made of other
> stuff.[58]

A single-minded pursuit of price competition, as advocated by the
orthodox model of competition law, can therefore have deleterious effects
on economic development. This is particularly true in more peripheral
countries, which have significant structural impediments – impediments
that extend beyond the quality of their regulatory system – to entering
into product-competitive markets.[59]

In fact, most, if not all, legal systems that have a competition law regime
also have a counterbalancing legal regime that compensates for this particular problem in the orthodox competition model. That is the regime of
intellectual property.[60] But, as noted by Schumpeter and others, intellectual
property's ability to compensate for this particular limitation is itself
limited, and does not cover a number of critical aspects of competitiveness
in product-competitive markets (cf. Jessop, Ch. 5, pp. 105–10).[61] As will be
explored in more detail immediately below, the orthodox model also seeks
to purify market competition by insulating competition law completely
from influence by other regulatory concerns.[62] In this way global competition law contests efforts to use competition law to promote capacity for
product competition and economic dynamism in those aspects of the
economy where intellectual property law, or its implementation, is

---

[58] Schumpeter, *Capitalism, Socialism, and Democracy*, pp. 84–5.
[59] Charlie Karlsson and Jan Larsson, 'Product and Price Competition in a Regional
Context', *Papers in Regional Science*, 69 (1990): 83–99.
[60] See R. Ian McEwin, 'Editor's Introduction', in McEwin, *Intellectual Property*, pp. 3–22;
William E. Kovacic, 'A Regulator's Perspective on Getting the Balance Right', in ibid.,
pp. 23–34.
[61] Crotty, 'Core Industries', p. 18. Cf. Anderson and Tushman, 'Managing through Cycles of
Technological Change'.
[62] See, e.g., Bork, *Antitrust Paradox*, p. 428.

insufficient. Perhaps the paradigmatic example of this in the context of Asian capitalism is the orthodox model's hostility to the 'developmental state' strategy for economic development and upgrading used by many Asian economies (see also Gerber, Ch. 2, pp. 41–3).

4. Public law and citizenship concerns

As noted above, orthodox competition theory assumes a regulatory environment in which public law concerns can be rigorously segregated from market concerns. This allows market regulation, including competition law, to focus exclusively on promoting market efficiency. This, in turn, maximizes the aggregate amount of goods and services available to society. It argues that, if and when distributional concerns come into play, these concerns are best addressed by regulatory systems other than market regulation, since compromising economic maximization of wealth in order to address distributional concerns would reduce the market's aggregate production of goods and services. Instead, we should assign responsibility for distribution concerns to the public law arena – and in particular to the tax system. This way, an economy can be both maximally efficient and sufficiently egalitarian at the same time.[63]

Not all economies are capable of maintaining such strict segregation, however. The regulatory segregation of public and private is a relatively recent invention, and one that there is good reason to believe is generally dependent on a prior industrialization of the economy. For lesser industrialized economies, maintaining such a distinction can be problematic.[64] And where this is the case, imposing egalitarian concerns directly on private market regulatory systems, including on competition regulation (see, e.g., what is sometimes referred to as 'fair trade' as contrasted with 'free trade'[65]) can make good economic and social sense.[66] (This issue is explored further in Dowdle, Ch. 9, pp. 210, 226.)

---

[63] See generally Louis Kaplow and Steven Shavell, *Fairness versus Welfare* (Cambridge, MA: Harvard University Press, 2002).

[64] See Hirschman, *The Passions and the Interests*. See also Peter Bratsis, 'The Construction of Corruption, or Rules of Separation and Illusions of Purity in Bourgeois Societies', *Social Text*, 21(4) (2003): 9–33.

[65] Lawrence S. Liu, 'In Fairness We Trust? – Why Fostering Competition Law and Policy Ain't Easy in Asia', unpublished paper dated 19 October 2004, available at SSRN, http://ssrn.com/abstract=610822.

[66] See, e.g., Mats Bergman, 'Antitrust, Marketing Cooperatives, and Market Power', *European Journal of Law and Economics*, 4 (1997): 73–92; Aravind R. Ganesh, 'The Right to

5.   Citizenship goods

Related to the distinction that the orthodox model draws between market regulation and distributional regulation is the distinction between ordinary market goods and what we might call 'citizenship goods'. As described above, the benefits of the orthodox model of competition come in part from its ability to promote allocative efficiency. But not all goods should be distributed simply on the basis of efficiency. Some have to be distributed on the basis of equality.[67] Common examples include access to education, minimal social and economic security, basic medical care (in Europe at least), access to transportation, and access to meaningful employment. Such goods are commonly seen as the *quid pro quo* that a state provides or otherwise guarantees to its citizens in exchange for their loyalty.[68] As citizens we are all equal, and we thus enjoy an equal claim to these particular goods independent of our individual capacity to pay and of whatever productive efficiencies that capacity to pay might promote. For convenience, we shall refer to these kinds of goods and services as 'citizenship goods'.[69]

As noted above, orthodox competition theory seeks to insulate private markets from the unique distributional concerns of citizenship goods. It sees private markets as properly existing purely to promote productive and allocative efficiency. When particular goods have to be allocated according to different criteria, it argues that the best regulatory response is to assign the allocation of those goods to the public sector, rather than to compromise the private market's ultimate goal of maximizing aggregate wealth generation.[70]

There are two problems with this idea, however. The first is that markets cannot always be isolated from the public realm in the way that the orthodox theory presumes (see, e.g., Dowdle, Ch. 9, p. 210, on the important and unavoidable social functionalities of raw-milk markets in

---

Food and Buyer Power', *German Law Journal*, 11 (2010): 1190–243. Cf. Jeffrey R. Fear, *Cartels and Competition: Neither Markets Nor Hierarchies*, HBS Working Papers Collection, Working Paper 07-011 (Cambridge, MA: 2006), available at www.hbs.edu/research/pdf/07-011.pdf (accessed 28 June 2012).

[67] See also Arthur Okun, *Equality and Efficiency: The Big Tradeoff* (Washington DC, Brookings Institution Press, 1975). See also Prosser, *Limits of Competition Law*, pp. 35–8.

[68] See T. H. Marshall, *Citizenship and Social Class, and Other Essays* (Cambridge University Press, 1950); see also Desmond S. King and Jeremy Waldron, 'Citizenship, Social Citizenship and the Defence of Welfare Provision', *British Journal of Political Science*, 18 (1988): 415–43.

[69] The author believes that what is captured by this notion of citizenship goods is largely the same as what Tony Prosser seeks to capture through his notion of 'citizenship rights'. Cf. Prosser, *Limits of Competition Law*, pp. 35–8.

[70] Kaplow and Shavell, *Fairness versus Welfare*.

rural China). Even in advanced economies, many markets have distinctly social functionalities that are not captured by a limited regulatory focus on efficiency. For example, access to meaningful employment is a paradigmatic citizenship good: a state that does not provide its citizenry with meaningful opportunity for employment will clearly lose its claim to their allegiance.[71] But in most, if not all, advanced industrial economies, the principal source for meaningful employment is the private labour market. Of course, this requires sacrificing some degree of market efficiency in these markets.[72] But the fact that all advanced industrial states choose to distribute this particular citizenship good by distributionally based regulation of private markets that may well compromise their maximal efficiency and capacity for aggregate wealth generation (at least as per the premises that drive the orthodox model of competition), rather than by building a parallel distributional apparatus for employment, strongly indicates that there is wide consensus that, even with its cost to productive efficiency, egalitarian distribution of employment through the private sector is less costly than distribution through parallel structures in the public sector.[73] Indeed, it is for this reason that the competition laws of the North Atlantic economies almost universally remove labour market competition from many aspects of their regulatory framework.[74]

When markets become involved in the allocation of citizenship goods, as they invariably are, the application of the orthodox model becomes problematic. This is because that model, as we have seen, cannot take the unique distributional needs of that kind of good into account and, at the same time, it cannot assign its distribution to the public law system. Indeed, in US law, the more dramatic consequences of these particular lacunae in market regulation are recognized and addressed through the federal government's formal capacity to issue federal emergency declarations and federal disaster declarations, whose purpose in part is to facilitate extraordinary interventions in private markets in order to secure

---

[71] See, e.g., Universal Declaration of Human Rights, Art. 23.1; International Covenant on Economic, Social and Cultural Rights, Art. 6.

[72] John A. Litwinski, 'Regulation of Labor Market Monopsony', *Berkeley Journal Of Employment and Labor Law*, 22 (2001): 49–98.

[73] Cf. Harold Demesetz, 'The Problem of Social Cost: What Problem? A Critique of the Reasoning of A. C. Pigou and R. H. Coase', *Review of Law and Economics*, 7 (2011): 1–13.

[74] See, e.g., Einer Elhauge and Damien Géradin, *Global Competition Law and Economics* (Oxford: Hart, 2007), pp. 32–4; *Albany International BV* v. *Stichting Bedrijfspensioenfond Textielindustrie*, [1999] ECR I-5751.

the more egalitarian distribution of necessary goods during times of extreme market disruption or failure.[75]

A second problem with the orthodox model in this regard is that that model contains no methodology for distinguishing citizenship goods from ordinary goods. This is problematic because, as we have just explored, some citizenship goods are best distributed through private markets. However, what constitutes a citizenship good can differ from polity to polity, due to differences in culture, levels of development, or local need. For example, studies by Ronald Ingelhart and others have shown that the citizenries of industrial societies have different preference structures and expectations from their government than the citizenries of lesser industrialized polities (and also from citizens of post-industrialized polities).[76] And, as noted above, many of the citizenship goods that derive from these particular preference structures and expectations will be, and will best be, distributed through private markets. When this is the case, however, the orthodox model has no way of determining whether some distribution-based restriction on market competition is a product of moral hazard or of the special distributional needs of a particular citizenship good that is best distributed through that market (see, e.g., Prosser, Ch. 10, pp. 233–6, looking at this problem in the context of European competition law).[77]

6.   Small economies

The orthodox model of competition also poses particular problems for what Michel Gal has identified as 'small economies' – economies that are

---

[75] See Bernadette Meyler, 'Economic Emergency and the Rule of Law', *DePaul Law Review*, 56 (2006): 539–67.

[76] Ronald Inglehart, 'Post-materialism in an Environment of Insecurity', *American Political Science Review*, 75 (1981): 880–900; idem, *Modernization and Postmodernization: Cultural, Economic and Political Change in 43 Societies* (Princeton University Press, 1997); Ronald Inglehart and Daphna Oyserman, 'Individualism, Autonomy and Self-Expression: The Human Development Syndrome', in Henk Vinken, Joseph Soeters, and Peter Ester (eds.), *Comparing Cultures: Dimensions of Culture in a Comparative Perspective* (Leiden: Brill, 2004), pp. 74–96.

[77] See, e.g., Pasuk Phongpaichit and Chris Baker, *Thailand's Crisis* (Singapore: Singapore Institute of Southeast Asian Studies, 2000), pp. 35–82. Raj Patel and Philip McMichael, 'A Political Economy of the Food Riot', *Review, A Journal of the Fernand Braudel Center*, 12 (2010): 9–35. See also Prosser, *The Limits of Competition Law*. Cf. Great Britain Board of Trade, 1 *Survey of International Cartels and Internal Cartels, 1944, 1946* (London: Central Library, Department of Industry, 1976) ('clearly cartels, directly or indirectly, served different national objectives', quoted in Fear, *Cartels and Competition*, p. 26).

too small to achieve a minimum efficient scale of production.[78] As is well known, the lure of mass production lies in its inverse relationship between production quantity and product costs. The more units a firm produces, the less each unit costs to produce. But this also means that, conversely, the fewer units a firm produces, the more it costs to produce that unit. At some point in this retrograde trajectory, the cost of production becomes inefficient. This point is referred to as the minimum efficient scale of production (MES). In other words, the MES tells us the minimum number of units that a firm needs to produce in order to be minimally efficient.

The fact that firms need to produce at some minimum level of scale in order to be efficient poses particular problems for 'small economies' – 'small' in this sense referring to national population rather than gross domestic product (GDP). Production capacity is determined in part by firm size. The smaller the economy, the fewer firms of efficient MES size it is able to support. Gal has shown that, in many cases, an economy can only support one or two firms operating at MES levels of product.[79] Promoting competition in smaller markets that can support only a limited number of MES-level firms can end up inhibiting that market's overall productive efficiency. But the orthodox competition model does not account for an economy's ability to support MES levels of production. In this way, too, the orthodox models of competition can become problematic. (See also Dowdle, Ch. 9.)

(As described by Maher in Chapter 3 (see p. 72), another problem for 'small economies' is the ability to recruit qualified competition law regulators. This is not so much a limitation of competition law as we are exploring it in this section, but a limitation to the implementation of competition law.)

IV.   Linking competition regulation to 'Asian capitalism': a preliminary mapping of the regulatory geography of competition regulation in Asia

With our investigation into the economic and geographic shape of Asian capitalism and its regulation of market competition, we are now able to develop a preliminary mapping of the regulatory geography of competition law in Asia. This regulatory geography will in turn provide a starting

---

[78] See generally Michal S. Gal, *Competition Policy for Small Market Economies* (Cambridge, MA: Harvard University Press, 2003).

[79] See, e.g., ibid., p. 19 (discussing Sweden).

conceptual framework from which we can construct this volume's larger investigation into the relationship between Asian capitalism and global competition law.

First, we can hypothesize that Asian capitalism as a whole would seem to have a more ambivalent relationship to 'competition' – at least the competition of the orthodox theory – than the North Atlantic varieties of capitalism (see also Gerber, Ch. 2, pp. 39–40). This ambivalence would derive both from its greater focus on export orientation and from its focus on exploiting flexibility (a particular form of economic volatility). Our discussion of the limits of competition in the context of small economies could also help to explain another global feature of Asian capitalism, and that is its use of developmental states. We might note that developmental states make a lot more sense in the context of small economies, since small economies are more likely to benefit from state restrictions on the number of participants in a particular market. At the time of their development, the economies of Asia were indeed relatively small, and one wonders whether that might have something to do both with their attraction to the developmental state model and with their successful emergence as advanced industrial economies under the auspices of that model. (Cf. Jessop, Ch. 5, pp. 107, 109–10.)

Insofar as Asia's internal, core–peripheral architecture is concerned, we would expect that competition and its regulation would become more complicated the further one moves into the periphery (in this volume see generally Gillespie, Ch. 8; Dowdle, Ch. 9). Here, too, export orientation and small economy status raise issues. Beyond this, lesser wealth and correspondingly lesser governmental capacity would likely cause markets to take an increasing social role.[80] At the same time, particular goods and services that are taken for granted by citizens in North Atlantic economies can become more scarce, promoting not only greater state intervention in markets, but also areas of intention that from the perspective of the orthodox competition model seem to be simply protectionist and anti-competitive[81] (see also Dowdle, Ch. 9, pp. 225–6; cf. Deyo, Ch. 12, pp. 285–6). The greater economic fragmentation of peripheral states could cause a corresponding fragmentation of the competition regime, making

---

[80] See, e.g., Frederic C. Deyo, 'Reforming Labor, Belaboring Reform: Structural Adjustment in Thailand and East Asia', in Yoichiro Sato (ed.), *Growth and Governance in Asia* (Honolulu: Asia-Pacific Center for Security Studies, 2004), pp. 97–114.

[81] See, e.g., Phongpaichit and Baker, *Thailand's Crisis*, pp. 35–82.

implementation of a coherent regulatory framework for competition more difficult (see, e.g., Zheng, Ch. 7; Gillespie, Ch. 8; Dowdle, Ch. 9, pp. 210–11, 219–22).

Of course, none of the observations above are particularly earth-shattering. We already know that Asian states have historically been reluctant to embrace global competition norms. We already know that the more peripheral environments in Asia are often even more resistant to such norms, formally adopting them in the guise of national competition legislation due to global pressures, but being very sporadic in their implementation.[82] But the general trope has attributed this resistance to a lack of political will, generally implying that this resistance is simply a reflection of what is termed 'moral hazard' – that is, of the political and economic elite colluding to put their own interests above that of their nation.[83] By contrast, our alternative explanation presented above suggests that the Asian states' resistant to North Atlantic models of competition could, at least sometimes, be working to serve legitimate social purposes. And, in this sense, what Jeffrey Fear said with regard to our understanding of cartels also applies to our efforts to understand competition in the context of Asian capitalism – namely, that studying competition in Asia simply through the lens of conspiracy also does a severe injustice to its empirical reality and short-circuits many important questions both about Asian capitalism and about the orthodox model of competition itself.[84]

---

[82] See also R. Ian McEwin, *Competition Law in Southeast Asia* (Cambridge University Press, forthcoming).

[83] See, e.g., Randall Morck, Daniel Wolfenzon, and Bernard Yeung, 'Corporate Governance, Economic Entrenchment, and Growth', *Journal of Economic Literature*, 43 (2005): 655–720. See also Phongpaichit and Baker, *Thailand's Crisis*, pp. 35–82.

[84] Cf. Fear, *Cartels and Competition*, p. 1 ('In short, studying cartels through the lens of conspiracy does a severe injustice to their empirical reality and short-circuits many important theoretical questions.').

2

Asia and global competition law convergence

DAVID J. GERBER

I. Introduction

Two topics have featured in discussions of transnational competition law over the last few years – the evolution of competition law in Asia and the global convergence of competition laws. The role of Asia, especially China, in global competition law development has attracted attention primarily because of the dramatically increased economic importance of the region and because of the resulting political and economic leverage that this economic importance has generated for the enforcement of the region's competition laws. Convergence is a central topic because it represents what is widely considered to be the only currently viable strategy for global competition law development. Curiously, however, the relationship between these two topics is seldom a focus of examination. This chapter sketches elements of that relationship. It introduces themes that are further developed in the chapters that follow.

Asia will necessarily play a central role in the evolution of competition law on the global level. Its economic and political importance will condition the potential effectiveness of any strategy for improving the legal framework of global markets.[1] Without widespread support from Asian countries, no such strategy can be successful. In particular, a strategy based on convergence of competition law systems can only be successful if it achieves such support. A central theme of this essay is, however, that the dynamics of competition law in Asia may limit the extent to which decision-makers there seek to move their competition law systems towards the 'Western' model that is envisioned in the current convergence strategy.

---

[1] I have dealt in depth with issues of global competition law in David J. Gerber, *Global Competition: Law, Markets and Globalization* (Oxford University Press, 2010). The book also contains extensive references to related literature. I refer the interested reader to that volume for further references.

My objective here is to identify some of the factors in the dynamics of Asian competition law systems that may influence Asia's role in convergence as a global strategy and thereby impact both the success of such a strategy and its shape. We focus here on decisions and on decisional influences – that is, factors that can be expected to influence decisions by relevant decision-makers.[2] Current Asian competition law regimes and experience with them represent one set of influences (see, e.g., Part III of this volume). Broader legal, political, and social factors produce another (see Part IV of this volume; see also Gillespie, Ch. 8). Our analysis focuses on competition law, but much of it also relates to larger issues concerning the role of Asia in legal globalization and in the evolution of 'varieties of capitalism'.[3]

II. Scope and key terms

Several key terms call for clarification of the ways in which we are using them here. One is the term 'Asia' itself. Geographically, it refers to a vast area whose borders are reasonably clear. Yet competition law experience in this region has been limited primarily to East Asia (basically, China, Japan, South Korea, and Taiwan).[4] Areas such as Southeast Asia have only recently begun to take competition law seriously.[5] As described in the first chapter by Dowdle, this volume includes both East and Southeast Asia within its use of the term. This chapter focuses primarily on the East Asian experience, tying it into larger Asian themes where appropriate.

'Competition law' here refers to a normative framework – institutions and processes – whose stated objective is to deter restraints on competition. The primary objective of this form of law is to provide a public good – namely markets that are more valuable to society because their operation is not distorted or restrained by private

---

[2] For fuller discussion of this methodology, see David J. Gerber, 'System Dynamics: Toward a Language of Comparative Law', *American Journal of Comparative Law*, 46 (1998), 719–37.

[3] Peter A. Hall and David Soskice (eds.), *Varieties of Capitalism: The Institutional Foundations of Comparative Advantage* (Oxford University Press, 2001).

[4] For an overview of the East Asian experience see Gerber, *Global Competition*, pp. 202–36.

[5] The countries of Southeast Asia often share basic issues with smaller, developing countries elsewhere. The leading analysis of competition law issues in small-market economies is Michal S. Gal, *Competition Policy for Small Market Economies* (Cambridge, MA: Harvard University Press, 2003).

conduct (see also Dowdle, Ch. 1, pp. 21–4). In the United States, the term used for this area of law is 'antitrust law'. In some countries, however, the term 'competition law' includes what is usually referred to as 'unfair competition law' – that is, legal regimes designed to protect competitors from conduct that is considered in some sense 'unfair'. Unfair competition law thus pursues aims that are fundamentally different from those of 'competition law' as described above, although their norms sometimes overlap.

Finally, the term 'convergence' is used here to refer to a process in which decision-makers decide *of their own accord* to move the characteristics of their competition law systems towards a common point, which we shall call a 'convergence point' (cf. Sum, Ch. 4).[6] It is important to emphasize that we are here exclusively concerned with decisions that are voluntary – that is, that are not made pursuant to obligation (e.g., through treaty) and are not subject to compulsion (e.g., political or economic compulsion such as may be created by the need to receive a loan from an international lender).

III.   Temporal contexts

The temporal context of Asian competition law experience influences not only the current operation of Asian competition law systems, but also their roles in the evolution of transnational competition law. It conditions the ways in which national and transnational decisions are interwoven. Asian competition law experience has a specific location in time that shapes the assumptions, judgements, and incentives of decision-makers, and that temporal location creates contexts for decision-making that differ in significant ways from experiences within the United States and Europe (see, e.g., Vande Walle's discussion of the historical evolution of competition law in Japan, Ch. 6).

In general, competition law experience in Asia has been recent, limited, wary, and ambiguous. These factors are often closely related to each other. Competition law is relatively new to Asia.[7] Very few countries had

---

[6] For more thorough discussion of the concept of convergence see Gerber, *Global Competition*, pp. 281–93.

[7] For overviews of early developments see Donald H. Brooks and Simon J. Evenett (eds.), *Competition Policy and Development in Asia* (New York: Palgrave Macmillan, 2005). For a more recent overview, see Toshiaki Takigawa and Mark Williams (eds.), *Antitrust Bulletin*, 54 (2009), *Symposium Part I: Asian Competition Laws*.

competition laws of any significance prior to the 1990s. One exception is Japan, but even there the actual implementation of competition law also remained weak during this period.[8] The US occupation authorities imposed competition law on Japan in the wake of World War II, but, again as described by Simon Vande Walle in Chapter 6, competition law played a relatively small role there prior to the globalization wave of the 1990s. This relatively shallow experience with competition law frames and influences many, if not all, competition law decisions in Asian countries.

Asian competition law experience is not only recent, but also generally limited in scope and depth. Even today, most Asian countries have had only limited experience in actually enforcing competition laws. As a result, countries other than Japan, Taiwan, and South Korea seldom have competition officials with significant enforcement experience or practical expertise. Even in those few countries where there has been some competition law enforcement (primarily Singapore), it is far more limited than is the enforcement experience in 'Western' jurisdictions such as the United States, Germany, and the European Union (see also Prosser, Ch. 10).

This is related to the third signal element in Asian competition law experience mentioned above – namely, wariness. Decision-makers in Asian competition law systems have moved slowly and carefully in implementing their competition law regimes. The distance between 'law on the books' and 'law in action' often remains great. With often limited and uncertain political backing, legislators and officials have avoided going 'too far too fast'. In Japan, for example, officials were very wary of enforcing competition law until the 1990s, and in recent years the Chinese have been similarly cautious, especially in areas other than merger control (which is subject to extensive foreign pressures and obligations) (see also Zheng, Ch. 7, pp. 151–60).[9]

Finally, Asian experience with competition law is often ambiguous. On the one hand, many officials and politicians assert the value of competition and claim to believe that competition law can be of value in establishing and maintaining it. Many statutes also follow

---

[8] Another notable exception is Taiwan, where competition law first acquired significant backing in the 1980s.

[9] For discussion of some of the factors at play in the Chinese context, see David J. Gerber, 'Constructing Competition Law in China: The Potential Value of European and U.S. Experience', 3 *Washington University Global Studies Law Review* 3 (2004), 315–31.

European or US models to a significant degree, and competition law officials often appear to follow the practices of their European and American counterparts. On the other hand, however, these claims and actions often appear to have limited political support and remain largely ineffectual in practice. For example, many states in the region have accepted competition law under pressure from external sources – for example, as a condition of receiving a loan from an international lending agency such as the International Monetary Fund (IMF) or the World Bank, and they are subject to pressures from foreign sources actually to implement them. Where statutes and decisions are coerced, incentives to apply and enforce them may meet with significant domestic resistance (see, e.g., Gillespie, Ch. 8). Domestic political and economic interests may impede competition authorities from applying competition law provisions seriously, especially if it harms their perceived interests. Under these circumstances, officials must often walk a narrow path in which they send mixed and sometimes even contradictory signals about their intentions and policies, depending on whether the intended audience is primarily foreign or primarily domestic. The contrasting 'pulls' of the two audiences – domestic and international – create uncertainty on the part of both the decision-makers and the audiences that seek to interpret their actions.

This temporal context has additional implications for decision-making in Asian competition law systems. I mention only two. One is that Asian decision-makers are continually faced with foreign models and operate under pressure from foreign sources to conform to those models. This presents a sharp contrast to the contexts in which US and European competition law evolved. In the United States, antitrust law developed for almost a century with limited concern for the impact of the outside world on it; and in Europe competition law also evolved for decades with limited influence from outside sources.[10] A second implication is that these countries are under pressure to play 'catch-up' – that is, to try to 'modernize' as quickly as possible, where 'modernize' means 'Westernize'. One result is that they often have incentives simply to 'put on a good show' for foreign audiences in order to buy time for themselves to develop competition law according to their own needs or not to develop it at all.

---

[10] For detailed analysis of European competition law development, see David J. Gerber, *Law and Competition in Twentieth Century Europe: Protecting Prometheus* (Oxford University Press, 1998).

IV.   Economic contexts

The economic contexts in which competition law has evolved in Asia also have distinctive traits that bear on the convergence strategy. Levels of economic development in Asia often differ dramatically among Asian countries and even within individual countries (see, e.g., Dowdle, Ch. 9). This makes generalizations particularly difficult, but three patterns that are often found in Asian countries deserve particular mention.

A.   State involvement

One pattern is the frequently high level of state involvement in the economy. In China, Vietnam, and some other countries this includes extensive state ownership of major enterprises, and this creates incentives for the government to avoid subjecting such companies to burdens that might impede their profitability.[11] Even where public bodies do not own a particularly large share of the country's productive capacity (e.g. Japan and South Korea), government officials often have significant capacity to influence and steer business decisions and thus to shape the direction of economic development.

B.   Domestic industry structures

A second component of the economic context that is common in Asia involves structures within the domestic economy. The prominence of the so-called 'hub and spokes' pattern of industrial structure (also known as 'production chains' or 'production networks') is a central concern (see especially Yeung, Ch. 11; see also Dowdle, Ch. 9). It is particularly prominent in Japan and South Korea, where the structures and relationships are relatively well defined and even have specific names (*keiretsu* and *zaibatsu* in Japan, *chaebol* in South Korea). Less clearly defined versions of it are also found in China and Vietnam as well as in many other countries. In this pattern, large networks of companies are structured around one or more large central industrial units and a related bank. The smaller firms typically supply the core industry and maintain close relationships with it. In effect, they

---

[11] For discussion, see Dali L. Yang, *Reshaping the Chinese Leviathan* (Stanford University Press, 2004).

function as dependent subcontractors – that is, they agree to provide particular goods or services to the core industrial unit, and in return they receive long-term purchasing obligations, favourable financing arrangements and other benefits, either from the industrial core unit itself or from a bank or other financial institution that is part of the hub and spokes group.

In many Asian countries the predominance of this pattern makes the relationships between the core units and their dependents a central concern of economic policy in general and of competition policy in particular. There are reports that in meetings among Asian competition law officials, these dependency relationships are often a major topic of discussion. These relationships raise issues of the use of economic power and 'fairness' that are often specific to this type of economic structure (see e.g. Dowdle, Ch. 9).

C. The international economic context

The international economic context also helps to shape competition law decisions in Asia. I mention two particularly prominent issues. One is the extent to which many Asian countries depend on foreign direct investment (FDI) for their economic advancement and often their political stability. The exceptionally rapid economic development in China and many other countries has been fuelled by foreign investment from the United States, Europe, and Japan. The main attraction has been lower labour and other factor costs. Although there is general recognition that the fuel of foreign direct investment is likely to diminish, most countries remain heavily dependent on it for the foreseeable future. This generates incentives for economic policymakers to tailor their policies and, above all, their *statements about policy* to the needs and expectations of potential foreign investors.

The international economic context also generates a perceived need for 'national champions' that is particularly prominent in Asian policy discussions, particularly in East Asia. In much of Asia, globalization has helped to generate the belief that domestic Asian companies require special protection in order to be able to 'catch up' with Western firms. They cannot be expected to compete effectively against foreign firms at this stage of development, so they must be given special advantages that counterbalance the 'head start' of Western and Japanese firms. This view of the relationship between domestic firms and the global economy is often used to justify government measures to support firms that are thought to be eventually capable of competing in global markets. The motivations for supporting and protecting 'national champions' include not only economic considerations, but also issues of international prestige and political influence.

These economic contexts create pressures on competition law decision-makers. Even the most independent competition law authorities are influenced by them. This does not necessarily, however, create pressures for greater conformity among competition law systems. It is often assumed that because all countries face similar international economic contexts, those contexts themselves will foster convergence among competition law systems. Yet this assumption deserves careful scrutiny. As explored by John Gillespie in Chapter 8, global economic pressures vary in the direction and intensity of their impact on particular states! The key issue is not the contexts themselves, but how decision-makers in individual countries perceive their relationship to these contexts. This may depend on numerous factors, such as, for example, the economic position of the state's economic units in relation to foreign markets and competitors and the state's international political obligations and interests. Moreover, these factors are always tempered with and shaped by domestic political and economic elites and their perceptions of these contexts.

V. Policy contexts

These temporal and economic contexts shape the issues to which decision-makers must respond, and competition law is increasingly seen as an important part of such policy responses. Competition law is, in turn, embedded in both domestic and political contexts that provide incentives, support, and constraints on competition law development. Historically, competition law has functioned well only when it has been part of a broader complex of policies that seeks to improve market functioning and enjoys political support for that mission. In Asia, however, the policy environments in which competition law is embedded often provide uncertain and fragile support. (This political aspect of Asian competition regulation is explored further by Tony Prosser in Ch. 10.)

A. The domestic policy environment

The domestic policy environment in Asian countries seldom provides strong support for competition law. As noted above, most institutional incentives and procedures in these systems have evolved within a context in which government officials are expected to control or strongly influence economic activity and economic development. This long-standing pattern in relations between the state and the market tends to conflict with the aims of competition law, which, by definition, seek to foster the competitive process rather than the state as the primary regulator of economic activity. Moreover, these domestic policy arrangements, patterns, and institutional cultures are often well established, and the political elites inhabiting them are often very powerful. This contrasts with the situation of most competition authorities, which are generally new and which frequently lack both experience and political clout. Often, therefore, domestic policy environments constrain rather than foster competition law development.

B. *International economic policy environments*

The international policy environment can sometimes provide a more hospitable climate for the development and effectiveness of competition law. The institutions of government that deal with transnational issues such as trade and investment often have incentives to advocate and support competition law. They are exposed to foreign pressure and influence, and their incentives to please foreign constituencies can be significant. Moreover, supporters of freer trade and/or greater international economic co-operation tend to share with competition law at least a basic appreciation of the importance of competition. Finally, to the extent that decision-makers in these institutions are concerned with international status for themselves or for their institutions and governments, they have incentives to follow models that are supported by leading players on the international level. Nevertheless, institutions dealing with foreign economic policy generally have less weight in domestic decision-making than their counterparts on the domestic sides, and this may be particularly true in Asia. Domestic policymakers tend to be more directly connected to sources of political and economic support than are foreign policy officials.

The policy environments within which officials can seek to implement competition law in Asia thus may provide some support for a global convergence strategy, but it is often fragile and not necessarily dependable or resilient. Moreover, while there are incentives to follow Western models at the formal, message-sending level, there are often significant obstacles to actually implementing competition policy in a sustained and serious way.

VI.   Defining the goals of competition law

Goals are the focal point of the convergence strategy. If all competition law systems move towards acceptance of the same set of goals, convergence at this level can be expected to lead towards convergence in outcomes and thereby generate an increasingly uniform normative framework for global competition. Statements of goals perform symbolic functions, and they are an important part of the convergence picture. Nevertheless, official statements about the goals of competition law often do not represent the objectives actually pursued by decision-makers.

In general, goals are taken more seriously where they correspond to a perceived societal need. Accordingly, the most effective way to set goals is to begin with the perceived problems and to develop legal tools specifically designed to solve them. In this procedure, the problems function as the starting point for fashioning competition law goals. Convergence as a strategy moves in the opposite direction. There the starting point is a solution that already exists rather than a harm which needs to be addressed. Moreover, it is a solution devised elsewhere by someone else. In current versions of global competition law convergence, the goals of competition law in the United States and Europe are used as the convergence point for others to emulate and approach. In short, instead of starting with the problems to be resolved, this strategy starts with a set of solutions and asks others to accept them (see also Sum, Ch. 4, pp. 88–92).

Decision-makers in many Asian countries may consider these solutions appropriate for their own contexts, and there may be valid reasons for urging their acceptance. For many Asian decision-makers, however, it is not clear that this set of responses is appropriate to the needs and problems of polities in the region (cf. Dowdle, Ch. 1, pp. 33–5). Where this is true, they are not likely to garner the political support necessary for effective implementation. For example, the predominance of 'hub and spokes' structures in many Asian countries foregrounds the potential impact of these relationships on competition. It raises concerns about the impact of relative economic power on the competitive process, and this in turn emphasizes related issues of fairness. In the United States and Europe these structures either do not exist or are of marginal concern. Not surprisingly, therefore, the current economics-based model of competition law does not address this form of harm. Similarly, the perceived need to control abuses of economic power by *foreign* corporations is a prominent topic in discussions of competition law in Asia, but the economics-based approach to competition law does not address this issue. Finally, economic development is a prominent, often the predominant, goal of economic policy in almost all Asian countries (with Hong Kong a possible exception). Again, the economics-based model does not address the issue, at least not directly. To the extent it fails to include development goals it may, therefore, have limited appeal.

Underlying these and other examples is a basic perception in many Asian countries that the protection of domestic producers is at least as important as the desire to benefit consumers. The economics-based model focuses on benefits to consumers, but in Asian countries the desire to benefit consumers cannot easily be divorced from the needs of producers. Regardless of whether the government owns and controls production firms, there is widespread agreement that economic policies should take the needs of producers into account, especially given that producers in the region are acknowledged to face major obstacles in competing with foreign firms. The contexts of competition law in Asia tend, therefore, to emphasize competition law goals that differ significantly from the relatively narrow set of goals pursued in the economics-based model that is the assumed convergence point for global convergence (see also Dowdle, Ch. 1, pp. 25–7). As is explored in greater detail in the final chapter of this volume, this suggests the need for a multi-goal concept of competition law. This is the form in which competition law developed in both the United States and Europe, and it has only recently been abandoned (in the United States) or narrowed (as in the European Union). The factors that have led decision-makers in the United States and Europe to move away from this model may urge Asian countries to move in the same direction, but this has not been established.

This divergence between goals common in Asia, on the one hand, and the economics-based goal structure used by the United States and Europe, on the other, may be a major obstacle in the evolution of convergence as a global competition law strategy. The economics-based model of the goals of competition law was developed in the United States, and it has been adopted to a significant extent by the European Union. It is a response to problems as perceived by decision-makers in the United States and the European Union. To the extent that Asian countries perceive different competition-related issues, convergence as a strategy may have limited appeal. Nevertheless, goals play a symbolic international role as well as a domestic role, and it may provide incentives for Asian countries to announce goals that send desired messages at the international level, regardless of the degree to which the goals are actually pursued by decision-makers on the domestic level.

VII.   Response tools: availability and use

Goals matter, but they mean little without implementation. How will goals be achieved? What factors will determine the actual role that competition law norms play in business decision-making? There would be little point in pursuing convergence in goals without considering their implementation and the capacity of competition law to influence business conduct. Notice that I use the term 'implementation' rather than the more common term 'enforcement' in this context. It refers to any measures or policies taken by public authorities or others for the purpose of increasing compliance with competition law norms (see also Maher, Ch. 3, pp. 75–8, for an extended examination of the distinction between enforcement and compliance). We look at two important factors in determining the availability and use of response tools – the characteristics of the legal system itself and the implementation capacity of the institutions related to competition law. Here again the risks of generalization are great, and there is much diversity in Asia on some of these points. Nevertheless, we can identify some basic patterns.

A.   Characteristics of the legal system

Several characteristics common to legal systems in Asia are particularly relevant for implementing competition law. One central fact is that formal legal institutions in Asia have been imported from 'the West' during the last century or so and sometimes only very recently. As a result, the attitudes and values associated with law as it is known in the United States and Europe tend to be less robust in Asia than they are in their source regions.[12] Most Asian countries have adapted concepts, procedures, and institutions of law from Western countries, but they have been imported into often very well-developed governance institutions with their own traditions, expectations, and preferences (see, e.g., Japan, as described by Vande Walle in Ch. 6). This has led to a process of blending in which formal legal institutions and practices interact with indigenous forms of governance and the expectations associated with them. Not unexpectedly, legal institutions and forms sometimes operate very differently in Asia than they do in their source areas of Europe and the United States.

---

[12] See, e.g., Harry Scheiber and Laurent Mayali (eds.), *Emerging Concepts of Rights in Japanese Law* (Berkeley, CA: The Robbins Religious and Civil Law Collection, 2007).

In particular, law as a formal and separately identified system of norms and institutions usually operates in Asia within governmental arrangements that feature a high degree of top-down control, on the one hand, and indigenous conflict resolution mechanisms and control structures, on the other. Dense populations and, in many cases, relatively recent histories of disruption and political instability have generated the perception – at least among political elites – that government must exercise strong controls over territory and people. These governance traditions seldom provide 'law' with the status and degree of independence that is often found in 'the West'. This history, and the attitudes and values it has generated, are reflected in many institutions and practices of law that are relevant to competition law implementation. Below are a few examples to illustrate the point. Some of the characteristics mentioned below can also be found in Europe and even the United States, but they tend to be significantly more prevalent and influential in the Asian context.

One example is legal education. In Asian contexts, education in law is often general and designed primarily to train bureaucrats rather than private legal practitioners or judges. In this there are some similarities to other so-called 'civil law' countries, but the focus on training for the bureaucracy and the close association between legal education and success in bureaucracies are particularly pronounced in many Asian countries, especially in countries where Confucian traditions have been emphasized. Moreover, the state frequently controls legal education in ways and to extents that are seldom seen elsewhere. Governments control not only the financing and administrative affairs (this is common in Europe) but often also the content and methods of legal education. The basic image tends to be that government establishes the law by enacting statutes; universities then promulgate these texts; and law students memorize the rules, both substantive and procedural. Memorization of rules tends to be the central feature of the educational mission. There is generally little emphasis on independent analysis, and criticism of the content of laws has generally not been encouraged, although reforms have recently been introduced in both Japan and South Korea to encourage critical legal thinking. This conception of legal education tends naturally to favour modes of governance that centre on control by the state.

Consistent with this role for legal education is the structure of the 'legal profession' (a concept which is itself somewhat strained in application to Asia). In contrast to many Western countries, bureaucrats tend to be at the top of the status hierarchy, with judges and private practitioners lower in status (sometimes far lower). One indication of this pattern is the fact that in many countries (Japan, China, and South Korea in particular) leading graduates of law faculties typically aspire to become bureaucrats rather than private practitioners or judges.

The roles assigned to law and legal professionals are related to this structure. The basic role for all law-trained individuals is to know what the formal rules are and how they are applied. Statutory texts are at the centre of the legal world. They represent the government – that is, the realm of government officials. Officials typically have strong political and cultural support in interpreting and applying these texts. The role of judges and private practitioners is to use knowledge of the texts to navigate the legal terrain shaped and largely controlled by administrative officials. Creative legal reasoning and argumentation tend to be less valued.

In this context, discretion in applying the rules becomes a central issue. Predictable interpretation of statutory rules is seen as fundamental to the legal system. It is portrayed as reducing the discretion of those who interpret the law (i.e. judges and private practitioners) and at the same time justifying the status and authority of those who write the laws. In many cases in Asia, however, other features of the social and political systems influence outcomes in indirect ways. In China, for example, 'guanxi' (the systematic use, development, and exchange of personal influence) often plays a significant role in decision-making.

This basic framework provides little support for the competition law model that is the assumed point for global convergence. It tends to support *dirigistic* control of an economy by bureaucratic officials rather than confidence in economic interactions by private firms and individuals. It favours clear rules, and it tends to provide limited space for open-ended norms based on evaluation of economic outcomes.

B. Institutional capacity

Institutional *capacity* available to pursue competition law objectives tends to be limited by these and other aspects of legal and political systems in Asia. Implementation measures must have support in order to be effective. They need economic and human resources as well as intellectual capacities appropriate to the tasks, and they must have sufficient independence from external constraints to pursue those tasks. Again, many Asian competition law institutions lack at least some of the appropriate capacity supports. (See, e.g., Dowdle's exploration of institutional capacity problems in rural China, Ch. 9, pp. 222–5).

Competition law authorities in the region are often new and untried. Their officials are still learning what competition law is about. Often they have had significant administrative experience, but in other areas of law that involve direct economic regulation – such as price controls – that have some similarities to competition law but nevertheless serve quite different purposes with quite distinct tools. Few have had significant practical experience in applying and enforcing competition law. Moreover, in many countries competition law agencies have limited resources that do not provide an adequate base for effective evaluation and application of competition law.

Courts also tend to be deficient in some or all of these respects. In many countries political and economic pressures limit the independence of courts to apply and enforce competition law, while in other countries such as Japan and South Korea judges have well-established judicial independence, but they may be subject to cultural and societal pressures and conventions that tend to impede competition enforcement. Competition law adjudication necessarily requires the capacity to investigate with some care complex factual scenarios, and this has proven to be an obstacle to competition law enforcement not only in Asia, but even in some European countries.

Finally, the specific capacity to use economic tools must be central to any discussion of a convergence strategy that seeks to implement an economics-based model of competition law. In that model, economics determines outcomes. Yet, as we have seen, the capacity of both courts and administrative officials to perform these operations effectively is significantly limited. Competition officials generally do not have significant training in economics, and training in competition law economics is rarer still. This is even more true with regard to judges, who seldom have training of any kind in economics. It is difficult, therefore, to envision convergence around a conception of competition law that requires high levels of capacity in the use and evaluation of economic data and analysis.

C. Implications for global convergence strategy

In general, therefore, the legal and political context in many Asian legal systems provides significant disincentives to adopting a model of competition law based entirely or even primarily on economics. Both the basic characteristics of the legal systems and the specific institutional capacities and capabilities available for competition law implementation tend to conflict with the basic requirements and assumptions behind the economics-based model of competition law. Even assuming that Asian countries want to accept the procedures and constraints of an economics-based model, they may not possess the tools and resources appropriate for implementing such a model. Moreover, even if the tools were made available, many Asian countries do not generally possess capacities necessary for using them as prescribed in the convergence model.

VIII.   Asian culture: phantom or factor?

The issue of culture plays elusive roles in discussions of competition law convergence. As magicians often say, 'Now you see it; now you don't.' On the one hand, there are frequent, almost routine references to the importance of developing 'competition culture', especially in countries with relatively new competition law regimes. The assumption behind these references is that acceptance of the value of economic competition is essential for the effective development of a market economy and that competition law contributes to achieving precisely that end. These references acknowledge that 'values' and 'societal expectations' are not only relevant but central to competition law objectives. On the other hand, few discussions of global competition policy make serious reference to national or other cultural traditions as a factor in assessing the potential for convergence (see also Sum, Ch. 4). 'Culture' in this sense is generally avoided, despite the fact that it refers to exactly the same kinds of factor involved in discussions of 'competition culture' – that is, widely shared values and community expectations. Not only does 'culture' represent a set of issues that can complicate discussions and that many may feel poorly equipped to discuss, but such references also amount to acknowledging obstacles to convergence that some would prefer not to acknowledge. Moreover, the language of economics tends to be rigorously allergic to considerations of culture. An American-style economics-based model is often lauded precisely because it is 'scientific'. This is thought then to have the advantage of avoiding or at least minimizing 'cultural' differences and thereby providing an attractive basis for convergence.

To avoid reference to 'culture' in discussing Asian competition law development is to ignore a major factor in decision-making in these countries. In East Asia, in particular, cultural traditions disfavouring reliance on competition as a social force and favouring reliance on bureaucratic leadership tend to play very important roles. These cultural traditions influence not only the decisions of leaders and administrators, but also political support for policies such as competition law. Ironically, as explored further by Tony Prosser in Chapter 10, progress in developing a 'competition culture' may require understanding, evaluating, and addressing cultural elements of varying kinds that can both support and impede such development.

IX.   Concluding comments

This brief review of the role of Asia in discussions of competition law convergence reveals the risks of assuming that Asian countries will readily and fully accept as their own the economics-based model of competition law that is currently assumed to represent a point of global convergence. The historical experience of Asian countries, their relationships with the global economy, the characteristics of their legal systems, and the political and cultural contexts in which they operate create significant obstacles to deep convergence around such a model.

These factors suggest an evolution in which these countries accept the value of certain elements of such a model of competition law and incorporate some of them, but also develop their own versions of competition law. Perhaps these versions will constitute variations on a theme proposed by the West, but they may also eventually represent a distinctively Asian theme.

PART II

The political economy of global competition law

3

The institutional structure of competition law

IMELDA MAHER

I. Introduction

The number of states adopting new domestic competition laws has grown exponentially over the last ten years.[1] This gives rise to the need to understand the challenges facing a new domestic competition regime, particularly with regard to the institutional design of that regime. Formal institutions are a necessary precondition for attaining the relevant equilibrium in the contexts of firm co-ordination in the market.[2] They are not, however, sufficient, and account also has to be taken of the hard law and soft law structures that give institutional shape to that regime. Even where these new statutes are able to provide a relatively complete formal image of the institutions and rules that are to give effect to agreed competition policies, they often represent, even at their best, what are in effect incomplete (social) contracts in which the competition agency is tasked with filling in the blanks (see also Jessop, Ch. 5) – a task complicated by what are sometimes competing principal/agent concerns of legitimacy and accountability.[3]

This chapter reflects on the role that institutional structure (as contrasted to that of regulatory norms) plays in the regulation of competition law at both the national and transnational levels. In this, it looks not only at statutory frameworks and agency design, but also through a lens of what is sometimes called a 'historical institutionalist perspective' that

---

[1] About 111 states with populations over 80,000 have competition laws. The peak decade was the 1990s, when sixty-three states adopted competition laws. See Anestis S. Papadopoulos, *The International Dimension of EU Competition Law and Policy* (Cambridge University Press, 2010), pp. 15–16.

[2] See Peter A. Hall and David Soskice, 'An Introduction to Varieties of Capitalism', in Peter A. Hall and David Soskice (eds.), *Varieties of Capitalism: The Institutional Foundations of Comparative Advantage* (Oxford University Press, 2001), p. 12.

[3] See, e.g., Brian Levy and Pablo T. Spiller, 'A Framework for Resolving the Regulatory Problem', in Brian Levy and Pablo T. Spiller (eds.), *Regulations, Institutions and Commitment* (Cambridge University Press, 1996), p. 4.

recognizes that 'institutional structures' do not merely comprise bureau-cratic architectures, but also include the formal and informal rules and procedures that, less overtly but just as critically, shape and constrain how these structures approach and implement their social mandates.[4]

At the transnational level, what we might call the 'institutional struc-tures of global competition law' include transnational networks that link domestic competition agencies; treaty arrangements that include terms affecting or implementing competition policy; and extraterritorial enforcement of competition law regimes that have been legislatively established at the national level. These will be discussed in section II. At the domestic level, this includes structural factors impacting the regulatory capacity of the competition agency, as well as its ability to withstand political pressures from the government and society. It also includes enforcement strategies and powers. These will be examined in section III. In examining all this, it is also acknowledged that despite a global pull towards formal isomorphism and homogeneity among the world's national competition regimes, culture, history, and different legal and economic contexts are still generating important divergences even among regimes that were highly isomorphic at the time of their founding. It might also be noted that many of the themes introduced in this chapter will be recapitulated specifically in the context of Asia by Tony Prosser in Chapter 10.

II.   Transnational structure: networks, treaties, and extraterritorial enforcement

The explosion of competition regulation as a global norm has been driven in large part by the zeal both of US antitrust officials[5] and of the European Commission. In the 1990s, the latter sought to replicate the European Union (EU) experience of a single, transnational competition agency on the world stage via trying to include development of a global competition law for WTO states in the WTO's Doha Round.[6] (See also

---

[4] Sven Steinmo and Kathleen Thelen, 'Historical Institutionalism in Comparative Politics', in Sven Steinmo, Kathleen Thelen, and Frank Longstreth (eds.), *Structuring Politics* (Cambridge University Press, 1992), pp. 2–3.

[5] John Braithwaite and Peter Drahos, *Global Business Regulation* (Cambridge University Press, 2000), p. 216.

[6] See, e.g., Leon Brittan and Karel Van Miert, 'Towards an International Framework of Competition Rules', *International Business Lawyer*, 24 (1996): 454–7; Imelda Maher, 'Competition Law in the International Domain: Networks as a New Form of Governance',

Sun, Ch. 4, pp. 83–4.) This effort failed, mainly due to the unlikely coalition of the United States, with its traditional rejection of multilateralism, and developing states whose earlier experience with the Agreement on Trade Related Aspects of Intellectual Property Rights (TRIPS) caused them to suspect that, like that agreement, WTO rules on competition, while dressed in the clothes of public good, would in fact prove to serve the interests primarily of Anglo-European multinational corporations (MNCs).[7]

In lieu of a global competition law, the Europeans eventually agreed to a US initiative to establish a new kind of global regulatory institution: the International Competition Network (ICN).[8] Comprising national competition agencies, this Network is largely virtual: it has no offices or secretariat. Officially it meets once a year, but it also organizes a number of workshops and 'webinars' (it has a website) in different locations. It provides materials on best practice and looks to facilitate mutual learning among its 114 members, of which 65 are from Asia. The competition bodies from the People's Republic of China are not members (due to the fact that the Network has admitted Taiwanese competition agencies as members). It is arguable that interactions facilitate greater trust between agencies so that experiences and 'grey' information can be exchanged more easily, not just face to face at the annual meeting but on a more ad hoc basis during the year. Such exchanges facilitate policy learning among network members. Membership can enhance the domestic standing of an agency both because it facilitates access to global information that can be critical to enforcement and because it makes the member agency a 'bearer of reputation' that can bring international attention to the domestic government's successes and challenges.[9]

Journal of Law and Society, 29 (2002): 112–36. See also David J. Gerber, *Global Competition: Law, Markets and Globalization* (Oxford University Press, 2010), p. 103.

[7] Josef Drexl, 'International Competition Policy after Cancun: Placing a Singapore Issue on the WTO Development Agenda', *World Competition*, 27 (2004): 419–57.

[8] Gerber, *Global Competition*, p. 115; Maher, 'Competition Law in the International Domain'. See also Merit E. Janow and James F. Rill, 'The Origins of the ICN', in Paul Lugard (ed.), *The International Competition Network at Ten: Origins, Accomplishments and Aspirations* (Cambridge: Intersentia, 2011), pp. 21–38; François Souty, 'From the Halls of Geneva to the Shores of the Low Countries: The Origins of the International Competition Network', in Lugard, *International Competition Network*, pp. 39–50. See also the International Competition Network's website at www.internationalcompetitionnetwork.org. The author of this chapter is a non-governmental advisor to the ICN.

[9] See generally Anne-Marie Slaughter, *A New World Order* (Princeton University Press, 2004), pp. 36–64.

The Network hosts a number of working groups on such topics as advocacy, agency effectiveness, cartels, mergers, and unilateral conduct – thus covering a range of substantive and institutional issues. In its ten-year existence, the Network has produced a fairly impressive array of papers and discussion documents. It will now on request also provide online or telephone assistance to member agencies with queries on how to implement recommended practices. Nevertheless, by being placed primarily in the hands of this largely informal network, international competition law has been, for now, relegated to the realm of informal governance – despite the fact that increased global trade and the growing global dominance of MNCs that increasingly transcend national jurisdictional borders mean that, as a consequence, anti-competitive conduct (or even a large merger) can now have significant impact on many states' economies.

The ICN is in fact one of a number of competition networks, most of which have emerged in the last twenty years (although the Nordic Co-operation Network was set up in the 1950s).[10] The Organization for Economic Co-operation and Development (OECD) and the United Nations Conference on Trade and Development (UNCTAD) both organize annual meetings of competition officials and look to facilitate policy learning and technical assistance among competition agencies and officials in Africa (UNCTAD), Asia (OECD), central Europe (OECD), and Latin America (both OECD and UNCTAD). The European Competition Network, comprising the agencies that enforce the EU's competition rules, is the most legalized of these networks. In Latin America, there is the Latin American Competition Forum (LACF), and the Ibero-American Competition Forum (which includes members from Latin America, Spain, and Portugal). The Lusophone Competition Network, created in 2004, brings together competition officials from the world's Portuguese-speaking countries. In Africa, there is the African Competition Network, established in 2010, and in Asia both ASEAN (Association of Southeast Asian Nations) and the APEC (Asia Pacific Economic Cooperation) Economic Forum have competition groups.

Beyond these networks, there are also many examples of multilateral and bilateral trade agreements that address competition issues. At the multilateral level, the EU has instituted a vigorous, regional-level competition regime that extends beyond private market behaviour to include

---

[10] Imelda Maher and Anestis S. Papadopoulos, 'Competition Agency Networks around the World', in Ariel Ezrachi (ed.), *Research Handbook on International Competition Law* (Cheltenham: Edward Elgar, 2012), pp. 60–88.

scrutiny of state subsidies and procurements. NAFTA and various multi-lateral regimes in Africa also include competition provisions, albeit with less enforcement rigour than the EU rules.[11] Many other multilateral trade agreements also include provisions on competition – underlining the symbiotic relationship between trade and competition in the international arena. These agreements address both substantive norms, most typically relating to restrictive agreements and abuse of dominance, and issues relating to enforcement.

Lucian Cernat suggests that one distinct feature of many regional trade agreements is that they generally include specific provisions relating to the content and enforcement of national competition laws: twenty-one agreements have such provisions, three-quarters of which are north–south (out of a total number of between 250 and 300 regional trade agreements). The EU in its trade agreements often requires the partner signatories to harmonize their competition laws with that of the EU. Some agreements require the establishment of trade and competition committees.[12] The existence of such provisions in these trade agreements underpins the importance of the link between trade and competition: removing formal trade barriers is of little real value if domestic markets can replace them with private restrictions on market entry. Finally, there are a small number of bilateral agreements relating to competition law enforcement, with the most comprehensive of these allowing for the exchange of confidential information.[13]

Alongside international negotiations and agreements, the United States and the EU both aggressively apply their competition rules extra-territorially. The United States has been doing this since the 1940s;[14] the EU began doing so more recently.[15] In the US context, the 'effects

---

[11] Papadopoulos, *International Dimension*, pp. 145–204.

[12] Lucian Cernat, 'Eager to Ink but Ready to Act? RTA Proliferation and International Cooperation on Competition Policy', in Philippe Brusick, Ana María Alverez, and Lucian Cernat (eds.), *Competition Provisions in Regional Trade Agreements: How to Assure Development Gains* (New York: United Nations Publications, 2005), pp. 1–34.

[13] For example Canada–United States; Australia–New Zealand; and Australia–United States. The United States and the EU have co-operation agreements, but these do not allow for the exchange of confidential information. For EU agreements, see generally Papadopoulos, *International Dimension*, pp. 52–92.

[14] See *United States* v. *Aluminium Company of America (Alcoa)*, 148 F.2d 416 (2d Cir. 1945).

[15] Damien Géradin, Marc Reysen and David Henry, 'Extraterritoriality, Comity and Cooperation in EC Competition Law', in Andrew T. Guzman (ed.), *Cooperation, Comity, and Competition Policy* (Oxford University Press, 2010), pp. 21–44.

doctrine' extends US competition law to cover any anti-competitive activity that has some effect in the United States. Harry First has argued that the application of this doctrine would allow the United States, with its vast experience and considerable resources, to police world competition.[16] Indeed, at one point there was suggestion that the effect at issue in the litigation simply had to parallel the effect in the United States of the complained-of activity. But, in *Empagran*, the US Supreme Court rejected this extension, holding that the plaintiffs' harm must have occurred at least in part directly in the United States.[17]

The EU developed its own version of the effects doctrine in 1988 in *Woodpulp*.[18] Beyond this, the European Court of Justice (ECJ) has also developed a 'single economic unit doctrine' that ignores the corporate veil for the purposes of competition enforcement, allowing parent firms to be found responsible for the action of their EU subsidiaries.[19] As far as the regulation of mergers is concerned, the EU has adopted a jurisdictional test that looks at the mix of the combined firms' world-wide and EU turnover and that therefore does not require any of the firms involved to have a corporate presence in the EU.[20] This regulation has been quite controversial. For example, the EU Commission blocked a proposed merger between General Electric and Honeywell.[21] Both are American firms and the proposed merger had been approved by the American authorities. This was one of the triggering events behind the American development of the ICN, one of the first working groups of which looked at merger regulation. (A more recent disagreement between the European Commission and the American Department of Justice regarding a transatlantic merger between the Bourse and the New York Stock Exchange was handled much more smoothly, however.[22])

---

[16] Harry First, 'The Vitamins Case: Cartel Prosecutions and the Coming of International Competition Law', *Antitrust Law Journal*, 68 (2001): 711–29.

[17] *F. Hoffmann-La Roche Ltd.* v. *Empagran SA*, 542 US 155 (2004).

[18] *A. Ahlstrom OY and others* v. *EC Commission*, [1988] ECR 5193.

[19] See, e.g., *Imperial Chemical Industries Ltd.* v. *Commission of the European Communities*, [1972] ECR 619.

[20] See Council Regulation (EC) No. 139/2004 of 20 January 2004 on the control of concentrations between undertakings (the EC Merger Regulation), [2004] OJ L24, 1–22. See, e.g., *Gencor/Lonrho*, Case IV/M.619, [1997] OJ L11, 30–72.

[21] *General Electric/Honeywell*, Case COMP/M.2220, [2004] OJ L48, 1–85. For a critical perspective see Eric R. Emch, '"Portfolio effects" in Merger Analysis: Differences Between EU and US Practice and Recommendations for the Future', *Antitrust Bulletin*, 49 (2004): 55–100.

[22] Compare United States Department of Justice, 'Press Release: Justice Department Requires Deutsche Börse to Divest its Interest in Direct Edge in Order to Merge with

Thus there is much regulatory activity at the international level, some directed by extraterritorial application of national rules – perhaps stretched to their limits[23] – and some directed by regional or bilateral trade or competition agreements. Given this, there is a tendency to view global competition policy as a relatively coherent and uniform homogeneous space (at least with regard to private conduct). But, in fact, global competition policy falls short of a formalized 'global competition law', or even of an agreed-upon system of international best practices. Instead, it reflects a patchwork of initiatives that is unified by a strong commitment to competition law on the part of both the United States and the EU, but is at the same time fragmented by the fact that these two powerful regimes have had very different theoretical and doctrinal approaches as to how economic competition should be structured – perhaps reflecting their different varieties of capitalism. Coherence is further compromised by the fact that the EU traditionally favours globalization via the development of multilateral rules, such as through the WTO, while the United States, on the other hand, has favoured globalization via the development of a 'hub and spoke' system of bilateral arrangements (with the United States at the hub).

III.   Domestic structure: the competition agency and competition enforcement

At the domestic level, the driving institutional motor behind effective implementation of competition policy is the competition agency. The competition agency is invariably an administrative agency, and is more likely than not structured as an 'independent regulatory agency'. But independence is not simply a matter of bureaucratic structure. As we shall see below, agency independence – particularly what we might call 'de facto' independence – depends on a variety of factors

---

NYSE Euronext', 22 December 2011 (available at www.justice.gov/atr/public/press_releases/2011/278537.htm), with European Commission, 'Press Release: Mergers: Commission Blocks Proposed Merger between Deutsche Börse and NYSE Euronext', 1 February 2012 (available at http://europa.eu/rapid/pressReleasesAction.do?reference=IP/12/94).

[23] For an overview see Joseph P. Griffin, 'Extraterritoriality in US and EU Antitrust Enforcement', *Antitrust Law Journal*, 67 (1999): 159–99; Imelda Maher, 'Transnational Legal Authority in Competition Law and Governance: Territoriality, Commonality and Networks', in Günther Handl, Joachim Zekoll, and Peer Zumbansen (eds.), *Beyond Territoriality: Transnational Legal Authority in an Age of Globalization* (Leiden: Brill Academic Publishers, 2012), pp. 414–38.

that lie outside the agency's bureaucratic and statutory architecture.[24] These include most importantly status endowments, resource endowments, the nature of its regulatory powers, and the cultural and constitutional constraints under which it must labour. The latter are also related to issues of enforcement. Here, as we shall see, formal legal enforcement is only part of the equation: much more important are the agency's efforts to internalize compliance via education and information sharing.

A.   The 'independent' competition agency

In terms of organization, the dominant global paradigm for the structuring of domestic competition enforcement agencies is that of the independent regulatory agency. 'Independence' – in the form of structural insulation from both government and 'politics' – is deemed necessary to protect the agency from the inevitable anti-competitive inclinations of both populist and political self-interest (but cf. Prosser, Ch. 10).[25] As David Gerber noted in Chapter 2, competition law is a highly technical area of the law which requires specialist lawyers and economists. Having committed to a competition policy and articulated it through legislation, the rationale then is that implementation should be delegated to a specialized independent agency that is able to comprehend the economic intricacies of market competition. Such delegation not only makes policy implementation and enforcement more efficient, it also gives political and populist interests reason to avoid intervening in the competitive forces of the market (by allowing them simply to blame the agency for politically unpopular competitive effects), it facilitates consistency over the electoral cycle, and it encourages market and economic development by demonstrating to potential new entrants a credible commitment to principles of free and fair competition.[26] Such credible commitment is particularly important where the new competition law is in response to

---

[24] This part develops ideas found in Imelda Maher, 'Networking Competition Authorities in the European Union: Diversity and Change', in Claus-Dieter Ehlermann, and Isabela Atanasiu (eds.), *European Competition Law Annual 2002: Constructing The EU Network of Competition Authorities* (Oxford: Hart Publishing, 2005), pp. 223–36.

[25] B. Guy Peters, 'United States Competition Policy Institutions: Structural Constraints and Opportunities', in G. Bruce Doern and Stephen Wilks (eds.), *Comparative Competition Policy* (Oxford: Clarendon, 1996), p. 48.

[26] Mark A. Pollack, 'Delegation, Agency, and Agenda Setting in the European Community', *International Organization*, 51 (1997): 99–134; Imelda Maher, 'Functional and

conditionalities that have been attached to trade agreements or World Bank or IMF arrangements, or where it is a pre-emptive response to the threat of increasingly internationalized enforcement by the domestic competition law regimes of other countries, principally those of Europe and the United States.

At the same time, there are major risks involved in such delegation. First, there is the functional problem that the agent (the competition agency) will depart from the policy preferences of the principal (the government).[27] From a competition policy perspective, this may not be a bad thing, especially where the state commits to a formal adoption of a competition regime without actually intending it to result in any substantive policy change.[28]

But even where this is the case, this 'independence' can also critically impact normative considerations of political accountability and political legitimacy.[29] There is a tension between, on the one hand, having an 'independent' competition agency that becomes the 'face' of competition policy and, especially if it has an advocacy role, becomes determinative of the legitimacy of such a policy; and on the other hand, the risk is that its innately opaque implementation of what is a highly technical area of the law can make that law seem illegitimate and contrary to existing (popular, business, and political) understandings of the relationship between markets, society, and the state (this issue is further explored in the context of Asia in Prosser, Ch. 10, pp. 255–8).[30]

Such remoteness also makes it less likely that business will engage in private enforcement, another point of increasingly global convergence for domestic competition law regimes. This is especially true where there is limited expertise at the Bar and no adjudicative fora with expertise in competition law matters. It contributes both to lack of predictability in enforcement and, through that, to diminished social understandings as to

Normative Delegation to Non-majoritarian Institutions: The Case of the European Competition Network', *Comparative European Politics*, 7 (2009): 414–34.

[27] Pollock, 'Delegation, Agency, and Agenda Setting', p. 108.

[28] Mathew D. McCubbins, Roger G. Noll, and Barry R. Weingast, 'Administrative Procedures as Instruments of Political Control', *Journal of Law, Economics, and Organization*, 3 (1987): 243–77; Mathew D. McCubbins, Roger G. Noll, and Barry R. Weingast, 'Structure and Process, Politics and Policy: Administrative Arrangements and the Political Control of Agencies', *Virginia Law Review*, 75 (1989): 431–82; Maher, 'Functional and Normative Delegation', 418.

[29] Colin Scott, 'Accountability in the Regulatory State', *Journal of Legal Studies*, 27 (2000): 38–60, 39.

[30] See, e.g., Bronwen Morgan, *Social Citizenship in the Shadow of Competition: The Bureaucratic Politics of Regulatory Justification* (Aldershot: Ashgate, 2003).

what the new competition regime demands from those subject to its authority – resulting in weaker overall compliance. This is particularly a problem for new competition regimes. A striking example of this is found in the early Irish competition regime, which was closely modelled substantively on the EU rules, but procedurally relied almost exclusively on private enforcement through the generalized court system (encouraged by the prospect of exemplary damages). It failed miserably, most private cases being brought against the state bodies themselves. The regime had to be substantially revised only seven years later.[31]

How competition policy is articulated within the founding statute is also significant. The vaguer the policy, the wider the margin for discretionary action on the part of the implementing agency. Concomitantly, there is a greater need for alternative accountability mechanisms that can show that the agency is indeed credibly committed to both government policy goals and the true promotion of economic competition. Such mechanisms might include parliamentary subcommittees, and reporting, budget, and audit requirements that reduce the risk of capture, shirking, or mission drift.[32] They also help to cement the legitimacy of the agency, allowing more effective resort to a technical expertise that is itself much more politically opaque.

Another such legitimacy mechanism is process: a strict adherence to transparent procedures adopted by the agency can be significant in enhancing credibility and legitimacy.[33] Strict adherence to procedures can help with compliance, as it can help to constrain and focus agency decision-making, making it more coherent and predictable.[34] Perhaps more importantly, however, compliance with procedure can be used to demonstrate agency embeddedness in the wider legal culture and to ensure that the agency is perceived as acting in accordance with the demands of the rule of law and is thus ultimately being 'fair' in its dealings. While fairness is a woolly concept, research on tax compliance has shown that even when subjects fall foul of the law, their willingness to

---

[31] See generally Imelda Maher, *Competition Law: Alignment and Reform* (Dublin: Round Hall Sweet & Maxwell, 1999), p. 51.

[32] Pollack, 'Delegation, Agency, and Agenda Setting', 99; see also McCubbins et al., 'Administrative Procedures'.

[33] Mark Thatcher and Alex Stone Sweet, 'Theory and Practice of Delegation to Non-majoritarian Institutions', *West European Politics*, 25 (2002): 1–22, 18. See also McCubbins et al., 'Administrative Procedures'.

[34] McCubbins et al., 'Administrative Procedures', 244; see generally Maher, 'Functional and Normative Delegation'.

comply in the future is strongly shaped by their perception of how fairly they were treated even when they were found to be in the wrong.[35]

Wilks and Bartle have shown that the establishment of a (relatively) independent competition agency has a strong symbolic element. Looking at the United Kingdom and Germany, they note how early symbolism with limited policy impact gave way over time to more entrenched agencies with considerably expanded expertise, having influence and setting priorities for enforcement and ultimately supported by governments with more overt preferences for competition policy.[36] There is a strong evolutionary dimension here, where the fledgling agency embeds over time, shapes expectations, and engages in advocacy to 'sell' competition law to those subject to its (potential) rigours, to public officials and politicians, and to the wider public. This experience may not have been lost on jurisdictions setting up more recent agencies, of course, where the motivation in any event has not come from home-grown commitment to competition policy as a public good, but more as a condition of access to global trade.[37] (But see Gerber, Ch. 2, p. 40, on the experience in Asia.)

B.   Factors that help to generate regulatory independence

In thinking about the 'independence' of competition agencies, we have to be careful not to confuse formal or statutory independence (i.e., the 'independent regulatory agency' model as advanced by many international economic development agencies) with actual independence. Competition agencies can still be de facto independent even where they lack formal independence. Perhaps most famously, the European Commission, which is effectively the governmental executive for the European Union, is also the chief competition agency for the EU. It is in this way not an 'independent' agency in the formal sense. But its de facto independence from politics in matters of competition policy enforcement is nevertheless well recognized. Indeed, calls made in the mid-1990s for the establishment of a statutorily independent competition agency were

---

[35] Michael Wenzel, 'The Impact of Outcome Orientation and Justice Concerns on Tax Compliance: The Role of Taxpayer's Identity', *Journal of Applied Psychology*, 87 (2002): 629–45.

[36] Stephen Wilks and Ian Bartle, 'The Unanticipated Consequences of Creating Independent Competition Agencies', *West European Politics*, 25 (2002): 148–72, 149, 170.

[37] Gerber, *Global Competition Law*, pp. 226–7.

quietly dropped, in part perhaps because member states feared creating an even more powerful enforcement body.[38] In the context of Asia, again as described by Tony Prosser in Chapter 10 (pp. **00**), the competition agencies in Singapore, Taiwan, and South Korea are not formally independent (each is set up as a part of government), but they have nevertheless exerted significant influence promoting a 'competition culture' in their respective countries, due precisely to their other endowments along the lines of those listed above.

As far as the agency's ability to embed itself in the country's larger competition culture is concerned, it is de facto independence rather than statutory independence that should receive the lion's share of our attention. Such de facto independence is the product, not simply or essentially of statutory status, but also of other social endowments, primarily status, resources, powers, and cultural, constitutional and accountability constraints.[39] Table 3.1 helps us better understand the kinds of factor that contribute to each of these endowments.

Of course, these endowments are closely interrelated, and it is often difficult to distinguish between them. For example, resources and powers are often tightly linked to status and constraints. Nonetheless, as we examine each in detail, disaggregating them in this way gives us a useful lens for thinking about what competition agencies require in order to embed themselves in the larger socio-economic environment.

1.   Agency status

There are a number of factors that affect agency status: the scope of its powers, its independence from the executive, its reputation (closely linked, I would suggest, to the agency's independence, and that of its head), its status vis-à-vis other domestic regulators, its international reputation, its standing among the media and public, and even the location of its headquarters.

The scope of the agency's powers (see column 3 in Table 3.1) is itself an important factor in determining the agency's status: an agency's

---

[38] Claus-Dieter Ehlermann, 'Reflections on a European Cartel Office', *Common Market Law Review*, 32 (1995): 471–86.

[39] For earlier analyses see Maher, 'Networking Competition Authorities'; see also Imelda Maher, 'Regulatory Compliance and the Rule of Law: Evaluating the Performance of the Australian Competition and Consumer Commission', in Michael Barker (ed.), *Appraising the Performance of Regulatory Agencies* (Canberra: Australian Institute of Administrative Law, 2004), pp. 208–27.

Table 3.1. *Agency endowments*

Status endowments	Resource endowments	Powers and authority	Cultural and constitutional constraints
Scope of powers	Size of budget	Arsenal of decision-making and enforcement powers	Rule of law considerations
Independence	Guaranteed budget?	Civil sanctions	Constitutional constraints
Domestic reputation (especially of its head)	Personnel	Trumping regulators	Cultural constraints
Location of headquarters	Equipment/offices	Scope of the law – unwritten exceptions especially vis-à-vis state actors	Accountability
Position vis-à-vis other domestic regulators	Access to expertise elsewhere, e.g. courts/police, external consultants	Criminal sanctions	
International reputation among other competition agencies	International networks	Prosecutorial role	
Media/public	Courts		

power to challenge conduct deemed inimical to competition, particularly when that conduct is by politically powerful actors, is an essential measure of its political standing. Closely aligned to this is the question of the agency's formal and de facto independence. We have already noted that agencies can lack formal independence but nevertheless enjoy de facto independence. Here, we should also acknowledge that, conversely, agencies can be formally independent under statute but nevertheless be highly vulnerable to political interference when actually trying to implement or enforce the competition law. For example, the Australian Competition and Consumer Commission (ACCC) is technically an independent regulatory agency. Its legislation allows for its chairman to be appointed by government for a maximum term of years. Implicitly, this means that the government can appoint for less than that maximum, so as to signal that their support for the chairman is less than complete, thus compromising the chairman and the commission's status and effectiveness despite their formally independent status. This is in fact what happened to Allan Fels, whose authority during his last term as chairman for the ACCC (c. 2000–4) was compromised by a governmental decision to limit his appointment to a term of three years and eight months rather than the standard five years.[40]

Other factors affecting de facto independence (other than formal independence) include security of funding, the presence of independently minded, professionalized staff with appropriate levels of training and expertise, and the way such staff are appointed (i.e., competitively via public advertisement vs. via secondment from other parts of the public service, although some combination of the two can help to educate the larger civil service in the value and workings of the competition regime and thus enhance the status of the agency within it[41]). The reputation and charisma of the head of the agency can also have a major effect on status and de facto independence. This, again, can be seen in the phenomenal impact Allan Fels had as the first chairman of the ACCC, where his excellent media skills made him very popular among the general public, if not among the political classes.[42]

International reputation can also be an important factor in agency status and de facto independence. After John Fingleton became the head of the relatively new Irish Competition Authority, a small competition agency with uncertain domestic political status, he was able to develop a strong international reputation through the quality of his contributions

---

[40] Fred Brenchley, *Allan Fels: A Portrait of Power* (Sydney: Wiley 2003) (see especially ch. 12, 'What Do We Do Now?').

[41] Clare Hall, Colin Scott, and Christopher Hood, *Telecommunications Regulation: Culture, Chaos and Interdependence inside the Regulatory Process* (London: Routledge, 1999), p. 35.

[42] Brenchley, *Allan Fels*.

to international conferences. This, in turn, helped to galvanize his domestic staff, and significantly enhanced the political status of his new agency. On the other hand, however, because agency heads normally serve only a limited term in office, there is a risk of their looking to enhance their own personal reputation rather than, and perhaps even at the expense of, that of their agency. This necessitates a clear public articulation of the agency's strategies and goals, so that the reputation of the head aligns with the actual needs of the agency.[43] Association with bodies such as the ICN (or in Europe, the European Competition Network[44]) can enhance the credibility and status of an agency, and also provide information, resources, and advice, especially when it is a fledgling, that puts it in a better position when advocating competition law domestically. In addition, networks can also act as a form of peer review, as sites where reputation matters. Thus the agency rankings of the Global Competition Review of Competition Agencies,[45] despite being derived from a relatively spurious methodology, are closely followed by many domestic competition authorities, especially by those ranked close to the top.

Even the location of the agency's headquarters can sometimes be a factor in its status. Location at some remove from that of centralized government can signal independence. On the other hand, distant location can also be used to marginalize the agency and demoralize its staff.

One of the more critical factors – one that goes to the fundamental question as to the role of competition policy as a tool for shaping national economic life – is the relationship between the agency and other regulators (cf. Prosser, Ch. 10, pp. 255–8). Within Europe, the relationship between national competition agencies and other national regulators has become increasingly blurred as sector-specific regulation grows closer to a competition model, leading in turn to more competition agency-like

---

[43] Timothy J. Muris, 'Principles for a Successful Competition Agency', *University of Chicago Law Review*, 72 (2005): 165–78; William E Kovacic, Hugh M. Hollman, and Patricia Grant, 'How Does Your Competition Agency Measure Up?' *European Competition Journal*, 7 (2011): 25–45, 27.

[44] See Recitals 15–18, Recital 32, and Arts. 11–12 of Council Regulation No 1/2003 of 16 December 2002 on the implementation of the rules on competition laid down in Articles 81 and 82 of the Treaty (European Council), [2003] OJ L 1, pp. L 1/4, L 1/10–L 1/11. See generally Maher, 'Functional and Normative Delegation'.

[45] See, e.g., Global Competition Review, *Ratings Enforcement 2012* (London: Law Business Research, 2012), available at www.globalcompetitionreview.com/surveys/survey/516/ Rating-Enforcement.

powers being given to these kinds of regulator.[46] As liberalization progresses and the regulatory turn in Europe leads to greater fragmentation of the 'regulatory state', there are also growing problems of the crowding of regulatory space as more and more sectoral regulators are created.[47] In practice, this means that stronger co-ordination mechanisms are necessary to ensure that conflicting decisions do not emerge, and to ensure that where both the competition authority and a sectoral regulator could have jurisdiction, there will be agreement as to who will take the lead.[48] Hierarchy is not necessarily required, provided there is a clear policy view as to the relationship of competition policy to other regulatory concerns in networked industries (cf. Prosser, Ch. 10, pp. 231–8).

Finally, the views of the media and the public, both of competition law in general and the agency in particular, can also be important. The Australian experience of the ACCC under Fels is salutary in this regard. The high public regard for that agency under Fels was significantly promoted by a positive public review of the agency's operations, but perhaps even more so by a famous press photo of agency officials removing boxes of papers from a company under investigation during a raid of that company's premises (an investigation that, perhaps somewhat ironically, would later collapse).[49] On the other hand, in the United Kingdom the effectiveness of competition authorities there is tempered by consumer attitudes to price fixing, which showed a general acceptance that price fixing is socially wrong, but not to such an extent as to warrant imprisonment. According to the overwhelming majority of respondents, fining and shaming would be sufficient and appropriate punishment.[50] In such cases – where the behaviour prohibited by competition law is not popularly regarded as having a damaging impact on individuals and on society, or is not deserving of the sanctions

---

[46] Nicholas Petit, 'The Proliferation of National Regulatory Authorities alongside Competition Authorities: A Source of Jurisdictional Confusion?', in Damien Géradin, Rodolphe Muñoz, and Nicolas Petit (eds.), *Regulation through Agencies in the EU: A New Paradigm of European Governance* (Cheltenham: Edward Elgar, 2005), pp. 180–214.

[47] See, e.g., Colin Scott, 'Regulating Everything: From Megaregulation to Metaregulation', *Administration*, 60 (2012): 57–85.

[48] See, e.g., United Kingdom, Competition Act 1998, 1998 Chapter 41, sec. 54, sch. 10. See generally Richard Whish, *Competition Law*, 7th edn (Oxford University Press, 2012), p. 437.

[49] Maher, 'Regulatory Compliance'.

[50] Andreas Stephan, 'Survey of Public Attitudes to Price-Fixing and Cartel Enforcement in Britain', *Competition Law Review*, 5 (2008): 123–45.

necessary to deter it – it can be very fruitful if the competition agency can make use of the media to educate the public about the benefits of its competition policy.[51]

2. Agency resources

Resources have an obvious link to status: an underfunded, poorly staffed, and poorly housed agency is unlikely to make a good job of implementing competition law.[52] Thus, irrespective of its formal powers and the statutory architecture, an agency's effective performance will be critically affected by its resources. This includes the size, certainty, and control of the budget; the resources necessary to recruit sufficient numbers of personnel with relevant expertise; appropriate offices and equipment; the ability to gain access to expertise elsewhere, either formally through secondment of civil servants and consultants or informally through support and advice from other agencies; and access to training and information through international networks.[53] The power to secure assistance from police where criminal sanctions are available, and to have the resources to go to court where required, as well as having access to the most appropriate court (ideally a specialist commercial court if there is one), can further facilitate effective enforcement.

A major consideration is that of the budget. This has a number of elements. An easy way to minimize the effectiveness of the agency is by reducing its budget. At the same time, however, a limited budget is not an absolute bar to an agency developing its role, although it can reflect ambivalence at government level about the desirability of an effective

---

[51] On the media and competition enforcement more generally, see Andreas Stephan, '"The Battle for Hearts and Minds": The Role of the Media in Treating Cartels as Criminal', in Caron Beaton-Wells and Ariel Ezrachi (eds.), *Criminalising Cartels: Critical Studies of an International Regulatory Movement* (Oxford: Hart, 2011), pp. 381–94.

[52] See generally International Competition Network, Competition Policy Implementation Working Group, 'Report on Agency Effectiveness', Seventh Annual Conference of the ICN, Kyoto, 14–16 April 2008 (available at www.internationalcompetitionnetwork.org/library.aspx?search=&group=13&type=0&workshop=0); International Competition Network, Competition Policy Implementation Working Group, 'Report on the Agency Effectiveness Project, Second Phase: Effectiveness of Decisions', Eighth Annual Conference of the ICN, Zurich, 3–5 June 2009 (available at www.internationalcompetitionnetwork.org/library.aspx?search=&group=13&type=0&workshop=0).

[53] For a discussion of some of these factors, see Kovacic et al., 'How Does Your Competition Agency Measure Up?'.

competition policy. In fact, where other government ministries control
the competition agency's budgets, this can constitute a form of indirect
control over enforcement priorities.[54]

The ability to recruit personnel with relevant expertise is also important.
This extends to being able to recruit overseas, especially for smaller
economies new to a competition regime which may not have the expertise
locally (a different kind of 'small economy' problem; cf. Dowdle, Ch. 1,
pp. 32–3). Expert support can also be garnered through attendance at
international conferences and participation in international agency networks, and other technical assistance programmes. Expertise can also be
secured on a temporary basis from consultants, especially where agencies
are relatively small, although there is a risk that over-reliance on consultants can cause the agency to lose internal expertise critical to its functioning.[55] Access to appropriate information technology (IT) facilities is
helpful, and the security of information is vital. This is because competition agencies invariably must work with commercially sensitive information, and some agencies will also have to conduct criminal investigations.
One of the most important resources an agency has is its reputation, so a
secure space where information will not be inappropriately leaked and
where business secrets are safe is essential. Should the agency lose its
credibility in this regard, its ability to garner information from whistle-
blowers or complainants will be much diminished if not entirely dissipated.

3. Agency powers

The powers of the agency are determined primarily but not exclusively by
legislation. This legislation will ideally set out what conduct is prohibited
and what are the consequences of breaching the prohibitions, who is
responsible for enforcing the law, and what the relationship is between
the agency and the government.[56] The powers of the agency include
advocacy and enforcement powers such as its ability to trigger

---

[54] See, e.g., OECD, *Regulatory Reform in Ireland: Enhancing Market Openness through
Regulatory Reform* (Paris: OECD Publications, 2001), p. 62.

[55] See also Jerry Mashaw, 'Accountability and Institutional Design: Some Thoughts on the
Grammar of Governance', in Michael W. Dowdle (ed.), *Public Accountability: Designs,
Dilemmas and Experiences* (Cambridge University Press, 2006), pp. 115–56, at pp. 137–8,
149–50.

[56] See UNCTAD, *Model Law on Competition: Substantive Possible Elements for a Competition Law, Commentaries and Alternative Approaches in Existing Legislations* (Geneva:
United Nations Publications, 2004) (available at http://r0.unctad.org/en/subsites/cpolicy/
docs/Modelaw04.pdf).

enforcement actions, particularly those that lead to sanctions, the range of sanctions at its disposal being important. The power to collect the information it needs to enforce the law – for example, to subpoena witnesses and fine firms for interfering with or refusing to handover evidence – is also significant.

The agency also needs the ability to trump other regulators, or at least to ensure that competition concerns are properly addressed by these other regulators in their decision-making (for a good demonstration of this problem, see Vande Walle, Ch. 6, pp. 126–31). One concern is that even if on the face of it the statute embraces a robust competition law, the legal context may be such that that law will not apply to state activity[57] (see generally Prosser, Ch. 10), or even to certain kinds of private economic activity that are sponsored by the state, such as perhaps most famously *keiretsu* in Japan and *chaebol* in the case of South Korea (see Prosser, Ch. 10, pp. 248–9). Such exceptions can make it difficult to develop competitive markets in certain sectors or contexts.

The ability to impose criminal sanctions ensures that competition law secures attention that it might not otherwise get in company board-rooms. Criminal convictions and, arguably, a meaningful and demonstrated threat of imprisonment, will generally cause companies to take prohibitions on anticompetitive conduct much more seriously. At the same time, the question of whether there should be criminal sanctions for anticompetitive behaviour is hotly debated.[58] Recall that a recent public poll in Britain found very little public support for criminal convictions leading to imprisonment for illegal anticompetitive behaviour.[59] Along these lines, criminal prosecutions are relatively common in the United States. But they are rare in Europe, with patchy invocation by member states of the criminal law provisions of their competition laws.[60] Linked to the availability of criminal sanctions is the division of agency

---

[57] See, e.g., the implicit exclusion of state monopolies under the old Greek competition law: Julia Pournara and Costas D. Vainanidis, 'Greek Anti-trust Law: A Critical Appraisal', *European Competition Law Review*, 14 (1993): 226–30, 229.

[58] See generally the contributions to Caron Beaton-Wells and Ariel Ezrachi (eds.), *Criminalising Cartels: Critical Studies of an International Regulatory Movement* (Oxford: Hart, 2011).

[59] See Stephan, 'Survey of Public Attitudes'; Andreas Stephan, 'How Dishonesty Killed the Cartel Offence', *Criminal Law Review*, 6 (2011): 446–55.

[60] The first successful European criminal competition cases were taken in Ireland in 2007; see Carolyn Galbreath, 'Criminalization of Cartel Offences in Ireland: Implications for International Cartels', paper presented at American Bar Association, Section for Antitrust Law Spring Meeting, San Francisco, April 2010, p. 3.

responsibilities in pursuing such sanctions. Some competition agencies have the power to bring prosecutions in their own right, but others have to rely on the state prosecutor to bring such cases. The involvement of the state prosecutor can be seen as a resource, given its expertise in prosecuting criminal activity, or it can be a constraint – white collar crime is generally not high on the enforcement priorities of a general prosecutor when she also has to deal with serious offences against the person.

Civil sanctions are less controversial. But as fines grow larger in the EU this, too, has generated concerns about procedures. With fines now reaching €1,000,000 and even €10,000,000, many argue that more robust adjudicative procedures are called for. One way of meeting these concerns is by separating investigation from judgment, as is done in US administrative agencies.[61] This model addresses concerns as to natural justice and the separation of prosecutor and judge, but at the same time its more elaborate institutional mechanisms can result in greater delay and greater cost in agency enforcement of the law.[62]

4.   Cultural, constitutional, and accountability constraints

Some of the legal constraints under which a competition authority works have already been referred to – notably the necessary constraint of accountability to the government and legislature to ensure compliance with the goals and objectives of the legislation. In addition, the rule of law is a fundamental constraint on the exercise of all public authority: a competition agency is not above the law in the exercise of its power and thus it must also comply with procedural norms to ensure that its decisions are not taken arbitrarily.[63] While the conventional understanding of the rule of law left little room for agency discretion, more recent articulations take account of the need for discretion to ensure individual

---

[61] Administrative Procedures Act (United States) (1946), 5 USC § 554(d). See, e.g., *Rausch v. Gardner*, 267 F. Supp. 4, 6 (E.D. Wis. 1967). See generally Kenneth Culp Davis and Richard J. Pierce Jr, *Administrative Law Treatise*, 3rd edn, 2 vols. (Boston, MA: Little, Brown, 1994), vol. 2, p. 95, §9.9. For application of such a principle to competition law enforcement see Michael J. Trebilcock and Edward M. Iacobucci, 'Designing Competition Law Institutions', *World Competition*, 25 (2002): 361–94; Michael J. Trebilcock and Edward M. Iacobucci, 'Designing Competition Law Institutions: Values, Structure, and Mandate', *Loyola University Chicago Law Journal*, 41 (2010): 455–71.

[62] But see Bernard Schwartz, 'Administrative Law', in Alan Morrison (ed.), *Fundamentals of American Law* (Oxford University Press, 1996), pp. 129–50, at pp. 139–40 (disputing this in the context of American experience).

[63] Maher, 'Functional and Normative Delegation', 414.

justice[64] and the extent to which the exercise of discretion is a norm of the political and legal system (see, e.g., Vande Walle, Ch. 6, p. 130 (on Japan); see also Prosser, Ch. 10, pp. 257–61).

A more heterarchical constraint is that which might be found in the constitution. In Ireland, for example, the constitution only allows courts to impose fines, which are regarded as criminal sanctions, and hence the competition agency only has power to request fines under the criminal law.[65]

As is well described by John Gillespie in Chapter 8 looking at Vietnam, cultural constraints can also be a significant factor. For example, the possible effect of the competition law on particular groups may have to be considered,[66] or it may be necessary to take account of historical patterns of discrimination and exclusion that may have been directed against particular minorities or classes.[67] Cultural limitations on enforcement style can also work important limitations on enforcement strategy, to which we now turn.

C. Enforcement and compliance

Enforcement style and strategy are also important in shaping agency effectiveness. But in this aspect there is greater normative diversity among nations than in the norms governing agency structures. This can be due to different domestic political pressures (see, e.g., Zheng, Ch. 7), different national legal enforcement traditions (see, e.g., Vande Walle, Ch. 6, pp. 126–131); different constitutional structures (see, e.g., Prosser, Ch. 10, pp. 232–4, 260); different forms of capitalism and industrial organization (see, e.g., Dowdle, Ch. 1; Dowdle, Ch. 9); and different cultural attitudes (see, e.g., Gillespie, Ch. 8; see also Gerber, Ch. 2, pp. 51–2).[68]

---

[64] Edward L. Rubin, 'The Concept of Law and the New Public Law Scholarship'. *Michigan Law Review*, 89 (1990): 792–836.

[65] For a critique of this interpretation of the constitution see Gerald FitzGerald and David McFadden, 'Filling a Gap in Irish Competition Law Enforcement: The Need for a Civil Fines Sanction', The Competition Authority, Dublin, 9 June 2011 (available at www.tca.ie/EN/Promoting-Competition/Presentations–Papers/The-need-for-civil-fines.aspx).

[66] See, e.g., Jon Altman and Sally Ward (eds.), *Competition and Consumer Issues for Indigenous Australians: A Report to the Australian Competition and Consumer Commission* (Canberra: Australian Competition and Consumer Commission, 2002).

[67] See, e.g., s. 2(f) of South Africa's Competition Act (as amended), which expressly states that one of the purposes of that Act is 'to promote a greater spread of ownership, in particular to increase the ownership stakes of historically disadvantaged persons'.

[68] See here generally Robert A. Kagan, 'Introduction: Comparing National Styles of Regulation in Japan and the United States', *Law and Policy*, 22 (2000): 225–44 (although he does

Even where the scope of sanctioning is the same, the intensity and frequency of application of those sanctions can differ across jurisdictions. We noted above, for example, how the United States is much more likely to deploy criminal sanctions for anticompetitive behaviour than are European countries (where they have criminal sanctions), despite the fact that they possess similar authority in this area. Another example of this enforcement variation is found by comparing the United States with Japan. The Japanese competition law derives from the US model. But US enforcement of its law is much more characterized by what Robert Kagan has famously termed 'adversarial legalism', in which the courts and (often private) adversarial litigation play a prominent role.[69] Regulatory enforcement in Japan, by contrast, often revolves around a kind of informal interaction between regulators and subjects called 'administrative guidance', a form of enforcement in which the courts play little part (see generally Vande Walle, Ch. 6, p. 130).[70] Of course, while competition agencies often conform with the dominant enforcement culture of the state, they do not always march in lockstep with that culture. Sometimes the particular enforcement culture of a competition agency differs significantly from the general cultural norm (as might be the case with regard to recent developments in competition regulation in Japan; see Vande Walle, Ch. 6, p. 130), such as was the case with regard to antitrust enforcement in the United States during the Reagan administration.[71] The enforcement style of an agency can also change over time (see, e.g., Vande Walle, Ch. 6, again discussing Japan).[72]

Enforcement styles also touch upon questions of enforcement strategy. The aim of competition law ultimately is to embed a 'competition culture' in the nation's business community such that enforcement actions are not required. In short, the successful competition agency is the one that simply has to nudge behaviour in the right direction, without

---

not specifically discuss competition law). On the need for 'informed divergence' in competition regimes, see John Fingleton, 'Competition Agencies and Global Markets: The Challenges Ahead', in Paul Lugard (ed.), *The International Competition Network at Ten: Origins, Accomplishments and Aspirations* (Cambridge: Intersentia, 2011), pp. 197–204.

[69] See generally Robert A. Kagan, *Adversarial Legalism: The American Way of Law* (Cambridge, MA: Harvard University Press, 2001).

[70] See also John O. Haley, *Authority without Power: Law and the Japanese Paradox* (Oxford University Press, 1992).

[71] See B. Dan Wood and James E. Anderson, 'The Politics of U.S. Antitrust Regulation', *American Journal of Political Science*, 37 (1993): 1–39.

[72] See also Gerber, *Global Competition Law*, pp. 220–2 (on South Korea).

much resort to formal enforcement, as firms themselves internalize the value of competition. In this sense, it is compliance, rather than formal 'enforcement' per se, that is the ultimate goal of any competition agency. And promoting compliance often involves much more than simply the effective imposition of the legal sanctions.

This is quite vividly demonstrated in the model of 'responsive regulation' developed by Ian Ayres and John Braithwaite.[73] In the context of competition regulation, responsive regulation would have regulators first and foremost seek to educate the public, public authorities, and firms as to (i) the value of competition, (ii) the demands and prohibitions set down by the competition law, and (iii) the consequences of non-compliance. Since people, as rational actors, are generally legally compliant and value their reputation as law-abiding, this minimizes the need for more invasive agency interventions in the market. But such emphasis on co-operation and education must nevertheless be backed up by the threat of deterrence and sanction. Firms must believe that the agency can and will act where appropriate, that it will act fairly and consistently regardless of who the subject of its attention is, and that it can and will impose sizeable sanctions when required. Thus formal sanctions are also a necessary part of the regulatory tool kit, as are appropriate procedures for their administration (including prosecutorial discretion).

Responsive regulation is thus represented by a pyramid (Figure 3.1). The pyramid rests on a fundamental foundation of education and advocacy. As one moves up the enforcement gradient, there is greater emphasis on the threat of, and ultimately the exercise of, sanction, albeit hopefully there will also be less need to resort to such emphasis. This ultimately culminates, again hopefully in only the fewest of cases, in the incapacitation of the most recalcitrant of violators (such incapacitation can involve bringing criminal actions against owners and directors, ultimately leading to imprisonment, and/or barring owners or directors barred from participating in the firm's corporate governance for a number of years).[74]

---

[73] Ian Ayres and John Braithwaite, *Responsive Regulation: Transcending the Deregulation Debate* (Oxford University Press, 1992), pp. 19–53; John Braithwaite, *Restorative Justice and Responsive Regulation* (Oxford University Press, 2002), pp. 29–44.

[74] See generally Ayres and Braithwaite, *Responsive Regulation*, p. 35. For a discussion on compliance in the context of competition law, see Christine Parker and Vibeke Lehmann Nielsen, 'Deterrence and the Impact of Calculative Thinking on Business Compliance with Competition and Consumer Regulation', *Antitrust Bulletin*, 56 (2011): 377–426.

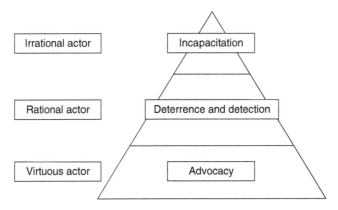

Figure 3.1. The 'regulatory pyramid', adapted from 'the enforcement pyramid', in Ian Ayres and John Braithwaite, *Responsive Regulation: Transcending the Deregulation Debate* (Oxford University Press, 1992), p. 35 (Fig. 2.1).

The pyramid explains why considerations over and beyond formal legal powers are so important in securing the prize of regulatory compliance. An agency that appears powerful and whose decisions and sanctions are widely reported, and that is seen as having influence in the way in which legislation is crafted to reflect a very public commitment to competition policy, can shape expectations so as to secure greater compliance without necessarily having to involve itself in greater 'enforcement'. This reputational quality is something that is built over time and must be maintained.

IV. Conclusion

The creation of an effective competition regime is a long road. Competition law and its effectiveness can ebb and flow depending on the context within which it operates – as evidenced by the emasculation of Japanese competition laws after the withdrawal of the Americans in 1955 (see Vande Walle, Ch. 6, pp. 126–31). While attempts at setting up formal international institutions have largely failed, less formal, competition 'networks' have emerged that facilitate agency effectiveness by promoting information sharing and mutual learning. While there is a large amount of shared commonality based on common substantive rules and a strong epistemic community of technical experts (lawyers and economists), national divergences remain. To explain and understand these variations it is important to go beyond the formal competition laws.

4

The cultural political economy of competitiveness, competition law, and competition policy in Asia

NGAI-LING SUM

I. Introduction

This chapter employs a cultural political economy (CPE) approach to examine the remaking of competition law and competition policy in Asia in the period following the WTO's Doha Round of trade liberalization. It is divided into six sections. Section 2 introduces the CPE approach and links it to the evolution of competition law and policy through three overlapping stages, from trade theory to economic theory and finally to simple managerialism. It focuses on the development of an international, neoclassical economic discourse on competition and competition law, a development that ended with the dropping of the issue of competition law from the Doha Round agenda of WTO negotiations.

The abandonment of this item from the Doha Round work programme prompted a search for other scales of action and other mechanisms to reintroduce competition law and policy into the international political economy agenda. Section 3 focuses on the efforts of the World Bank and its regional counterpart, the Asian Development Bank, to develop an alternative way to promote competition law globally, or, failing that, to promote a market-friendly governance of competition. This strategy reflects the fact that, following the Doha Round decision, competition law is no longer tied primarily to the discourse and practices of 'trade liberalization', but has been re-articulated as a device for promoting 'pro-poor growth' and 'competitiveness' in the Asian region. This discursive shift is discernible from policy documents and proceedings of the World Bank, the Asian Development Bank (ADB), and the Asian Development Bank Institute (ADBI).

Section 4 then shows how this discursive shift has also been accompanied by the managerialization of competition law and competition policy. This has occurred in a context, especially following the 1997 Asian economic crisis, when the World Bank reinvented itself as a

'knowledge bank' to organize the management of development knowledge. Similarly, the ADB has also assumed an active focus on producing
knowledge and developing capacity through toolkits and training workshops on effective management of competition law and policy. This kind
of neoliberal legal managerialism can be seen, in neo-Foucauldian terms,
as an assemblage of 'apparatuses of rule' that involve micro-technologies
of steering, assessment, and capacitation. The fifth section discusses how
this 'regime of truth' is supported in different ways and to different
degrees by national states in the region, and how it both complements
and challenges the state-sponsored, exportist mode of growth found in
many Asian economies. In this regard, competition law continues to be a
key site of contestation and negotiation between the modified neoliberal
and the state-sponsored exportist type. Section 6 concludes with some
observations on the evolving nature of competition law, policy, and
discourse in Asia.

II. The cultural political economy of competition law and policy discourses

CPE is a broad theoretical current that takes the 'cultural turn' (i.e., a
concern with discourse and inter-subjective meaning-making) seriously
and combines it with critical political economy. It explores the interface
between the discursive and the material in political economy, paying
particular attention to the semiotic and material bases of power in the
reproduction and remaking of neoliberal capitalism.[1] Accordingly, this
approach calls attention to the importance of discursive moments
(instances of the making of social meanings, subjectivities, identities,
modes of calculation, and structures of feeling) and to the remaking of
social relations across different sites and scales. CPE considers several
social and discursive features of the discursive-material interactions that
characterize political economy in this regard. Two are worth

---

[1] Ngai-Ling Sum, 'From Regulation Approach to Cultural Political Economy', EU Framework 6 DEMLOGOS Project, Work Package 1 (2005), available at http://demologos.ncl.ac.
uk/wp/wp1/papers/cpe2.pdf.; Bob Jessop and Ngai-Ling Sum, 'Towards a Cultural International Political Economy: Post-structuralism and the Italian School', in Marieke de
Goede (ed.), *International Political Economy and Poststructural Politics* (Palgrave Macmillan, 2006), pp. 157–76; Ngai-Ling Sum, 'The Production of Hegemonic Policy Discourses: "Competitiveness" as a Knowledge Brand and Its (Re-)Contextualizations',
Critical Policy Studies, 3 (2009): 50–76; Ngai-Ling Sum and Bob Jessop, *Towards a
Cultural Political Economy* (Cheltenham: Edward Elgar, forthcoming, 2013).

mentioning here. One is the changing economic, legal, and political imaginaries that simplify and represent complex social realities in order to facilitate social action. These imaginaries (e.g., 'competition for competitiveness', cf. Jessop, Ch. 5) are not neutral, but privilege different entry points and standpoints to interpreting and changing the world. Of particular interest in the present context are changing conceptions of competition, competitiveness, and the extra-economic as well as economic conditions that bear on this. (See, e.g., Yeung, Ch. 11; Deyo, Ch. 12; cf. Dowdle, Ch. 13.) A second feature is the creative deployment of the insights of some neo-Foucauldian scholars[2] about the knowledge–power nexus and its associated normalizing, disciplinary, and governmentalizing technologies (see, e.g., Gillespie, Ch. 8).[3] CPE supplements these neo-Foucauldian analyses of governmental technologies by highlighting the role of negotiations, adaptations, and resistance across different sites and scales and the unevenness of these discursive and material practices.[4]

Given this broad agenda, this chapter mainly concentrates on the discursive side of the global project to incorporate neoliberal models of competition law and policy into the transnational legal-managerial regime. The production and promotion of policy discourses have a long history. They are especially prevalent in the market discourses developed during the era of neoliberal globalization: a notable example in the present context is the 'law and economics' movement, with its multi-site promotion of neoclassical economics as a basis for competition law.[5] This chapter starts by providing a brief outline of the three overlapping stages in the discourses of competition law and policy – from its academic origin in neo-classical economics, to a theory of economic development, and finally to a simple, managerial component of economic governance.

The first stage in the development of modern competition law and policy involved the elaboration of diverse economic and business theoretical paradigms (as described by Dowdle in Ch. 1, pp. 21–4)

---

[2] See, e.g., Mitchell Dean, *Governmentality: Power and Rule in Modern Society* (Thousand Oaks, CA: Sage, 1999); Peter Miller and Nikolas Rose, *Governing the Present: Administering Economic, Social and Personal Life* (Cambridge: Polity Press, 2008).

[3] For an application to the global economy see Wendy Larner and William Walters (eds.), *Global Governmentality: Governing International Spaces* (London: Routledge, 2006).

[4] For further details see Sum, 'From Regulation Approach'; Sum, 'Production of Hegemonic Policy Discourses'.

[5] Jamie Peck, *Constructions of Neo-liberal Reason* (Oxford University Press, 2010).

and their application to the organization of firms and markets.[6] This stage has its origins in classical political economy and political theory (e.g., Adam Smith and Jeremy Bentham respectively). It was supplemented in the United States by the progressive movement (with its anti-monopoly campaigns and the passage of the Sherman Act in 1890,[7] the Clayton Act in 1914,[8] and later antitrust legislation[9]) (see also Dowdle, Ch. 13, pp. 313–6) and in continental Europe by, among others, the German Freiburg School with its ordoliberalism.[10] Also included in this first stage, from the late nineteenth century onwards, is the application of neoclassical economic theory and also, in the second half of the twentieth century, Coasean transaction cost economics as applied to legal decision-making (see also Jessop, Ch. 5).[11]

In order to highlight the contrast between the first stage and the second and third stages, it is worth noting a shared feature of the different economic and business theories that were mobilized in this stage to legitimate competition law and policy. In CPE terminology, this involved the creating of particular economic and legal imaginaries (or 'construals') regarding the nature and dynamic of a profit-oriented, market-mediated economy and the role of law in securing the conditions for economic efficiency, prosperity, and consumer welfare. For example, in the progressive and neoclassical traditions, competition law is framed in terms of restricting monopoly rents of various kinds in order to benefit consumers or to enhance welfare more generally. These traditions argue that competition can enhance the natural 'efficiency' of the market and secure the naturally 'optimal' allocation of resources that markets work to

---

[6] See Spencer W. Waller, 'The Language of Law and the Language of Business', *Case Western Law Review*, 52 (2001): 283–338. Cf. Sum, 'Production of Hegemonic Policy Discourses', pp. 186–7.

[7] Sherman Antitrust Act (1890), 15 USC §§ 1–7.

[8] Clayton Antitrust Act (1914), 15 USC §§ 12–27, 29 USC §§ 52–53.

[9] See generally United States Code, Title 15, Chapter 1 – 'Monopolies And Combinations In Restraint Of Trade' (15 USC §§ 1–38).

[10] For an argument that the extension of competition law in post-Second World War Europe has its own indigenous roots and is not a simple imposition of US antitrust law, see David J. Gerber, *Global Competition: Law, Markets, and Globalization* (Oxford University Press, 2010), pp. 159–204.

[11] See, e.g., Francesco Parisi, 'Positive, Normative and Functional Schools in Law and Economics', in Jürgen G. Backhaus (ed.), *The Elgar Companion to Law and Economics*, 2nd edn (Cheltenham: Edward Elgar, 2005), pp. 58–73. For an interesting study of changing rhetorics of competition policy representing competing views of the role of competition in promoting equality and/or liberty, see Rudolph J. R. Peritz, *Competition Policy in America, 1888–1992: History, Rhetoric, Law* (Oxford University Press, 1996).

provide. Consumers, who are seen as rational and armed with perfect information, will then naturally act to enhance social welfare in this environment. What corrupts this natural dynamic, according to the competition-law narrative, is that some firms have sufficient power (through natural, technological, de facto, or legal monopolies) that they 'distort' the naturally efficient operation of market forces, generating super-normal profits or rents and thereby reducing social welfare. Antitrust law (as per the United States) or competition law (as per the United Kingdom and Europe) is necessary to prevent this problem from occurring (see also Dowdle, Ch. 1, pp. 21–4). The overall effect of these discourses is to visibilize problems of market 'distortion' and, in stages two and three of the effort to roll out competition law, to objectivize legal and managerial fixes as appropriate solutions to the policy gap.

(Of course, this approach has been challenged by some in the Chicago school 'law and economics' movement, which provided a different narrative about monopolies, arguing that they are less threatening than most earlier economic and business theories have suggested and, indeed, may even benefit consumers.[12] But notwithstanding the rise of the Chicago school approach in the United States, and its attempts to train elite international lawyers in this new way of thinking,[13] the effort to extend competition law on a global scale has been much more influenced by the traditional antitrust, pro-competition approach of more orthodox US approaches to competition regulation (see also Dowdle, Ch. 13, pp. 315–19). This reflects the broader consensus in North America, the United Kingdom and its former dominions and some colonies, and the European Union.[14]

But whereas the first stage mainly concerned the development of national legal traditions and national competition policies deemed appropriate to national business models and conditions, the second stage attempted to harmonize competition law and policy across different national economies, to bring about convergence, and to develop a global

[12] See, e.g., Robert H. Bork, *The Antitrust Paradox*, 2nd edn (New York: Free Press, 1993); Richard A. Posner, *Economic Analysis of the Law*, 7th edn (New York: Aspen, 2007). See generally Steven M. Teles, *The Rise of the Conservative Legal Movement: The Battle for Control of Law* (Princeton University Press, 2008); Peck, *Constructions of Neo-liberal Reason*.

[13] Yves Dezalay and Bryant G. Garth, *The Internationalization of Palace Wars: Lawyers, Economists, and the Contest to Transform Latin American States* (University of Chicago Press, 2002).

[14] See Gerber, *Global Competition*, pp. 19–52.

competition law.[15] This became especially significant after the Second World War, with an emerging consensus in the West against monopolies and protectionism and a provisional commitment to promote inter-nationalization. The broad post-war consensus rested on the competition mode of knowing/seeing, according to which extending competition law and policy is seen as a solution to the problem of market 'distortion'. Competition law/policy became pervasive, the European Union using it to promote a single market and with American attempts to export the Sherman Act. The emergence of the Washington Consensus with its neoliberal premises was significant here in combination with a steep increase in levels of world market integration. In 1996, at the WTO's first ministerial conference, in Singapore, competition law was placed on the agenda for the upcoming Doha Round of trade negotiation. However, no consensus could be reached on this issue during that round, and efforts to globalize competition law were dropped at the Cancún Minis-terial Meeting in September 2003, at the instigation of an improbable alliance between the United States and 70 developing countries.[16] In its subsequent 'July 2004 package', which was formally adopted on 1 August 2004, the WTO General Council announced that competition policy issues would not be included in the Work Programme within the WTO for the Doha Round.

This (semi-)closing of the WTO door for competition law occurred in the general context of the shift from the Washington Consensus to the post-Washington Consensus. Most problematically, the neoliberal restructuring promoted through structural adjustment programmes (SAPs) advocated under the Washington Consensus had given rise to uneven development. The Asian crisis (1997–8) and massive social protests on the destructive effects of SAPs in developing countries severely dented the legitimacy of the WTO, the World Bank, and the IMF.[17] In these circumstances, international organizations and regional actors were searching for new theoretical orientations that would help to construct a softer or more 'inclusive neoliberalism' under the post-Washington Consensus.

---

[15] See generally Gerber, *Global Competition*.

[16] Josef Drexl, 'International Competition Policy after Cancun: Placing a Singapore Issue on the WTO Development Agenda', *World Competition*, 27 (2004): 419–57.

[17] Marcus Taylor and Susanne Soederberg, 'The King is Dead (Long Live the King?): From Wolfensohn to Wolfowitz at the World Bank', in David Moore (ed.), *The World Bank: Development, Poverty, Hegemony* (Scottsville: University of KwaZulu-Natal Press, 2007), pp. 453–78.

This general shift provided fertile ground for these actors to modify and recast the competition 'regime of truth'. New sites and scales as well as new discursive links are forged to modify the meaning of neoliberalism. More specifically and in relation to competition law and policy, international organizations (e.g. World Bank, OECD), worldwide networks (e.g. the US-sponsored International Competition Network), and regional organizations (e.g. the EU and the ADB) became nodal sites and scales for the remaking of this legal-policy regime. The next two sections will use the case of the World Bank–ADB nexus in particular as an example to illustrate stages two and three in the development of competition law and policy discourses and practices from a recontextualized doctrinal framework into a set of management toolkits.

III.   The recontextualization of competition law and policy by the World Bank in Asia: pro-poor growth and competition for competitiveness

The difficulties in pursuing a straightforward competition law agenda during the Doha Round led to a recontextualization of concerns with competition policy. There was a shift from an explicit focus on consumer interests (linked in part, it must be conceded, to concerns to open up Third-World markets to US and European companies) to a focus on wealth maximization and poverty reduction. With the general shift from the Washington Consensus to the post-Washington Consensus, the discourses and practices of the market were being modified. The World Bank was quick to re-hegemonize developmental policy by engaging in a process of reform via adjusting its theoretical and policy discourses largely in the direction of 'growth' and 'poverty reduction'. More specifically, it renamed its neoliberal 'enhanced structural adjustment facility' as the 'poverty reduction and growth facility'. It also increased its efforts to show how developing countries (now seen as 'development partners') 'owned' this pro-poor model by producing a series of national Poverty Reduction Strategy Papers. Together with its Asian counterpart, the ADB, it appropriated 'poverty reduction' as the main object of competition policymaking.

In order to drive this new mode of thought forward, the World Bank also re-identified itself as a 'knowledge bank', which enabled it to dominate the developmental process through 'information sharing'.[18] This

---

[18] Thomas K. Wanner, 'The Bank's Greenspeak and Sustainable Development', in David Moore (ed.), *The World Bank: Development, Poverty, Hegemony* (Scottsville: University of

can be seen in its development of the *World Development Reports* and *Doing Business Reports*, which are said to provide information that would enable the South to 'catch up' through knowledge acquisition and transfer. In making this shift, the World Bank was particularly influenced by a new form of economic thinking called 'new institutional economics'. New institutional economists such as Douglass North had criticized neoclassical economic theory for ignoring the institutional contexts within which markets operate. Institutions, considered as both the formal rules designed by the states and the cultural norms and informal codes of conduct that shape human interaction,[19] operate either to increase or to reduce the costs of market transactions.

The growing influence of this perspective is well evinced by the Bank's *World Development Report* for 1997 and 2005. The *World Development Report 1997: The State in a Changing World* highlighted the ways in which a 'capable state' was needed to support markets. A clearer and more coherent statement of the World Bank's modified neoliberal approach was provided in the *World Development Report 2005: A Better Investment Climate for Everyone.*[20] Among other key issues on development, the report revived the 'competition' mode of knowing/seeing, but refocused it in the direction of 'pro-poor growth'. This modified neoliberalism linked 'competition' with 'improvement in private sector investment climate' that can 'unleash competitive and productive economy' and, thereby, can create jobs and reduce poverty[21] (Table 4.1).

This selective recontextualization of 'competition' into a pro-poor agenda by the World Bank can be examined on two levels. First, the neoliberal 'market distortion' narrative of the need for competition law and policy to counteract monopoly condition that emerged from the domestic ambit (e.g., cartels, price-setting activities) was retained under the rhetoric of 'market failure'. Second, this neoclassical version was rearticulated using ideas derived from new institutional economics regarding

---

KwaZulu-Natal Press, 2007), p. 163; Bill Cooke and Sadhvi Dar, 'Introduction: The New Development Management', in Sadhvi Dar and Bill Cooke (eds.), *The New Development Management: Critiquing the Dual Modernization* (London: Zed Books, 2008), pp. 1–14, pp. 8–11.

[19] Douglass C. North, *Institutions, Institutional Change, and Economic Performance* (Cambridge University Press, 1990), p. 3.

[20] World Bank, *World Development Report 2005: A Better Investment Climate for Everyone* (Oxford University Press, 2004). See also Taylor and Soederberg, 'The King is Dead', p. 458.

[21] World Bank, *World Development Report 2005*, pp. 95–106.

Table 4.1. *Some examples of 'information sharing' as a device for maintaining neoliberal influence over development*

Scale	Example of institutions involved	Example of reports/programmes on competition law and competitiveness
Global	World Bank	Poverty Reduction Strategy Papers *World Development Report* 1997 and 2005
Regional	Asian Development Bank/ADBI	Asian Development Outlook 2005 Competition Law Policy Roundtable 2006 Competition Law Toolkit 2006 AEGC Workshops 2008–2010
	ASEAN	ASEAN Competition Law Project Series 2001 ASEAN Guidelines on Competition Law 2008 ASEAN Handbook for Competition Law and Policy 2010

the importance of effective institutional structure as an integral part of development policy.[22] It is now ineffective institutions, which are narrated as 'government failure' (e.g., corruption, rigidity, information problems, 'moral hazard'), that are said to prevent or hinder the poor from effectively enjoying the benefits of the market. In this regard, this modified competition gaze combined the 'market distortion' view of neoclassical economics with the new, 'government failure' perspective of new institutional economics. It is through balancing 'markets' and 'governance', it was claimed, that a 'good institutional fit' can be achieved that can reduce 'barriers to competition' and thereby promote pro-poor growth.

The ADB, which is the regional counterpart of the World Bank, echoed the latter's neo-institutional approach in the making of competition law and policy. In order to increase further the reverberation of the World Bank's new perspective in the region, the ADB added another discursive layer to the construction. It thickened it by linking competition law and policy to the idea of 'competitiveness' – a body of discourse with strong resonance in Asia via the work of Michael Porter, management schools, business media, and so on (for a critique of this discourse, see Jessop, Ch. 5, pp. 102, 105–10).[23] This discursive thickening is discernible in the policy documents of the ADB/ADBI as well as those

---

[22] See, e.g., North, *Institutions, Institutional Change.*
[23] See Sum, 'Production of Hegemonic Policy Discourses'.

of ASEAN. In the Report and Proceedings of the ADB's Competition Law and Policy Roundtable meeting on 16 and 17 May 2006 in New Delhi, 'competition' and 'competitiveness' were used as the title of both the Preface and of the IMD Index, illustrating the importance (and the power) of 'competitiveness' in classificatory-hierarchical terms.[24] Within this report, one of its contributors, Dr V. Krishnamurthy, chairman of the National Manufacturing Competitiveness Council in India, was reported as saying, 'Competition laws trigger competitiveness; they provide the framework necessary to achieving competitiveness.'[25] This means–end link between competition law and 'competitiveness' provides the basis for a functional-cum-pragmatic reasoning that is conducive to regional strategizing and planning. In the same document, it was reported that Allan Fels, the charismatic first chairman of the Australian Competition and Consumer Commission (see Maher, Ch. 3, p. 68), referred to a 'Competition Policy Strategy Model' by highlighting 'that regulatory institutions as well as the judiciary need capacity building and international technical assistance can play an important role in this regard.'[26] These twin emphases on 'capacity building' and 'technical assistance' mark the third stage in the development of a globalized competition law and policy, a move towards the managerialization of competition law promotion strategies.

IV.   The managerialization of competition law by the Asian Development Bank: intervention via toolkits and training workshops

The third stage in the development of the globalization of a competition law and policy discourse can be seen as a 'management stage', in which neo-institutional knowledge on pro-poor competition law and policy is implemented at the level of daily practice. Some insights into what is at stake here can be drawn from David Craig and Doug Porter's examination of World Bank project implementation in Vietnam, Uganda, Pakistan, and New Zealand.[27] They argued that new institutional economics visibilizes the institutional gaps in these countries; dictated the design of technical-managerial tools for intervention; and, in the cases that they examined, led

---

[24] See also ibid.

[25] Asian Development Bank and Christine Veloso Lao, *Report and Proceedings from the Competition Law and Policy Roundtable, 16–17 May 2006, New Delhi, India* (Manila: Asian Development Bank, 2006), p. xii.

[26] Ibid., p. xv.

[27] See generally David Craig and Doug Porter, *Development Beyond Neoliberalism? Governance, Poverty Reduction and Political Economy* (London: Routledge, 2006).

to an agenda for a three-pronged framework of intervention encapsulated in the slogan 'Inform, Enforce, Compete'.[28] This framework offers good insights into understanding how implementing this policy framework in the Asian region worked to intensify the effects of disciplinary and governmentalizing power. Let us consider each of the three elements of this slogan in turn.

In this slogan, 'inform' refers to the way in which the ADB provides information about competition law – in the form of a 'toolkit'. In 2006, it formulated an on-line 'toolkit' called the 'Competition Law Toolkit',[29] as part of the legal-managerial technologies it designed to help realize its objectives. This toolkit has many elements but, for illustrative purposes, one can simply concentrate on its 'Overview of Practices Controlled by Competition Law'.[30] The Overview reveals a shift in rhetoric from an emphasis on 'competition-competitiveness' to a simpler focus on what is simply 'beneficial' or 'harmful' to the competition process (Table 4.2). This redirection of the discourse by identifying 'harm/benefit' intensifies its effect on governmentalized power by providing a form of easily applied, diagnostic knowledge that offers an easy assessment grid that distinguishes between good and bad competition practices; brings regional-national actors into the competition-law fold; and guides formative judgements and related 'soft' policy recommendations (see Table 4.2).

In addition, the toolkit also provides programmes for technical assistance and specifies the appropriate enforcement mechanisms, which include independent competition authorities (see also Maher, Ch. 3), the role of courts and 'administrative guidance', and so on. This way of mapping legal-managerial organization, technical assistance and regulatory procedures subjects regional and national actors to formalist-disciplinary designs of competition law.

The 'enforce' part of Craig and Porter's framework can be seen in the deployment of managerial practices that build institutions and strengthen the technical expertise of law providers (see also Maher, Ch. 3). An example of this can be seen in the training workshops organized by the Asian Development Bank Institute (ADBI) (the executive arm of the ADB), together with the US Federal Trade Commission (USFTC) and

---

[28] Ibid., p. 102.

[29] Asian Development Bank, 'Competition Law Toolkit', available at www2.adb.org/Documents/Others/OGC-Toolkits/Competition-Law/default.asp (dated 31 October 2006).

[30] Asian Development Bank, 'Competition Law Toolkit: Overview of Competition Law Practices', undated, available at www2.adb.org/Documents/Others/OGC-Toolkits/Competition-Law/complaw020000.asp.

Table 4.2. *Neoliberal perspectives on anti-competitive practices*

Practices	Harms	Benefits of eliminating	Recommended actions
Anti-competitive agreements (e.g., price fixing, output restriction)	Ill effects of preventing, restricting and distorting competition	Competitive markets are beneficial to consumer welfare	Regulation
Abusive behaviour (e.g., monopoly or dominant firm)	Predatory pricing of dominant firms or monopolists	Benefits of competition (allocative efficiency)	De-monopolization Regulation
Mergers (e.g., mergers of independent firms)	Reduction in rivalry of firms in the market, with detrimental consequences for consumer welfare	Competitive markets are beneficial to consumer welfare	Regulation
Public restrictions on competition (e.g. state subsidies, licensing rules)	State distorting competition	Benefits of market power (allocative and productive efficiency)	Privatization Disinvestment Regulation

Source: Author's compilation from Asian Development Bank, *Competition Law Toolkit.*

the ASEAN Secretariat. Their third AEGC (ASEAN Expert Group on Competition) workshop, on 'Costs and Benefits of Competition Policy, Law and Regulatory Bodies' in Kuala Lumpur on 18–19 May 2009, was 'part of the capacity building program to assist ASEAN countries to develop and harmonize competition laws and policies by 2015.'[31] Its

[31] ADBI, '3rd AEGC Workshop: Costs and Benefits of Competition Policy, Law and Regulatory Bodies', undated, available at www.adbi.org/event/3070.3rd.aegc.workshop/.

participants consisted of '[a]bout thirty mid-senior government officials and representatives of competition and related agencies in ASEAN member countries and the ASEAN Secretariat', who were encouraged to adopt the Workshop's 'best practices' in assessing the regulatory impact of competition laws and policy. 'Best practices' were defined in cost–benefit terms, and encouraged targeted groups to imbue these terms with competition-competitive meanings. These techno-economic means of calculation contributed towards the shaping of 'choices' and elicited particular modes of support and advocacy for competitive practices.[32]

Managerialist practices of this kind can also be seen as the rise of a modified neoliberal legal managerialism. In neo-Foucauldian terms, these toolkits and workshops can be seen as 'apparatuses of rule'. They involve micro-technologies of steering, assessment, and capacitation that target and 'assist' states, firms, mid-ranking officials, and delegates of related agencies, whom they steer towards a competitiveness order based on market-competition calculations. These targets are encouraged to learn and adopt skill-based toolkits and best practices with regard to regulatory design, advocacy, and assessment. These micro-technologies refashion the self and reproduce neoliberal visions of competitive usefulness among 'experts' on competition law and policy. They intensify the mode of ruling over everyday policy life and are designed to 'change hearts and minds of actors and stakeholders in policy, plan and programme procedures'.[33]

The 'compete' part of Craig and Porter's framework refers in the Asian context to the promotion of market forces and of market-friendly mentalities via the integration of pro-competition rules into understandings of good governance in general and norms of corporate governance in particular. The intention behind this agenda is that this kind of 'governing at a distance' will limit the scope for cronyism, corruption, and bureaucratic inefficiencies, both through the institution of 'new rules of the game' and through internalization and self-regulation. By generalizing rules, norms, and practices of good corporate governance, it is expected that competition will be fostered, opportunities for rent-seeking

[32] Ibid.
[33] Ross Marshall and Thomas B. Fischer, 'Regional Electricity Transmission Planning and SEA', *Journal of Environmental Planning and Management*, 49 (2006): 277–99, 284. See also Bronwen Morgan, *Social Citizenship in the Shadow of Competition: The Bureaucratic Politics of Regulatory Justification* (Aldershot: Ashgate, 2003).

behaviour reduced, and reciprocal monitoring and self-monitoring encouraged. The technology of competition-competitiveness is extended beyond a commitment to the 'rule of law' in a narrow, juridico-political sense, to include the creation of individual and corporate mentalities who have internal commitment to a 'level playing field' as defined by neoliberal theories of competition. Where successful, these governing technologies help to intensify the penetration of norms of competition-competitiveness into the everyday life of the region. Of particular importance is the penetration of these norms into the micro-pores of society, introducing the ideology of competitiveness into local economies that are somewhat autonomous from broader regional, national, or supranational frameworks.

V.   The remaking of social relations and its challenges in Asia

The support for this legal-managerial regime varies significantly across national states because it challenges fundamentally the state-sponsored, exportist mode of growth found in many Asian economies.[34] (Cf. Dowdle, Ch. 1, p. 25. For a description of why Asian capitalism might have evolved in that direction, see Vande Walle, Ch. 6, p. 127.) Compared with the competition law regime presented above (Table 4.2), this exportist mode of growth is premised on a different set of harm/benefit calculations (Table 4.3).

Competition law and policy remains a key site of contestation and negotiation between these two types of economic regime (i.e., modified neoliberalism versus state-sponsored exportism) and their related interests. (See also Gerber, Ch. 2.) They are discursively sutured together via the shared discourses of 'pro-poor growth' and 'competition for competitiveness'. This may increase the general appeal of competition law and policy to a variety of social actors and diffuse possible oppositions (see, e.g., Gillespie, Ch. 8, pp. 185–91). However, the two regimes differ in terms of their economic embeddedness (see, e.g., the use of state-owned enterprises and state-picked 'national champions' by Asian exportism versus the laissez-faire orientation of neoliberalism), contrasting harm/benefit calculations, strategic priorities (compare Table 4.2 and Table 4.3), and the technical-managerial emphasis of neoliberalism

---

[34] See generally Bob Jessop and Ngai-Ling Sum, *Beyond the Regulation Approach: Putting Capitalist Economies in Their Place* (Cheltenham: Edward Elgar, 2006), pp. 152–86.

Table 4.3. *The exportist mode of growth: practices, threats, and benefits*[1]

Practices	Threats and possible harms	Benefits	Examples of recommended actions
Export competitiveness	Sluggish export markets (slowdown in Europe and United States)	Export-driven trade surpluses, income and growth	Nurturing of export and production/ service chains
Investment and reinvestment	Slowdown of FDI and exports	FDI, state investment, etc. enhance growth	Promotion of FDI and state capacity and support
Industrial and supply-side policies	Overproduction and inflation	Innovation, industrial and technological upgrading	Industrial and cluster policies, science and technology policies, creative industries
Factor costs	Rising wage rates, rents, and administrative costs	Human resource enhancement	Manpower policy Land policy, industrial parks
Foreign exchange	Weak dollar relative to local currency	Strong dollar relative to local currency	Monitoring exchange rate policy

[1] Summarizing Jessop and Sum, *Beyond the Regulation Approach*, pp. 152–86.

versus the state-centred emphasis of exportism[35] (see also Prosser, Ch. 10, pp. 255–8). These are some of the possible sites of tensions in this amalgam of discourses and practices surrounding competitiveness-competition legal regimes on the one hand and Asian exportist regimes on the other.

[35] Verena Fritz and Alina Rocha Menocal. 'Developmental States in the New Millennium: Concepts and Challenges for a New Aid Agenda', *Development Policy Review*, 25 (2007): 531–52, 534.

VI. Concluding remarks

Competition law and policy necessarily sit at the interface of the economic and legal systems, and reflect the hegemonic or dominant economic and legal imaginaries. They also pose questions about the relative primacy of the criteria of economic freedom and market efficiency and legal criteria such as legality, equity, and justice. (See also Jessop, Ch. 5, p. 120.) The work involved in establishing the 'law and economics' movement, which gave more or less exclusive priority to maximizing market efficiency, is only one of many examples of this broad point. As Will Davies notes,

> Until the mid-1970s, American antitrust policy had been used to pursue various political and moral goals, from defence of small businesses, to ensuring public accountability of cartels and monopolies, to redistributing wealth, to attacking organized crime. These were all abandoned in less than a decade, as the Chicago definition of efficiency was recognized as the only coherent objective.[36]

Competition law and competition policy are being recontextualized in the context of Asia. Whereas the traditional global competition law movement attempted to purge competition law of all extraneous, non-utilitarian baggage, in Asia such baggage has been reintroduced, at least rhetorically, and linked to new discourses and techniques of economic governance (see especially Gerber, Ch. 2; cf. Dowdle, Ch. 13, pp. 306–13). Changes on this scale are not achieved overnight and, as this chapter demonstrates, a wide range of discursive and material techniques and mechanisms are being mobilized to produce this reorientation.

As noted at its outset, this chapter adopts a cultural political economy approach that focuses on discursive moments in the transition from Washington Consensus to post-Washington Consensus and finally to managerialism. During this transition, competition law and policy has been re-scaled and re-calibrated through regional and managerial routes set up by the World Bank, the ADB/ADBI, ASEAN, the OECD, and so on. Despite the prevalence of these global discourses and practices in the region, global competition law is still faced with challenges that are linked to the exportist, state-dominated

---

[36] William Davies, 'Economics and the "Nonsense" of Law: The Case of the Chicago Antitrust Revolution', *Economy & Society*, 39 (2010): 64–83, 65.

mode of growth found in many Asian economies (see also Gerber, Ch. 2). Competition law remains a site of contestation and negotiation both in the development of Asian capitalism, and in organizations such as the World Bank and the ADB seeking to build a modified neoliberalism in Asia on the regional scale.

5

The complexities of competition and competitiveness: challenges for competition law and economic governance in variegated capitalism

BOB JESSOP

I. Introduction

Competition is the external expression of the internal drive of capital *as capital* to expand and to produce surplus value and realize it in the form of profit. It is through competition that the contingent necessities of the differential accumulation of particular enterprises, clusters, or sectors and the differential growth of particular economic spaces are realized. Competition takes many forms and plays out in many ways (cf., e.g., Gillespie, Ch. 8; Dowdle, Ch. 9; and Deyo, Ch. 12). It is not confined to any particular type of economic activities, although, in today's world, financial innovation and competition are especially significant. The ultimate horizon of competition is the world market, but the world market is not a constant (see, e.g., Yeung, Ch. 11). It changes not only through the anarchic effects of market-mediated competition (and the crises that this periodically produces), but also through competing hierarchical or heterarchic efforts to redesign its rules and institutional architecture, and to govern the conduct of the economic (and extra-economic) forces with stakes in the competitive game.

The capacity to compete is grounded in turn in diverse sources of competitiveness, both economic (broadly considered) and extra-economic. As the forms of competition and the sources of competitiveness change (partly in response to changing forms of regulation and the opportunities for regulatory arbitrage), we also observe changes in the modes of regulation, whether through legal or extra-legal means (see, e.g., Yeung, Ch. 11; Deyo, Ch. 12). This chapter seeks to put flesh on these bare bones statements and to link them to the nature and limits of competition law.[1]

---

[1] This chapter draws in part on work for my Professorial Fellowship on the Cultural Political Economy of Crises of Crisis-Management (RES-051-27-0303), funded by the Economic and Social Research Council (ESRC). It also builds on my earlier work on

Specifically, it aims to put competition law in its place in relation to different modalities of competition and the changing bases of competitiveness in profit-oriented economies of an increasingly integrated world market – one in which Asian economies have once again become global forces to be reckoned with. It draws on critical political economy to show how changing forms of competition, changing forms of competitiveness, and changing forms of world market integration combine to make it harder to achieve the purported objectives of competition law (cf. Yeung, Ch. 11).

In this regard, my chapter contributes to this volume's discussion in at least three ways. First, it looks at competition from the perspective of actually existing capitalism and its differential accumulation, rather than from the perspective of how to regulate or govern competition from the viewpoint of its purported role as a public good (cf. Dowdle, Ch. 1; Gerber, Ch. 2). While there is a rational kernel to the perspective of competition itself as a per se public good, it is typically interpreted in ways that merit at least a sceptical interrogation (again, see also Dowdle, Ch. 1; Gerber, Ch. 2), if not a more radical ideological critique. Second, it looks at competition law in terms of the complexities of its object, rather than in terms of its mechanisms, its institutional architecture, its advocates, facilitators, co-ordinators, targets, and agents. Without paying attention to these complexities, there is a tendency to blame regulatory failure on the inadequate design of competition law rather than on the inherent ungovernability of its object. And, third, it also looks at competition law as one among several means in which economic and political forces seek to design social modes of regulation to promote the differential accumulation of some capitals at the expense of others. In this sense, it looks at competition law as one element in the overall governance of accumulation on a world scale.

The argument progresses through four 'moments' that overlap rather than being segmentable into distinct packages. The first moment concerns the modalities of competition and competitiveness, locating them materially and discursively. A second moment concerns intermittent reflections on the role of competition law in relation to the complexities residing in these modalities, exploring the limits that these different

metagovernance. See Bob Jessop, 'The Rise of Governance and the Risks of Failure: The Case of Economic Development', *International Social Science Journal*, 155 (1998): 29–46; Bob Jessop, 'Metagovernance', in Mark Bevir (ed.), *The SAGE Handbook of Governance* (London: Sage, 2011), pp. 106–23.

modalities impose on that law's effectiveness. A third moment involves the problems of both governing competition and at the same time boosting competitiveness in a world market that is becoming more integrated. And a fourth moment, developed towards the end of this chapter, raises the possibility that there has been a shift from the use of competition law from one of regulating a particular national or regional variety of capitalism towards efforts at multi-spatial metagovernance of competitiveness in a variegated market – in which law is but one element in a more complex form of 'collibration'. In these regards, then, my analysis directs attention away from firm-centred, market-centred, and state-centred analyses of competition to a more governance-centred analysis of competitiveness concerned with the ways in which competition law relates to the dynamic of differential accumulation in different varieties of capitalism and to the emerging dynamic of the world market based on the internal and external relations among these varieties.

II.   Competition

Competition is a general feature of social life – but it is not its most essential feature, nor one that should be esteemed above all others. It acquires distinct forms in the capitalist mode of production, which is based on the generalization of the commodity form to labour-power, making labour into a 'fictitious commodity' (such as land, money, and, more recently, knowledge).[2] The resulting extension of property rights, contracts, and markets to include labour leads to distinct laws (in the descriptive-sociological sense rather than normative-legal sense) of competition that distinguish capitalism from other modes of production (see below).

Through his detailed discussion of the sociological laws of supply and demand, and their mediation through market competition, Adam Smith introduced the idea of competition into economics as a comprehensive science and as a general organizing principle of economic society.[3]

---

[2] Cf. Karl Marx, *Capital, Volume III: The Process of Capitalist Production as a Whole* (London: Lawrence & Wishart, 1963 [1894]); Karl Polanyi, *The Great Transformation: the Political and Economic Origins of our Time* (Boston, MA: Beacon Press, 2001 [1944]). On knowledge as a fictitious commodity see Bob Jessop, 'Knowledge as a Fictitious Commodity: Insights and Limits of a Polanyian Analysis', in Ayse Buğra and Kaan Ağartan, (eds.), *Reading Karl Polanyi for the 21st Century: Market Economy as a Political Project* (Basingstoke: Palgrave Macmillan, 2007), pp. 115–34.

[3] Adam Smith, *An Inquiry into the Nature and Causes of the Wealth of Nations*, 2 vols. (Oxford: Clarendon, 1976 [1776]).

Indeed, through this and other routes, competition became the basis and rationale for classical political economy. Thus, as John Stuart Mill argued,

> Only through the principle of competition has political economy any pretension to the character of a science. So far as rents, profits, wages, prices, are determined by competition, [sociological] laws may be assigned for them. Assume competition to be their exclusive regulator, and principles of broad generality and scientific precision may be laid down, according to which they will be regulated.[4]

For some seventy years after Smith, classical political economists treated 'competition' as an ordering force that was based on exchange relations characterized by many buyers and sellers. The greater the degree of competition, and the greater its transparency, the more likely that it was to benefit the public good. (Compared with the preceding pre-capitalist period, there was some merit to this claim.) Thus classical political economists focused on the ways in which market exchange was organized. But they neglected the role that changes in the *labour process* or in the *organization of production* played as bases of competition. In this way, they reflected the mercantile capitalist's concern with price formation as the basis for profit and loss, and regarded what today we would identify as competition 'law' (loosely defined) as simply a means to avoid market manipulation to the benefit of one of the parties in a market transaction.

A continuing problem during this period was the determination of the centre of gravity around which market prices fluctuated. Nassau W. Senior made a breakthrough here in 1836, when he introduced the idea of perfect competition:

> But though, under free competition, cost of production is the regulator of price, its influence is subject to much occasional interruption. Its operation can be supposed to be perfect only if we suppose that there are no disturbing causes, that capital and labor can be at once transferred, and without loss, from one employment to another, and that every producer has full information of the profit to be derived from every mode of production. But it is obvious that these suppositions have no resemblance to the truth. A large portion of the capital essential to production consists of buildings, machinery, and other implements, the results of much time and labour, and of little service for any except their existing purposes . . . few capitalists can estimate,

---

[4] John Stuart Mill, *Principles of Political Economy: With Some of Their Applications to Social Philosophy*, abridged edn, ed. Stephen Nathanson (Indianapolis: Hackett Publishing, 2004 [1848]), p. 113.

except upon an average of some years, the amount of their own profits, and still fewer can estimate those of their neighbors.[5]

In line with this, other classical political economists explored the role of competition in organizing production and, through the allocation of capital among alternative investments, its role in forming the general rate of profit. Criticism arose when firms took action alone or in collusion to hinder the role of competitive markets in forming a general rate of profit or, which is the same thing, to secure above average rates of profit through anti-competitive or non-competitive forms of competition. This indicated a tension between the interests of *particular capitals* to secure above average rates of profit at the expense of other capitals through anti-competitive forms of competition, such as via cartels or monopolies, and those of *capital in general* in securing the free play of market forces so that no particular capitals are disadvantaged. It is such tensions that competition law is expected (cognitively and/or normatively) to resolve.

But it is a tension that is easier to resolve in relation to anti-competitive competition in market exchange (e.g., manipulating market prices) than it is in relation to anti-competitive competition in the sphere of production prices (as per Marx, reorganizing parts or all of the circuit of profit-producing capital in an effort to win an above-average rate of return on capital invested in a given product or process). For it is hard for state power to penetrate formally, let alone substantively, into the heart of the corporation as a productive organization – even more so when that corporation is organized on a global scale and exploits zones of opacity to disguise some of its operations (cf. Yeung, Ch. 11).

Karl Marx elaborated the relation between these (and other) forms of competition (i.e., competition in market price and competition in cost of production) by focusing on the circuit of productive capital in developing his distinctive critique of political economy. Taking account of the metamorphosis of capital as it travels through this circuit of production, distribution, and exchange, he showed that capitalist competition is not simply for market share or for sales, but also for profit earned on investment – for the capitalist's key strategic decision where to invest. The defining characteristic of capitalist competition is thus in the mobility of investment, both among different commercial, financial, and industrial activities and across space–time.

[5] Nassau William Senior, *An Outline of the Science of Political Economy* (New York: Farrar & Rinehart, 1939 [1836]), p. 102.

Along these lines Marxists distinguish three forms of profit-oriented, market-mediated competition. The first is to reduce the *socially necessary labour-time* required for producing commodities for sale. The second is to reduce the *socially necessary turnover time* of capital through innovations in money, credit, commercial capital, means of transportation, and so on. And the third is to reduce the *naturally necessary (re)production time of nature* (e.g., plants, animals, raw materials) through its direct or indirect manipulation (e.g., through bio-technology, genetic engineering, factory farming, etc.).

This leads Marxist analysis in a different direction, from a concern with market prices towards a concern with production prices. Thus Marx noted that whereas merchant capital continually compares purchase and sale prices for its merchandise because this is the source of mercantile profit, '[t]he industrial capitalist always has the world-market before him, compares, and must constantly compare, his own cost-prices with the market prices at home, and throughout the world.'[6] While this puts production at the heart of competition in an integrated world market, it still depends (increasingly, one might argue) on the role of the credit system in promoting competition on the world market.

Whereas Marx was already well aware that, through competition, 'one capitalist always kills many',[7] in the sense that capitalist development was marked not only by the centralization of capital but also its concentration under the control of a limited number of capitals, he actually paid little attention to the specific dynamic of monopoly capitalism. Later Marxist analyses have studied in various ways and from rival perspectives the dialectic of competition and monopoly. This initially reflected the emergence at the end of the nineteenth and start of the twentieth century of trustification, finance capital, and giant firms that collectively monopolized national markets.[8] Yet, even if monopoly tends to suppress the anarchy of capitalist competition on the market at the national level, there is still competition to gain advantage in the organization of other parts of the productive circuit of capital, and competition thus re-emerges in an even more intensified but disruptive form at the global level.

---

[6] Marx, *Capital, Volume III*, p. xx.
[7] Ibid., p. 714. See also Karl Marx, *Capital, Volume I: A Critique of Political Economy* (London: Lawrence & Wishart, 1963 [1894]).
[8] Nikolai I. Bukharin, *Imperialism and the World Economy* (London: Merlin Press, 1972 [1915]).

Thus, for Bukharin and other leading contemporary theorists of imperialism, the concentration and centralization of capital produce, not an end to competition, but a change in its form and scale. For example, Lenin, following Bukharin, argued that the trend to monopoly did not exclude competition. It continued to operate among the small and medium enterprises subordinated to monopoly domination, among the monopolists themselves, and among competing imperialist powers.[9] Marxist specificities aside, this idea is also reflected in the focus of recent neoliberal scholarship on competition in the context of the global contestability of monopoly positions and the quest for dynamic Schumpeterian competition (cf. Yeung, Ch. 11).

The role of competition continued to exercise classical political economists in the nineteenth century, and from mid-century onwards they discussed the growing importance of natural monopolies such as railroads, public utilities, and the growth of large industrial enterprises. In contrast, during that time a new discipline, that of *neo*classical economics, emerged that began the turn to mathematical formalization, in the process demanding a more precise definition of ideal market competition. Thus, the 'perfect' competition of Nassau Senior became the benchmark for defining the allocative efficiency of markets and for evaluating other forms of market competition.[10]

As a result, the classical political economic conception of competition and the neoclassical economic concept of competition became incompatible. Whereas classical political economy regarded 'competition' as a steering mechanism of actual economic development and differential accumulation, one based on the formation of production costs and/or market prices, neoclassical economics regarded 'perfect competition' as an abstract or idealized condition of equilibrium in which there was no long-term competitive advantage between firms. As Hayek put it, 'if the state of affairs assumed by the theory of perfect competition ever existed, it would not only deprive of their scope all the activities which the verb 'to compete' describes but would make them virtually impossible'.[11]

---

[9] Vladimir I. Lenin, *Imperialism: the Highest Stage of Capitalism* (Eastford, CT: Martino, 2011 [1918]).

[10] Qyvind Horverak, 'Marx's View of Competition and Price Determination', *History of Political Economy*, 20 (1988): 275–98.

[11] Friedrich A. Hayek, *Individualism and Economic Order* (University of Chicago Press, 1948), p. 96.

This obviously poses interesting questions for competition law. Should it be oriented to promoting competitive behaviour in dynamic markets, or to achieving the conditions for perfect competition? And how has the balance between these goals changed as competition and antitrust law have been modified over the years? An interesting observation in this regard comes from Franz Neumann, the German critical theorist. In his remarks on the attempts of the Nazi regime to limit the operation of market forces through top-down planning, he noted,

> Disruption of the 'automatism' of market reactions does not abolish the market. The fact that the tendencies of production-agents to react are checked and subject to restrictions does not annihilate them. When an individual production agent is prevented through monopoly or administrative regulation from making profits by raising prices, he will try to increase his sales or cut down his costs, or both, in order to secure his goal as a producer of commodities. When he is not allowed to market more than a definite quantum of goods, he will have to raise prices, and when both prices and marketing quotas are set by regimentation or monopoly, he must alter the set-up of cost elements in manufacturing processes through pressure on the costs of raw materials, manufacturing equipment, use of labour and capital, as well as through changes in the manufacturing process itself, both organizational and technological.[12]

Just as planning cannot fully eliminate competition, competition law cannot fully eliminate anti-competitive behaviour. For example, it cannot address problems with competition as it operates within corporations: in the allocation of capital to different activities within the corporation in the expectation that this will increase profits of enterprise (see also Dowdle, Ch. 1, pp. 27–9; cf. Yeung, Ch. 11). This is an example of what is sometimes termed dynamic allocative efficiency, a form of competition that, as we shall see below, is often thought to be difficult to regulate through the lever of competition law[13] (although the principle of shareholder value sometimes makes a valiant effort to substitute for it).

Related to the distinction between competition in market exchange and competition in the organization of production is that between competition in the routine activities of firms in a stable competitive market oriented to price competition and competition in the disruptive, creatively destructive, effects of entrepreneurship in dynamic markets

---

[12] Franz Neumann, *Behemoth: The Structure and Practice of National Socialism* (London: Gollancz, 1942), p. 256.

[13] See also Cosmo Graham and Fiona Smith (eds.), *Competition, Regulation and the New Economy* (Oxford: Hart, 2004).

(see also Dowdle, Ch. 1, pp. 26–9). This distinction is conventionally associated with Joseph Schumpeter.[14] He rejected the notion of perfect competition both in reality and as an abstract reference point for analysing imperfect competition. He also disputed the idea that markets tended towards equilibrium. He argued that entrepreneurship disrupts equilibrium through the 'creative destruction' caused by innovation, and that that is constantly altering the pace and direction of economic growth.

Schumpeter identified five areas of innovation. These are: (i) the introduction of a new good or a new quality of a good; (ii) the introduction of a new method of production or a new way of commercially handling a commodity; (iii) the opening of new markets for one's own products; (iv) securing a new source of supply of raw materials or half-finished goods; and (v) the reorganization of an industry – for example, the creation of a new cartel or monopoly position, or the breaking up of existing cartels or monopolies.[15] Successful competition in these areas produces monopoly profits in the short term. But, in a well-functioning market, these higher profit levels will eventually be competed away as other firms adopt these innovations or seek to counter them with their own innovations (whether competitive or anti-competitive). Without directly following Schumpeter's arguments, the Austrian School of Economics, which also rejects the ideal of a perfect competition (see Hayek above), is another theoretical paradigm that emphasizes the importance of dynamic competition vis-à-vis static, price and production cost competition.

The relative importance of static competition focusing on the formation of market prices, on the one hand, and dynamic competition focusing on innovation, on the other, varies significantly. The latter is especially important during those punctuated evolutionary periods in which a previously dominant form of productive technology and/or associated forms of firm organization and finance is overtaken by some other. Such transitions tend to disrupt competition law, which lags behind changes in products, processes, marketing, sourcing, and corporate organization. A particular system of competition law can weather the relatively minor disruptions and crises associated with contiguous

---

[14] See generally Joseph A. Schumpeter, *The Theory of Economic Development: An Inquiry into Profits, Capital, Credit, Interest and the Business Cycle* (Cambridge, MA: Harvard University Press, 1962); Joseph A. Schumpeter, *Capitalism, Socialism, and Democracy*, 3rd edn (New York: Harper & Row, 1975).

[15] Schumpeter, *Theory of Economic Development*, pp. 129–35.

day-to-day developments; the more serious crises that accompany the punctuated transitions from one technological epoch to another will sooner or later trigger a corresponding search for a new regulatory system.

III. Competitiveness

The idea of 'competitiveness' is conceptually ambiguous, politically controversial, and ideologically charged. Essentially it comprises the key set of resources and abilities that underpin competition. It refers to the capacity to engage in competition and prevail in the struggle over differential accumulation – whether or not this capacity is fully realized is another, contingent matter. As such, competitiveness varies with the forms and modalities of competition. There are many ways to define and measure it, and past and current legal and policy debates over its nature indicate the political issues that are at stake.

Definitions of competitiveness and their associated discourses are liable to change: mercantilist notions from the seventeenth century can be contrasted with those of 1890s imperialism or with recent worries about structural competitiveness vis-à-vis emerging market economies. A well-known periodization is that proposed by Michael Porter, who initially distinguished four stages in the development of competition among nations, and then generalized this to competition among cities, regions, and regional blocs. These are factor-driven competition (based on static comparative advantage); investment-driven competition (based on dynamic allocative advantage); innovation-led competition (or 'product competition'; as per Dowdle, Ch. 1, pp. 27–9) (based on Schumpeterian entrepreneurship leading to creative destruction); and wealth-driven competition (based on the legacies and prestige of past success – for example, in luxury goods, art markets, or consultancy).[16] Another interesting periodization of the discourse in competition, this time addressing the private sector, is found in three distinct discursive periods that make up the global competition law discourse following the end of the Cold War as described by Ngai-Ling Sum in Chapter 4.

Institutional economists sometimes distinguish between micro-, meso-, and macro-forms of competitiveness. Traditionally, competition law seeks to regulate micro-economic competitiveness – that is, competition in the structure and behaviour of firms. This is often measured through

---

[16] See generally Michael E. Porter, *The Competitive Advantage of Nations* (New York: Free Press, 1990).

market share, profits, and growth rates. There is an extensive body of managerial and industrial economics literature that argues that 'firm-specific advantages' – that is, factors that are unavailable in the short term to competing firms – are the key basis for this kind of competitiveness. Such advantages are the basis of monopolistic competition. They might originate in factors of production (patent rights, know-how, research and development capacity) or in marketing capacity (design, image, knowledge of likely demand, sales networks). But they can also derive from extra-legal or illegal activities (e.g., predatory pricing, political deals, Mafia-like conduct). It is at this micro-level of competitiveness that the paradox discussed in the previous section between the interests of particular capitals in securing above-average profit rates (facilitating their differential accumulation at the expense of less profitable firms) and the interest of capital in general in the formation of an average rate of profit, an average rate of interest, and so on, is located.

The meso-level looks at the larger institutional complexes – such as the clusters or economic regions – in which a particular population of firms is embedded and on which they depend for their competitiveness (see, e.g., Yeung, Ch. 11; cf. Deyo, Ch. 12). An increasing array of institutions is being identified as relevant here in affecting the capacities of firms to compete in technology, delivery, and after-sales service and to develop other forms of firm-specific advantages. This is an area where industrial policy has a key role to play, and often finds itself in conflict with competition law (see, e.g., Vande Walle, Ch. 6 (discussing Japan); see also Prosser, Ch. 10, pp. 258–61; cf. Deyo, Ch. 12). Indeed, for the Parisian *école de la régulation* ('Regulation School' economics[17]), the enterprise form and its associated forms of competition constitute just one of five key sites of the 'regulation' (or, more precisely, the 'regular-ization' or normalization[18]) of capital accumulation. Other areas of capitalist 'regulation' include capital–labour relations, monetary and financial systems, the state, and international regimes. While certain aspects of the capital–labour relation can be managed at the level of the firm, this and the other sites of regulation are better seen as meso- or macro-level problems that emerge from the firm's larger environment.

---

[17] On the following forms and on regulation more generally, see the comprehensive survey in Robert Boyer and Yves Saillard (eds.), *Régulation Theory: State of the Art*, trans. Carolyn Shread (London: Routledge, 2002).

[18] In French, *'régulation'* refers to processes of standardization, as contrasted with *'règle-mentation'*, which refers to 'regulation' in the political-legal sense of the term.

This is where competition law, competition policy, and competitiveness intersect, and may prove complementary or may prove contradictory (see, e.g., Dowdle, Ch. 9).

Conventionally, the macro-level of competitiveness is equated with national economies. Relevant measures of competitiveness here include employment levels, growth rates, exports, and profits. But this is doubly misleading. First, it is the world market, not the national market, that is the ultimate site and horizon of accumulation, and even beneath this there are also sub-national and supra-national conditions that work to sustain (or handicap) competitiveness outside the reach of national institutions. And second, and self-evidently nowadays, many leading firms and banks are transnational in their manifestation, with complex internal divisions of labour and with complex forms of embedding into global production chains and financial flows that transcend the reach of national regulatory systems (see, e.g., Yeung, Ch. 11).

For this reason, a more inclusive range of factors influencing macro-level competitiveness should include:

> the size of domestic markets, the structure of domestic production, relationships between different sectors and industries ... the distribution and market power of supplier firms ... the characteristics and size distribution of buyers, and the efficiency of non-market relations between firms and production units.[19]

And it might further depend on:

> no exaggerated conflict in the field of income distribution, price stability, flexibility, and the adaptability of all participants in the market ... a balanced economic structure based on small, medium-sized, and big companies ... the acceptance of new technology, favourable scientific and technological infrastructure and realistic requirements for risk containment and environmental protection.[20]

Once macroeconomic competitiveness is deemed relevant, it can be targeted for action. But the definition of competitiveness, the target variables, and the strategies adopted are all discursively constituted and will vary from case to case. Insofar as that competition is mediated through market forces, it will depend on the struggle to increase efficiency. But in other cases, extra-economic factors – such as tariff and non-tariff barriers to trade, or access to state subsidies – can prove crucial.

---

[19] OECD, 'Science Technology Industry', *STI Review*, 1 (1986): 84–129, 91–2.
[20] Ibid., 91–2.

Competitiveness in modern capitalist economies is said to depend increasingly on such extra-economic factors, and this is leading tendentially to the subordination of the whole social formation to the imperatives of accumulation and competition. This occurs because of the growing importance that is attached to structural or systemic competitiveness and to cultivating the knowledge base as a critical source of dynamic competitive advantage. It extends economic competition to a virtual competition between entire social worlds, as mediated through the audit of the world market, and it increases pressures to valorize a wide range of previously social and extra-economic institutions and relations. Among many examples, consider the importance that 'social capital', 'social trust', 'collective learning', 'institutional thickness', 'untraded interdependencies', 'local amenities', and even 'culture' are now said to play in global competitiveness. Likewise, discourses and strategies of structural or systemic competitiveness now emphasize not only firm-level and sectoral-level factors, but also the role of an extended range of the social and extra-economic institutional contexts and socio-cultural conditions in which economic actors also 'compete' (see, e.g., Deyo, Ch. 12). They are linked to the rapid expansion of (competing!) benchmarking exercises and services concerned to construct league tables and offer recommendations on how to enhance such competitiveness. This is reinforced by the growing importance attached to the knowledge-base in post-Fordism and thus to knowledge production and transfer in the wider society. (See also Sum, Ch. 4, pp. 85–8, exploring this specifically in the context of competition regulation.)

These changed discourses and strategies mean in turn that hard economic calculation increasingly rests on the mobilization of soft social resources that are both irreducible to the economic and resistant to such calculation.[21] The competitiveness of cities and regions, for example, is now said to depend not only on narrow economic determinants, but also on the localized untraded interdependencies, knowledge assets, regional competencies, institutional thickness, social capital, trust, and capacities for collective learning mentioned above, as well as on distinctive and attractive local amenities and aspects of culture.[22] Similarly, there is also

---

[21] Pierre Veltz, *Mondialisation, villes et territoires: l'économie d'archipel* (Paris: Presses Universitaires de France, 1996), pp. 11–12.

[22] Allen J. Scott and Michael Storper, 'Regional Development Reconsidered', in Huib Ernst and Verena Meier (eds.), *Regional Development and Contemporary Industrial Response* (London: Belhaven, 1992), pp. 3–24.

growing emphasis on improving the interface between business, on the one hand, and previously non-economic institutions such as universities and the state, on the other, to promote competition in the new, knowledge-based economy (see, e.g., Deyo, Ch. 12).[23]

As attention has turned from micro-level competitiveness to meso- and macro-level competitiveness, the role of the state with regard to competition also changes. This is reflected in the concepts of the developmental state (oriented to catch-up competitiveness) and the so-called 'competition state'. The latter notion was introduced by Philip G. Cerny and has been further developed by myself.[24] A parallel notion was introduced in German by Elmar Altvater and Joachim Hirsch.[25] Cerny initially described the competition state as a new form of state that prioritized the pursuit of global competitiveness on behalf of its national territory and domestic capital (in subsequent works, he gave it a more complex definition).[26] In general, the competition state is one that aims to secure economic growth within its borders and/or to secure competitive advantages for capitals based in its borders, even where they operate abroad, by promoting the economic and extra-economic conditions that are currently deemed vital for success in economic competition with economic actors and spaces located in other states. The leading Asian newly industrialized economies (NIEs) illustrate this tendency well (see, e.g., Deyo, Ch. 12). The same tendency is equally evident in the leading Western economies in terms of the organization of regional and global outsourcing, and regional and global commodity chains, and in the organization of global finance (see also Yeung, Ch. 11). Paradoxically, offshore, more peripheral national economies can themselves be an element in this struggle for competition, insofar as they can be sponsored (or tolerated) by the competition state in order to secure competitive

---

[23] Loet Leydesdorff and Henry Etzkowitz (eds.), *Universities and the Global Knowledge Economy. A Triple Helix of University–Industry–Government Relations* (London: Thomson Learning, 1997).

[24] Philip G. Cerny, *The Changing Architecture of Politics: Structure, Agency and the Future of the State* (London: Sage, 1990); Bob Jessop, *The Future of the Capitalist State* (Cambridge: Polity Press, 2002).

[25] Elmar Altvater, 'Operationsfeld Weltmarkt oder: Die Transformation des souveränen Nationalstaats in den nationalen Wettbewerbsstaat', *Prokla: Zeitschrift für Kritische Wissenschaft*, 24 (1994): 517–47. Joachim Hirsch, *Der nationale Wettbewerbsstaat* (Berlin: Edition ID-Archiv, 1995).

[26] Philip G. Cerny, 'Paradoxes of the Competition State: The Dynamics of Globalization', *Government and Opposition*, 32 (1997): 251–74.

advantages for domestic or international capitals based in their own territories (such as via transnational supply chains).[27]

Although the competition state's strategies may be targeted at specific places, spaces, and scales, and even directed against particular competitors, these strategies are always mediated through the operation of the world market as a whole – especially as efforts are made to widen and deepen the reach of that market through strategies of neoliberal globalization. This is reflected in the transnationalization of competition law – that is, global competition law (see generally Gerber, Ch. 2). Here, we can observe the emergence of new, state-centred structures of 'global competition law' (as defined in Dowdle, Ch. 1, pp. 21–4), such as transnational networks that link together national competition agencies; treaty arrangements affecting state-level responsibilities for implementing competition policy; and inter-state arrangements for the transnational enforcement of national competition law regimes (see Maher, Ch. 3, pp. 56–61).

At the same time, however, the competition state still tends to prioritize strategies that are intended to create, restructure, or reinforce – as far as it is economically and politically feasible to do so – the overall competitive advantages of its particular territory, population, built environment, social institutions, and economic agents. The same idea is sometimes expressed in the notion of 'entrepreneurial state'. And just as there are different forms of competition, so, too, are there different forms of competition state, depending on which particular strategy or strategies the state uses to promote competitiveness (cf. Dowdle, Ch. 13, discussing competition at this level in the context of Asian capitalism). Along these lines, we can distinguish, for example, between a neoliberal competition state, a dirigiste competition state, and a social-democratic competition state.[28]

We also find a proliferation of spatially specific competitiveness strategies operating at many other scales and sites of economic and political action, strategies that are associated with and promoted by differently scaled entrepreneurial actors and/or competition regimes (see, e.g., Gillespie, Ch. 8, discussing Vietnam). As we noted above, the state is not the only level of space through which macro-competitiveness manifests itself.

---

[27] Ronen Palan, 'The Emergence of an Offshore Economy', *Futures*, 30 (1998): 63–73.

[28] See generally Cerny, 'Paradoxes of the Competition State'; Jessop, *Future of the Capitalist State*.

IV.   Varieties of capitalism

There is no best way to organize and govern capitalism and, notwith-standing claims about long-term convergence, several varieties of capit-alism persist due to the heterogeneity of the goods and services (including fictitious commodities) produced for sale, and due to the inevitable embedding of capitalist production and markets in broader sets of social relations. Such variation is evident in the wide range of firms, industries and sectors, complexes and clusters, local and regional associations, national economies, plurinational systems, transnational networks, and trading blocs found in capitalist environments. Advocates of a one-size-fits-all model of competition law, particularly those that come from liberal market economies (LMEs), tend to ignore this diver-sity – especially where the model for this derives from liberal market economies themselves. From this LME perspective, varieties of capital-ism simply represent path-dependent frictions within the larger trajectory of the neoliberal realization of economic efficiency, shareholder value, and freedom of choice. From the viewpoint of co-ordinated market economies (in all the heterogeneity of their forms of co-ordination), however, this diversity represents the path-dependent economic and extra-economic legacies of different specializations in producing and marketing, the production of different types of commodities, and differ-ent trajectories of insertion into a multi-scalar and still-fragmented world market. This latter perspective indicates that there should be different forms of competition law for different varieties of capitalism. (In the context of Asian capitalism, see Dowdle, Ch. 1, pp. 15–18.)

Seen in these terms, we should examine how different modes of inter-firm competition and/or co-operation in different varieties of capitalism in a variegated world market lead to the relative dominance of formal market exchange in some circumstances and of different forms of net-working in securing the conditions of valorization, innovation, and so on in others (see also Gillespie, Ch. 8; cf. Dowdle, Ch. 1; Dowdle, Ch. 9). These sets of factors operate initially at the level of specific branches and sectors (for example, in the organization of the labour process, in the structure of labour markets, in training regimes, or in the differential development of paternalism and occupational welfare). But depending on the relative dominance of specific economic sectors and fractions of capital, and their particular hegemonic capacities, the effects of these factors on competition can become more general (or even universal) within particular regional or national formations.

Competition law is one such factor, but only one – there are many others. And of course, these factors must be balanced against one another. The relative weight of these different factors can also vary not only across capitalisms, but also between different stages of a particular capitalism. The recent rise of finance-dominated accumulation vis-à-vis production-dominated accumulation, particularly in LMEs, provides only the most recent example of this. And it is producing critical challenges to competition law, both as regards the governing of finance and the neoliberalized world more generally.

The literature on varieties of capitalism tends to focus on what Max Weber called 'rational capitalism' – that is, profit-oriented, market-mediated economic organization based on formal-rational calculation of opportunities for profit on the market and the allocation of capital and organization of economic activities with a view to maximizing profits. Rational capitalism encompassed two of the six different orientations to economic profitability that Weber identified (Figure 5.1).[29] The two orientations associated with rational capitalism include (i) trade via free markets and the rational organization of capitalist production in the light of calculations about expected rate of return, and (ii) trade in money and credit instruments, together with speculation in these instruments (modes #1 and #2 in Figure 5.1). Weber also contrasted rational capitalism against what he called political capitalism, which consisted of three other approaches to generating profit. These included (i) securing profits through political-predatory means; (ii) pursuit of market profits through private force and domination; and (iii) pursuit of profit via unusual deals with political authority (modes #3, #4, and #5 in Figure 5.1 respectively). (Weber also identified a sixth kind of orientation that revolved around traditional (pre-modern) forms of trade or money deals (see mode #6, Figure 5.1), but which need not concern us here.)

Competition law is clearly oriented to Weber's rational version of capitalism. At the same time, it has particular problems with 'political capitalism'.[30] Perhaps for this reason, those who look at competition from an LME or neoliberal perspective have often associated 'Asian capitalism' with the latter (others have referred to other parts of Weber's economic analysis, focusing not on his typology of capitalism but on his

---

[29] Max Weber, *Economy and Society: An Outline of Interpretive Sociology*, ed. Guenther Roth and Claus Wittich, trans. Ephraim Fischoff et al. (Berkeley: University of California Press, 1978), vol. 1, pp. 164–6.

[30] See, e.g., Colin Crouch, *Post-Democracy* (Cambridge: Polity Press, 2004).

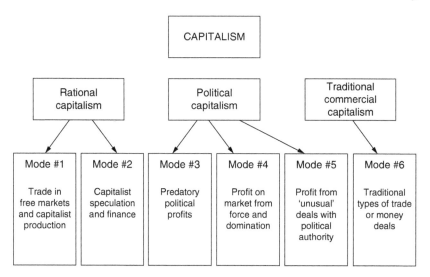

Figure 5.1. Weber's modes of capitalism, based on Richard Swedberg, *Max Weber and the Idea of Economic Sociology* (Princeton University Press, 1998), p. 27.

analysis of patrimonial and prebendal societies[31]). While the developmental state analysis and claims about 'crony capitalism' (which are often disingenuous, especially when advanced by the same authors who once praised East Asia's developmental state) can be subsumed under one or more forms of political capitalism, the more recent developments in East Asian capitalism as it moves beyond catch-up competitiveness and develops distinctive forms of competition state are harder to fit into his scheme (see also Dowdle, Ch. 13, pp. 313–19). Simon Vande Walle (Ch. 6) provides a good illustration of the problems that this produces in Japan – the original reference point for discussions of the developmental state – in his analysis of the continued tensions between Japan's competition law and its industrial policy. This survives today, and not just in Japan, as East Asian economies move from what Porter would call factor- and investment-driven competitiveness into innovation-driven (or Schumpeterian) competitiveness with their distinctive forms of co-ordinated market economy (see also Deyo, Ch. 12). Asian capitalism's current incompatibility with the neoliberal vision of competition law could be a reflection of its creative adaptation of 'post-Fordist' accumulation within regimes that are less marked by the supposedly typical

---

[31] See especially Weber, *Economy and Society*, vol. 1, pp. 235–6; ibid., vol. 2, pp. 1073–7.

institutional separation between the economy and polity systems that is
said to characterize Western liberal market economies (see, e.g., Dowdle,
Ch. 9, pp. 222–7; see also Prosser, Ch. 10, pp. 255–61).

V.   Some implications and generalizations

Competition occurs on a stratified terrain rather than a level playing
field. As the hierarchy of forms of competition and competitive players
alters, the dynamics of competition also change. These hierarchies can be
approached from several directions: (i) changes in the relative importance of different markets in setting the parameters of competition; (ii)
changes in the relative super- and sub-ordination of different forms of
competition; and (iii) changes in firm organization associated with
advantage in given fields of competition. It is also important to note that
economic competition includes social and other 'extra-economic' factors,
forces, and capacities.

The first hierarchy concerns the *relation among four types of markets*,
which comprise financial, industrial, and commercial markets, together
with emerging 'meta-markets' in the ever more central field of intellectual
property. These can be considered both within national economies (e.g.,
the dominance of City interests in Britain) and across national economies
(e.g., the emergence of an 'international intellectual property regime' as
part of the high-tech neo-mercantilist strategies pursued by the United
States and Japan). Along these lines, financial market transactions
prompted by short-term money-making opportunities have grown at
the expense of long-term industrial (or producer) interests, and have
engineered massive restructuring of firms through new financial instruments. Likewise, as technologies become more knowledge-intensive,
access to 'meta-markets' of technological know-how (licences, databases,
patents, technology transfer, etc.) becomes crucial to effective competition, and the appropriation of knowledge becomes a key factor in
competitive success.

The second hierarchy is more complex and concerns the *relation
among different forms and/or bases of competition*. Thus, as well as the
economic interactions characteristic of the conventional categories of
'pure' markets (for example, perfect, imperfect, monopolistic, oligopol-
istic, and monopsonistic), we can also cite other, supposedly less 'pure'
forms of economic interaction, such as networks or strategic alliances,
that can also serve as agents for competition. To these can be added a
concern with the bases along which these different forms of economic

interaction operate (e.g., costs and prices, various forms of rent, state subsidies, etc.). This is not simply a question of which competition forms per se exist, but of their relative sub- and super-ordination. Thus, even where liberal competition survives in current capitalism, it is often subordinate to monopolistic competition in particular circumstances, such as in the case of suppliers to retail chains.[32] Conversely, as new technologies, processes, or product innovations become more widespread, the dynamic economies associated with Schumpeterian innovation decline and neoclassical allocative efficiencies become more significant again.

The third hierarchy concerns the *corporate form* assumed by the competition setters in different markets and/or forms of competition. The peak of the global corporate hierarchy is currently occupied by denationalized, transnational banks that offer a full range of financial services at the global level and by 'stateless' multinational firms that specialize in high-tech, high-value-added groups of products such as specialty chemicals, advanced transport, and energy resources (see also Yeung, Ch. 11).

Combining these hierarchies, we can say that the dominant competitive forces are those that set the terms of competition in the most important market. This can be linked to ecological dominance within the broader ecology of different markets.[33] And, as the forms of competition and competitive strategy shift, patterns of competitive advantage will do so as well. In turn, this implies that the state's capacity to promote competitiveness depends on its ability to pursue dynamic competitive strategies that adapt to the ever evolving position of the national economy within these evolving and co-evolving hierarchies. (See also Dowdle, Ch. 13, expanding on this conclusion.)

Markets must also be socially constructed via a set of agreed-on or imposed rules of the game. There is no 'natural' or 'spontaneous' implementation of market mechanisms. If specific markets seem to be self-equilibrating mechanisms, this results from adherence to sophisticated regulations concerning the quality of goods exchanged, the inner

---

[32] Cf. John Kenneth Galbraith, *The New Industrial State*, 3rd rev. edn (Boston, MA: Houghton Mifflin, 1967).

[33] Bob Jessop, 'The Continuing Ecological Dominance of Neoliberalism in the Crisis', in Alfredo Saad-Filho and Galip L. Yalman (eds.), *Economic Transitions to Neoliberalism in Middle-Income Countries: Policy Dilemmas, Economic Crises, Forms of Resistance* (London: Routledge, 2009), pp. 24–38.

organization of transactions, the legal penalty for non-compliance, and so on. Without such surveillance mechanisms, private-sector opportunism and corporate self-interest would severely distort the alleged smooth adjustment process of supply and demand (see, e.g., Dowdle, Ch. 9, for an example of this).[34]

'The market' is *both* a self-description for the interactions among profit-oriented economic agents – hence a social construct – *and* the actual form of movement of a complex material substratum of economic interactions that are more or less embedded in a wider nexus of social relations. It is impossible to regulate the market in this second sense and, as I hope to have shown above, to regulate its competition in all its complexity. Indeed, as the preceding analysis suggests, competition occurs not only between economic actors (e.g., firms, strategic alliances, networks) but also between political entities representing specific spaces and places (e.g., cities, regions, nations).

Likewise, as we have also seen, competition and competitiveness depend on extra-economic as well as economic conditions, capacities, and competencies. At best, then, social forces can identify a subset of interactions among profit-oriented economic agents, isolate them as an object of regulation or governance, and then seek to govern them through the development of appropriate rules, regulations, agencies, mechanisms, and institutions (all steps being contested). Even here, however, the pronounced influences of the 'unmarked' and the 'unobserved' persist, forming a 'constitutive outside' that continues to shape the development of the actual form of movement of market forces, resisting regulatory capture. This is one of the sources of market and regulatory failure.

This becomes all the more significant the more integrated the world market becomes in real time. For this integration tends to universalize competition – to rebase the modalities of competition and reinforce its treadmill effects for all forms of competition, and to intensify the contradictions of capital accumulation that exist on a world scale. Indeed, the recent ascendancy of financialization over industrialization, together with the enormous expansion of liquidity associated with derivatives and securitization, has enhanced the primacy of financial capital over productive capital. This imposes competitive pressures on other capitals to meet rates of return compatible with financial capital, and establishes a

---

[34] See also Robert Boyer, 'State and Market: a New Engagement for the Twenty-first Century?', in Robert Boyer and Daniel Drache (eds.), *States against Markets: the Limits of Globalization* (London: Routledge, 1996), pp. 84–114.

new form of commensuration that allows for the further universalization and standardization of competition.[35] New forms of competition law are being developed here in the hope that this increasingly inclusive spread of competition will conform to market-liberal standards. But, as my earlier discussion of post-Fordism suggests, one suspects that this hope is in vain.

VI. Conclusions

Competition and competitiveness are extraordinarily complex phenomena and, as such, resist regulation and governance. Matters can be simplified a little by relating them to the periodization of capitalism and to varieties of capitalism, but this comes at the price of neglecting the complexities of variegated capitalism in the world market with all its uneven and combined development. Thus, unless we recognize that the capital relation, including the role of competition in mediating the drive to differential accumulation, is inherently contradictory in structural terms, that it poses major strategic dilemmas, and that it is subject to all manner of paradoxes, we shall never fully understand the complexities of regulating and governing capitalism – including through competition law – and that the inherent tendency for all forms of governance of capitalism is to fail.

There are several modes of differential accumulation, associated with different kinds of competition and different bases of competitiveness. Competition law tends to target just one sub-type, that of 'rational capitalism', and even here it is better suited to regulate competition based on static allocative efficiency than it is the dynamic, destructive creation associated with Schumpeterian innovation. This indicates a tension between competition within static or stable markets on the one hand, and entrepreneurial activities in turbulent conditions on the other. Yet every mode of differential accumulation rests on a balance of competition and entrepreneurship. The former is hard to regulate without undermining innovation. At the same time, however, the celebration of innovation can often serve as a legitimating cloak for predatory activities, such as in the recent examples of what one might call 'financial criminnovation'.[36]

---

[35] Cf. Dick Bryan and Michael Rafferty, *Capitalism with Derivatives: A Political Economy of Financial Derivatives, Capital and Class* (Basingstoke: Palgrave Macmillan, 2006).

[36] The term is mine. For more on the idea see William K. Black, 'When Fragile Becomes Friable: Endemic Control Fraud as a Cause of Economic Stagnation and Collapse', paper

Efforts to regulate competition are further complicated by the fact that competitiveness has many bases, many of which (notably extra-economic ones) are unsuited to competition law. The expanding world market and the plurality of states create further regulatory problems, such as with regard to the role of international private law, how to handle conflicts of laws, and the reach of extraterritoriality.

One response to this, much discussed in the last fifteen years or so, is the shift from a one-sided emphasis on specific forms of governance – for example, the anarchy of the market, the hierarchy of command, the heterarchy of self-organization, and the solidarity of collective commitments – to efforts at metagovernance, or collibration. Building on efforts by Andrew Dunsire, Jan Kooiman, and myself, this can be defined as an approach to governance that involves the judicious mixing of market, hierarchy, networks, and solidarity to achieve the best possible outcomes from the viewpoint of those engaged in metagovernance.[37] (See also Dowdle, Ch. 13, pp. 319–25, for a discussion of collibration in the context of both Asian and future global competition regulation). Governments have a key role to play here, but even this kind of 'metagovernance' is fallible. The emerging system is a complex, multi-scalar, hybrid, and tangled system of metagovernance. But it continues to operate in the shadow of the continued dominance of competition law by the Western model (which means, in particular, the US model) as advanced by the continued national dominance (if no longer the continued hegemony) of both the US economy and the American state in the world market. Yet the very complexity of the interweaving of different forms of governance and government on different scales means that the resulting system is more complex than any state, or political or social entity, can understand, and its overall evolution lies beyond the control of a state or its society.

In conclusion, let me recapitulate some of the problems confronting the role of competition in securing a level playing field for different capitals seeking to benefit from differential accumulation. First,

---

presented at the IDEAS Conference, New Delhi, 19–20 December 2005; William K. Black, 'How The Servant Became the Predator: Finance's Five Fatal Flaws', Next New Deal: The Blog of the Roosevelt Institute, available at www.nextnewdeal.net/how-servant-became-predator-finances-five-fatal-flaws, 12 October 2009.

[37] See Andrew Dunsire, 'Tipping the Balance: Autopoiesis and Governance', *Administration and Society*, 28 (1996): 299–334; Jessop, 'Rise of Governance'; Jan Kooiman, *Governing as Governance* (London: Sage, 2003). See also Colin Scott, 'Spontaneous Accountability', in Michael Dowdle (ed.), *Public Accountability: Designs, Dilemmas and Experiences* (Cambridge University Press, 2006), pp. 174–91.

competition, as an *actual* process, is inherently disequilibrating and, when it takes a Schumpeterian form, is creatively destructive. Second, competitiveness is a set of *real capacities or powers* that affect the ability of agents to engage in competition and prevail in the struggle over differential accumulation. Competitiveness has many bases, especially if viewed in meso-, macro-, and meta-terms (not just micro-), and in relation to modes of capitalism and their requirements. Understandings of competition and competitiveness are discursively shaped by specific frames, categories, strategies – original, mimetic, or imposed – that simplify what would otherwise be too complex to observe, calculate, manage, regulate, or otherwise govern. Different framings of competition and competitiveness involve different forms of action with uneven impact on positioning of firms, sectors, regions, nations, and continents, as well as on the balance of economic and political forces in and beyond the state system itself. And if competition is hard to regulate through law, it is impossible to govern the factors making for the 'competitiveness' that competition law is supposed to serve.

Competition does not occur in a social vacuum, but depends on complex sets of institutions and broader social frameworks. This is one of the bases of distinguishing modes of production, stages of capitalist development, and varieties of capitalism – and, in the work of scholars like Karl Polanyi, of examining the consequences of de-institutionalization or disembedding.[38] The instituted nature of competition is reflected in the development of competition law, their regulatory institutions (e.g., antitrust departments), and other mechanisms to limit, shape, guide, or extend competition.

Contemporary economists disagree about the relevant units of competition. Notably, some argue that it is only the owners of economic resources, such as firms and workers, that compete, and that it is mistaken to treat cities, regions, nations, or supranational blocs (such as the European Union) as units of competition.[39] Others argue that these entities can, indeed, compete.[40] The extent and manner to which this is literally true, metaphorically feasible, or merely rhetorically useful needs to be investigated. Overall, while the critics are right that 'economies' are not really agents or subjects, they err insofar as real agents or

---

[38] Polanyi, *Great Transformation.*

[39] See, e.g., Paul Krugman, 'Competitiveness: A Dangerous Obsession', *Foreign Affairs*, 73 (2) (1994): 28–44.

[40] See, e.g., Porter, *Competitive Advantage.*

subjects do identify economies as being strategically engaged in 'competition', and act on this perception. Such competition is perceived in political or military as well as economic arenas, and is closely linked to the organization of world society in and through nation-states.

Finally, with growing concerns about the environment, and about the effects of growing inequalities in income and wealth, there is also the question of whether competition needs to be tempered and moderated in the name of moral economy. The logic of competition in the capitalist mode of production is connected to the principle of unending, ever-expanding accumulation. Perhaps it is time to compete to find ways to block the effects of this growth-oriented dynamic. And, in this context, perhaps it is time to return to the ancient and medieval doctrines of 'fair price', the limitations on competition in the name of solidarity, and a willingness to cancel odious debt in the name of social justice.

PART III

Competition regulation in representative Asian countries

6

Competition and competition law in Japan: between scepticism and embrace

SIMON VANDE WALLE

I. Introduction

Japan's engagement with international models of competition law has been decidedly ambiguous and cyclical in its economic performance. During times of prolonged economic growth, Japan's attitude to Western styles of competition regulation has been predominantly sceptical, if not hostile. During times of economic stagnation, it has been much more positive. The next section of this chapter charts the development of competition law in Japan in the post-war period. Competition law was introduced in Japan by the US occupation authorities after the Second World War. Initially, it was met with scepticism and hostility. In the 1950s and 1960s it conflicted with Japan's industrial policy and enforcement became anaemic. There was a revival in the 1970s, when the oil crisis wreaked havoc on the Japanese economy, but momentum was lost again in the 1980s. Finally, in the 1990s and 2000s, competition law gained increasing acceptance among policymakers seeking ways to revive a stagnating economy. In the third section we shall explore the link between competition law and Japan's specific form of capitalism.

II. The development of competition law in post-war Japan

A. The Enactment of the Japanese Antimonopoly Act in 1947

Japan was the first Asian country to import and enact a competition law. After the end of the Second World War in September 1945, the US occupation authorities embarked on a large-scale effort to demilitarize and democratize the archipelago. In the US government's view, democratization required not only political freedoms and a new constitution but also 'economic democratization', which included the democratization of industry.[1]

---

[1] Mitsuo Matsushita, *International Trade and Competition Law in Japan* (Oxford University Press, 1993), p. 77.

The idea was to give 'equal opportunity to firms and individuals to compete in industry, commerce, finance, and agriculture'.[2] The two main measures to achieve this were the dissolution of the large *zaibatsu*, the family-owned conglomerates that had oligopolized the Japanese economy immediately prior to and during the war,[3] and the enactment of a competition law. The *zaibatsu* were viewed by the United States as partly responsible for Japan's imperialist and militarist policies.[4] Dissolving them was therefore of immediate concern to the US occupation authorities.[5] But breaking up the *zaibatsu* was a 'surgical', one-time-only measure.[6] To prevent excessive concentration and to ensure free competition in the future, a more permanent measure was necessary: the enactment of a robust competition law. This was the Antimonopoly Act, enacted by the Japanese Diet in 1947.[7]

On its face, the Antimonopoly Act was the strictest competition law in the world at the time of its enactment, although, in truth, only a few countries had a competition law at that time. Like the American Sherman Act, it prohibited 'unreasonable restraints of trade'[8] and 'private monopolization'.[9] Like the Federal Trade Commission Act, it also prohibited 'unfair methods of competition', such as boycotts, price discrimination, dumping, and exclusive dealing or tying contracts.[10] But the law went beyond US antitrust law, being much more detailed and stringent. This was because the Americans feared that 'against the background of traditional Japanese thinking' the general standards of American antitrust law alone would be interpreted in such a way as to render them meaningless.[11] For example, the Japanese

---

[2] SCAP (Supreme Command for the Allied Powers), 'Directive No. 244 on the Dissolution of Holding Companies', 6 November 1945, repr. in T. A. Bisson, *Zaibatsu Dissolution in Japan* (Westport, CT: Greenwood Press, 1976), p. 244.

[3] Act for the Elimination of Excessive Concentration of Economic Power (Kado keizai shūchū haijo hō), Law No. 207 of 1947, repr. in Bisson, *Zaibatsu Dissolution*, p. 262. For a definition of *zaibatsu*, see Hidemasa Morikawa, *Zaibatsu: The Rise and Fall of Family Enterprise Groups in Japan* (University of Tokyo Press, 1992), p. xvii. On the *zaibatsu* programme, see generally Bisson, *Zaibatsu Dissolution*.

[4] Harry First, 'Antitrust in Japan: The Original Intent', *Pacific Rim Law and Policy Journal*, 9 (2000): 1–71, 21–9. See also Mission on Japanese Combines, *Report of the Mission on Japanese Combines....: A report to the Department of State and the War Department* (Washington, DC: United States Government Printing Office).

[5] Bisson, *Zaibatsu Dissolution*, p. 1.   [6] Ibid., p. 180.

[7] Act on Prohibition of Private Monopolization and Maintenance of Fair Trade (Shiteki dokusen no kinshi oyobi kōsei torihiki no kakuho ni kan suru hōritsu), Law No. 54 of 1947 (as amended, hereinafter Antimonopoly Act).

[8] Antimonopoly Act, Art. 3; compare with the Sherman Antitrust Act, 15 USC §1.

[9] Antimonopoly Act, Art. 3; compare with the Sherman Antitrust Act, 15 USC §2.

[10] Antimonopoly Act, former Art. 2(6)(i)–(vi) (revised in 1953) and Art. 19.

[11] Mission on Japanese Combines, *Report*; first, 'Antitrust in Japan', p. 25.

law completely forbade any merger or acquisitions between competitors,[12] and required that all mergers and acquisitions, regardless of size, first be approved by the Japan Fair Trade Commission (JFTC), the agency in charge of competition enforcement (see below).[13] To prevent the *zaibatsu* from ever emerging again, the law also contained a blanket prohibition on holding companies as principal businesses:[14] corporations were not allowed to hold shares in other corporations, and even non-holding companies could only hold shares in corporations after receiving authorization from the JFTC.[15] Furthermore, to prevent international cartels, the Antimonopoly Act subjected any international agreement to JFTC approval.[16] Another far-reaching provision, also clearly inspired by the fear of the *zaibatsu* re-emerging, allowed the JFTC to break up companies when 'undue substantial disparities in bargaining power exist'.[17] The Antimonopoly Act also banned 'interlocking corporate directorships' – that is, it prohibited directors from holding an executive post in two or more competing firms.[18]

The occupation authorities were also concerned about Japan's trade associations. Prior to and during the war, so-called private control organizations (*tōsei dantai*) had been used by the government as tools to implement cartels. To prevent this, one year after the enactment of the Antimonopoly Act the United States had the Trade Association Act enacted,[19] which stringently limited the activities in which trade associations could engage.[20] It prohibited not only more obvious transgressions, such as price fixing and output allocation,[21] but also a wide range of conduct that would be perfectly acceptable elsewhere, such as dispute arbitration[22] and lobbying (i.e. 'unduly influencing legislation or government policy').[23]

---

[12] Antimonopoly Act, former Art. 15. See also Yoshio Kanazawa, 'The Regulation of Corporate Enterprise: The Law of Unfair Competition and the Control of Monopoly Power', in Arthur Taylor von Mehren (ed.), *Law in Japan: The Legal Order in a Changing Society* (Cambridge, MA: Harvard University Press, 1963), pp. 480–506, 486.

[13] Antimonopoly Act, former Art. 15 (on mergers) and former Art. 16 (on asset acquisitions).

[14] Ibid., former Art. 9.

[15] Ibid., former Art. 10. Prior to amendment in 2002, Art. 11 of the Antimonopoly Act mandated that financial companies could hold a maximum of 5 per cent of shares of another company.

[16] Ibid., former Art. 6(1). See also Masako Wakui, *Antimonopoly Law – Competition Law and Policy in Japan* (Bury St Edmunds: abramis, 2008), p. 14.

[17] Antimonopoly Act, Art. 8 (this article was repealed by Law No. 259 of 1953).

[18] Ibid., Art. 13.

[19] Trade Association Act (Jigyōsha dantai hō), Law No. 191 of 1948. The particular articles of that Act referenced in this chapter are translated into English in Wakui, *Antimonopoly Law*, p. 319.

[20] Trade Association Act, Art. 4.   [21] Ibid., Art. 4.

[22] Ibid., Art. 5(16).   [23] Ibid., Art. 5(17).

The central player in this new regime was the JFTC, a newly created and independent[24] agency modelled after the US Federal Trade Commission. The JFTC effectively monopolized enforcement authority as far as Japan's competition law framework was concerned. It was the only administrative body that could enforce the law directly through administrative proceedings. Public prosecutors could prosecute firms for anti-competitive behaviour, but only on the request of the JFTC.[25] Private parties seeking enforcement of the Antimonopoly Act through civil litigation could only bring such a suit if the JFTC had first found an infringement,[26] although case law would later establish that plaintiffs could seek damages on the basis of tort law even without any prior JFTC decision.[27] The Americans thought that concentrating enforcement in one single independent agency would be most effective for enforcing the law,[28] although the future would show that, in fact, in Japan, this single agency model made that agency much more vulnerable to political pressure and hence that enforcement could easily become ineffective.

All in all, the Antimonopoly Act and the Trade Association Act established a very constraining regulatory framework. Its many structural provisions and its draconic measures to prevent concentration of economic power corresponded to late New Deal-era US thinking about the proper role of business and competition in a democratic society.[29] The large enterprise as such was deemed suspect, and an atomistic market structure was considered ideal. Hence the justification for introducing competition law was not so much economic (as would be the case today – see Sum, Ch. 4; Jessop, Ch. 5) as also, and even primarily, political – that is, to avoid the anti-democratic political pressure that could be caused by excessive concentration of economic power.

B.   The 1950s and 1960s: industrial policy trumps competition policy

In April 1952, Japan regained its independence and the occupation ended. This was also the start of two decades of rapid economic growth, annual real GDP growing by around 10 per cent on average. But for the Antimonopoly Act and the JFTC, the 1950s and 1960s were years

---

[24] Antimonopoly Act, Art. 28.   [25] Ibid., Arts. 74(1) and 96(1).   [26] Ibid., Art. 26(1).

[27] *Satō* v. *Sekiyu renmei*, 43(11) Minshū 1340, 1477 (Yamagata District Ct., 31 March 1981).

[28] Bisson, *Zaibatsu Dissolution*, p. 182.

[29] Michael L. Beeman, *Public Policy and Economic Competition in Japan: Change and Continuity in Antimonopoly Policy, 1973–1995* (Routledge, 2002), p. 15.

of retreat. The competition laws left behind by the Americans quickly came became subordinated to Japan's industrial policymaking, and the Antimonopoly Act was amended, interpreted, and enforced accordingly.

1. The conflict between competition policy and industrial policy

'Industrial policy' is a broad term that is used to designate any government policy that causes the market to allocate resources differently from what would be the case under free market conditions. In the case of Japan, industrial policy was primarily geared to achieving international competitiveness.[30] Japan has virtually no natural resources and therefore imports much of its resources in significant quantities. Hence exports have always been of crucial importance to Japan in order to obtain the foreign currency necessary to buy the raw materials for its economy. The export industries on which Japan's industrial policy focused in the 1950s and 1960s were heavy industries, such as steel, cars, aluminium, and petrochemicals.[31]

Some industrial policy measures, such as tax incentives, can perfectly well coexist with competition law. Other measures are bound to come into conflict with it. This conflict has been particularly sharp in the case of Japan because its industrial policy has traditionally been built on two assumptions. The first is that efficiency is associated with firm size, so the higher the market concentration, the more efficient the use of resources (see also Dowdle, Ch. 1, pp. 32–3). The second is that price competition destroys the 'orderly growth' necessary to achieve international competitiveness[32] (see also Dowdle, Ch. 1, pp. 27–9). For these reasons, Japan's industrial policy encouraged mergers between large companies to create national champions[33] and encouraged cartels that would prevent 'excessive [price] competition' (katō kyōsō).

Given these assumptions, politicians, bureaucrats, and large businesses perceived the stringent Antimonopoly Act and the Trade Association Act as obstacles to economic growth. The Trade Association Act was abolished in its entirety, only a few of its restrictions surviving by being relocated into the Antimonopoly Act.[34] The Antimonopoly Act itself

---

[30] Matsushita, *International Trade and Competition Law*, p. 274.   [31] Ibid., p. 274.

[32] Ulrike Schaede, *Cooperative Capitalism: Self-Regulation, Trade Associations, and the Antimonopoly Law in Japan* (Oxford University Press, 2000), p. 50.

[33] Matsushita, *International Trade and Competition Law*, p. 274.

[34] Act to Partially Amend the Act on the Prohibition of Private Monopolization and Maintenance of Fair Trade (Shiteki dokusen no kinshi oyobi kōsei torihiki no kakuho ni kan suru hōritsu no ichibu wo kaisei suru hōritsu), Law No. 259 of 1953, Art. 2.

was also heavily amended. A first series of amendments was passed in 1949, when the focus of the US occupation shifted from preventing concentrations of economic power so as to prevent a return of Japanese militarism, to rebuilding Japan's heavy industries in order to prevent communist infiltration.[35] Further amendments were made in 1953[36] at the insistence of Japanese businesses. The amendments included giving the JFTC power to authorize certain kinds of cartels, namely 'recession cartels' and 'rationalization cartels', which respectively set output quotas during downturns and implemented joint measures to rationalize specific industries.[37] Vertical price-fixing – that is, resale price maintenance – was also authorized for certain products.[38] The JFTC's power to restructure enterprises that had 'undue disparities in bargaining power' was repealed.

It should also be noted, however, that although the amendments to the Antimonopoly Act were far-reaching, the law itself was not gutted. Core provisions, such as the prohibition on unreasonable restraints of trade and private monopolization, survived. And, in one area, the law was actually strengthened to address distinctly Japanese concerns about competition. The section on 'unfair methods of competition' (fukōseina kyōsō hōhō) as prohibited by the pre-amended law was relabelled 'unfair trade practices' (fukōseina torihiki hōhō) and a new type of conduct was added to the list of prohibited conduct, namely unjust use of one's bargaining position.[39] This type of conduct did not require any market power, let alone a dominant position, on the part of the infringer. Instead, it was a provision aimed at protecting the weaker party in a transaction.[40] In fact, the entire concept of 'unfair trade practices' would long be interpreted with little regard for any actual anticompetitive effect,[41] reflecting a Japanese concern for fair competition rather than free competition.

See generally Mitsuo Matsushita, *Introduction to Japanese Antimonopoly Law* (with John D. Davis) (Tokyo: Yūhikaku, 1990), p. 3.

[35] Matsushita, *International Trade and Competition Law*, p. 79.

[36] Act to Partially Amend the Act on the Prohibition of Private Monopolization, Law No. 259 of 1953.

[37] Antimonopoly Act, Arts. 24-3 (depression cartels) and 24-4 (rationalization cartels) (both repealed in 1999).

[38] Ibid., Art. 23 (previously Art. 24-2).

[39] Ibid., Art. 2(9)(v) (previously Art. 2(6)(v)).

[40] Matsushita, *International Trade and Competition Law*, p. 81.

[41] Masahiro Murakami, *The Japanese Antimonopoly Act = Nihon no Dokusen Kinshihō* (Tokyo: Shōji Hōmu, 2003), p. 47.

Enforcement of the Antimonopoly Act also became correspondingly anaemic.[42] During the occupation (1947–1951) the Antimonopoly Act had been strongly enforced,[43] but after the occupation ended the JFTC ceased initiating criminal actions. The number of JFTC administrative actions dwindled to a handful per year, and most of these focused on the so-called 'unfair trade practices', which as noted above did not necessarily have to do with competition per se.[44] The number of private suits was negligible,[45] and at one point there was talk in the governing party about abolishing the JFTC altogether.[46]

2. The proliferation of cartels

Consequently the 1950s and 1960s saw a large number of cartels come into existence. By 1966 there were 1,079 cartels in operation, not including quasi-legal and illegal cartels.[47] These included not just recession cartels and rationalization cartels, which, as we saw, were exempt from the Antimonopoly Act's ban on cartelization, but also cartels exempted from the Antimonopoly Act by special laws. Most of the new cartels that emerged after the ending of occupation were of this sort.[48] These special laws generally did not subject cartels to the approval of the JFTC but to that of the Ministry of International Trade and Industry (MITI), whose

---

[42] Kanazawa, 'Regulation of Corporate Enterprise', p. 505.

[43] Mitsuo Matsushita, 'Reforming the Enforcement of the Japanese Antimonopoly Law', *Loyola University Chicago Law Journal*, 41 (2010): 521–3.

[44] Hiroshi Iyori and Akinori Uesugi, *The Antimonopoly Laws and Policies of Japan* (New York: Federal Legal Publications, 1994), p. 213; see also Kanazawa, 'Regulation of Corporate Enterprise', p. 491.

[45] Makoto Murayama, 'Private Enforcement of Antitrust Law in Japan', in Clifford A. Jones and Mitsuo Matsushita (eds.), *Competition Policy in the Global Trading System: Perspectives from the EU, Japan and the USA* (Leiden: Kluwer Law International, 2002), pp. 243–54, at p. 253.

[46] Beeman, *Public Policy and Economic Competition*, p. 20.

[47] Kōtaro Suzumura, 'Formal and Informal Measures for Controlling Competition in Japan: Institutional Overview and Theoretical Evaluation', in Edward M. Graham and J. David Richardson (eds.), *Global Competition Policy* (Washington, DC: Institute for International Economics, 1997), pp. 439–74, at p. 447; Douglas E. Rosenthal and Mitsuo Matsushita, 'Competition in Japan and the West: Can the Approaches Be Reconciled?', in Edward M. Graham and J. David Richardson (eds.), *Global Competition Policy* (Washington, DC: Institute for International Economics, 1997), pp. 313–38, at p. 317; Iyori and Uesugi, *Antimonopoly Laws*, p. 359.

[48] Schaede, *Cooperative Capitalism*, p. 86.

attitude towards cartelization was much more favourable. Cartels established through special legislation ranged from cartels in textiles, machinery, coal, fertilizer, insurance to those in saké and beauty salons.[49] Such cartels were often used to protect small and medium enterprises,[50] as well as to control exports and/or imports.[51]

MITI also sponsored the formation of cartels that were not based on any statutory exemption. For this, it used a particular form of 'administrative guidance' (gyōsei shidō) to limit production called kankoku sōtan[52] (administrative guidance is a form of government 'advice' that is not formally binding in law, but which can be enforced by (tacit) agency threat to withhold assistance or support in other regulatory matters). Such cartels were often formed with the support of industry itself. They clearly violated the Antimonopoly Act, and the JFTC objected to them at first. But MITI argued that because such cartels were the product of an act of government, they did not constitute private collusion as prohibited by the Act. In the end, the JFTC decided to avoid taking formal action against these 'quasi-legal cartels'. There were also many blatantly illegal cartels that existed without statutory exemption and without administrative guidance. At the time, cartels of all kinds – legal, quasi-legal and illegal – were so numerous that Japan earned itself the nickname of 'the cartel archipelago'.[53]

In sum, the Antimonopoly Act's strong prohibition against private cartelization paradoxically resulted in businesses seeking the cloak of government support for their cartels. This had the effect of fostering the close government–business co-operation that would become the hallmark of Japan's political economy for much of the post-war period. According to Michael Beeman, the Antimonopoly Act 'clearly constituted a major reason why business moved closer to the state during this

---

[49] John Owen Haley, Antitrust in Germany and Japan: The First Fifty Years, 1947–1998 (University of Washington Press, 2001), p. 54; Beeman, Public Policy and Economic Competition, p. 18.

[50] Special Measures Act for the Stabilization of Designated Medium and Smaller Enterprises (Tokutei chūshō kigyō no antei ni kan suru rinji sochi hō), Law No. 294 of 1952, which was later replaced by the Small and Medium Enterprises Organization Act (Chūshō kigyō dantai soshikihō), Law No. 185 of 1957.

[51] Export–Import Transactions Act (Yushutsunyū torihiki hō), Law No. 299 of 1952.

[52] Alex Y. Seita and Jirō Tamura, 'The Historical Background of Japan's Antimonopoly Law', University of Illinois Law Review, 1 (1994): 115–85, 181.

[53] Beeman, Public Policy and Economic Competition, p. 40. See also Patricia L. Maclachlan, Consumer Politics in Postwar Japan: The Institutional Boundaries of Citizen Activism (New York: Columbia University Press, 2002), p. 160.

era'.[54] Government involvement in industry cartels 'became the implicit guarantee that the JFTC would not act against otherwise illegal business behavior'.[55] Likewise, Chalmers Johnson suggests that the tension between competition law and industrial policy, between the JFTC and MITI, may have constituted one of the greatest – though unintended – contributions of the occupation to Japan's economic miracle.[56]

C. The 1970s: the strengthening of competition law

The oil shock of 1973 ended a period of extremely rapid growth of the Japanese economy.[57] At the same time, major corporate scandals and charges of corruption and collusion between big business and government seriously undermined public trust in business and government.[58] Corporate responsibility, or rather the lack thereof, became a major theme in political discourse.[59] Support for stricter competition law enforcement grew among the public and consumer groups.[60] It was against this background that the JFTC felt that it had sufficient backing to embark on more aggressive enforcement and take the initiative to strengthen the Antimonopoly Act.

Between April 1973 and March 1974, the JFTC took sixty-nine formal administrative actions, nearly all of them against cartels.[61] It was an all-time high for the JFTC and a dramatic change from the 1950s and 1960s, when only a handful of cases were brought each year.[62] In 1974, the JFTC also initiated Japan's first criminal prosecution since the occupation for price fixing.[63] The case went all the way to the Supreme Court and resulted in convictions. Eleven companies were fined and twelve individuals received prison sentences, although none of them actually went to jail because the sentences were suspended. This case served as an important check on MITI's increasing power. The main defence of the price-

---

[54] Beeman, *Public Policy and Economic Competition*, p. 19. [55] Ibid., p. 19.

[56] Chalmers A. Johnson, *MITI and the Japanese Miracle: The Growth of Industrial Policy, 1925–1975* (Stanford University Press, 1982), p. 175.

[57] Naoyuki Yoshino and Eisuke Sakakibara, 'The Current State of the Japanese Economy and Remedies', *Asian Economic Papers*, 1 (2002): 110–26, 113; see also Haley, *Antitrust in Germany and Japan*, p. 59.

[58] Beeman, *Public Policy and Economic Competition*, p. 41. [59] Ibid., p. 41.

[60] Maclachlan, *Consumer Politics in Postwar Japan*, p. 159; Matsushita, *International Trade and Competition Law*, p. 82.

[61] Iyori and Uesugi, *Antimonopoly Laws*, p. 214. [62] Ibid., p. 213.

[63] *Japan v. Idemitsu Kōsan K.K.*, 28(2) Shinketsushū 299, 985 Hanrei Jihō 3, 8 (Tokyo High Ct., 26 September 1980).

fixers had been that they acted in accordance with MITI's administrative guidance. This defence was rejected, thus casting doubt on MITI's authority to authorize 'quasi-legal' cartels.[64]

The JFTC also worked to strengthen the Antimonopoly Act, which was amended in 1977.[65] The most important change concerned its enforcement mechanisms. The amendments raised tenfold the maximum criminal fines that could be imposed by the courts. They also introduced a new penalty for unreasonable restraints of trade – an administrative fine referred to as a 'surcharge' (*kachōkin*) that allowed the JFTC, on finding that a company had engaged in an unreasonable restraint of trade, to impose a penalty ranging from 0.5 per cent to 2 per cent (depending on the industry) of the turnover of the goods that had been subject to the unreasonable restraint.[66]

D.   The 1980s: competition law enforcement wanes again

As inflation rates returned to normal and the pro-business Liberal Democratic Party regained its dominant position in politics, the JFTC's standing waned and the regulatory role of competition law diminished. The JFTC toned down enforcement and avoided taking formal enforcement measures.[67] Instead, it relied more on informal mechanisms, such as cautions and warnings, and tried to increase awareness and compliance with competition law by issuing guidelines on various topics.

In areas where competition law really clashed with existing practices, it was mostly the existing practices that survived and competition law that was adjusted. Many major Japanese manufacturers had established a large degree of control over their distribution and supply channels through so-called vertical *keiretsu*. These close relationships between manufacturers and their suppliers and distributors were often character-ized by vertical restraints of dubious legality (e.g., exclusive purchasing obligations and territorial exclusivity) or blatant illegality (e.g., resale price maintenance). Yet the JFTC's efforts to tackle these practices

---

[64] Johnson, *MITI and the Japanese Miracle*, p. 301.

[65] Act to Partially Amend the Act on the Prohibition of Private Monopolization and Maintenance of Fair Trade (Shiteki dokusen no kinshi oyobi kōsei torihiki no kakuho ni kan suru hōritsu no ichibu wo kaisei suru hōritsu), Law No. 63 of 1977.

[66] Antimonopoly Act, former Art. 7(2) and former Art. 48(2).

[67] Beeman, *Public Policy and Economic Competition*, p. 129.

proved largely ineffectual. When it tried to issue guidelines to curtail these practices, it had to retreat under stark opposition from businesses.[68]

E. From the 1990s onwards: economic stagnation and the reinvigoration of competition law

Japan's second long period of economic growth ended abruptly at the beginning of the 1990s, when the so-called 'bubble economy' collapsed. What followed was a decade of low growth and stagnation, known as the 'lost decade'. Although the economy started growing again in 2002, growth was subdued and in 2008 the economy went into recession again. Some commentators, such as the former prime minister Yasuhiro Nakasone, now speak of two lost decades.[69]

For competition law the 1990s and 2000s were years of renewed appreciation, strengthened enforcement, and convergence towards the EU and US models. Initially, these changes were triggered by outside pressure, particularly from the United States. But they also became part of a domestic policy that increasingly saw Western-style competition law as a means of returning to sustained economic growth.

The outside pressure had been building up since the 1980s, when the United States' enormous trade deficit with Japan prompted demands that Japan open up its market to American companies. The United States identified weak enforcement of the competition law as one of the 'structural impediments' to entry. Hence the issue was taken up in the Structural Impediments Initiative negotiations, the round of bilateral trade negotiations between the United States and Japan that lasted from 1989 to 1992.

To placate the United States, the Japanese government pledged to strengthen competition law enforcement and implemented a number of changes. The staffing of the JFTC was increased and the agency resumed the more aggressive enforcement posture it evinced in the 1970s. A 1992 amendment to the Antimonopoly Act raised the administrative penalties for antitrust violations fourfold, bringing it to a maximum of 6 per cent of a company's turnover generated from the illegal activity. The maximum criminal fine was increased twenty-fold, from 5 million yen to 100 million yen. The JFTC also started using

---

[68] Ibid., pp. 118–21.
[69] Yasuhiro Nakasone, 'Japan Adrift in a Changing World', *Japan Times*, 16 September 2010.

criminal actions again,[70] something it had not done since the 1970s. In parallel, and also in response to international pressure, the JFTC issued guidelines on distribution practices that effectively led to some changes in the operation of vertical *keiretsu*.[71]

As the stagnation of the Japanese economy continued throughout the 1990s, the move towards more effective enforcement, initially triggered by outside pressure, gradually became part of the domestic policy agenda. To stimulate the economy the Japanese government tried a range of macroeconomic measures, such as lowering interest rates and offering stimulus packages, but these failed to bring sustained growth. A consensus emerged that the sluggish performance of the Japanese economy was not just a cyclical downturn, but the result of structural defects in the economy.[72]

One of Japan's key structural problems was, and still is, the comparatively low productivity of a large part of its economy – namely the domestically oriented companies, particularly in the agriculture, construction, and service industries. Japan has what is effectively a dual economy. On the one hand, there are highly efficient companies that compete internationally and are export-oriented. These include well-known companies such as Sony, Toyota, Honda, and Canon, and their productivity is around 20 per cent higher than that of their US counterparts.[73] But these industries make up only 10 per cent of Japan's economy, the other 90 per cent of Japan's economic activity taking place in companies that do not export but cater to the domestic market, and their productivity level is only 63 per cent of that of their US counterparts.[74] One would expect more efficient enterprises, domestic or foreign, to enter these inefficient markets and replace the inefficient companies.

---

[70] Tony A. Freyer, *Antitrust and Global Capitalism, 1930–2004* (Cambridge University Press, 2006), p. 228.

[71] JFTC, Guidelines Concerning Distribution Systems and Business Practices under the Antimonopoly Act (Ryūtsū torihiki kankō ni kan suru dokusenkinshihōjō no shishin), 11 July 1991, translated into English at www.jftc.go.jp/en/legislation_guidelines/ama/pdf/distribution.pdf. See, on the actual impact of these guidelines, Beeman, *Public Policy and Economic Competition*, p. 154.

[72] See, e.g., Michael E. Porter and Mariko Sakakibara, 'Competition in Japan', *Journal of Economic Perspectives*, 18 (2004): 27–50; McKinsey Global Institute, *Why the Japanese Economy is Not Growing: Micro Barriers to Productivity Growth* (Washington: McKinsey Global Institute, 2000), p. 1; Akinori Uesugi, 'How Japan Is Tackling Enforcement Activities against Cartels', *George Mason Law Review*, 13 (2005): 349–65, 350.

[73] McKinsey Global Institute, *Why the Japanese Economy Is Not Growing*, p. 1.

[74] Ibid., p. 1.

Apparently that is not happening because these industries are shielded from new competition by entry barriers and collusive practices.

This realization has led to a renewed interest in competition regulation in Japan. As one recent study suggests, the sectors where competition was restricted through interventionist industrial policies today tend to concentrate in the unproductive economy, whereas sectors in which firms were traditionally left to compete today tend to concentrate in the productive economy.[75] The government has again begun pushing stronger competition enforcement as one of the remedies for Japan's structural problems. A policy speech given in 2001 by Junichirō Koizumi immediately after taking office as Prime Minister illustrates Japan's second turn towards competition law. He stated that 'the structures that hitherto served [Japan] so well may not be appropriate for our society in the twenty-first century', and stressed the need for regulatory reform and increased competition enforcement under the slogan 'no growth without structural reform'.[76]

Since 1997, the number of cartels exempted from the Antimonopoly Act has been significantly reduced, and now only a handful remain. In 1999, the exemption for recession and rationalization cartels was repealed. The number of products for which resale price maintenance is allowed was also reduced and currently only copyrighted works still benefit from an exemption.[77]

Recent years have seen a further strengthening of competition law, particularly in the field of enforcement. A 2005 amendment strengthened the JFTC's investigative powers and again increased administrative surcharges. For large companies that have been found to have participated in a cartel, the maximum rate now stands at 10 per cent of the sales of the product subject to the cartel. In 2009, the Antimonopoly Act was yet again amended. This time, the conduct for which administrative fines can be imposed was extended to include exclusionary types of unilateral conduct and certain unfair trade practices. Sanctions were strengthened once again: administrative fines for cartel ringleaders were raised to 15 per cent of the illegal turnover and the maximum prison sentences for individuals were lengthened.

The 2005 amendments also introduced a leniency programme, akin to that existing in the United States and the European Union, under which

---

[75] Porter and Sakakibara, 'Competition in Japan', p. 35.
[76] Junichirō Koizumi, 'Policy Speech by Prime Minister Junichirō Koizumi to the 151st Session of the Diet', 7 May 2001. See also Uesugi, 'How Japan Is Tackling Enforcement Activities', 350.
[77] Antimonopoly Act, Art. 23(4).

'whistleblowers' are afforded immunity from fines in return for confessing to cartel involvement and helping the JFTC to punish the other offenders.[78] Many had predicted that such a leniency programme would never see the light of day in Japan, given the opposition from business groups, who contended that whistle blowing was at odds with Japanese culture and society. In fact, Japan's leniency programme has been relatively successful, with over 500 leniency applications made since the start of the programme in 2006,[79] although many of those were probably filed after the JFTC had initiated surprise raids.

Even private enforcement, long absent in Japan, has evolved from virtual non-existence to a level where around a dozen new cases are filed each year.[80] Through these cases, antitrust victims have recovered tens of billions of yen in damages (hundreds of millions of euros).[81] An amendment of the Antimonopoly Act that took effect in 2001 gave private individuals and companies a right to seek injunctive relief against unfair trade practices,[82] whereas before they could only seek damages. Of course, this level of private enforcement is still a far cry from that in the United States. Indeed, Japan, like most countries in Europe, still relies primarily on administrative sanctions rather than on private enforcement and criminal enforcement. All in all, however, there has been increasing convergence between Japanese competition law and EU and US competition law.

III.   The link between competition law and Japan's specific blend of capitalism

A.   The Antimonopoly Act as a legal irritant

The conventional view has long been that Japan's Antimonopoly Act was a 'translated amalgamation' of US antitrust law and, as such, an entirely alien concept forced on the Japanese by the US occupation authorities.[83]

---

[78] Ibid., Art. 7-2(7)–(9) (currently Art. 7-2(10)–(12)).

[79] Takujirō Kōno, 'Leniency Program of Japan Fair Trade Commission', presentation at the ICN Cartel Workshop 2011, 12 October 2011; JFTC, 'Concerning the Publication of the Enterprises to Which the Leniency System Has Been Applied [Kachōkin genmen seido no tekiyō jigyōsha no kōhyō ni tsuite]' (continually updated), available at www.jftc.go.jp/dk/genmen/kouhyou.html.

[80] Simon Vande Walle, 'Private Enforcement of Antitrust Law in Japan: An Empirical Analysis', *Competition Law Review*, 8 (2011): 7–28, 16.

[81] Ibid., 16.   [82] Antimonopoly Act, Art. 24.

[83] Schaede, *Cooperative Capitalism*, p. 75; Murakami, *Japanese Antimonopoly Act*, p. 41; Seita and Tamura, 'Historical Background of Japan's Antimonopoly Law', p. 122.

In fact, so alien that the Japanese had difficulty understanding the meaning of it. The Japanese government official who had to translate the first draft submitted by the Americans to the Japanese government later wrote that 'it seems laughable today, but then we didn't really know what they were talking about'.[84]

Recent scholarship has partly corrected this conventional view. The historic records show that the Japanese government quickly came to understand the key issues and that there were intense negotiations between the occupation authorities and the Japanese side.[85] Through these negotiations, the Japanese did have significant influence on the final version of the Act. For example, Japanese negotiators were responsible for curtailing the possibilities for private enforcement of the Antimonopoly Act.

However, this correction of the conventional view does not detract from the fact that the Antimonopoly Act was a foreign element in the Japanese legal and economic order. Even though the Japanese government understood the law, they did not necessarily agree with its foundational presumptions. The pre-war experience had convinced most Japanese policymakers that large companies were efficient, that cartels were a good way of avoiding overproduction, and that strong governmental guidance of industry was essential for promoting economic growth. Hence the Antimonopoly Act had very little indigenous support. One former MITI official, Maeda Yasuyuki, has described the views of the MITI bureaucrats in the immediate post-war years as follows:

> Most of them thought that enforcing the Antimonopoly Law was part of Japan's punishment. Getting even with Japan, somehow. For example, Mitsui Bussan had been divided up into ten or twenty separate companies. In the beginning, the SCAP [Supreme Commander of the Allied Powers] concept of antitrust was very severe,

---

[84] Johnson, *MITI and the Japanese Miracle*, p. 175. See also Mitsuo Matsushita, 'The Antimonopoly Law of Japan', in Edward M. Graham and J. David Richardson (eds.), *Global Competition Policy* (Washington, DC: Institute for International Economics, 1997), pp. 151–97, at p. 151.

[85] Nobufumi Nishimura and Fumio Sensui, 'The Enactment of the Original AMA and its Implications for the Current AMA [Genshi dokusenkinshihō no seitei katei to genkōhō he no shisa]', 2006, available at www.jftc.go.jp/cprc/english/cr-0206.pdf; Nobufumi Nishimura and Fumio Sensui, 'The Enactment of the Original AMA and its Implications for the Current AMA – the JFTC's Organization, Judicial System, Damages and Criminal System [Genshi dokusenkinshihō no seitei katei to genkōhō he no shisa – kōtorii no soshiki, shihōseido, songaibaishō, keijiseido]', 2008, available at www.jftc.go.jp/cprc/english/cr-0408.pdf. See also First, 'Antitrust in Japan'.

and we thought it was a form of punishment. We didn't really understand the idea of free enterprise then.[86]

There is another historic fact that shows how different from US ideas about competition regulation were those of Japanese policymakers. At the very start of the drafting process, the occupation authorities had requested the Japanese Ministry of Commerce and Industry to come up with a draft statute. But the draft produced by the Japanese expressed completely the opposite of US ideas of competition law. Based primarily on pre-war legislation, it did not outlaw cartels, rather it promoted them.[87]

Unsurprisingly, this first draft was considered wholly inadequate by the Americans,[88] who subsequently drafted their own proposal, known as the Kime draft, and, although the Japanese government managed to shift the discussion to a counter-proposal they had introduced, the Kime draft nonetheless provided the basic foundation for what would eventually become the Antimonopoly Act. This, of course, had very little to do with any genuine Japanese support for US theories of economic competition but everything to do with the political realities of the occupation.

Yet the foreign character of Western-style competition law does not mean that it was or is doomed to fail in Japan. As well noted by Gunther Teubner, the problem with the metaphor of legal transplants is that it gives the misleading impression that the foreign law is either rejected or accepted, like an organ that is transplanted into an organism. In fact, Teubner argues, most legal transfers are better analogized as 'legal irritants': a fundamental irritation which triggers a whole series of new and unexpected events.[89] This irritation leads to a double transformation along the lines of what Teubner calls co-evolving trajectories. On the one hand, the transferred rule will be transformed – that is, recontextualized in its new environment – and, at the same time, the rule will trigger changes in the social system. Teubner predicts that it can take a long time before this process of mutual irritation comes to a preliminary equilibrium. This will especially be the case if there is a tight coupling between the transferred law and parts of

---

[86] William Chapman, *Inventing Japan: The Making of a Postwar Civilization* (New York: Simon and Schuster, 1991), p. 104.

[87] Schaede, *Cooperative Capitalism*, p. 246 (2000). Cf. Seita and Tamura, 'Historical Background', 135–9 (discussing pre-war legislation).

[88] Iyori and Uesugi, *Antimonopoly Laws*, p. 16.

[89] Gunther Teubner, 'Legal Irritants: How Unifying Law Ends up in New Divergences,' in Peter A. Hall and David W. Soskice (eds.), *Varieties of Capitalism: The Institutional Foundations of Comparative Advantage* (Oxford University Press, 2001), pp. 417–41, at p. 418.

society.[90] Competition law is closely connected to a range of economic institutions, making a protracted process of mutual irritation likely. As the next subsection shows, in the case of the Antimonopoly Act in Japan, the mutual irritation process is still ongoing after more than sixty years.

B.   The 'irritation' of Japanese capitalism

For four decades after the Second World War, Japan experienced remarkable economic growth. Many have attributed its phenomenal success to a set of economic institutions specific to Japan. Key characteristics of this form of capitalism were said to include close collaboration between companies and the government and a distinctly co-operative relationship among companies that in the West would be competitively rather than co-operatively aligned. Based on these features, the Japanese form of capitalism has been characterized as 'collaborative capitalism' (stressing the collaboration between government and business)[91] and 'alliance capitalism' (stressing the co-operation between businesses, especially in *keiretsu*).[92] Chalmers Johnson emphasized the state's role in fostering economic development, and called Japan a 'capitalist developmental state'.[93] Journalists used the term 'Japan Inc.' to indicate the close ties between business and government. Ulrike Schaede, in her recent analysis of Japan's pervasive trade associations, suggests that while the developmental state is a thing of the past because of deregulation, even today co-operation between companies remains a hallmark of Japan's capitalism, resulting in what she has termed 'co-operative capitalism'.[94]

Such a form of capitalism was bound to come into conflict with the US model of competition law introduced in 1947. This incompatibility led to a process of mutual irritation, through which competition law was reconstructed while at the same time changing Japan's capitalism.

As the preceding subsection made clear, throughout the post-war period the Japanese have indeed changed, interpreted, and enforced their competition law in ways to make it compatible with Japan's form of capitalism, in fact, so much so that Japan's particular approach towards

---

[90] Ibid., p. 426.
[91] Andrew A. Procassini, *Competitors in Alliance: Industry Associations, Global Rivalries, and Business-Government Relations* (Westport, CT: Quorum, 1995), p. 37.
[92] See generally Michael L. Gerlach, *Alliance Capitalism: The Social Organization of Japanese Business* (Berkeley: University of California Press, 1997).
[93] Johnson, *MITI and the Japanese Miracle*, p. 130.
[94] Schaede, *Cooperative Capitalism*, p. 4.

competition law was said to be a key institutional ingredient of Japan's capitalism,[95] challenging the orthodox view that Western-style competition law was essential for a well-functioning capitalist system. Without this approach it would not have been possible for the government to implement its national industrial policy, which steered production through cartels and fostered national champions, and it would not have been possible for companies to co-operate to the extent they did.

But while competition law underwent fundamental and continuous change, it also triggered change itself in Japan's social and economic order, sometimes in unexpected ways. As explained in the previous part, the stringent ban on cartels pushed companies in the 1950s and 1960s to seek the cloak of government approval for cartels, thus strengthening the close ties between businesses and government that became characteristic of Japan's capitalism. Likewise, the atomistic market structure pursued by the US occupation authorities and the Antimonopoly Act's ban on holding companies were probably two of the factors that drove Japanese businesses to reunite through cross-shareholdings, leading to the formation of the notorious *keiretsu* groups.[96] Of course, not all change brought about by competition law was unexpected or unintended. In more recent times, the JFTC's stricter policy towards vertical restraints, as embodied in its 1991 guidelines, has led to some changes in vertical relationships,[97] and the JFTC's crackdown on cartels and bid-rigging, especially in the past decade, has undoubtedly led to less collusion among firms.[98]

This reciprocal transformation of the legal framework and society is likely to continue for some time to come. Japan's lacklustre economic growth over the past two decades has led many policymakers, scholars, and export-oriented corporations to call for a more Western-style approach to competition law.[99] They argue that while the lax competition regime and the form of capitalism it fostered may have been effective when

---

[95] Ibid., p. 4; Gerlach, *Alliance Capitalism*, p. 23. See, e.g., Chalmers A. Johnson, *Japan, Who Governs? The Rise of the Developmental State* (New York: W. W. Norton, 1995), pp. 77–8 (using the example of lax enforcement against bid-rigging).

[96] Iyori and Uesugi, *Antimonopoly Laws*, p. 320.

[97] Beeman, *Public Policy and Economic Competition*, p. 154.

[98] See, e.g., 'Four General Contractors: "No More Bid-rigging" [Zenekon yon sha "dangō to ketsubetsu"]', *Asahi Shimbun*, 29 December 2005, 1 (reporting the declaration of Japan's four major construction companies to cease bid-rigging and step up compliance efforts in response to stricter enforcement of the Antimonopoly Act).

[99] See, e.g., Porter and Sakakibara, 'Competition in Japan', 47; Edward J. Lincoln, *Arthritic Japan: The Slow Pace of Economic Reform* (Washington, DC: Brookings Institution Press, 2001), p. 38; Uesugi, 'How Japan Is Tackling Enforcement Activities against Cartels', 351.

Japan was a developmental state, it does not seem to be working for the post-developmental state that Japan now is.

On the other side, policymakers, scholars, and many small and medium-sized enterprises point out that the Japanese economy has been and is characterized by intense competition in most sectors, something confirmed by several studies,[100] although perhaps less on price and more on quality and innovation than in the United States.[101] Hence they view rigorous application of Western-style competition rules as unnecessary and counterproductive, in that it would lead to a single-minded focus on destructive price competition as opposed to competition through quality and innovation.[102]

Others raise more fundamental concerns about the trend towards a more Western-style implementation of competition law. They point out that, in spite of two decades of low growth and stagnation, the Japanese system has shown remarkable social resilience. In contrast to many other advanced industrial countries of the Euro-American 'West', there has been no mass unemployment, no social conflict, no conspicuous gap between the rich and the poor and no community breakdown. Hence Japan's form of capitalism and its concomitant approach to competition law is still highly valued, not, perhaps, because it leads to economic efficiency but because it achieves other goals that are deemed equally or more important. Although the exact role of Japan's approach to competition law in enabling these favourable social outcomes is uncertain, many perceive it to play a positive role.

For instance, Japan's long-time lenient approach towards vertical restraints – before a 2009 amendment[103] there was essentially no penalty for anti-competitive vertical agreements[104] – coupled with

---

[100] See, e.g., Porter and Sakakibara, 'Competition in Japan', 28.

[101] Andrew R. Dick, 'Japanese Antitrust: Reconciling Theory and Evidence', *Contemporary Economic Policy*, 11 (1993): 50–61, 51–2.

[102] See, e.g., Japan Chamber of Commerce and Industry, 'Views Concerning the "Outline of Proposed Amendments to the Antimonopoly Act", ["Dokusenkinshihō kaisei (an) no gaiyō" ni tai suru iken]', 25 June 2004, available at www.jcci.or.jp/nissyo/iken/ 040625dokkinhou.htm. See also Uesugi, 'How Japan Is Tackling Enforcement Activities against Cartels', 352.

[103] Act to Partially Amend the Act on the Prohibition of Private Monopolization and Maintenance of Fair Trade [Shiteki dokusen no kinshi oyobi kōsei torihiki no kakuho ni kan suru hōritsu no ichibu wo kaisei suru hōritsu], Law No. 51 of 2009.

[104] *K.K. Asahi shimbunsha et al.* v. *JFTC*, 2 Hanrei Jihō 8 (Tokyo High Ct, 9 March 1953) (holding that the prohibition on unreasonable restraints of trade only applies to horizontal agreements). But see *Japan* v. *Toppan mūa et al.*, 840 Hanrei Taimuzu 81, 88 (Tokyo High Ct, 14 December 1993) (expressing doubts as to the validity of this view).

other entry barriers[105] are often said to contribute to Japan's inefficient and overly complex distribution system, which is characterized by a high number of small retailers (mom-and-pop stores). Yet these small stores may well serve an important social function, for example by keeping town centres habitable and safe and by increasing social cohesion.

Another example is Japan's resale price maintenance system for books. Such a system violates competition law orthodoxy but it is perceived to lead to a more diverse offering of books. Indeed, when the JFTC proposed to abolish the system, this led to an overwhelmingly negative response from authors and the public.[106] Eventually, the JFTC had to backtrack.[107]

The continuing tendency to take into account broader societal concerns when implementing competition policy is also evidenced by the JFTC's concern to protect the weaker parties in subcontracting relationships, a concern also found in many other Asian countries. Indeed, Japan's competition authority each year spends significant time and resources on the enforcement of a law aimed at protecting subcontractors,[108] which are often small and medium-sized enterprises. In 2010, for instance, the JFTC handled 4,226 cases under this law, an all-time high.[109]

Ultimately, these examples lay bare the large gap that remains between Japanese views on the goals and role of competition law and those in the West, particularly the United States. Japan has never subscribed to the view, now commonplace in the United States, that competition law's sole concern should be economic efficiency (see Dowdle, Ch. 1, pp. 23–4). As noted above, competition law was originally introduced in Japan to achieve the political goal of economic democratization and, over time,

---

[105] See, e.g., Act on the Measures by Large-Scale Retail Stores for Preservation of the Living Environment (Daikibo kouritenpo ricchi hō), Law No. 91 of 1998, and its predecessor, Act Concerning the Adjustment of Retail Business Activities of Large-Scale Retail Stores (Daikibo kouritenpo ni okeru kourigyō no jigyōkatsudō no chōsei ni kan suru hōritsu), Law No. 109 of 1973 (repealed by Law No. 91 of 1998).

[106] JFTC, 'Concerning the Treatment of the Resale System for Copyrighted Works [Chosakubutsu saihan seido no toriatsukai ni tsuite]', 23 March 2001, available at www.jftc. go.jp/sosiki/chosakuken.pdf (Annex 1).

[107] Ibid., p. 1.

[108] Act against Delay in Payment of Subcontract Proceeds, etc. to Subcontractors (Shitauke daikin shiharai chien nado bōshi hō), Law No. 120 of 1956.

[109] JFTC, Annual Report 2010 (Heisei 22 nendo kōsei torihiki iinkai nenji hōkoku), Chart 5-2, available at www.jftc.go.jp/info/nenpou/h22/table/table_05.html#t5-2.

its goals have come to encompass a mix of both economic and non-economic elements.[110] As pointed out in Chapter 2 by David Gerber, this divergence between competition law's goals in Asia and the narrow economic-based goals in the United States may present a major obstacle to any convergence. Other obstacles to convergence identified by Gerber, such as institutional capacity, may present less of an obstacle in Japan than in other Asian countries, but fundamental differences are nonetheless likely to remain. In sum, competition law in Japan will likely continue to evolve, in parallel with Japan's capitalist system itself and conditioned by the performance of that system, along a trajectory that is distinct from that of the West.

---

[110] Shūya Hayashi, 'The Goals of Japanese Competition Law', in Josef Drexl, Laurence Idot and Joël Monéger (eds.), *Economic Theory and Competition Law* (Cheltenham: Edward Elgar, 2009), pp. 45–69, at p. 49.

State capitalism and the regulation of competition in China

WENTONG ZHENG

I. Introduction

The formal regulation of competition in market economies is done primarily through competition law. Having its origin in the United States as a response to industrial concentration and social changes during the mid to late nineteenth century, competition law – known in the United States as antitrust law – has now been adopted in more than one hundred jurisdictions. This proliferation of competition law has been particularly notable since the early 1990s, when a number of developing countries and former communist countries began adopting such regimes.[1]

As of 2010, the most recent major country to join the expanding competition law club is China, whose first comprehensive competition law, the Antimonopoly Law (AML), was adopted on 30 August 2007 and went into effect on 1 August 2008.[2] To a large extent, the AML is a transplant of the competition law models used in Western economies. Like competition law in Western economies, the AML contains provisions dealing with restraints or potential restraints on competition in three areas: agreements in restraint of trade, abuse of dominant market position, and mergers. Specifically, the AML's provisions on agreements in restraint of trade and abuse of dominant market position borrow heavily from the Treaty on the Functioning of the

---

[1] See generally David J. Gerber, *Global Competition: Law, Markets, and Globalization* (Oxford University Press, 2010).

[2] Antimonopoly Law of the People's Republic of China (Zhonghua Renmin Gongheguo Fanlongduan Fa) (China), effective 1 August 2008, available at www.gov.cn/flfg/2007-08/30/content_732591.htm. Unofficial English translation available at https://www.amcham-china.org.cn/amcham/upload/wysiwyg/20070906152846.pdf. See generally Xiaoye Wang, 'Highlights of China's New Anti-monopoly Law', *Antitrust Law Journal*, 75 (2008): 133–50; Zhenguo Wu, 'Perspectives on the Chinese Anti-monopoly Law', *Antitrust Law Journal*, 75 (2008): 73–116.

European Union,[3] and the AML's provisions on mergers 'appear to be drawn from the European Union Merger Regulation'.[4] Some provisions of the AML also show influences of US antitrust law.[5]

However, efforts to regulate competition through a formal competition law face particular challenges in China. As John Haley succinctly summarized in 2004, the competition law models that originated in the United States and Europe 'were designed to deal with problems in advanced capitalist states in which the influence of private actors in national and international markets often seemed to outmatch the role of the state'.[6] None of these models, Haley continued, 'were concerned with state power or the need of the state to create conditions for effective market competition'.[7] (See also Prosser, Ch. 10, pp. 255–8; cf. Jessop, Ch. 5.) Because they 'do not adequately address the basic underpinnings of monopoly power and barriers to free and competitive markets in East Asia or in most other developing states',[8] Haley predicted that questions might be raised 'whether these models have any applicability to China and other parts of East Asia'.[9]

This chapter sets out to examine the main themes of China's 'state capitalism' and how the extensive role of the state in China's economy affects the regulation of competition through the AML. In particular, this chapter explores three themes that shape competition law and policy in China: China's current transitional stage, China's market structures, and the pervasive state control of China's economy. It analyses how these themes have prevented China from pursuing a rigorous anti-cartel policy; how they have led to a mismatch between monopoly abuses that are prohibited under the AML and monopoly abuses that are most prevalent in China's economy; and how they have prevented the merger review process under the AML from being meaningfully applied to domestic firms. It concludes that, despite having a Western-style competition law,

---

[3] Susan Beth Farmer, 'The Evolution of Chinese Merger Notification Guidelines: A Work in Progress Integrating Global Consensus and Domestic Imperatives', *Tulane Journal of International and Comparative Law*, 18 (2009): 1–92, 6.

[4] Ibid., 9 n. 43.

[5] See Salil K. Mehra and Meng Yanbei, 'Against Antitrust Functionalism: Reconsidering China's Antimonopoly Law', *Virginia Journal of International Law*, 49 (2009): 379–429, 398 n.81.

[6] John O. Haley, 'Competition Policy for East Asia', *Washington University Global Studies Law Review*, 3 (2004): 277–84, 277.

[7] Ibid., 277.   [8] Ibid.   [9] Ibid.

China has not developed and likely will not develop a Western-style
competition law jurisprudence in the near future, due to these themes.

II.   State capitalism in China: economic transition, market
structure, and state control

Understanding China's path of transition towards a market economy is
of the utmost importance for understanding the regulation of competition in China. The following discussions provide overviews of certain key
aspects of China's transition that have shaped its current economic
conditions pertaining to competition.

A.   Price liberalization

According to Western competition theory, the principal mechanism
through which a market economy allocates resources is price (but see
Dowdle, Ch. 1, pp. 23–4). Beginning in the early 1980s, China gradually
moved away from price controls in an effort to expand the role of
markets in determining prices. But despite the overall success of price
reforms, price controls still play a significant role in certain sectors in
China. The Price Law enacted in 1997 explicitly allows the government to
control prices in certain important sectors, including natural resources,
sectors characterized by natural monopolies, and public utilities.[10] In
those sectors, the government could either directly set prices or set
'guidance prices' that limit the fluctuation of market prices within a
specified band.[11] In 2001, thirteen items appeared in the catalogue of
products or services whose prices were controlled by the central government.[12] While the number of controlled prices seems small, the significance of price control in China nowadays is definitely greater than that
number would suggest, given that many of the controlled prices are for
important products or services such as electricity, basic telecommunications, and gasoline.

---

[10] Price Law of the People's Republic of China (Zhonghua Renmin Gongheguo Jiage Fa),
effective 1 May 1999, available at www.gov.cn/banshi/2005–09/12/content_69757.htm,
Art. 18.

[11] Ibid., Arts. 3(5) and 3(4).

[12] Catalog of Prices Controlled by the National Development & Planning Commission and
Other Central Government Agencies (Guojia Jiwei he Guowuyuan Youguan Bumen
Dingjia Mulu), 4 July 2001, available at www.ndrc.gov.cn/zcfb/zcfbl/zcfbl2003pro/
t20050707_27540.htm.

B. Decentralization

On the founding of the People's Republic of China in 1949, China structured its industries in a decentralized fashion. Each region in China was relatively self-sufficient, and regional governments assumed considerable responsibility for co-ordinating production and distribution within the region. Economic reforms since the late 1970s have further strengthened the trend towards decentralization.[13] Starting in 1980, fiscal reforms granted local governments a greater share of revenues generated by local enterprises, and granted more autonomy to local governments in setting budgets and deciding on expenditures. The direct outcome of these fiscal reforms was that local budgets became highly dependent on the financial health of local enterprises. Coupled with the further decentralization of the investment control regime in the reform era, these fiscal reforms created enormous incentives, as well as pressures, for local governments to seek more revenues through the creation of new local enterprises.[14]

C. Market concentration

As a result of decentralization, China's industries are structured in a cellular manner, with duplication of a single industrial pattern in each province. A World Bank study has found that, by the early 1990s, the degree of differences in industrial structures across regions in China was much less than in the United States or the EU. And each of the major industrial groups examined by the World Bank was present in virtually all provinces in the early 1990s.[15] Consequently, market concentration ratios in China are low. Official statistics indicate that market concentration ratios in China have been unusually low when compared with both developed and developing economies.[16] Between the mid 1980s and

---

[13] See Yingyi Qian and Barry R. Weingast, *China's Transition to Markets: Market-Preserving Federalism, Chinese Style* (Stanford: Hoover Institutions), p. 10–21.

[14] Christine P. W. Wong, 'Fiscal Reform and Local Industrialization: The Problematic Sequencing of Reform in Post-Mao China', *Modern China*, 18 (1992): 197–227, 197; Jean C. Oi, 'Fiscal Reform and the Economic Foundations of Local State Corporatism in China', *World Politics*, 45 (1992): 99–126, 102. See also OECD, *China in the World Economy: The Domestic Policy Challenges* (Paris: OECD Publications), pp. 659–77.

[15] World Bank, *China: Internal Market Development and Regulation* (Washington, DC: World Bank Publications, 1994), pp. 13, 18–19.

[16] See, e.g., Minxin Pei, *China's Trapped Transition: The Limits of Developmental Autocracy* (Cambridge, MA: Harvard University Press, 2006), p. 258 n.148.

the mid 1990s, the average market concentration ratio for the largest one hundred firms in various sectors hovered between 10 and 16 per cent. In the mid-1990s, in eighteen out of thirty-nine major sectors, the largest eight firms in each sector accounted for less than 10 per cent of the market share.[17]

D. Market entry restrictions

Since the start of economic reform, China has seen a great expansion of private and foreign enterprises in its economy. In certain sectors, however, private and foreign enterprises still face substantial government-imposed barriers to market entry. In the case of foreign enterprises, the government periodically publishes a guidance catalogue on the sectors and industries in which entry is prohibited or restricted.[18] In the case of private enterprises, market entry restrictions are imposed mainly through stringent licensing and minimum capital requirements, and the sectors or industries that carry market entry restrictions tend not to be clearly spelled out.

E. The transformation of state-owned enterprises

In the official lexicon of the Chinese political economy, 'state-owned enterprises [SOEs]' refer to enterprises owned by the 'whole people', whose ownership rights are exercised by governments at various levels, from the central government down to county governments.[19] During the planned economy era, SOEs were little more than productive units of the state; managers (or, more accurately, government officials) at SOEs simply followed government orders regarding what to produce, how much to produce, and the prices at which the products would be sold. They turned all resulting profits (or losses) over to the government.

---

[17] Ibid., p. 130.

[18] For the most recent edition (as of 2012) of the guidance catalogue, see National Development and Reform Commission (Guojia Fazhan he Gaige Weiyuanhui) and Ministry of Commerce (Shangwu Bu), 'Guidance Catalog on Foreign Investment [Waishang Touzi Chanye Zhidao Mulu]', 2007, available at www.sdpc.gov.cn/zcfb /zcfbl/2007ling/ W020071107537750156652.pdf.

[19] Yingyi Qian and Chenggang Xu, 'Why China's Economic Reforms Differ: The M-Form Hierarchy and Entry/Expansion of the Non-state Sector', *Economics of Transition*, 1 (1993): 135–70, 138.

Beginning in the late 1970s, China has sought to reform SOEs along numerous lines. These reforms notwithstanding, China's SOEs still differ in material respects from profit-maximizing firms in market economies. Although most SOEs are now generally responsive to market signals, profit maximization is not the sole objective of SOEs and often gives way to other objectives such as the provision of employment and social services and the generation of tax revenues (cf. Dowdle, Ch. 1, pp. 29–32). Every SOE in China still carries a political rank, and many of the largest SOEs, such as the central SOEs supervised by the State-owned Assets Supervision and Administration Commission of the State Council (SASAC), are politically very powerful.[20] Finally, China's SOEs still have implicit, and sometimes even explicit, financial backing from the government. The 'soft budget constraints' of SOEs – that is, their ability to transfer firm debt to the government – give rise to the moral hazard problems typically associated with not having to be fully responsible for operating failures.[21]

F.   The changing regulatory landscape

In the planned-economy era, government ministries directly managed China's major industries, obviating the need for government regulation as it is practised in more market-oriented economies. As China continues its transition towards a market economy, the question arises as to how to redefine the nature and extent of state involvement in that market economy.

China has responded by using different strategies for different industries. In industries that the government believes should be opened up to market competition and that state capital should eventually exit, China has gradually reduced the role of the government through numerous rounds of government restructuring.[22] Those industries, known as 'competitive industries' in China, include coal, machinery, metallurgy, chemical, light, textile, building materials, and

---

[20] Erica S. Downs, 'Business Interest Groups in Chinese Politics: The Case of the Oil Companies', in Cheng Li (ed.), *China's Changing Political Landscape: Prospects for Democracy* (Washington, DC: Brookings Institution Press, 2008), p. 122.

[21] William L. Megginson, *The Financial Economics of Privatization* (Oxford University Press, 2005), p. 40.

[22] See generally OECD, *China: Defining the Boundary between the Market and the State* (Paris: OECD Publications), pp. 92–5.

non-ferrous metal. The central government ministries overseeing those industries were first downgraded in 1998, before being abolished altogether in 2001.[23]

In industries in which the government decides to retain control of state capital – that is, 'monopoly industries' such as electricity, banking, insurance, telecommunications, petroleum, civil aviation, and railways – government reforms have generally focused on separating the government's role as regulator from its role as owner of the major enterprises. In some of the monopoly industries, China established new 'independent' regulatory bodies that assumed the regulatory functions of the government, including the China Insurance Regulatory Commission (established in 1998), the General Administration of Civil Aviation (established in 2002), the State Electricity Regulatory Commission (established in 2003), and the China Banking Regulatory Commission (established in 2003).[24]

Regulatory reforms in China, however, are by no means complete. In industries where the government has abolished its formal regulatory roles, the informal roles of the government are still preserved to varying degrees through so-called 'industrial associations'. Many of these industrial associations are officially 'affiliated' (*guakao*) with various government agencies.[25] Furthermore, in many of the industries where the government has retained its regulatory presence, the impartiality of the regulators remains questionable. Although the original intent of regulatory reforms in those industries was to separate the government's regulatory functions from its operating functions, politically powerful SOEs still regularly receive favourable regulatory treatment. In addition, it is still not uncommon for a government agency either to directly own or otherwise have financial deals with 'affiliate companies' that are subject to its regulation.[26] With such financial interests at stake, it is the partiality rather than impartiality of the regulators that seems all but assured.

---

[23] 'State Economic & Trade Commission Abolishes Nine National Bureaus Including Domestic Distribution Bureau [Jingmaowei Chexiao Guojia Guonei Maoyi ju Deng Jiu Ge Guojia Ju]', *Sina*, 19 February 2001, available at http://finance.sina.com.cn/g/37340. html.

[24] OECD, *China: Defining the Boundary*, p. 94.

[25] See Jianhua Liu, *China's New Market Order [Zhongguo Shichang Xin Zhixu]* (Beijing: Tsinghua University Press, 2006), p. 178 & n.1.

[26] See Bing Song, 'Competition Policy in a Transitional Economy: The Case of China', *Stanford Journal of International Law*, 31 (1995): 387–422, 407.

III.   The regulation of competition in China

The main themes of China's 'state capitalism' have a great impact on the regulation of competition in China. The discussion below will explore how these themes have affected the effectiveness and relevance of the Western antitrust models incorporated in the AML. It demonstrates that in all three major areas of antitrust – cartels, abuse of dominant market position, and merger review – China's local conditions have prevented the AML from becoming an integral part of China's market environments.

A.   Cartels as regulatory price-control mechanisms

In a perfect competitive market, firms make production and sale decisions independently of – and in competition with – one another, driving prices down and volumes of production up to socially optimal levels. However, if competitors could reach, and enforce, an agreement among themselves – that is, form a cartel – regarding certain areas of competition such as price, the resulting constraints on competition will disrupt market discipline and cause losses to consumer (and presumably social) welfare. For this reason, most national competition laws today forbid cartelization in general (although they allow for exceptions).

China, however, faces a fundamental challenge in devising a coherent cartel policy: excess capacities caused by widespread structural distortions. Many of China's industries suffer from chronic excess capacity. In the mid 1990s, for example, there was excess capacity in sixty-one of China's ninety-four major categories of industrial products, and the capacity utilization rate was below 50 per cent in thirty-five of them.[27] The excess capacity in many of China's industries has persisted until today, and in some industries has reached staggering levels. According to governmental figures, the capacity utilization rate in 2008 was only 76 per cent for steel, 75 per cent for cement, 73 per cent for aluminium electrode, 88 per cent for flat glass, 40 per cent for methanol, and 20 per cent for poly-crystalline silicon (a key raw material for solar cells). And on top of this, if we adjust these figures to include the additional capacity of projects still in the pipeline, they

---

[27] Pei, *China's Trapped Transition*, p. 129.

would be 71 per cent for steel, 59 per cent for cement, 72 per cent for plate glass and, breathtakingly, 4 per cent for poly-crystalline silicon.[28]

There are several reasons for China's chronic excess capacity. First, China's abnormally high savings and investment rates lead to constant expansions of production relative to consumption. Second, the capacity-creating process in China is predominantly a government-driven one. Governments at various levels have the authority to approve investment and are also the largest investors. In 2006, for example, investments made by state entities (including SOEs and entities that are majority-controlled by the state) accounted for about 48 per cent of all investments in urban areas.[29] Many of the investments made by the local governments are copycat investments made for the primary purpose of competing against other localities for both tax revenues and higher economic growth rates.[30] These investments further add to the duplication of industries at local levels. Third, the capacity-elimination process in China is distorted by the role of these governments, too. In China, many of the duplicate investments are made by SOEs, particularly SOEs supervised by local governments. As discussed earlier, despite China's efforts to reform SOEs, many of them still shoulder responsibilities apart from profit considerations, such as the provision of employment and social services. For this reason, when SOEs become insolvent, the government is very reluctant to let them go into bankruptcy.

The excess capacity in many of China's industries, coupled with China's low market concentration ratios, leads to enormous competitive pressures in those industries (see also Dowdle, Ch. 9, detailing this phenomenon in China's raw milk market). In fact, competition is so intense in many of China's industries, and the industries affected are so

---

[28] See generally National Development and Reform Commission, 'Notice on Opinions Concerning Inhibiting Excess Capacity and Duplicate Construction in Certain Industries in Order to Guide Healthy Industrial Development [Guanyu Yizhi Bufen Hangye Channeng Guosheng he Chongfu Jianshe yindao Chanye Jiankang Fazhan de Ruogan Yijian]', 26 September 2009, available at www.sdpc.gov.cn/zcfb/zcfbqt/2010qt/t20100513_346554. htm.

[29] National Bureau of Statistics of China (Zhonghua Renmin Gongheguo Guojia Tongjiju), 'People's Republic of China 2006 National Economic and Social Development Statistics [Zhonghua Renmin Gongheguo 2006 nian Guomin Jingji he Shehui Fazhan Tongji Gongbao]', 28 February 2007, available at www.stats.gov.cn/tjgb/ndtjgb/qgndtjgb/ t20070228_402387821.htm.

[30] Yasheng Huang, *Inflation and Investment Controls in China: The Political Economy of Central–Local Relations during the Reform Era* (Cambridge University Press, 1996), pp. 70–3.

wide-ranging, that a new term was coined in the Chinese lexicon to describe just this phenomenon: 'excessive competition' (*guodu jingzheng*). In almost all of the reported instances of excessive competition, intense price competition has driven industry profits to abnormally low or even negative levels. Not surprisingly, the only firms that could remain standing under such intense competition and heavy losses were SOEs.

When competitive pressures are up, so are the incentives to organize illegal cartels. China has proven no exception to this rule. In 1993, in what appears to be China's first price cartel in modern history, five top retail outlets for electrical appliances in Beijing conspired to increase by 10 per cent the price of washing machines sold at their stores.[31] That was only one year after the price control for light industry goods, which included washing machines, was abolished.

Ever since the first price cartel in 1993, China's cartel policy has been caught in a tug of war between two forces brought about by China's price reforms. On the one hand, the general trend towards price liberalization requires the setting of prices by the market, and any interference with the setting of prices by the market, including efforts by cartels to fix prices, is undoubtedly against the fundamental neoliberal goal of price liberalization. As a result, as price reforms deepened, China has sought to ban cartels, at least in principle. The 1997 Price Law, enacted after the bulk of China's price liberalization was completed, contained China's first legal provision banning price fixing.[32] Price fixing also topped the list of prohibited pricing conduct in a regulation issued by the National Development and Reform Commission (NDRC) in 2003[33] and, more recently, in the AML.[34]

On the other hand, government regulators in China continue to see a positive role for cartels in addressing structural distortions caused by the incompleteness of price reforms. Government regulators soon found out that due to these structural distortions, unbridled competition would only lead to unbridled price wars, which in turn would lead to the draining of the state's coffers and the pile-up of non-performing loans

---

[31] World Bank, *China*, p. 134.

[32] Price Law, Art. 14(1) (instituting a ban on collusive behaviour that manipulates market prices and causes detriment to others operating in the market or to consumers).

[33] Provisional Provisions on Prohibition of Monopoly Pricing (Zhizhi Jiage Longduan Xingwei Zhanxing Guiding), National Development and Reform Commission (NDRC) Order No. 3, 18 June 2003, Art. 4(1).

[34] Antimonopoly Law, Art. 13(1) (prohibiting monopoly agreements among competing operators that fix or change the price of a commodity).

in state-owned banks. As a result, China's government regulators have, as discussed below, looked to cartels as a means of reinstating some sort of price control that was abolished in the price reforms. (Cf. Dowdle, Ch. 9, p. 227 n. 115.)

The tension between the need for market pricing and the need for addressing structural distortions has led to a wide gap between how cartels are treated under formal laws and how cartels are treated in practice. On the one hand, there are laws and regulations that strictly prohibit cartels. On the other hand, there are public, widespread attempts at cartels, so public and so widespread that the media routinely reports them with a sense of resignation or even normalcy. In the colour television industry, for instance, five publicly reported attempts were made to organize nationwide price or production cartels by China's largest colour television manufacturers during a period of two years between April 1998 and June 2000.[35] In the VCD player industry, three publicly reported attempts were made to organize nationwide price cartels between May 1997 and May 2000.[36] In late 2005, twenty-three of China's largest aluminium electrode producers announced the formation of a production cartel to jointly reduce their volumes of production by 10 per cent.[37] In the airline industry there have been repeated attempts at price cartels to curb ever-increasing price competition. It was reported that in March 2005 almost all China's airline companies were involved in a 'price coalition' aimed at propping up ticket prices for flights between Beijing and seven major Chinese cities.[38] In April 2009, eight months after the AML went into effect, a 'price coalition' reappeared in the airline industry, this time in the form of a new industry price-quoting system that lowered the basis for calculating price discounts.[39] Similarly, the ocean shipping industry operating Sino-Japanese shipping routes has seen

---

[35] Scott Kennedy, *The Business of Lobbying in China* (Cambridge, MA: Harvard University Press, 2005), p. 113.

[36] Ibid., Table 4.2, p. 113.

[37] 'Twenty-Three of China's Largest Aluminum Electrode Manufacturers to Jointly Reduce Production by Ten Percent [Zhongguo 23 Jia Dianjielü Gugan Qiye Jiang Lianhe Jianchan 10%]', Xinhua, 2 December 2005, available at http://news.xinhuanet.com/fortune/2005–12/02/content_3868498.htm.

[38] 'China's Airline Companies Form Price Coalition: Air Ticket Prices Increase [Guonei Hangkong Gongsi Dacheng Jiage Tongmeng; Jipiao Jiage Pubian Shangsheng]', *Beijing Xiandai Shangbao* (*Beijing Modern Business Journal*), 4 April 2005, available at http://finance.sina.com.cn/chanjing/b/20050404/07401484238.shtml.

[39] 'Five Airline Companies Suspected for Colluding to Raise Prices; Scheme Approved by General Administration of Civil Aviation [Wu Da Hangkong Gongsi Yi Gongmou

repeated attempts to organize price cartels as a means of stopping zero or negative shipping charges. One such attempt was made in summer 2005,[40] followed by another attempt in August 2009.[41]

The government's attitude towards cartels, not surprisingly, has been ambivalent. Only in very few cases has the NDRC rigorously enforced the anti-cartel provisions of the Price Law, the AML, and its own 2003 regulation on monopoly pricing. In recent years, the NDRC has taken enforcement action against only three price cartels, all in the food or agricultural sector.[42] All those cases involved daily necessities and likely implicated non-antitrust concerns such as social stability. In the remaining cases, the NDRC and other government regulators have been silent about cartels, or even have played an active role in organizing cartels themselves.[43] This tolerance or promotion of cartels is in essence an effort to reinstate some sort of price control in an economy where incomplete price reforms have led to widespread structural distortions. An argument could be made that under such structural distortions, the government's tolerance or promotion of cartels, if successful, would not be as welfare-reducing as it would be in a typical market economy, or may even be welfare-improving, because the 'market' prices prevailing under such structural distortions do not necessarily represent maximum economic efficiency (see also Dowdle, Ch. 1, pp. 24–9). In addition, the government's tolerance or promotion of cartels, if

Zhangjia; Fangan Huo Minhangju Renke]', *Guangzhou Ribao* (*Guangzhou Daily*), 22 April 2009, available at http://finance.jrj.com.cn/2009/04/2209124197055.shtml.

[40] 'CCTV in Focus Interview: Ocean Shippers Discover "Negative Rates" [Yangshi Jiaodian Fangtan: Hayun Jingxian "Fuyunjia"]', Sohu, 22 September 2006, available at http://news.sohu.com/20060922/n245477144.shtml.

[41] 'Fourteen Shipping Companies Operating in Sino-Japan Shipping Routes Form Self-Discipline Coalition [14 Jia Riben Hangxie Chuandong Zucheng Yunjia Zilü Lianmeng]', *Tianjin Ocean Network*, 30 July 2009, available at www.dolphin-gp.com/cn/content.php?id=1248417093.

[42] See, e.g., Hannah Ha, John Hickin, and Gerry O'Brien, 'China Steps Up Antitrust Capacity Building – Cartels a Focus', *Mondaq*, 20 July 2010, available at www.mondaq.com/article.asp?articleid=105788 (NDRC action against mung bean cartel); Kala Anandarajah and Dominique Lombardi, 'China's First Public Anti-Cartel Action Under the Anti-Monopoly Law,' *Mondaq*, 11 June 2010, available at www.mondaq.com/article.asp?articleid=102700 (NDRC action against rice noodle cartel).

[43] See, e.g., 'China's Big Four Airlines Jointly Set Prices to Increase Profits [Zhongguo Si Da Hangkong Lianshou Zhiding Piaojia Yi Tisheng Lirun]', Xiamen Huoyun Wang (Logistics Website of the City of Xiamen), 15 March 2010, available at www.xmwuliu.net/WuLiuXinWen/20100315/89748.html (airline industry); 'Fourteen Shipping Companies' (ocean shipping industry).

successful, may not harm consumers as much as it would in a typical market economy, as consumers would have incurred harms of a comparable magnitude, albeit indirectly, in the form of SOE losses but for successful cartels.

Leaving these normative issues aside, the bottom line seems to be that China, despite all its stringent anti-cartel laws on the books, is unlikely to develop a rigorous anti-cartel policy before structural distortions in its economy are removed, which likely will take a while, if it happens at all.

B. Abuse of dominance

A central task of competition law is to prevent abuses of dominant market position. Competition law has generally recognized two kinds of abusive conduct: exclusionary conduct and exploitative conduct. Exclusionary conduct seeks to exclude competitors from the market and create or maintain the dominant firm's market power. Exploitative conduct involves the exploitation of one's market position to charge excessive prices to consumers or, sometimes, to extort excessively low prices from suppliers. Competition law in Western countries has generally focused on exclusionary conduct.[44]

This exclusion-focused paradigm appears also to have been adopted by the AML. Article 17 of the AML provides a non-exhaustive list of six types of conduct that are each considered to be an abuse of a dominant market position. Those six types of conduct are referred to as excessive pricing, predatory pricing, refusal to deal, exclusive dealing, tying, and price discrimination in US and EU competition laws. Article 17, however, is ambiguous as regards whether it is concerned primarily with the exclusionary or the exploitative aspects of these behaviours. It is clear that Article 17 prohibits one type of purely exploitative conduct – excessive pricing. But the other types of prohibited conduct could be either exclusionary or exploitative, or both. For example, 'refusal to deal' as prohibited under Article 17(3)

---

[44] See, e.g., Brian A. Facey and Dany H. Assaf, 'Monopolization and Abuse of Dominance in Canada, the United States, and the European Union: A Survey', *Antitrust Law Journal*, 70 (2002): 513–91, 544; Massimo Motta and Alexandre de Streel, 'Excessive Pricing and Price Squeeze Under EU Law', in Claus-Dieter Ehlermann and Isabela Atanasiu (eds.), *European Competition Law Annual 2003: What is an Abuse of a Dominant Position?* (Oxford: Hart, 2006), pp. 91–125.

could be exclusionary if the dominant firm refuses to deal with a supplier who is also dealing with a competitor, but could also be exploitative if the dominant firm refuses to deal with a consumer, harming the consumer directly. But this lacuna appears to have been filled by another article: Article 6, one of the AML's 'general provisions [*zongze*]', provides that 'undertakings that have a dominant market position are prohibited from abusing that position *to exclude or impede competition*' (emphasis added). Article 6 thus appears to limit the conduct prohibited under Article 17 to exclusionary conduct only, perhaps with the exception of excessive pricing, which is specifically listed under Article 17 but is purely exploitative.

However, for there to be exclusionary abuses there must be competitors or at least potential competitors that, but for regulatory intervention, would be excluded. This condition is to varying degrees not satisfied in China's monopoly industries, where the state tightly controls the number of incumbent firms as well as market entry by new firms. In extreme scenarios, where the state allows only one firm in an industry and strictly prohibits entry by others, that industry will not see any exclusionary conduct within the meaning of competition law, because, with the exclusion of competitors and potential competitors already carried out by the state, the monopoly firm will not need to resort to exclusionary conduct itself.

A competition law that focuses on exclusionary conduct, therefore, is powerless to address this kind of abuse of dominance. In such industries, for exclusion-based competition law even to become relevant, competition must be first 'created' – that is, by breaking up the state-sanctioned monopoly and/or allowing the possibility of entry by new firms.[45] But these efforts would take place outside the framework of the AML. If these efforts are successful, China's monopoly industries might see more exclusionary abuses because there will be more competitors to exclude. But until then the AML will have only limited relevance to the regulation of abuse-of-dominance in those industries.

C. *Merger review*

As with antitrust laws in most jurisdictions, the AML provides a merger review regime – a regime in which parties to a proposed merger or

---

[45] Song, 'Competition Policy in a Transitional Economy', 387–8.

'concentration' are required to notify the government of the proposed transaction and to wait for government review of the likely effects on competition of the transaction before the transaction can be officially consummated. Prior to the AML, a merger review process existed for foreign companies seeking to acquire domestic Chinese companies, but there was no corresponding merger review process for domestic mergers.[46] This was changed by the AML, at least in theory. By virtue of applying to 'monopoly conduct in economic activities within the People's Republic of China', the AML seems to extend its merger review regime to domestic mergers as well.[47]

Two years later, however, the AML appeared not to have significantly changed China's merger review landscape. As of August 2010, the Ministry of Commerce, the agency charged with merger review, had since the AML went into effect rejected one proposed merger and approved six others with conditions.[48] All seven transactions involved foreign companies, and six of them were transactions initiated overseas between multinational corporations with operations in China. In terms of mergers notified to ministry officials, foreign companies accounted for the majority of them also. According to statistics provided by the ministry, as of June 2009, of the fifty-eight mergers accepted by the ministry for review under the AML, forty involved multinational corporations.[49] The more recent statistics on merger review cases, released in August 2010 in a press conference, did not provide the exact number of notified mergers involving foreign companies, but a senior ministry official stated at the press conference that 'the majority of mergers accepted for review involved foreign companies'.[50]

---

[46] Provisions on Acquisitions of Domestic Enterprises by Foreign Investors (Guanyu Waiguo Touzizhe Binggou Jingnei Giye De Guiding) (Ministry of Commerce Order No. 10, 6 August 2006); English translation available at www.sipf.com.cn/en/lawsandregulations/linvestors/otherlawsandregu/10/6658.shtml.

[47] Antimonopoly Law, Art. 2.

[48] For Ministry of Commerce merger decisions in these cases (in Chinese), see http://fldj.mofcom.gov.cn/ztxx/ztxx.html?3161571153=3993603634 (accessed 14 June 2012).

[49] 'Antimonopoly Law One Year On: Multinational Corporations Involved in Sixty-Nine Percent of Cases [Fanlongduan Fa Shishi Yinian: Kuaguo Gongsi Canyu Anjia Zhan 69%]', Franchise Attorneys, 17 November 2009, available at www.fclaw.com.cn/Details.asp?id=13994.

[50] 'Ministry of Commerce: No Discrimination Against Foreign Companies in Antimonopoly Merger Review [Shangwubu: Fanlongduan Shencha Wei Qishi Qaizi]', *Morning Post*, 12 August 2010, available at www.morningpost.com.cn/xwzx/jjxw/2010–08–12/66994.shtml.l.

The first reason why the AML's merger review process has not involved many domestic firms is the market structure of China's industries. As discussed earlier, most of China's industries, with the exception of the monopoly industries, are characterized by small-scale firms and low market concentration ratios. Mergers among small firms in non-concentrated markets hardly pose a threat to competition, and a merger review process that aims to prevent only mergers that have anticompetitive effects typically does not, and should not, extend to those mergers.

The second reason why the AML's merger review process has had only limited relevance to domestic firms has to do with the treatment of SOE mergers. First of all, subjecting SOE mergers to merger review would be problematic from a conceptual point of view. If a merger among private firms that are subsidiaries of a common parent should be exempted from the merger notification requirement, why should a merger among SOEs that are also owned by one common parent – that is, the state – not be exempted, too? One plausible answer to this question appears to be that there is an implicit assumption when exempting mergers among subsidiaries of private firms from merger review, and that assumption is that such subsidiaries are not in a competitive relationship with one another. Such an assumption does not hold, the answer would go, for China's SOEs that are, or are at least intended to be, competitors with one another.

This answer, while intuitive, actually underscores the paradoxical nature of China's SOEs. In a continuum between a pure state entity at one end and a pure market entity at the other, China's SOEs appear in the middle. They have moved far enough in the process of becoming market entities to be in a competitive relationship with one another, but have not moved far enough in that process to be completely independent of state control. So when the state merges two SOEs, to what extent is that merger an 'economic activity' (see Article 2) subject to the AML?

In addition to the conceptual issue discussed above, subjecting SOEs to merger review would also create tensions between competing policy goals. China has long had a policy favouring SOE mergers, a policy that dates back to the early 1980s. As time went on, China appeared to keep adding new justifications for this policy. Initially, beginning in the early 1980s, SOE mergers were intended primarily as a response to low market concentration and market segmentation across provinces.[51] Beginning in

---

[51] Song, 'Competition Policy in a Transitional Economy', 397.

the early 1990s, along with the need to address market segmentation, the government's strategic repositioning of SOEs in the national economy – a strategy referred to as 'grasp the large, let go of the small' – became a major factor driving SOE mergers. Most recently, in addition to the need for addressing market segmentation and the need for carrying out the government's overall SOE strategy, a third factor – that is, the need for forming China's 'national champions' – appeared to have made its way to the expanding list of policy considerations favouring SOE mergers. All three policy goals driving SOE mergers appear to be at least equally as important as, if not more important than, the anti-market-concentration goal of the AML. As a result, even if SOE mergers were indeed notified to the Ministry of Commerce, it would be exceedingly difficult for the ministry to exercise independent merger review to override these competing policy goals.

In sum, what appeared to be one of the AML's most significant breakthroughs – the creation of a merger review regime for domestic mergers – has not had a significant impact on domestic mergers. Before China's domestic industries become more concentrated, and before China reconciles its SOE policies with its merger control policy, the merger review process under the AML will likely remain a process largely focused on foreign companies.

IV.   Why was the Antimonopoly Law enacted?

A recurring pattern emerges from the analyses above: despite having been widely regarded as a historic step for China, the AML has not yet become an integral part of China's competition policy. The transitional stage that China is currently in, China's market structures, and pervasive state control of China's economy have limited the reach and applicability of the AML in all three major areas of antitrust: cartels, abuse of dominant market position, and merger review. The question brought to the forefront by the above analyses is then this: if the AML appears to be ill-suited to address the most pressing competition issues in China today, why was it enacted in the first place?

Short of having access to documentation of the behind-the-scenes deliberations that eventually led to the consensus within the government on the need for a formal competition law, the original intent of the AML may never be completely known. Nevertheless, publicly available information about the AML's drafting process can, and does, provide significant clues.

As has been observed elsewhere, among the driving forces behind the AML were the government's desires to promote the development of the market and to contain abusive state power.[52] These 'domestic incentives', however, were not strong, and certainly not strong enough to make the idea of enacting a formal competition law a quick sell.[53] It has been widely noted that the AML was first placed on the government's legislative agenda in 1994. Its drafting process, however, 'languished for a decade', and it was not until 2004 that the drafting efforts were 'suddenly revived and expedited'.[54]

What happened? Based on Chinese media reports, it was apparently a 2003 incident involving the alleged anticompetitive practices of a foreign company in China that led to the sudden acceleration of the drafting process for the AML. In 2003, Tetra Pak, a Swedish company specializing in aseptic packaging equipment and supplies for dairy and beverage products, was accused of tying the sale of packaging equipment to the sale of packaging supplies in China.[55] After receiving complaints from domestic firms competing with Tetra Pak for packaging supplies, SAIC and the Ministry of Commerce conducted a series of investigations into anticompetitive conduct by foreign companies in China.[56] In April 2004, SAIC reported in an internal publication the findings of its investigations. In its report, SAIC gave a detailed – albeit somewhat exaggerated – account of the market shares of foreign companies in China in seven product groups or industries, and warned of a trend of foreign companies monopolizing Chinese markets.[57]

The Tetra Pak incident and the ensuing investigations by SAIC and the Ministry of Commerce took place against the backdrop of the more

---

[52] Yong Huang, 'Pursuing the Second Best: The History, Momentum, and Remaining Issues of China's Anti-Monopoly Law', *Antitrust Law Journal*, 75 (2008): 117–31, 121–2.

[53] David J. Gerber, 'Economics, Law and Institutions: The Shaping of Chinese Competition Law', *Journal of Law and Policy*, 26 (2008): 271–99, 282.

[54] Huang, 'Pursuing the Second Best', 119.

[55] Jia Hepeng, 'Country Fighting against Monopolies', *China Daily*, 5 December 2004, available at www.chinadaily.com.cn/english/doc/2004–12/05/content_397413.htm.

[56] 'The Antimonopoly Law's Bumpy Journey of Twenty-One Years [Fanlongduan Fa 21 Nian Fengyu Licheng]', *Zhongguo Jingji Shibao* (*China Economic Times*), 29 July 2008, available at www.competitionlaw.cn/show.aspx?id=3984&cid=13.

[57] 'State Administration for Industry & Commerce [SAIC] Report: Multinational Giants Show Signs of Monopolizing China's Markets [Guojia Gongshang Zongju Baogao: Kuaguo Jutou Zai Hua Jian Xian Longduan Taishi]', *Xinwen Chenbao* (*Morning News Daily*), 15 November 2004, available at http://news.xinhuanet.com/fortune/2004-11/15/content_2221465.htm.

globalized Chinese economy of the WTO era. On its accession to the WTO in 2001, China made a broad range of commitments, including on tariff reductions, which were binding for a large number of products, and on trade in services in a large number of sectors. The direct outcome of these WTO commitments is enhanced access to the Chinese market by foreign companies. With the elimination of many policy tools that used to be available to protect China's domestic industries from multinational corporations, Chinese firms are to an increasing degree facing direct competition from multinational corporations, which are generally considered in China to be stronger competitors because of their advantages in financial resources, technologies, and management skills. It is therefore not surprising that the alleged anticompetitive practices of Tetra Pak and possibly other multinational corporations gave rise to a strong reaction in China.

The Tetra Pak incident and the SAIC report appear to have led to a broad consensus that China needed a formal competition law as a precaution against anticompetitive practices of multinational corporations. After the issuance of the 2004 SAIC report, the drafting process for the AML accelerated,[58] culminating in its adoption in August 2007.

The adoption of the AML did not, however, alter the fact that there was still not a consensus on the need to have a formal competition law to deal with domestic competition issues. In the WTO era, China could not really enact a competition law that would apply to foreign firms only. But subjecting domestic firms, particularly SOEs, to the new competition law would pose numerous conceptual and policy challenges. In the last three years of the AML's drafting process, therefore, efforts appear to have been made to draft a law that would, at least nominally, conform to antitrust principles but would at the same time accommodate the status quo, rather than a law that would require the status quo to conform to antitrust principles. This minimalist approach is largely made necessary by China's unique local conditions as discussed earlier in the chapter. Before these local conditions become more compatible with a coherent competition policy, and before there is a consensus on the role of competition in the domestic sectors, the AML will likely remain a minimalist law, and China's competition policy will likely continue to

---

[58] 'Drafting of Antimonopoly Law Accelerates after Ten Years in the Making: Foreign Companies Rebut Monopoly Charges [Fanlongduan Fa Yunniang 10 Nian Jiasu Chutai: Waiqi Fanbo Longduan]', *Beijing Qingnian Bao (Beijing Youth Daily)*, 28 May 2004, available at http://hyconference.edu.cn/chinese/law/574907.htm.

be shaped more by ad hoc government action initiated outside the AML than by the more globalized understanding of competition regulation that law sought to capture (see also Prosser, Ch. 10).

V. Conclusion

This chapter demonstrates that due to the extensive role of the state in China's economy, the regulation of competition in China takes place under conditions that are not entirely compatible with global competition law models, even as they are incorporated in China's positive competition law regime, the AML. These conditions – chiefly the transitional nature of China's economy, its attendant market structures, and the state's continuing, pervasive control of that economy – have limited the reach and applicability of the AML in all three major areas of competition regulation, namely cartels, abuse of dominant market position, and merger review. Despite having a Western-style competition law, China has not developed and likely will not develop Western-style competition law jurisprudence in the near future due to these local conditions.

8

Managing competition in socialist-transforming Asia: the case of Vietnam

JOHN GILLESPIE

I. Introduction

The recent adoption of global models of competition law in China and Vietnam provides an excellent opportunity to explore how competition law interacts with Asian capitalism. Socialist-transforming Asia evinces an economic framework that is historically unsuited to the capitalist-market presumptions embedded in the global competition law model. More than anywhere else in Asia, this region relies on state-led industrial planning and relational governance to regulate competition – modes of regulation that are not generally considered compatible with market-based competition laws, but which are often considered hallmarks of Asian capitalism (see Dowdle, Ch. 1, pp. 17–21). Understanding how global models of competition laws interact with these very different, pre-existing regulatory systems promises valuable insights into how Asian capitalism more generally interacts with transplanted competition law drawn from the North Atlantic forms of capitalism.

It is possible to view this interaction in Polanyian terms, as a function of disembedded markets. As Karl Polanyi noted over half a century ago, laws designed to privilege market freedoms and to protect property rights often lack social and economic relevance in developing and not-yet-industrialized societies, where markets are not disembedded from non-economic, social forces such as relational networks, village spirituality, and traditional identities.[1] He argued that markets dis-embed from societal forms of ordering as they move away from traditional relational transactions to more arm's-length, industrial modes of commerce. One implication often drawn from Polanyi's work is that as industrial and post-industrial markets dis-embed, there is an inevitable convergence towards governance through abstract rules such as market-based competition laws.

---

[1] Karl Polanyi, *The Great Transformation: The Political and Economic Origins of Our Times* (Boston, MA: Beacon Press, 2001 [1944]), p. 61. See generally Gareth Dale, *Karl Polanyi: The Limits of the Market* (Cambridge: Polity Press, 2010).

This chapter aims to demonstrate, in the context of socialist-transforming Asia, that rather than converging towards disembedded markets and law-based governance, the introduction of Euro-American competition law has produced in socialist-transforming Asia an economy, and corresponding regulatory space, that is variegated and uneven. Firms and actors that are more deeply embedded in the traditional state-capitalist nexus have little need for new competition-law models, and are able to resist their influence. They rely on the Communist Party of Vietnam (CPV) and sympathetic state administrators to 'manage' their markets to ensure that they rather than consumers capture more of the surplus value of the production. Conversely, newer firms operating outside this nexus are more likely to embrace the form of economic competition that these Euro-American transplants seek to catalyse.

This chapter is developed in three sections. The first sets out the theoretical approach. It argues that the competitive markets associated with Euro-American varieties of capitalism do not represent natural points of convergence towards which firms in formerly socialist economies will automatically gravitate. Rather, they are something in which these firms have to learn to operate, and this epistemological transformation primarily takes place in dialogical exchanges that circulate in and around business networks. The second section reviews the regulatory environment in which these business networks interpret and respond to competition regimes. In the third section, three case studies will be presented in order to explore the three main types of business networks that are emerging in transforming Vietnam. I shall show how each of these kinds of network interacts with the imported competition model in a different way. The chapter concludes that market-based competition law will often struggle to find regulatory coherence in the context of Asian capitalism, where business networks more commonly rely on relational regulation to order their markets.

II. Analytical framework

Much discussion about market regulation in China and Vietnam[2] is animated by the commercialization thesis,[3] which holds that capitalism resulted from the division of labour, leading to increased efficiency of

---

[2] See Barry Naughton, *Growing Out of the Plan: Chinese Economic Reform 1978–93* (Cambridge University Press, 1996), pp. 23–4; Adam Fforde, *Vietnamese State Industry and the Political Economy of Commercial Renaissance: Dragon's Tooth or Curate's Egg?* (Oxford: Chandos, 2007).

[3] Ellen Wood, *The Origin of Capitalism: A Longer View*, rev. edn (London: Verso, 2002), p. 36.

production, which in turn generated the progressive development of trade, greater accumulation of wealth, and the advancement of science. This commercialization thesis focuses on the quantitative expansion of existing natural human tendencies, rather than on the qualitative transformations that require economic actors to learn new practices[4] (see also Dowdle, Ch. 1, pp. 23–4; Jessop, Ch. 5, pp. 99–100). It assumes that industrial capitalism emerges naturally out of markets, and that since markets exist in every society, the shift from non-market to market forms of economic ordering, such as the current transformation in China and Vietnam, is a natural corollary of having more markets.

However, as Carol Rose observed in relation to post-Soviet Russia: 'capitalist production has a kind of moral and cultural infrastructure that we may have mistakenly thought was simply natural, whereas in fact it is learnt through sustained commercial practice'[5] (see also Jessop, Ch. 5, p. 102). Victor Nee and Annette Miae Kim have made similar observations about the development of capitalism in China and Vietnam.[6] This scholarship suggests that the adoption of a capitalist competition law in socialist Asia not only requires exposure to new economic modes of production, but also some kind of epistemological transformation.

A growing body of research shows that this kind of capitalist-regulatory learning primarily occurs in dialogical exchanges within, and among, business networks.[7] Seen from the distance of systems theory, this kind of communication has both an internal and an external dimension. Internally such exchanges revolve around narratives that are the product of a deliberate design to steer members of business networks towards common epistemic and regulatory assumptions.[8] Externally, networks use these exchanges strategically, sometimes to compete with

---

[4] Annette Miae Kim, *Learning To Be Capitalists: Entrepreneurs in Vietnam's Transition Economy* (Oxford University Press, 2008), pp. 1–20.

[5] Carol M. Rose, 'Propter Honoris Respectum: Property as the Keystone Right?', *Notre Dame Law Review*, 71 (1996): 329–65, 354.

[6] Victor Nee, 'Organization Dynamics of Institutional Change: Politicized Capitalism in China', in Victor Nee and Richard Swedberg (eds.), *The Economic Sociology of Capitalism* (Princeton University Press, 2005), pp. 53–74; Kim, *Learning to Be Capitalists*, pp. 31–52.

[7] See, e.g., Victor Nee and Richard Swedberg (eds.), *The Economic Sociology of Capitalism* (Princeton University Press, 2005); Hugh Collins, 'The Weakest Link: Legal Implications of the Network Architecture of Supply Chains', in Marc Amstutz and Gunther Teubner (eds.), *Networks: Legal Issues of Multilateral Co-Operation* (Oxford: Hart, 2009), pp. 187–210.

[8] Richard M. Buxbaum, 'Is "Network" a Legal Concept?', *Journal of Institutional and Theoretical Economics*, 149 (1993): 698–705, 702–5; Collins, 'Weakest Link'.

and sometimes to negotiate with other regulatory institutions (including those of the formal state) that also seek to manage the markets in which the business networks are involved. Over time, the interactions among the business networks and these other regulatory institutions work to reconcile differences, identify common objectives, and allow the institutions to 'co-evolve'.[9] (Cf. Vande Walle, Ch. 6, pp. 134–43.)

Despite providing a useful macro structure for understanding dialogical learning, systems theory does not enquire into the micro-exchanges that make regulatory change possible. In particular, it fails to explain adequately why economic actors tend to coalesce into like-minded communities, such as business networks, in the first place. In this regard, theorists from various schools of social constructionism offer more nuanced insights about the internal architecture of regulatory communities.[10] Social constructionists see business networks as epistemic communities. They argue that business networks create evaluative frames of reference that build consensus about internal and external regulatory practices.[11] Business networks straddle the interface between individual practices and collective action, sometimes compelling economic actors to regard particular regulators and their procedures and outcomes as supportive of, if not necessary to, the network's own agenda, sometimes compelling them to regard other efforts at regulation as alien and threatening to the values and goals of the network and its members.

III.   Mapping business networks in socialist-transforming Asia

A burgeoning literature suggests that business networks are the main market regulators in socialist-transforming Asia[12] (see also Yeung, Ch. 11). Studies have identified three main types of business network in China and Vietnam. These loose groupings comprise both vertical and

---

[9] Bob Jessop, 'Regulationist and Autopoieticist Reflections on Polanyi's Account of Market Economics and the Market Society', *New Political Economy*, 6 (2001): 213–32, 217–18.

[10] See, e.g., Susan S. Silbey, 'After Legal Consciousness', *Annual Review of Law and Social Science*, 1 (2005): 323–68; Paul DiMaggio, 'Culture and Cognition: An Interdisciplinary Review', *Annual Review of Sociology*, 23 (1997): 263–87. See generally Peter L. Berger and Thomas Luckmann, *The Social Construction of Reality* (Garden City, NJ: Anchor Books, 1967).

[11] Tom R. Tyler, 'Psychological Perspectives on Legitimacy and Legitimation', *Annual Review of Psychology*, 57 (2006): 375–400.

[12] See, e.g., Roselyn Hsueh, *China's Regulatory State: A New Strategy for Globalization* (Ithaca, NY: Cornell University Press 2011), pp. 9–24; Martin Gainsborough, *Vietnam: Rethinking the State* (London: Zed Books, 2010).

horizontal regulatory dimensions: 'vertical', in the sense of disaggregation into state, non-state, and trans-state regulatory spaces; 'horizontal', in the sense of disaggregation into public, private, and corporatist regulatory spaces. Each kind of business network has a different regulatory need and expectation, and consequently has responded in different ways to the importation of Euro-American forms of competition law.[13]

The first type of network is associated with 'cadre-capitalism', a term used to describe the large state-owned-and-controlled firms which form a series of interconnected business networks. The firms comprising this network were created by and controlled by the state and work to further that state's industrial policies. They draw extensively on economic resources that are controlled by the state, and rely on the state to monitor and enforce their network. Although these kinds of network are dominated by state-controlled firms, they sometimes include foreign investors and private firms in their complex webs of cross-ownership and control.[14] In both China and Vietnam, these networks control the 'commanding heights' of the economy and are responsible for approximately 40 per cent of non-farm production (NFP).

The second type of business network we shall call the 'LME network'. LME networks consist of large and medium-sized private or foreign firms. These firms and their business networks are comparatively independent of CPV and state control, and operate at the periphery of the cadre-capitalist network. The firms in the LME network are often linked to transnational corporations via production chains, making them more open to global regulatory ideas than cadre-capitalists. Firms in LME networks collectively generate about 30 per cent of non-farm production in both Vietnam and China.[15]

---

[13] See generally Yusheng Peng, 'Kinship Networks and Entrepreneurs in China's Transition Economy', *American Journal of Sociology*, 109: 1045–74; Barry Naughton, 'SASAC and rising corporate power', *China Leadership Monitor*, 24 (Spring 2008): 1–9, available at http://media.hoover.org/documents/CLM24BN.pdf; Berhanu Abegaz, 'The Diversified Business Group as an Innovative Organisational Model for Large State-Enterprise Reform in China and Vietnam', *International Journal of Entrepreneurship and Innovation Management*, 5 (2005): 379–400; Melanie Beresford, 'The Development of Commercial Regulation in Vietnam's Market Economy', in John Gillespie and Albert Chen (eds.), *Legal Reforms in China and Vietnam* (London: Routledge, 2010), pp. 254–68.

[14] Yi-Chein Chiang, Tung Liang Liao and Yu-Ling Liu, 'Performance and Investments in China from Industrial Perspectives: Evidence from Taiwan Firms', *Review of Pacific Basin Financial Markets and Policies*, 11 (2008): 331–46.

[15] Barry Naughton, *The Chinese Economy: Transitions and Growth* (Boston, MA: MIT Press, 2007), pp. 297–326; UNCTAD, *Investment Policy Review: Viet Nam* (New York: United Nations Publications, 2008), pp. 5–10.

The third type of business network is what we shall call the 'SME network'. SME networks consist of small and medium-sized enterprises (SMEs) that are embedded in smaller, relational markets. Along these lines, what distinguishes SME networks from LME networks is not so much firm size or degree of formality per se, but rather level of education, exposure to international markets and information, and identification with relational transactions and the business network per se. Firms in SME networks only infrequently interact with firms in the other two kinds of network, and often strategically avoid interaction with state regulators. Although they are increasingly linked to regional production networks, these SME networks draw their private ordering strategies from local rather than global regulatory sources. Conservative estimates show them contributing 30 per cent of both China's and Vietnam's NFP.[16]

All three kinds of business network function within a state regulatory system that projects power both through formal legal and administrative instruments and through personal networks based on party and state linkages. Each facet of this complex system influences how business networks engage with the competition laws.

IV.   Developing a market competition regime

A key difference between the transformations from socialism in Asia on one hand and eastern Europe on the other is that in China and Vietnam reforms did not bring about regime collapse.[17] In both China and Vietnam the party-state survived intact, and continue to play a central role in the development of market capitalism.

In tandem with (partially) dismantling the command economy during the 1980s, both China and Vietnam enacted legislative frameworks that promoted and offered greater protection for private commercial activities. These included laws that incrementally extended state protection to private property and contractual rights; company laws that gave state and non-state firms a legal framework through which they could attract

---

[16] Naughton, *Chinese Economy*, pp. 297–326; Jean-Pierre Cling, Nguyễn Thị Thu Huyền, Nguyễn Hữu Chí, Phan T. Ngọc Trâm, Mireille Razafindrakoto, and François Roubaud, *The Informal Sector in Vietnam: A Focus on Hanoi and Ho Chi Minh City* (Hanoi: The Gioi, 2010), pp. 74–86.

[17] Peter Nolan, *China's Rise, Russia's Fall: Politics, Economics and Planning in the Transition from Stalinism* (New York: St. Martin's Press, 1995); Phong Dang and Melanie Beresford, *Authority Relations and Economic Decision-Making in Vietnam: An Historical Perspective* (Copenhagen: NIAS Publications, 1998).

private investment; and laws that enabled both state-owned and private firms to sell their businesses and use land and buildings as collateral. As part of this framework, and following years of internal debate, Vietnam enacted a competition law in 2004 and China followed in 2008.

Consistent with global standards, the competition laws of both China and Vietnam have sought to introduce three core ideas into their new economic environments:[18]

- the principle of non-discriminatory competition, which prohibits state authorities from discriminating against private enterprises in regulating market activity;[19]
- prohibiting cartels and other forms of anti-competitive behaviour among competing firms (except in particular economic sectors);[20] and
- preventing economic concentrations that impede competition.[21]

Although leaving considerable room for flexible interpretation, these core ideas invoke a clearly neoliberal approach to market regulation. They suggest that principles of market competition override industry policies in regulating the market. They further suggest that the state will not intervene except to correct market failures caused by anti-competitive behaviour. Such signalling carries out an important function, 'not only because it helps set the rules by which market activity takes place, but it also makes a larger statement about government priorities'.[22] But, as we shall see, such signalling can lack credibility where there is significant divergence between the message and the everyday experience of state governance.

---

[18] David J. Gerber, 'Economics, Law and Institutions: The Shaping of Chinese Competition Law', *Washington University Journal of Law and Policy*, 26 (2008): 271–99; Alice Pham, 'The Development of Competition Law in Vietnam in the Face of Economic Reforms and Global Integration', *Northwestern Journal of International Law and Business*, 26 (2005): 547–64, 547; see also Bruce M. Owen, Su Sun, and Wentong Zheng, 'China's Competition Policy Reforms: The Antimonopoly Law and Beyond', *Antitrust Law Journal*, 75 (2008): 231–68.

[19] Cf. Competition Law (Luật Cuộc thi), No. 27/2004/QH11 (hereinafter Competition Law (Vietnam)), Arts. 1, 5 and 6, with Antimonopoly Law (China), Arts. 32–37.

[20] Cf. Competition Law (Vietnam), Arts. 8, 9, with Antimonopoly Law (China), Arts. 13–16.

[21] Cf. Competition Law (Vietnam), Arts. 17–24, with Antimonopoly Law (China), Arts. 20–31.

[22] See Curtis J. Milhaupt and Katharina Pistor, Law and Capitalism: *What Corporate Crises Reveal about Legal Systems and Economic Development Around the World* (University of Chicago Press, 2008), p. 34.

A. *The regulatory framework*

Before examining how the different kinds of business network have responded to the introduction of new competition laws, it is instructive to analyse briefly the regulatory framework for competition found in both China and Vietnam. China and Vietnam are sometimes portrayed as representing a distinctive 'East Asian model' of economic development that revolves around a singular export-oriented, globally open, but not particularly neoliberal regulatory state.[23] But there are problems with this portrayal. First, the regulatory experiences of China and Vietnam diverge from those of the rest of the East Asian developmental states in several important respects. Both China and Vietnam have liberalized foreign direct investment to a greater extent than have other developing East Asian states.[24] This has enabled more intensive competition in some sectors, but, nevertheless, the party-state has been able to retain greater control of markets both through selective intervention across the economy and by retaining direct control over the 'commanding heights' of the economy via control of the large state-run firms associated with cadre-capitalism (cf. Zheng, Ch. 7, pp. 159–60). China and Vietnam have also been significantly less willing than other Asian developmental states 'to permit law to function as a framework to facilitate private transactions'.[25] At the same time as they have rhetorically supported the law-based state, central and local governments in both China and Vietnam are routinely prepared to ignore formal property rights when pursuing particular socio-economic goals (or even the regulator's personal benefit).[26]

In addition, both countries' regulatory systems have been constructed out of a wide diversity of regulatory sources, both neoliberal and non-neoliberal. Both are also evolving rapidly, and both vary considerably from local region to local region (see, e.g., Dowdle, Ch. 9). In this context, it does not make sense to talk about a single, coherent regulatory model – that is, an 'East

---

[23] See Randall P. Peerenboom, *China Modernizes: Threat to the West or Model for the Rest?* (Oxford University Press, 2007); see also Hsueh, *China's Regulatory State*, pp. 16–18.

[24] Peerenboom, *China Modernizes*, pp. 10–18.

[25] Xianchu Zhang. 'Commentary on "Legislating for a Market Economy in China"', *China Quarterly*, 191 (2007): 586–9, 586.

[26] Donald C. Clarke, 'Economic Development and the Rights Hypothesis: The China Problem', *American Journal of Comparative Law*, 51 (2003): 89–111; Donald C. Clarke, 'Nothing but Wind: The Past and Future of Comparative Corporate Governance', *American Journal of Comparative Law*, 59 (2011): 75–110; Ronald J. Gilson and Curtis J. Milhaupt, 'Economically Benevolent Dictators: Lessons for Developing Democracies', *American Journal of Comparative Law*, 59 (2011): 227–88.

Asian model'. Rather, what we have is a bifurcated regulatory framework in which central and local levels follow somewhat different regulatory logics.

B.   Central-level regulation

At the central level, regulators have been somewhat more receptive to neoliberal models of economic competition. One of the main regulatory objectives in China and Vietnam over the last two decades has been to make cadre-capitalist state-owned enterprises (SOEs) more competitive by recasting them in the image of capitalist corporations. This has involved introducing into these firms more capitalist models of corporate governance, and opening them up to private sources of capital and their associated forms of corporate oversight (euphemistically called 'corporatization' in China and 'equitization' in Vietnam).

Similarly, when the party-state has sought to stimulate competition in key economic sectors – what is sometimes called 'managed competition' – competition has ultimately remained under state control. For example, when the governments in both countries sought to improve the efficiency of electricity generation by introducing market competition in this sector, they did so by exposing SOE monopoly suppliers to competition *from other state-controlled competitors* rather than from private firms. This form of 'managed' or 'limited' competition in markets constructed around 'national champions' (such as in telecommunications, electricity generation, and construction – see below) ensures that the state retains control over the 'competing' firms.[27] In less strategic sectors, such as textiles, regulators have been willing to take a more arm's-length approach to competition regulation.[28] Overall significant divergences from the neoliberal model remain firmly in place at the central level. Most particularly, as intimated above, the dynamics of economic 'competition' remains tightly tethered to the political control of the party-state. Rather than developing a politically insulated bureaucratic elite as advocated by global competition law, key state officials in China and Vietnam are normatively expected to be responsive to party-based political policies. (Cf. Prosser, Ch. 10.)

In fact, their Leninist organizational systems, which symbiotically link the state to the party, play an important co-ordinating function in the interpretation and implementation of the competition laws. Party

---

[27] Barry Naughton, 'China's Distinctive System: Can It Be a Model for Others?', *Journal of Contemporary China*, 19 (2010): 437–60; Beresford, 'Development of Commercial Regulation'.

[28] Hsueh, *China's Regulatory State*, pp. 54–7.

organization departments appoint the leaders not only of government agencies, but also of the state-owned and privatized companies that control the cadre-capitalist networks.[29] Party policies are transmitted by 'party cells' that are set up in these firms and departments. In this system, there is less need for 'law' as an intermediating device for converting policy decisions into collective action. The party and the state can convey administrative directives through personal exchanges[30] that co-ordinate and fine-tune the behaviour of cadre-capitalist networks.

In a Leninist system, the very notion of 'agencification' generates profound anxiety.[31] Competition authorities are to be subordinated not only to the party and state agencies, but also to the managers of large state-owned-and-controlled companies, whose Leninist backgrounds make them uncomfortable both with arm's-length, politically neutral forms of regulation characteristic of competition regulation, and with the idea of (unfettered) economic competition more generally.[32] As Le Dang Doanh, a prominent Vietnamese intellectual, recently noted, 'the law creates legal foundations to fight against monopoly and abuse of dominant position in the market, but the extent to which such fights can be realized depends upon whether state authorities want to touch enterprises that they have been supporting'.[33]

---

[29] Richard McGregor, *The Party: The Secret World of China's Communist Rulers* (London: Allen Lane, 2010), pp. 70–103.

[30] For China see Peter J. Buckley, Jeremy Clegg, and Chengqi Wang, 'Is the Relationship between Inward FDI and Spillover Effects Linear? An Empirical Examination of the Case of China', *Journal of International Business Studies*, 38 (2007): 447–559. For Vietnam see Eric Ramstetter and Phan Minh Ngoc, *Changes in Ownership and Producer Concentration after the Implementation of Vietnam's Enterprise Law*, Working Paper Series Vol. 2007-06 (Kitakyushu: International Centre for the Study of East Asian Development, 2007), available at http://file.icsead.or.jp/user04/760_210_20110623101822.pdf.

[31] McGregor, *Party*, pp. 70–103; Frank K. Upham, 'From Demsetz to Deng: Speculations on the Implications of Chinese Growth for Law and Development Theory', *New York University Journal of International Law and Politics*, 41 (2009): 551–602.

[32] Naughton, 'China's Distinctive System', 445–6, 456–7; Sebastian Heilmann, 'Regulatory Innovation by Leninist Means: Communist Party Supervision in China's Financial Industry', *China Quarterly*, 181 (2006): 1–21.

[33] Tan Duc and Thien Nhan, 'Competition Law: Concerns over Its Implementation [Luat Canh Tranh: Ban khoan Cau chuyen thuc hien]', 2 August 2005, available at http://vietbao.vn/Kinh-te/Luat-canh-tranh-ban-khoan-chuyen-thuc-hien/20474629/87/. For comments on this view, see Le Thanh Vinh, 'Development Thinking and the Competition Law Enforcement in Vietnam [Tu duy phat trien va van de thuc thi Luat Canh tranh tai Viet Nam]', *Tap chi Nghien cuu Lap phap* (*Legislative Studies*), 176 (15) (2010): 42–7.

Even in their efforts to make SOEs more competitive by recasting them in the image of capitalist corporations, research suggests that the dominant effect of these efforts has been to rearrange rather than sever the relationship between the party-state on one hand and the SOE on the other.[34] The organizational departments of the central committees of both the CPV and the Communist the Party of China (CCP)[35] still appoint and monitor the performance of senior managers of SOEs. Many of these managers are also linked to the party through familial ties with party leaders.[36] Shaun Breslin claims that cadre-capitalist networks in China still continue to reproduce a 'symbiotic relationship (at the very least) between state elites and new economic elites', and that '[t]hey have effectively co-opted each other into an alliance that ... mutually reinforces each other's power and influence, not to mention personal fortunes'.[37] As Barry Naughton has observed in relation to China, the CCP 'creates an unusually strong and pervasive system of monitoring that allows the SOE system to continue functioning despite the incentives for corruption and personal enrichment.'[38]

Following a policy of 'grasp the large and release the small', both China and Vietnam have concentrated their developmental efforts on administratively providing selected SOEs and economic conglomerations with the resources to become 'national champions'. In China, the Jinghu High Speed Rail Company is a good example of the party-state co-opting state banks and SOEs to underwrite the development of advanced technology and to help secure export markets by subsidising a marginally profitable domestic rail network.[39] Far from withering away, a reduced number of state-owned or state-controlled firms in both countries have not only

---

[34] With regard to China, see Nee, 'Organization Dynamics', pp. 53–74; with regard to Vietnam, Martin Gainsborough, 'The (Neglected) Statist Bias and the Developmental State: The Case of Singapore and Vietnam', *Third World Quarterly*, 30 (2009): 1317–28.

[35] Naughton, 'China's Distinctive System', 456.

[36] Bruce J. Dickson, *Red Capitalists in China: The Party, Private Entrepreneurs, and Prospects for Political Change* (Cambridge University Press, 2003); Scott Cheshier and Jonathan Pincus, 'Minsky au Vietnam: State Corporations, Financial Instability and Industrialisation', in Daniela Tavasci and Jan Toporowski (eds.), *Minsky, Crisis and Development* (Basingstoke: Palgrave Macmillan, 2010), pp. 188–206.

[37] Shaun Breslin, *Capitalism with Chinese Characteristics: The Public, the Private and the International*, Working Paper 104 (Perth: Murdoch University Asia Research Centre, 2004), available at http://dspace.cigilibrary.org/jspui/bitstream/123456789/12979/1/Capitalism%20with%20Chinese%20Characteristics%20the%20Public%20the%20Private%20and%20the%20International.pdf.

[38] Naughton, 'China's Distinctive System', 456; see also Heilmann, 'Regulatory Innovation'.

[39] 'Five High Speed Rail Systems Are Suffering Losses because of Lack of Passengers [Zhongguo 5 tiao yiyunying gaotie kuisun yanzhong shang zuoludi shi zhuyin]', Yahoo

increased their share of economic production; they now dominate the list of the top five hundred firms.[40]

In sum, while China and Vietnam have liberalized their economies somewhat to comply with neoliberal requirements (often as demanded by the conditions of their membership in the WTO), at a micro level state management of the economy continues. State regulators manage competition on a sectoral basis. The commanding heights of the economy remain tightly controlled. But if neoliberal market-based competition is not the driving force of China and Vietnam's socialist capitalism, what are the principles that underlie competition regulation in these countries?

In describing China as a 'competition state', Bob Jessop and Ngai-Ling Sum point to a regulatory strategy that is both clearly formed and yet divergent from that associated with neoliberal models of competition.[41] (See also Jessop, Ch. 5, pp. 109–10.) By 'competition *state*', they mean that, at the central level, the party-state and its cadre-capitalist firms work as partners in a network of relations that aim to mobilize 'soft social resources' such as knowledge, social capital, and research and development to advance *proactively* the innovative capacities that are essential for sectoral upgrading into higher-value-added activities in world markets. State regulations seek to increase the international competitiveness of domestic firms by ensuring that they benefit more fully from technology transfers and other spillovers stemming from their international supply chains relationships (see also Deyo, Ch. 12). Through this, regulators seek to help domestic firms to move up the value chain in the supply networks that increasingly control intra-Asian trade. In short, the Chinese state – like Japan and South Korea before it – seeks to promote *international* competitiveness without believing that *domestic* market competition is a necessary mechanism for achieving this objective (see also Vande Walle, Ch. 6, pp. 127–31, discussing Japan). Vietnam has followed a similar regulatory path.

News (Chinese edition), 25 June 2011, available at http://news.cn.yahoo.com/ypen/ 20110625/434652.html.

[40] For China, see Geng Xiao, Xiuke Yang and A. Janus, 'State-Owned Enterprises in China: Reform Dynamics and Impacts', in Ross Garnaut, Ligang Song, and Wing Thye Woo (eds.), *China's New Place in a World in Crisis* (Canberra: ANU E Press, 2009), pp. 155–78, at p. 158. For Vietnam see Gainsborough, *Vietnam: Rethinking the State*, pp. 72–3; Markus Taussig, *A Policy Discussion Paper: Business Strategy during Radical Economic Transition: Viet Nam's First Generation of Larger Private Manufacturers and a Decade of Intensifying Opportunities and Competition* (Hanoi: United Nations Development Programme Viet Nam, 2009), p. 8.

[41] See Bob Jessop and Ngai-Ling Sum, *Beyond the Regulatory Approach: Putting Capitalist Economies in their Place* (Cheltenham: Edward Elgar, 2006), pp. 201–6.

C. Local-level regulation

Local-level governance in China and Vietnam has been even less accommodating to neoliberal visions of economic competition. In Polanyian terms, city- and provincial-level governments in China and Vietnam are the principal loci of the 'double-movement' counter-response that invariably accompanies market liberalization at the central level (see also Dowdle, Ch. 9). As noted above, Polanyi argued that market liberalization threatens more traditional, societal forms of economic organization. For this reason, efforts to liberalize markets are often met with countervailing societal responses that insulate key societal economic spaces from such liberalization. Consistent with this, in both China and Vietnam local-level authorities have been much less inclined than central regulators to support global models of market competition, looking instead for new ways of preserving the traditional, proactive forms of economic regulation associated with the older system of 'state economic management'. For example, local officials often use a complex system of licences and permits, embedded in a larger regulatory environment of policy uncertainty, in order to restrict market entry, protect local cartels, and otherwise disrupt the co-ordinating power of the competition law, and thus preserve the role of relational networks in the regulatory system. They show considerable ingenuity in subverting deregulatory reforms and increasing their discretionary power.[42]

V. Case studies

This section presents the three case studies that are representative of cadre-capitalist, LME, and SME networks in Vietnam.[43] The studies examine what firms think about competition laws and how their interaction with state regulatory authorities shapes these views. They show how the three types of business network – cadre-capitalists, LMEs and SMEs – do indeed respond to the transplantation of more globalized, neoliberal models of

---

[42] See generally Donald C. Clarke, 'Legislating for a Market Economy', *China Quarterly*, 191 (2007): 567–85; John Gillespie, 'Testing the Limits to the "Rule of Law": Commercial Regulation in Vietnam', *Journal of Comparative Asian Development*, 12 (2009): 245–72.

[43] This section draws on more than five hundred interviews with sixty firms in construction, wood processing, copper wire, sunglasses and batteries trading, and computer and footwear manufactures. The interviews were conducted in northern and central Vietnam by the author with the assistance of Vietnamese law firms (N.H. Quang and Associates and Investconsult) and research assistants between March 2004 and April 2010.

competition regulation in significantly different ways. Although these studies are drawn from Vietnam, subsequent interviews by the author in southern China suggest that China's business environments evince a similar topology of networks with a similar relationship to national efforts to introduce neoliberal models of competition.

A.   Competition regulation in the context of cadre-capitalist networks: the construction industry

This study is based on interviews with construction firms in Nam Dinh and Nghe An provinces in north and central Vietnam.

During the command economy, provincial people's committees supervised the operations of state-owned construction companies, and government officials decided administratively which companies worked on particular projects. Contrasting with industries such as telecommunications and electricity generation, which remained closed to private investment, following the dismantling of the command economy in the 1980s the government removed formal regulatory barriers to private participation in the construction industry. With considerable prompting from international donors providing soft infrastructure loans, the government enacted tendering regulations, based on neoliberal templates, to regulate state-funded projects.[44] The Competition Law 2004 appeared to reinforce further competitive tendering and market competition. What this study shows, however, is that state funded construction remains tightly integrated into cadre-capitalist networks. Unperturbed by market liberalizations, party-state actors use the tendering system to defend state-owned and -controlled construction firms against private competition.

Interviews with senior managers of construction companies in these provinces revealed that, although the state tendering system outwardly complies with market principles, in practice business networks known as 'construction groups [thau con]' regulate the industry. The groups typically comprise senior officials from the provincial-level party state, as well as the senior managers of state-owned or state-controlled construction enterprises. To avoid the appearance of collusion, each group divides

---

[44] Circular No. 2 on the Management of Construction Projects, 29 January 1993; later replaced by Decree 88-1999-ND-CP of the Central Government Promulgating the Regulations on Tenders, 1 September 1999; and then again by the Law on Tendering, No. 61-2005-QH11, effective 1 July 2006.

itself into two coalitions, the 'green army [*quan xanh*]' and the 'red army [*quan do*]', which take turns bidding for tenders.

The senior managers of these firms spent their formative years working for the government or for SOEs. Socialist regulatory traditions such as 'state economic management', which they absorbed during this period, continue to condition their regulatory outlook more than two decades after market reforms began. As the command economy dissolved, they – like many other senior managers[45] – relied on state resources to promote the economic interests of both their firms and themselves.

These managers meet and socialize regularly with provincial party and state officials to discuss corporate plans and lobby for favourable state policies. In addition to enjoying close personal connections with each other, they are integrated into the construction groups through interlocking ownership and profit-and-loss-sharing arrangements. One way this is done is to structure transactions so that profit accrues to private firms involved in bids, but losses are absorbed by state-owned or state-controlled enterprises. The officials and managers own these private firms through family members.

As partners in a common venture, party and state officials do not dictate from above, but rather negotiate socio-economic objectives with firm managers.[46] In return for regulatory protection and access to state resources, party and state officials expect construction firms to stabilize markets, invest in key government projects, and, above all else, reinvest profits to innovate and become internationally competitive. These are the regulatory objectives of the 'competition state' as described by Jessop and Sum and discussed above.[47]

From a legal perspective, this collaboration between the party-state and the construction groups appears corrupt, because they deploy state power to serve private as well as state interests. But it is perhaps better interpreted as a type of 'responsive regulation', in which the state joins with construction firms in order to promote the distinctly managed

---

[45] Martin Rama, *Making Difficult Choices: Vietnam in Transition*, Commission on Growth and Development, Working Paper No. 40 (Washington, DC: International Bank for Reconstruction and Development/The World Bank Commission on Growth and Development, 2008), pp. 17–21.

[46] Gainsborough, '(Neglected) Statist Bias', 265–70.

[47] See also 'State Businesses Form the Core of the Economy', Voice of Vietnam Online, 10 March 2010, available at http://english.vov.vn/Home/State-businesses-form-the-core-of-economy/20103/113374.vov.

competitiveness of the 'competition state': a co-operative strategy that simultaneously serves the public interests of the party-state and the private interests of the firms it is supposed to 'regulate'.[48] A similar dynamic has also been observed in China.[49]

The senior managers of these firms strongly support this form of responsive regulation, to the point where they questioned the legitimacy of the state's tendering and competition laws. They regard, with some justification, market-based tendering principles as foreign impositions designed to appease international donor agencies. They also think that tendering rules disrupt long-standing collaborative practices that deliver high-quality outcomes. Competitive tendering cannot provide predicable outcomes, they explained, because firms operating outside the disciplining effects of these construction groups cannot be trusted to limit their corruption and ensure that building standards are strictly followed. By themselves, state regulators and abstract legal codes are incapable of effectively safeguarding building standards.

Implicitly these senior managers conveyed a sense of entitlement to their privileged access to state resources and state support. Scott Cheshier describes this particular mindset as being characteristic of what he calls the 'New Class'.[50] Although the law has always stipulated that socialist property belonged to the people and is to be managed by the state, members of this New Class instinctively feel that it is really their property. During the command economy, many of these senior managers were responsible for administering socialist property as part of the party-state. They were allowed to benefit in myriad ways from their control over socialist property, such as by living in superior housing and enjoying preferential access to travel, food, and luxury consumer items. Market reforms offered new opportunities to benefit from socialist property. As

---

[48] See, e.g., Cheshier and Pincus, 'Minsky au Vietnam', pp. 18–19; Taussig, *Business Strategy during Radical Economic Transition*, pp. 7–9. Cf. Ian Ayres and John Braithwaite, *Responsive Regulation: Transcending the Deregulation Debate* (Oxford University Press, 1992).

[49] Compare Guosheng Deng and Scott Kennedy, 'Big Business and Industry Association Lobbying in China: The Paradox of Contrasting Styles', *The China Journal*, 63 (2010): 101–25, 116–17.

[50] Scott Cheshier, 'The New Class in Vietnam', Ph.D. dissertation, School of Business and Management, Queen Mary, University of London, 2010, available at https://qmro.qmul.ac.uk/jspui/bitstream/123456789/443/1/CHESIERNewClass2010.pdf. A similar phenomenon has been observed in Eastern bloc countries. See, e.g., Lawrence Peter King and Iván Szelényi, *Theories of the New Class: Intellectuals and Power* (Minneapolis: University of Minnesota Press, 2004).

members of the New Class, the senior construction managers continue to feel allegiance to, and identify with, senior provincial party and state officials. They regard the new tendering and competition laws with ambivalence. They convey an overriding impression that state property, such as construction contracts, is properly reserved for their use, provided they use it to support the 'competition state' model and reinvest profits so as to move up the value chain and engage in product competition based on product quality rather than simply on price.

As far as they are concerned, the regulation of competition properly resides more in the personal interactions among members of the construction groups and between these members and the party-state than in the abstract and socially disembedded legal frameworks being imported from abroad.

B.   Competition regulation in the context of peripheral LME networks: the case of computer manufacturing

This second case study examines the interaction between Vietnam's new competition law framework and an LME business network. This kind of network operates outside the protective web of cadre-capitalism, but still under the somewhat protective shadow of the managed competition of the competition state. In 2000, four friends (the 'founders') founded separate firms to assemble and sell personal computers. They met while working for FPT, a privatized, cadre-capitalist firm that controls Vietnam's largest computer and software conglomerate. Operating as separate entities, their firms struggled to compete with the much larger FPT.[51] Eventually the founders established a network to bulk-buy components and jointly assemble computers. This computer network, which currently employs approximately 400 staff, now competes profitably in the northern Vietnamese computer market.

According to the founders, Vietnam's computer industry is divided into two segments. The high end is dominated by FPT, which presides over an array of subsidiaries engaged in computer assembly, software design, finance, and other non-core businesses. Its founder is a quintessential New Class insider, and the FPT network is closely integrated into other cadre-capitalist networks in Vietnam. FPT's main customers are

---

[51] Nguyen Sa, 'Vietnamese Companies Join Forces to Regain Laptop Market Share', VietNamNet Bridge, 1 October 2007, republished at http://duongcodon.blogspot.sg/2007/01/vietnamese-companies-join-forces-to.html.

state agencies and large SOEs. The founders have tried to win supply tenders with high-end government buyers, but for the reasons discussed in the construction industry case study, members of the New Class enjoy an absolute advantage in catering to such markets. Finding the high end of the market monopolized by cadre-capitalist networks, the founders aimed their products at the small, private enterprises occupying the budget end of the market. (Studies reveal similar cleavages separating cadre-capitalist and LME networks elsewhere in Vietnam.[52] For example, in Ho Chi Minh City, cadre-capitalist firms monopolize the major land development projects, while 'outsiders' are left to compete for less profitable, lower-end projects.)

To profit in this intensely competitive market, the founders routinely violate the law. For example, they illegally sell counterfeit computers under the Dell brand name, and import components from Malaysia, Singapore, and Taiwan without paying the full import tariffs. Although their claims are difficult to substantiate, they insist that customs agents and market control authorities apply the law with *hop ly* ('reasonableness') to ensure that domestic computer manufacturers are able to compete with foreign imports and move up the value chain. The founders maintain that state authorities are also prepared to overlook these infractions as part of their promotion of the competition state. This flexibility in the application of the formal law must frequently be greased by bribes, and is consequently less stable and predictable than the 'partnerships' between party-state officials and enterprise managers enjoyed by cadre-capitalist networks.

Network members meet regularly to share market information and to discuss production, distribution, and the creditworthiness of customers. As the network developed, their business relationships have become intertwined with *tinh cam* (sentiment). They now socialize frequently at weddings, funerals, and other family gatherings; and actively cultivate family-like sentiments by referring to each other as '*anh em*' (a sentimental term for 'brother') and integrating their social lives. Members not only believe that these relational networks (*mang luoi*) generate solidarity and minimize opportunistic behaviour, but also that they are morally superior to the anonymous, arm's-length business transactions characteristic of neoliberal marketization. To build and reinforce solidarity, network members adopt shared tropes that depict their network as an

---

[52] Kim, *Learning To Be Capitalists*, p. 93; Gainsborough, *Vietnam: Rethinking the State*.

ethical island floating in an unscrupulous and predatory ocean. For example, interviewees commonly repeated a creation myth about the need to form a network to protect themselves from hyper-competition. They worry about *cuc bo*, where firm employees immorally appropriate confidential information to establish their own rival businesses. This practice is common at the budget end of the computer market, increasing the intensity of price competition and further lowering already low profit levels. As the founders explain, for them tax avoidance and smuggling are the most effective ways to generate profits, which in turn are necessary to fuel innovation and movement from price-competition to product-and-service competition, as per the demands of the competition state.

LME network members do not belong to the CPV or to the New Class. They are cynical about the grandiose nation-building rhetoric emanating from the New Class, and are careful to portray themselves as modern, globally connected professionals. Being younger than most New Class managers, they have only second-hand knowledge of the revolutionary period and the command economy. They are university educated, travel often to neighbouring countries, and admire the orderly world that law-based markets seem to offer in Singapore and Japan.

All this would suggest that the network might enthusiastically support the competition law with its potential to prise open cadre-capitalist networks to outsiders. However, a more complex, conflicted position emerges. While these members are intellectually drawn to 'rule of law' imagery and its rigorous enforcement of neoliberal forms of market competition, this imagery does not resemble the world in which they live. Their success depends on the competition state model and its flexible application of import duties. In their world of hyper-competitive price competition, only tightly knit business networks can produce at sufficient economies of scale to generate the profits necessary to move up the value chain and begin competing on the basis of product quality and service rather than simply on the basis of price. Their ultimate goal is to become a part of the cadre-capitalist network system, like FPT, rather than simply to compete with such networks via strong legal enforcement of the new competition laws. Behind their jokes about the founder of FPT, Truong Gia Binh, lies a deep admiration for the way he leveraged his relationship with General Vo Nguyen Giap, one of Vietnam's revolutionary immortals, for his firm's (and his own) benefit. Although well aware that their chances of cultivating their own personal ties of this sort are low, the members of this LME network still put their ultimate faith in cadre-capitalism rather than the competition law regime.

C. Competition regulation in the context of a local SME network: a case from the copper wire industry

This case study looks at competition and competition regulation as it manifests in Vietnam's local (or so-called 'informal') economic sectors. In this case, it is a local SME network consisting of copper wire wholesalers based in Hanoi. In contrast to the other two kinds of networks examined above, this distinctly local network operates, by and large, with complete disregard for global competition norms. It uses relational connections to control a large import and distribution system. Members closely identify with the network and actively resist external ideas – especially the global, neoliberal models of market competition that appear contrary to the network's own way of doing business.

Operating in a non-essential industrial sector, participants in this network have little engagement with the competition state. In contrast to the members of the LME network described above, members in this network have little desire to become cadre-capitalists, or to move up the value chain. The formal regulatory state's hold over them is therefore significantly muted.

The network expressly rejects 'Western' models of economic market interaction, choosing instead to only transact with suppliers who follow what its members call an 'Asian business style'. By this, they mean firms that can be trusted to rely on relational connections that are in turn anchored in 'sentimental' bonds (*tinh cam*) rather than contractual and legal formalities. Despite the complexity and value of their transactions (some deals are worth millions of US dollars), sales agreements are formalized only to satisfy customs declarations. The underlying transactions are actually founded on handwritten notes that pay little regard to global or domestic laws. The network routinely flouts the Competition Law 2004, using its dominant market position to price competitors from the south out of the northern market.

The history of the network actually dates back to the 1920s, when shops selling and repairing electronic goods began to open in Hang Bong Street in the old trading quarter in Hanoi, selling among other things copper wire. In the 1960s, the state collectivized these businesses into a small industrial co-operative (*hop tac xa tieu thu cong ng hiep*) to produce electric transformers. When the Politburo decriminalized household businesses in 1986,[53] that

---

[53] Decision 146 on Developing a Household Economy, Council of Ministers, 26 November 1986.

co-operative dissolved and out of it emerged four private wholesale firms dealing in copper wire.

Today, these four wholesalers sit at the centre of a large network of wholesalers that controls approximately 70 per cent of the market in northern Vietnam for industrial-grade copper wire. Although local in its direct geographic situs, the network actually oversees a global production chain that links South Korean copper-wire manufacturers to Vietnamese SOEs that manufacture electrical appliances. This network consists of two distinct spheres of co-operation: an inner group comprising the four original wholesalers, who are bound together by familial relationships and direct the management of the network as a whole, and an outer group of approximately fifteen wholesalers who derive benefits from being in the network but do not participate in its governance. Members of the inner group trade with those of the outer group, but do not admit members from this outer group into their circle.

Through this network, the four dominant wholesalers collect and share information about prices, quality, supply, and the creditworthiness of customers, as well as extend short-term trade credit to one another and other network members. They frequently visit South Korea to cultivate personal ties with the copper-wire manufacturers there. They conduct their governance of the network through 'tea club' meetings that both demonstrate solidarity and formulate the business norms that guide the copper-wire market. These norms include, for example, encouraging the outer group of wholesalers to value market stability over short-term profits; promoting the image of copper-wire traders; and avoiding sharp business practices, misleading advertising, poaching customers by paying high commissions and kickbacks, and selling counterfeit goods.

One of the things that distinguishes the members of this network, particularly its core group, from those of LME networks is their high level of identification with the network. The core wholesalers and their families spent the high-socialist period earning a precarious living in the underground economy, and in many ways continue to operate at the very periphery of the state-backed economy. Friendships formed in the earlier co-operative have been maintained over the intervening years through frequent social engagements and intermarriage. The resulting strong, mutual support has been crucial for allowing them to persist in such an environment. When predatory provincial officials outside Hanoi demanded bribes to allow copper-wire deliveries to manufacturers located there, the leading members of the wholesale group acted collectively to mobilize their political connections and the power of the network as a whole to successfully oppose these officials, sending them and others a message that even in other provinces officials cannot interfere with one member of the network without dealing with the network as a whole. Due to this and similar experiences, network members see no difference between the 'mutual assistance' (*tuong tro lan nhau*) that cements their trading network and the 'sentiment' (*tinh cam*) that underpins their social relationships. As noted above, they show little interest in moving up the value chain and becoming cadre-capitalists. Their membership in the copper-wire network defines who they are as well as what they should do, both economically and socially.

VI. Learning to be capitalists

This chapter began by arguing that capitalism is not inherent in all societies, but rather it is something that must be learned. What the case studies show is that, except for a few LME networks, many cadre-capitalist and SME networks have not 'learned' capitalism (at least in its neoliberal guise) and consequently have little affinity for market-based competition laws. A shortcoming with the Polanyian-convergence account is that it fails to explain why some business networks have been able to make this cognitive shift, but not others.

We cannot explain the differing regulatory responses of these networks simply by referring to their knowledge about tendering and competition regimes. A recent survey shows that most business networks demonstrated relatively high levels of awareness of the law.[54] 'Learning', as distinct from acquiring knowledge, only occurs when new evidence *changes* our beliefs and leads to the *replacement* of one regulatory approach by another.[55] Such learning is also socially constructed, in the sense that new evidence is interpreted by reference to socially received normative and epistemic assumptions.

---

[54] Ministry of Trade, Vietnam, 'Survey of the Community's Understanding about the Competition Law [KHẢO SÁT MỨC ĐỘ NHẬN THỨC CỦA CỘNG ĐỒNG ĐỐI VỚI LUẬT CẠNH TRANH]', unpublished report, Hanoi, 2009.

[55] See Zachary Elkins and Beth Simmons, 'On Waves, Clusters and Diffusion: A Conceptual Framework', *Annals of the American Academy of Political and Social Science*, 598 (2005): 33–51; Covadonga Meseguer, 'Policy Learning, Policy Diffusion and the Making of a New Order', *Annals of the American Academy of Political and Social Science*, 598 (2005): 67–82.

This would suggest that firm learning about new market laws is intermediated through conceptual frameworks that stem from these existing business networks. This is consistent with the findings of these cases studies, which shows a correlation between market embeddedness and responsiveness to global competition regime. Cadre-capitalist and SME networks are largely embedded in relational settings and thus resist neoliberal models of competition. In contrast, LME networks are more integrated into socially disembedded, global markets and generally demonstrate more receptiveness to global commercial laws.

A.   Socially constructed patterns of learning

The case studies show that basic cost–benefit calculations influenced how firms evaluated market-based laws, but this alone does not explain why they changed their regulatory preferences. Consider the senior managers of the construction groups. They were profit-motivated, but saw profit-making as part of an overarching moral mission to fulfil party socio-economic objectives (i.e., those associated with the competition state). This balance between profit and socio-economic objectives was constantly negotiated and renegotiated by the key players in this network. The managers did not consider these socio-economic objectives as transaction costs, but rather as moral obligations that attached to their membership in the New Class. Within this context, neoliberal arguments that competitive markets are good because they promote 'consumer welfare' or 'consumer sovereignty' seemed unconvincing, even morally suspect.

Similarly, members of the locally embedded copper-wire network were also profit motivated, but did not attribute any negative cost to the social relationships that bound their business network. They maintained these complex connections to fulfil familial and social obligations. It is complying with the formalities of the commercial laws that is considered costly and time-consuming. In this transactional context, claims that neoliberal forms of regulation can promote economic gain by reducing transaction costs thus lack credibility.

Members of the LME computer network, on the other hand, derived fewer material and social benefits from relationally embedded markets. On a pure cost–benefit analysis, law-based competition seems indeed to offer a more profitable world. However, the credibility of this regime is undermined by its inability to open cadre-capitalist networks to entry. Such entry is of value to them, not simply because of its lucrative business opportunities (which effective enforcement of competition law could provide), but also because of the elite social status enjoyed by the members of the New Class, a status that simple success in neoliberal market competition could not provide. Put differently, the anticipated outcomes of market competition are offset not only by the failure of this system to deliver on its promise actually to open the economic system, but equally by the network's cognitive preference for the prestige that attaches to membership in the very tightly knit 'New Class' social networks that operate outside market dynamics.

It is instructive to compare the attitudes of members of the LME computer network to those of the Vietnamese managers of a large foreign-owned footwear manufacturing network that operates in northern Vietnam.[56] The managers in this network were initially hostile towards corporate governance rules that had been imposed on them by a foreign buyer as a condition for inclusion in that buyer's production network. But as the imported regime took hold, the managers became much more accepting, due to the increased profits that accrued from greater workplace specializations, clearer hierarchical lines of authority, and more precise monitoring of manufacturing processes that these rules introduced into the manufacturers' production processes.

A major difference between the members of the computer network and the footwear managers was how the latter were able to 'learn' the regulatory regime of global capitalism from a cultural intermediary. In particular, the introduction of global corporate governance techniques into the footwear manufacturing network was supported by the foreign investor who controlled that network. According to the managers, he acted as a cultural intermediary by translating foreign ideas into local idioms and contexts. The managers trusted him and accepted his assurances that the imported regime, which severed the managers' longstanding relational connections with other trusted staff members, would improve profit and stabilize the network. In this way, the cultural intermediary not only facilitated technical learning, he also reduced anxiety about the uncertainty of the new regulatory practices. Without his personal intervention, the managers say they would have consented formally (*hinh thuc*) to the new regime without fundamentally changing their underlying beliefs.

---

[56] For more details see John Gillespie 'Exploring the Role of Legitimacy and Identity in Framing Responses to Legal Globalization in a Transforming Socialist Asia', *Wisconsin International Law Journal*, 29 (2011): 534–608.

Other studies confirm the importance of cultural intermediaries to learning and preference change (see, e.g., Yeung, Ch. 11, pp. 277–80). For example, Chinese professionals working in the Beijing branches of transnational firms learned the tacit and unwritten linguistic conventions that govern global business environments from their contact with other Chinese professionals working outside China in these and similar firms.[57] In another example, firms in the Thai car-parts industry were able to learn the workings of the production networks linking their industry to Japanese car assemblers through the assistance of cultural intermediaries who translated Japanese manufacturing know-how and production techniques into a Thai context.[58]

B.   Collective identities and learning

In addition to cultural intermediaries, collective identity also informs the way in which business networks learn about regulatory regimes.[59] The main thrust of the collective identity literature is that when people 'take on the same identity, experience the same reality, and observe one another's parallel emotions and collateral behaviours, a sense of common destiny and empathic connection arises'.[60] Collective identities serve as an organizational force, guiding actors with shared ideas and emotional connections towards common responses to particular regulatory regimes.

Boundary narratives seemed to determine how strongly the different business networks identified with specific regulatory traditions. These narratives not only establish who is in and who is out of the network, they also establish the epistemic assumptions that order the network. The cadre-capitalist construction managers, for example, demonized private competitors as free-market opportunists trying to use competition laws to erode New Class leadership. As well as relegating private competitors

---

[57] Qing Zhang, 'A Chinese Yuppie in Beijing: Phonological Variation and the Construction of a New Professional Identity', *Language in Society*, 34 (2005): 431–66.

[58] Frederic C. Deyo and Richard F. Doner, 'Dynamic Flexibility and Sectoral Governance in the Thai Auto Industry: The Enclave Problem', in Frederic C. Deyo, Richard F. Doner, and Eric Hershberg (eds.), *Economic Governance and the Challenge of Flexibility in East Asia* (Lanham, MD: Rowman & Littlefield, 2001), pp. 107–36.

[59] See generally George A. Akerlof and Rachel E. Kranton, *Identity Economics: How Our Identities Shape Our Work, Wages, and Well-Being* (Princeton University Press, 2010).

[60] Timothy J. Owens, Dawn T. Robinson, and Lynn Smith-Lovin, 'Three Faces of Identity', *Annual Review of Sociology*, 36 (2010): 477–99; James L. Gibson, 'Group Identities and Theories of Justice: An Experimental Investigation into the Justice and Injustice of Land Squatting in South Africa', *Journal of Politics*, 70: 700–16.

to the 'out-group', this narrative legitimizes the relational connections that order cadre-capitalist networks. It stresses the importance of party-state socio-economic objectives and the modernizing role played by the New Class managers of the cadre-capitalist network. In addition, the narrative re-signified the tendering laws. It urged construction managers to follow the procedural rules governing tenders – because these rules co-ordinated interaction between state authorities and construction groups – but at the same time to reject market competition principles that might allow out-groups to gain access to state tenders.

Inhabiting a world much more at the periphery of state power, the copper-wire traders constructed an identity based on self-reliance, one that avoided the state in all its manifestations. Like the construction group, they believed in the moral superiority of their network. This conviction was reinforced by the network's effectiveness in generating profit and monitoring and enforcing a global production network that linked South Korean and Vietnamese manufacturers. Rather than experimenting with new identities to deal with global traders, the copper-wire wholesalers turned inward for inspiration. They drew on traditional relational forms of regulation to order the global and local networks.

Strong boundary narratives and collective identities made members of the construction and copper-wire networks unreceptive to ideas that did not originate from within their regulatory traditions. For the copper-wire wholesalers, the competition law seemed alien and imported, since it embodied ideas that were beyond their cognitive horizon. As Victor Nee observed in relation to Chinese business networks, 'if the formal rules are aligned against the identity and perceived interests of members of close-knit groups, oppositional norms are likely to emerge to counter the formal rules'.[61]

Even so, the construction managers and copper-wire traders were not entirely closed to global ideas and they responded positively to new knowledge that appeared compatible with their regulatory traditions – new wine in old bottles. For example, members of the construction groups imported ISO Building Construction Codes to improve the finishes on corporate buildings. Although the codes primarily contained technical know-how, some aspects related to team management and standards monitoring that resembled the corporate governance rules adopted by the footwear managers. More research is required to ascertain

---

[61] Nee, 'Organization Dynamics', p. 55.

whether this new regulatory know-how has stimulated broader regulatory change within the construction network.

In contrast with these other networks, the computer and footwear manufacturers were less convinced that their networks were cohesive and morally superior. They did not express the same level of antagonism towards rival regulatory groups and they were consequently more open to new ideas. Their flexible interaction with global regulatory regimes corresponds to Mark Granovetter's observation that there is strength in weak network ties and identities because, in contrast to the stronger ties that bind the construction and copper-wire networks, weak ties allow firms more fluidity to adjust to new regulatory conditions.[62]

Firms in LME networks are more prepared than firms in other kinds of network to learn from global governance. The computer manufacturers were cognitively open to orderly market regulation, yet remained sceptical as to whether competition and tendering laws were capable of taming cadre-capitalism. It is difficult to predict whether their views would change if the competition authority began rigorously enforcing the law, particularly given their yearning for the financial security and higher social status offered by possible membership in the New Class.

As they learned about the corporate governance regime, the footwear managers' identity slowly changed from that of a paternal overseer of a corporate family to that of a modern bureaucratic professional. This shift was marked by changing lifestyles – tennis clubs, foreign education for children, holidays abroad, and socializing with Hanoi's expatriate business community. These managers moved further than the computer manufacturers in acting out modern cosmopolitan identities, which put them more in direct contact with global regulatory ideas and the foreign business community. This, in turn, encouraged them to enter the global, neoliberal regulatory world and learn to be modern capitalists.

Taken together, these studies show how collective identities shape the way that business networks learn (or do not learn) from the imported competition law regime. They reveal that business networks with strong collective identities are generally less receptive to external regulatory ideas than more loosely constituted networks. Boundary narratives not only erect epistemological barriers to learning, they also make it more difficult to form personal connections with outsiders who can translate external knowledge into familiar concepts and idioms. Above all, these

---

[62] Mark Granovetter, 'The Impact of Social Structure on Economic Outcomes', *Journal of Economic Perspectives*, 19 (2005): 33–50, 34–5.

studies demonstrate the importance of agency and interpersonal connections to transmitting and interpreting regulatory knowledge.

VII. Globalization and relational organization

Contradicting conventional tropes, this study shows that integration into global production networks does not inexorably lead to convergence with global regulatory models. Rather, it suggests that relationally based business networks, such as the cadre-capitalist and SME networks, are capable of building and maintaining sophisticated global production networks that are not founded on neoliberal forms of economic ordering. Moreover, as previously mentioned, such networks together account for over 75 per cent of NFP in socialist Asia. The cadre-capitalist networks dominate the 'commanding heights' of the economy, while SME networks employ more than half the workforce. The economic success of business networks based on relational connections exposes the difficulty in promoting neoliberal market-based competition regulation in this region.

To explore the region's potential for change, it is instructive to look more closely at the co-evolution between the business networks and global trading partners. Evidence from China and Vietnam suggests that the New Class, which presides over cadre-capitalist networks, is tightly knit and self-referential. Its members are epistemologically unreceptive to new regulatory ideas – such as the competition law regime – that might disrupt the concentration of economic and political benefits within this network. Compounding their isolation, they have limited opportunities to form close personal links with the 'cultural intermediaries' who are critical to translating new knowledge and building trust in untried regulatory regimes.[63]

It is unclear whether global integration will necessarily change the regulatory preferences of cadre-capitalists. Many state-owned or state-controlled companies in China and Vietnam successfully compete with foreign investors and domestic private firms. They attract the most capable employees, invest profits to innovate and diversify, and have unquestionably benefited from the regulatory policies of the competition state.[64] Further complicating this inquiry, some studies indicate that the

---

[63] Taussig, *Business Strategy during Radical Economic Transition*, p. 8. See also Yasheng Huang, *Capitalism with Chinese Characteristics: Entrepreneurship and the State* (New York: Cambridge University Press, 2008).

[64] Buckley et al., 'Relationship'; Ramstetter and Phan, *Changes in Ownership*.

party-state views law-based governance as a threat to its relational control over cadre-capitalist networks.[65]

What happens when cadre-capitalist networks move offshore and are exposed to different regulatory environments? More research is required to answer this empirical question, but extant studies suggest that the networks both adapt to foreign competition law regimes and create relational networks to 'manage' markets in foreign countries.[66] For example, Chinese SOEs conform to Western competition regimes in many countries and have developed highly skilled regulatory compliance departments. Over time it is possible that the head offices in China will learn from 'cultural intermediaries' within these firms. Research also shows that Chinese firms invest in OECD countries to acquire industrial technology and know-how.[67] As previously mentioned, even technical knowledge has the potential to change regulatory preferences.

Other studies show a different side to global integration.[68] Chinese firms establish relational connections with foreign-based Chinese business and cultural associations to secure a foothold in offshore locations.[69] Take for instance the Chinese SOEs working in Mexico that mobilize local Chinese communities to secure political access to the state. Other Chinese SOEs are following similar strategies in Africa. Although this pattern of global integration does not rule out convergence with market-based laws, it presents different pathways where a different kind of regulatory learning could well occur.

As we saw above, trade-exposed LME networks, such as the footwear network, are more likely to learn from law-based market models. Domestic LME networks, such as the computer network, are also open to law-based market models, but perhaps less so. They are less profitable and more exposed to international competition than cadre-capitalist, and thus more willing to explore new regulatory approaches that promise greater efficiencies. And since their group identities are rather loose and permeable, they are less constrained than the cadre-capitalists and more able to experiment with fluid identities and reach out and learn from new regulatory systems. But their domestic embeddedness encourages in

---

[65] McGregor, *Party*, pp. 70–103; Cheshier, 'New Class'.

[66] Hinrich Voss, *The Determinants of Chinese Outward Direct Investment* (Cheltenham: Edward Elgar, 2011), pp. 56–107.

[67] Ibid., pp. 157–9.   [68] Ibid., pp. 157–9.

[69] See Adrian H. Hearn, *The Politics of Trust: China's Relations with Cuba and Mexico* (Durham, NC: Duke University Press, in press).

them an ambition to join the locally based New Class rather than the more cosmopolitan class of global entrepreneurs, and this constrains their regulatory flexibility vis-à-vis the footwear network.

These studies also demonstrate the critical role played by trusted 'cultural intermediaries' in translating global legal models and persuading local managers to have confidence in untried regulatory regimes. Recent studies in China and Vietnam show that imported regulatory regimes do not readily spill over into upstream domestic firms.[70] For example, a study funded by the United Nations Conference on Trade and Development in Vietnam found that foreign-owned entities 'operate as enclaves, with relatively few linkages with national firms through supplier or buyer contracts'.[71] Even when linkages exist, without 'cultural intermediaries' the learning process is attenuated. This research suggests caution in assuming that global regulatory ideas spread rapidly and easily among firms in production networks.

The case studies also suggest that the SME networks are more inward looking and steeped in relational connections than LME networks. Yet, as the copper-wire case study shows, these relational connections are capable of building and sustaining complex global production networks without resorting to neoliberal regulation. This network drew on allegedly 'Asian' regulatory traditions to govern global as well as domestic trading networks. Over several decades, it has proved flexible and enduring, delivering market stability, transparency and predictability for network members. Given this success, the copper-wire wholesalers unsurprisingly demonstrated little interest in global regulatory models such as the competition law regime.

Further reinforcing these SME networks are the tightly knit collective identities binding network members. Rather than experimenting with new identities to deal with global trading partners, members of the copper-wire trading network have synthesized a type of inter-Asian production and trading model that draws on Vietnamese and South Korean business characteristics. It promotes sentimental relational ties and demonizes the impersonal and professionalized trading associated with Western production networks. This collective identity disclines network members to engage with 'cultural intermediaries' who might dispel anxiety that global regulatory models will undermine the sentimental foundations of the network.

[70] Buckley et al., 'Relationship'; Ramstetter and Phan, *Changes in Ownership*.
[71] UNCTAD, *Investment Policy Review*, p. 125.

Studies show that inter-Asian production networks now dominate transnational trade in East Asia.[72] Although the literature suggests considerable variation within these networks, it also implies less attachment to market laws than the production networks constructed by Western transnational corporations. As the volume of intra-Asian trade increases following the global financial crisis in 2008, the exposure of businesses in socialist-transforming Asia to market-based laws is likely to diminish.

Finally, despite the insistence of social theorists such as Weber and Durkheim that modernization erodes relational ties, the case studies suggest a different story. Much more consistent with the observations of Polanyi, they show that relational-based economies are remarkably resilient and can readily adapt to the new trading conditions created by international economic integration. From a competition perspective, this finding has significant implications. Most particularly, it seems unlikely that competition law will make inroads into the relationally embedded cadre-capitalist and SME networks in the short term.

VIII.   Conclusion: from socialist-transforming Asia to Asia

What do our observations tell us, not simply about socialist-transforming Asia, but about Asia more generally? Are China and Vietnam *sui generis*, or are they particularly lucid demonstrations of regional trends? The competition state model is not unique to China and Vietnam, but through the Leninist organizational system it has reached a level of political integration in these countries that is arguably unparalleled elsewhere in Asia. Even at its height, administrative guidance in north-east Asia did not generate similar levels of political-economic symbiosis as cadre-capitalism has created in China and Vietnam. Whether this is simply a matter of degree, rather than a qualitative difference, and China and Vietnam will over time come to resemble north-east Asia remains unclear.

What is clear is that transformational capitalism in China and Vietnam is likely to evince a much more fragmented response to the

---

[72] See Tomohiro Machikita and Yasushi Ueki, *Spatial Architecture of the Production Networks in South East Asia*, ERIA Discussion Paper Series ERIA-DP-2010-01 (Jakarta: Economic Research Institute for ASEAN and East Asia, 2010); Ikuo Kuroiwa, 'Formation of Inter-country Production Networks in East Asia: Application of International Input–Output Analysis', paper presented at the 15th International Conference on Input–Output Techniques, Beijing: 27 June–1 July 2005).

introduction of competition law than occurred, for example, in Europe in the 1970s. Neoliberal competition laws are predicated on distinct state and non-state boundaries that dissolve in cadre-capitalist networks, where decisions are negotiated within state and enterprise hierarchies. As Dowdle will show in the last chapter of this volume, the real nature of the 'East Asian Model' is that it does not evince a monocratic structure, but rather a distinctly pluralist regulatory space (due to reliance on networks), which ultimately has to rely on collibration for its regulatory coherence.

PART IV

Asian capitalism and competition regulation in operation: selected issues

9

Competition in the periphery: melamine milk adulteration as peripheral 'innovation'

MICHAEL W. DOWDLE

I. Introduction

Orthodox competition theory – what others in this volume are often referring to as 'neoliberal' theory – presumes that the regulatory best practices for competition regulation are the same for all economies. This chapter will use China's recent experiences with melamine milk adulteration to challenge that presumption. It will argue that the regulation of market competition in peripheral economies faces a different set of concerns than does the regulation of market competition in more advanced industrial economies, and therefore peripheral regulation needs to adopt different foundational practices. In particular, competition regulation in the periphery cannot and should not isolate itself from counterbalancing social concerns in the way it does in more industrially advanced countries, and in the way advocated by orthodox competition theory and the international 'best practices' that derive from that theory (see, e.g., Maher, Ch. 3).

In autumn 2008, China and much of the world became gripped by the discovery that much of China's domestically produced milk powder was contaminated with toxic levels of a melamine, a chemical used primarily in the making of plastics. Some eighteen months earlier, producers and collectors of raw milk had begun adding melamine to raw milk to make it look as if it had a higher protein content than it actually did. But melamine also promoted kidney failure, particularly in infants – who were some of the principal consumers of this milk powder (milk powder is used to make baby milk formula). By the time this contamination was discovered, it had caused at least 51,900 infants to be hospitalized, and would be implicated in at least eleven infant deaths.

China's melamine contamination has generally been portrayed, at least in the anglophone world, as the product of dysfunction in China's authoritarian political system. But this does not in fact appear to be the case. China's authoritarian system did contribute to a local cover-up of the problem, and also to a suppression of popular mobilization in response to the problem, but it did not facilitate adulteration prior to discovery, and in fact was generally successful in stopping adulteration once it was discovered by the central government.

In this chapter it will be argued that melamine milk adulteration was caused primarily by market competition of the kind that the orthodox competition model seeks to promote. From the perspective of that model, this adulteration was simply a kind of product innovation, *economically* indistinguishable from the kinds of innovation that market competition is supposed to facilitate.

Of course, the key qualifier in all this is the term 'economically'. Melamine milk adulteration is clearly distinguishable from other more paradigmatic examples of market innovation, such as UHT (ultra-high temperature) milk, on social and moral grounds. But markets are not concerned with issues of morality or of social meaning (see also Jessop, Ch. 5, p. 117). They are, to use Hayek's famous adjective, spontaneous: driven, as famously described by Ronald Coase, by economic forces that are innately blind to issues of social or moral good that lie outside the reach of productive, distributive, or dynamic efficiency.[1] And, indeed, scholars working in the area of competition law theory make a strong argument that for this reason, competition law – what we shall here call competition regulation – should itself focus purely on promoting market efficiencies, and leave non-efficiency concerns, such as distributional concerns, to other components of the legal system (see below).

The problem is that this is much harder to do in peripheral economies. This is the real lesson of the melamine milk adulteration tragedy. As we shall see, peripheral socio-economic space is generally too fragmented to allow other, independent, regulatory frameworks to compensate for the ancillary social harms that can result from a market's unfettered and inevitably morally blind pursuit of productive efficiency.

What all this means is that, again from a social perspective, the regulation of market competition will often work differently in peripheral economic environments than it does in the advanced industrial environments from which orthodox competition theory is derived. Most particularly, it means that in peripheral regions, competition law cannot

---

[1] F. A. Hayek, 'The Use of Knowledge in Society', *American Economic Review*, 35 (1945): 519–30; Ronald H. Coase, 'The Problem of Social Cost', *Journal of Law and Economics*, 3 (1960): 1–44.

be cordoned off from non-economic concerns in the way that it is in advanced industrial countries, and in the way advocated by most in the developmental community.

The remainder of this chapter will unpack and expand on this claim. The next section looks at the history of China's melamine milk adulteration tragedy, showing that it was not a product of some specific political failure, but instead, a natural product of the pre-industrialized structure of China's national market for raw milk interacting with the largely industrialized market for consumer milk products. Melamine milk adulteration was simply a market innovation that was spurred by competitive pressures to reduce production costs. From the market's perspective, the tragedy that followed was simply an externality, since the people affected, the ultimate consumers, were not a part of that particular market.

The chapter will then explore what China's tragedy has to tell us about market competition and its regulation in more economically peripheral regions. In advanced industrial economies, externalities such as this one would be handled by other parts of the regulatory system. But, in China, the greater fragmentation of the national socio-economic environment made this very difficult. And China is not unique in this regard: peripheral economies generally feature more significantly fragmented national socio-economic space than is typical of advanced industrial countries. This means that the orthodox competition model's emphasis on focusing competition regulation solely on issues of market efficiency is highly problematic for such regions. In peripheral regions, markets and their regulation, including competition regulation, need to consider a much wider variety of competing social concerns than do their counterparts in advanced industrialized countries.

II. Anatomy of the tragedy

In spring and summer 2008, large numbers of nursing-age infants drinking certain brands of infant milk formula being produced and sold in China were reported to have experienced kidney stones and kidney failure. Subsequent investigation revealed that the cause of this was melamine adulteration of the raw milk being used to make that milk formula. As at December 2008, the Chinese Ministry of Health estimated that over 290,000 infants had been affected by consuming contaminated milk formula, some 51,900 having been hospitalized and with at least eleven suspected deaths (three confirmed).[2]

Melamine is an organic compound used primarily in the manufacture of plastics and acrylics, and also as fertilizer. It is mildly toxic to adults. But for infants, ingestion of significant amounts increase the chances of developing kidney stones by some 700 per cent. Moreover, the kidney stones that result from melamine ingestion are asymptomatic compared with ordinary kidney stones: they do not show up under the more standard techniques for testing for kidney stones and therefore are much more difficult to treat before causing significant kidney failure.[3]

Melamine was being added to raw milk by small-scale producers and collection agents in order to increase its apparent protein content. Melamine has a high nitrogen content; China's dairy industry tested for nitrogen as a way of measuring protein content. When melamine was mixed into raw milk, the nitrogen it contained was impossible to distinguish from the nitrogen found in milk protein under then existing testing processes. Adding melamine to raw milk could increase the apparent protein content of that milk by up to 25 per cent.[4]

Reports of melamine milk contamination begin appearing in the Chinese press as early as 2005. These reports triggered official investigation, but nothing was confirmed. At that time, melamine was widely thought to be only mildly toxic to humans. Its particular effects on kidney functioning were unknown.[5] Complaints linking consumption of infant formula with urinary tract problems began appearing in December 2007. By April 2008, these complaints had reached such a volume as to cause China's largest producer of milk powder formula, the

[2] Changbai Xiu and K. K. Klein, 'Melamine in Milk Products in China: Examining the Factors that Led to Deliberate use of the Contaminant', *Food Policy*, 35 (2010): 463–70, 464.

[3] See Na Guan, Qingfeng Fan, Jie Ding, Yiming Zhao, Jingqiao Lu, Yi Ai, Guobin Xu, Sainan Zhu, Chen Yao, Lina Jiang, Jing Miao, Han Zhang, Dan Zhao, Xiaoyu Liu, and Yong Yao, 'Melamine-Contaminated Powdered Formula and Urolithiasis in Young Children', *New England Journal of Medicine*, 360 (2009): 1067–74; Craig B. Langman, 'Melamine, Powdered Milk, and Nephrolithiasis in Chinese Infants', *The New England Journal of Medicine*, 360 (2009): 1139–41.

[4] Hao Xin and Richard Stone, 'Tainted Milk Scandal: Chinese Probe Unmasks High-Tech Adulteration with Melamine', *Science*, 28 November 2008: 1310–11. See also Austin Ramzy, 'China's Tainted Milk Scandal of 2008', *Time Magazine*, 26 September 2011, available at www.time.com/time/world/article/0,8599,1844750,00.html.

[5] David Bradley, 'Melamine in Milk', Sciencebase: Science News and Views, 17 September 2008, available at www.sciencebase.com/science-blog/melamine-in-milk.html (citing the United Kingdom's MSDS (Material Safety Data Sheet) for melamine c. 2007).

Sanlu Group, to conduct an internal inspection into the matter. That inspection revealed that Sanlu's milk formula often contained high amounts of 'non-protein nitrogen' – up to six times the amount found in other milk powders.[6] (Trace amounts of melamine are commonly found in raw milk, even in advanced industrial countries, due to its being used as a fertilizer in the production of cattle feed and in the production of the plastic tubing used to collect milk during milking.[7])

Sanlu officials began to suspect that the 'non-protein nitrogen' was coming from melamine. Small-scale farmers throughout China had long known that melamine could be used to increase the apparent protein content of raw food. Previously, it had been discovered that melamine was being used to boost the apparent protein content of animal feed.[8] In 2007, melamine adulteration in Chinese wheat gluten, a protein supplement commonly (and legally) added by American pet-food companies to increase (actual) protein content in pet food, caused the death of a large number North American pets.[9] Melamine adulteration was also discovered in imported Chinese rice protein concentrate, another protein additive commonly used in pet food manufacture,[10] and in imported Chinese vegetable protein used in chicken feed.[11] In fact, it was through that scandal that Western health administrators first became aware of a link between melamine consumption and kidney problems.[12] But as of

---

[6] Chenglin Liu, 'Profits above the Law: China's Melamine Tainted Milk Incident', *Mississippi Law Journal*, 79 (2009): 371–417, 384–5.

[7] Xiu and Klein, 'Melamine in Milk Products', 467.

[8] David Barboza and Alexei Barrionuevo, 'Filler in Animal Feed Is Open Secret in China', *New York Times*, 30 April 2007, available at www.nytimes.com/2007/04/30/business/worldbusiness/30food.html?pagewanted=all.

[9] FDA, 'Pet Food Recall: Frequently Asked Questions', 2 April 2007, available at http://web.archive.org/web/20070407113721/www.fda.gov/cvm/MenuFoodRecallFAQ.htm.

[10] FDA, 'Consumer Update: 'Contaminant Found in Second Pet Food Ingredient', 23 April 2007, available at www.fda.gov/ForConsumers/ConsumerUpdates/ucm048190.htm.

[11] FDA, 'Joint Update: FDA/USDA Trace Adulterated Animal Feed to Poultry', press release, 30 April 2007, available at www.fda.gov/NewsEvents/Newsroom/PressAnnouncements/2007/ucm108902.htm; FDA, 'Important Alert: Detention without Physical Examination of All Vegetable Protein Products from China for Animal or Human Food Use Due to the Presence of Melamine and/or Melamine Analogs', 2 May 2012, available at www.accessdata.fda.gov/cms_ia/importalert_267.html.

[12] Birgit Puschner, Robert H. Poppenga, Linda J. Lowenstine, Michael S. Filigenzi, and Patricia A. Pesavento, 'Assessment of Melamine and Cyanuric Acid Toxicity in Cats'. *Journal of Veterinary Diagnostic Investigation*, 19 (2007): 616–24; Anthony Kai-ching Hau, Tze Hoi Kwan, and Philip Kam-tao Li, 'Melamine Toxicity and the Kidney', *Journal of the American Society of Nephrology*, 20 (2009): 245–50.

2008 it was still unclear whether that effect was limited to animals, or whether it also extended to humans.[13]

When the Sanlu Group began in spring 2008 to receive large numbers of complaints of kidney stones developing in infants consuming its milk formula, its management recalled the earlier pet food scandal and began to suspect possible melamine contamination.[14] In summer 2008, Sanlu secretly tested its milk powder for melamine. It anonymously sent sixteen samples of its milk formula, each labelled with a fake brand name so as to disguise its place of origin, to the Hebei Frontier Inspection and Quarantine Bureau for testing (Sanlu's headquarters and production facilities are based in Shijiazhuang, the capital of Hebei province). Testing revealed that fifteen of these sixteen samples contained melamine in amounts sufficient to pose a serious health threat to animals.[15]

On becoming aware of these findings, Sanlu's president, (Ms) Tian Wenhua, called an emergency meeting to determine how Sanlu should respond. The meeting consisted of all of Sanlu's senior management, all its marketing managers, and representatives from the New Zealand dairy co-operative, Fonterra, which owned a 43 per cent stake in Sanlu. Fonterra is the world's largest exporter of dairy products, and Sanlu was a key supplier in its international production network. Fonterra's representatives urged a total public recall of all affected products.[16] But Sanlu decided instead secretly to replace all the unsold stock of tainted formula with new stock of untainted product – a 'trade recall' instead of a general recall. Sanlu also reported the problem and its proposed response to the municipal authorities of Shijiazhuang (alternative accounts say that Fonterra reported this situation to the Shijiazhuang authorities). Municipal authorities not only supported this response, but also helped to facilitate the cover-up by not reporting the incident to provincial authorities as they were required to do by law.[17]

---

[13] See, e.g., Na et al., 'Melamine-Contaminated Powdered Formula'; Langman, 'Melamine, Powdered Milk'.

[14] Liu, 'Profits above the Law', 385.   [15] Ibid., 385.

[16] David Barboza, 'Former Executive Pleads Guilty in China Milk Scandal', New York Times, 1 January 2009, A10.

[17] Jamil Anderlini and Peter Smith, 'Officials Knew of Tainted Baby Milk', Financial Times, 16 September 2008, available at www.ft.com/intl/cms/s/0/d75a0d08-8388-11dd-907e-000077b07658.html#axzz1yxlmjBc3; Tania Branigan, 'China Milk Scandal Company "Asked Government to Help in Cover-Up"', Guardian, 1 October 2008, available at www.guardian.co.uk/world/2008/oct/01/china.milk.

The clandestine trade recall began on 6 August 2008.[18] Evidence suggests that Sanlu's management was sincere in its intentions. But a quiet replacement on such a scale was simply impossible. The supply of known untainted raw milk was insufficient to produce the quantity of untainted replacement necessary to make the recall work. In fact, demand for Sanlu dairy products was dramatically increasing due to China's upcoming Mid-Autumn Festival. By 13 August it was clear to Sanlu's management that an effective (and effectively quiet) trade recall was impossible, and it was decided instead to try simply to reduce melamine contamination to seemingly marginally safe levels of 15 mg/kg – an amount derived from EU standards allowing 20 mg/kg (today, the international standard for the maximum allowable level of melamine in dairy products is 2.5 mg/kg, but this was not set until the end of 2008). But even this proved impossible. Between 2 August and 12 September Sanlu ended up producing and selling 813 tons of baby formula that its officials knew to contain dangerously high levels of melamine.[19]

Throughout this period, Fonterra officials were trying to find ways of increasing pressure on Sanlu to implement a public, general recall. Finding the Shijiazhuang officials unco-operative, it began releasing information to New Zealand embassy personnel in Beijing, first in informal cocktail conversation, and later through increasingly formal requests for advice on how to proceed. Eventually, on 1 September, New Zealand's ambassador to China informed the New Zealand government about the problem. On 8 September, after discussion with her senior cabinet, New Zealand's prime minister, Helen Clark, ordered the ambassador to inform the relevant central authorities in China directly. Two days later the ambassador informed senior Chinese officials of the problem.[20] On that same day, reports began appearing in the Chinese media detailing the contamination and Sanlu's cover-up efforts. The next day, 11 September, China's central government publicly announced a general recall of all Sanlu milk powder, a recall involving over 10,000 tons of milk powder.[21]

Unfortunately, the tragedy did not end there. On 17 September, further government testing revealed that of 265 samples of milk

---

[18] Anderlini and Smith, 'Officials Knew'.
[19] See generally Liu, 'Profits above the Law', 385–6.
[20] Fran O'Sullivan, 'Embassy Officials Slow to Call Toxic Alert', *New Zealand Herald News*, 21 September 2008, available at www.nzherald.co.nz/nz/news/article.cfm?c_id=1&objectid=10533363.
[21] 'China to Destroy 10,000 Tons of Tainted Baby Formula', Xinhua News Agency, 16 September 2008, available at www.china.org.cn/health/2008–09/16/content_16464641.htm.

powder produced by 154 companies prior to 14 September, 31 samples originating from 22 companies contained significant concentrations of melamine.[22] These included samples coming from the three dairy companies that, along with Sanlu, had been designated 'Chinese famous brands' by the China Promotion Committee for Top Brand Strategy: the Yili Group, the China Mengniu Dairy Company, and the Shanghai Bright Dairy and Food Company.[23] Sanlu, Yili, and Mengniu products were stripped of their 'Chinese top brand' status after this finding.[24]

Once it felt that it had gained a handle on the problem, Beijing appears to have begun ordering the state-run media to cease reporting on the problem.[25] Internet discourse about the tragedy was also suppressed. Local courts refused to accept civil lawsuits stemming from the tragedy, and lawyers and families who persisted in pressing such claims, or in otherwise demanding greater political accountability for the tragedy, were harassed and subjected to detention and arrest.[26] At the same time, however, the central government was generally effective in stopping the milk contamination once they became aware of it. Testing processes were updated so as to detect melamine adulteration. Supply networks were streamlined, and all 20,000 milk collection stations were inspected to ensure that they had the equipment necessary for effective testing – some 5,000 of these stations were closed down for not having such equipment. New regulations were also enacted that clarified testing responsibilities of local governments, collecting stations, and dairy processors.[27]

---

[22] 'China Seizes 22 Companies with Contaminated Baby Milk Powder', Xinhua News Agency, 16 September 2008, available at http://news.xinhuanet.com/english/2008–09/17/content_10046949.htm.

[23] 'Most Liquid Milk in China Does Not Contain Melamine', Xinhua News Agency, 18 September 2008, available at http://news.xinhuanet.com/english/2008–09/19/content_10076616.htm.

[24] 'Administration of Quality Inspection and Supervision [AQSIQ]: Mengniu, Yili, Guangming Liquid Milk Removed from Chinese Famous Brands Product', CCTV.com, 22 September 2008, available at http://news.cctv.com/china/20080922/101235.shtml.

[25] David Bandurski, 'Press Controls Feed China's Food Problem', Wall Street Journal Asia, 7 October 2008, available at http://online.wsj.com/article/SB122332462058208791.html.

[26] Ng Tze-wei, 'Lawyers Warned to Shun Milk Suits', South China Morning Post, 23 September 2008, A2; Edward Wong, 'Courts Compound Pains of China's Tainted Milk', New York Times, 17 October 2008, A1.

[27] Xiu and Klein, 'Melamine in Milk Products', 467–8.

The remainder of this chapter, however, focuses on the evolution of this tragedy rather than on China's regulatory and political response. China's post-discovery response does have important things to tell us about China's political system, and in particular its concern – or lack thereof – for social justice. But it does not tell us much about why the tragedy came about in the first place. It does not tell us about the particular regulatory needs and incapacities that allowed this practice of contamination to develop and spread prior to regulatory discovery. And it is through these issues that the distinctive capitalist dynamics of the periphery, both in China and elsewhere, are revealed.

III. Melamine contamination as a product of market competition

The melamine milk tragedy has sometimes been attributed to particular flaws in China's political system – in particular, to economic planning, to corruption, and to the political unaccountability of China's authoritarian party-state. But, in fact, nothing in the story above suggests a significant role for any of these in the evolution of that tragedy (although, as discussed above, they did play a role in shaping China's regulatory and political response to it). We cannot blame the tragedy on China's propensity to intervene in free market operations, because both its market for raw milk and its dairy industry as a whole have operated without state interference for the better part of two decades, and all the significant actors involved in the development of the tragedy were privately run.[28] Insofar as the dairy industry, and its attendant markets, were concerned, the role of the state was indeed in the form of that paradigmatic 'night watchman' that is the basis of neoliberal economic theory: namely to legislate and monitor the testing and handling of raw milk once it got to collection.

There are no reports suggesting that bribery or corruption contributed significantly to the development of the tragedy either. Nor should this surprise us, despite China's pronounced reputation for official corruption. What made melamine adulteration attractive was precisely that it was not detectable by then existing testing routines.[29] One does not need to bribe officials to look away from what they cannot see in the first place.

The cover-up by municipal officials in Shijiazhuang does not appear to have been motivated by corruption, either. Shijiazhuang had plenty of non-corrupt incentives to support the cover-up and the continued operation and profitability of Sanlu.[30] Sanlu was an important source of

---

[28] See generally ibid., 464–6.   [29] Ibid., 468.   [30] Cf. ibid., 466.

employment and public revenue. It directly employed over 10,000 people in Shijiazhuang.[31] It was also the keystone that supported Hebei's regional dairy industry, one of China's largest, and a key source of public revenue (via taxation) to Shijiazhuang: in 2007, the year before the crisis, Sanlu paid 330 million renminbi (US$48.5 million) in tax revenue to the municipality.[32] Sanlu also brought significant social capital to the city; it had been widely celebrated for its innovations in manufacturing (including the rigour of its product testing).[33]

Similarly, it is hard to find anything in this narrative that is unique or even distinctive to non-democratic or other otherwise non-accountable political systems. The Chinese had long acknowledged that its raw milk supply had significant problems with adulteration, even before the discovery of melamine.[34] In 2007, China's state-run television ran a national investigative programme on the problem specifically as it involved milk powder. The central government conducted an investigation in response to that programme, but that investigation revealed nothing (probably because melamine contaminations would not show up in ordinary testing).[35]

International observers seem generally to agree that as of the middle part of the 2000s, the Chinese authorities were honestly devoted to doing what they could to address the general problem of raw milk adulteration.[36] Consistently with this, the state's authoritarian political establishment showed no hesitation in addressing the problem of melamine adulteration once it became aware of it. The general recall was publicly announced within twenty-four hours of the state's discovery, and Sanlu's

---

[31] 'Sanlu Liquid Milk Back on Chinese Market after Melamine Scandal', Xinhua News Agency, 13 November 2008, available at http://news.xinhuanet.com/english/2008-11/13/content_10353146.htm.

[32] Willy Lam, 'Milk Scandal Sours China's "Soft Power"', Asia Times Online, 10 October 2008, available at www.atimes.com/atimes/China/JJ10Ad02.html.

[33] 'CCTV Investigative Report of Sanlu Milk Powder: Thousands of Tests before Leaving Factory', Cnfol.com, 12 September 2008, available at http://news.cnfol.com/080912/101,1603,4759687,00.shtml (reporting on CCTV programme that aired on 2 September 2007).

[34] Gordon Fairclough, 'Tainting of Milk is Open Secret in China', Wall Street Journal, 3 November 2008, available at http://online.wsj.com/article/SB122567367498791713.html. See also Waikeung Tam and Dali Yang, 'Food Safety and the Development of Regulatory Institutions in China', Asian Perspectives, 29 (2005): 5–36.

[35] Fairclough, 'Tainting of Milk'.

[36] See, e.g., Tam and Yang, 'Food Safety', 29–34; United Nations, Office of Resident Coordinator in China, 'Advancing Food Safety In China', occasional paper, March 2008, pp. 4–5, available at www.un.org.cn/cms/p/resources/30/841/content.html.

operations were shut down. Comprehensive testing of milk powder sold in China was immediately ordered, and the (quite damning) results made public.[37]

Nor was Sanlu's attempted cover-up, via its clandestine trade recall as opposed to an open public recall, particularly distinctive of China's non-democratic, authoritarian political culture. Corporate efforts to cover up dangerous product defects are well known even in advanced industrial democracies. In the United States, the Ethyl Corporation effectively suppressed knowledge of the dangerous effects of its lead-based, anti-knock gasoline additive for almost forty years, from the late 1920s well into the 1960s.[38] American tobacco companies did the same with regard to the harmful health effects of second-hand smoke for around a decade beginning in the 1980s.[39]

A.   The structure of China's dairy industry

The real culprit in the melamine milk adulteration tragedy in China seems quite simply to be 'the market' itself – not 'the market' in the sense of a particular market with idiosyncratic 'Chinese characteristics', but 'the market' in the archetypical sense as used, for example, by neoliberal economics.

China's dairy industry has been a poster child for neoliberal market-ization in China. Since its founding, it has generally been highly competitive and free of state intervention. It has also been one of China's fastest growing industries.[40] China did not even have a national dairy market prior to the 1990s.[41] But beginning in 1994, per capita milk consumption began growing at rates constantly in excess of 10 per cent

---

[37] See, e.g., Andrew Jacobs, 'Chinese Release Increased Numbers in Tainted Milk Scandal', *New York Times*, 2 December 2008, available at www.nytimes.com/2008/12/03/world/asia/03milk.html; 'China seizes 22 Companies'.

[38] Bill Bryson, *A Short History of Nearly Everything* (New York: Broadway Books, 2003), pp. 149–60.

[39] Suzaynn Schick and Stanton A. Glantz, 'Philip Morris Toxicological Experiments with Fresh Sidestream Smoke: More Toxic than Mainstream Smoke', *Tobacco Control*, 14 (2005): 396–404. See also *McCabe v. British American Tobacco Australia Services Limited*, [2002] VSC 73, No. 8121 of 2001.

[40] Frank H. Fuller, Jikun Huang, Hengyun Ma, and Scott Rozelle, *The Rapid Rise of China's Dairy Sector: Factors behind the Growth in Demand and Supply*, Working Paper 05-394 (Ames, IA: Iowa State University Center for Agricultural and Rural Development, 2005), pp. 2–5, 11–12.

[41] Xiu and Klein, 'Melamine in Milk Products in China', p. 466.

per annum, and would continue to do so into the next century. This occurred across the economic spectrum. Milk consumption in households in the lowest 10 per cent of income distribution doubled their dairy consumption between 1995 and 2002. For that same period, higher income groups tripled consumption.[42]

As demand for dairy products skyrocketed, so too did the production of raw milk. In 1994, China produced less than 6 million tons of milk per year. That output tripled in little less than a decade, reaching 18 million tons in 2003. It then doubled again between 2003 and 2007.[43] But this expansion of milk production had been driven primarily by an expansion in the number of milk cows and in the number of small, milk-producing farms, not by increases in productivity. As of 2008, when melamine contamination was discovered, 80 per cent of China's raw milk was still produced by small, family-based dairy farms, each having on average three to five cows.[44] Milk production per cow and per man-hour was largely the same as it had been in the 1980s.

China's failure to industrialize the supply base for raw milk was due to a number of factors. China's milk production industry emerged out of subsistence farming practices, and this gave such production a more complex social function (and social meaning) than it has in more modern, neoliberal markets. In many regions, milk production was still regarded by many of its family producers as a means for ensuring the survival of the family, and not simply as a means of generating economic growth through profits from outside sales.[45] Most such farmers had very limited access to capital and only a very meagre education, and thus the milk production industry had very little capacity for industrial upgrading at the point of initial production.[46]

Things were different, however, as one moved down the production stream. During the 1990s, there was significant consolidation among downstream dairy processing firms – the firms that convert raw milk

---

[42] Fuller, et al., *Rapid Rise*, p. 3.

[43] FAO, *Food Outlook: Global Market Analysis No.2*, December 2006, available at ftp://ftp.fao.org/docrep/fao/009/j8126e/j8126e00.pdf, p. 29.

[44] Liu, 'Profits above Law', 380.

[45] Xiu and Klein, 'Melamine in Milk Products', 466. On the relative complexity of the social function and meaning of basic goods in non-commodified societies, see Karl Polanyi, *The Great Transformation: The Political and Economic Origins of our Time* (Boston, MA: Beacon Press, 2001).

[46] Xiu and Klein, 'Melamine in Milk Products', 466; Fuller et al., *Rapid Rise*, p. 16. Cf. Tam and Yang, 'Food Safety', 27–8.

into the dairy products being consumed by the general public. Originally, these firms were largely regional in scope, reflecting their origins as state-run rural collectives that had been established during the Mao era. But in the latter part of the 1990s, four national 'mega-milk processing firms' emerged that grew to dominate the national consumer market. By 2007, half the dairy products sold to consumers in China came from one of four processing firms, one of which was the Sanlu Group.[47] Due to their ability to exploit economies of scale, these mega-firms were quite profitable, and their production and distribution processes were (and are) quite industrialized. Here there were significant productivity increases due to industrial upgrading.[48]

In short, China's overall dairy industry was, and to a large extent still is, bifurcated into a non-industrialized upstream production sector that consists of a huge number of small-scale, low-tech producers, on the one end, and a hi-tech downstream processing sector dominated by a handful of very large, advanced brand-name firms on the other. Such industrial bifurcation creates co-ordination problems, namely, how does an advanced industrial processing system that is based on centralized co-ordination and monitoring of a highly standardized and task-specialized production process come to grips with a supply system that is highly dispersed, highly localized, and highly non-standardized and irregular?[49]

Within China's dairy industry there were three different industrial responses to this problem.[50] One is found in the perseverance of smaller regional processors that largely continue to operate along pre-reform lines. These processors, which tend to be in the form of state-run collectives, solved the problem of a pre-industrial supply network by largely forgoing large-scale industrialization themselves and retaining a localized production and marketing focus.[51] Another response was for the processor to simply set up its own technologically advanced dairy-producing farms. Because this response requires significant amounts of investment, however, and could not match the levels of milk supplied by the small-scale-farm portion of the production industry, this was the response primarily of the more upscale (value-added) segment of

[47] Xiu and Klein, 'Melamine in Milk Products', 465.   [48] Ibid.
[49] See also Fuller et al., *Rapid Rise*, pp. 20–1.
[50] See generally William D. Dobson, *Drivers of Change in China's Dairy Industry – Implications for the U.S. and World Dairy Industries*, Babcock Institute Discussion Paper 2006-4 (Madison, WI: Babcock Institute for International Dairy Research and Development, 2006), pp. 1–12, 22.
[51] Xiu and Klein, 'Melamine in Milk Products', 465, 466.

the industry (the segment that sold fewer dairy products overall but at higher return on sales) – a segment that was and is dominated by more technologically advanced, transnational dairy firms such as Mead Johnson, Wyeth, Dumex, and Fonterra.[52]

For domestic mega-producers competing at the more price-sensitive end of the consumer market, however, neither of these responses could provide the quantity of raw milk necessary to meet consumer demand. Their response, one that was actually invented by Sanlu itself, was to set up a large, geographically extended and industrially disaggregated supply network that linked small-scale family farms to centralized production facilities through an intermediary known as the 'milk collection station'. This became known as the 'Sanlu model'.[53]

Milk collection stations were places where small-scale farmers could take their milk cows to be milked:

> An ordinary milk collection station is a big sheltered room with necessary equipment (including milking machines and simple quality inspection equipment) that can handle a certain number of dairy cows (usually less than 100) for milking. The regular activities of a milk collection station include sterilization of cows' udders, milking, milk storage and shipment.[54]

These milk collection stations were largely privately run enterprises, established by local third parties operating under contract with one of the mega-processing firms. On average, each milk collection station serviced around 200 cows, and monopolized milk collection within its particular territory.[55] Milk collection stations were also responsible for quality inspection, although this would generally only be undertaken when there were specific complaints from the tied processor about the quality of its milk. As of 2008, there were over 20,000 milk collection stations operating throughout China.[56]

The Sanlu model was crucial for tying together the industrialized and non-industrialized ends of China's raw milk supply networks.[57] As far as its often impoverished rural suppliers were concerned, it reduced start-up

---

[52] Ethel Lu, 'Radical Shifts in China's Milk Market', *China Today*, 14 January 2009, available at http://china.org.cn/business/news/2009-01/14/content_17105973.htm. See also Dobson, *Drivers of Change*, p. 17.

[53] Liu, 'Profits above Law', 378–9. See also Fred Gale and Dinghuan Hu, 'Supply Chain Issues in China's Milk Adulteration Incident', paper presented at the International Association of Agricultural Economists' 2009 Conference, Beijing, China, 16–22 August 2009.

[54] Xiu and Klein, 'Melamine in Milk Products', 466.   [55] Ibid., 466.

[56] 'China Closes Thousands of Milk Collection Stations', *China Daily*, 3 June 2009, available at www.chinadaily.com.cn/business/2009–06/03/content_8038447.htm.

[57] See Gale and Hu, 'Supply Chain Issues', pp. 5–7.

and maintenance costs by alleviating the need for farmers to purchase and maintain sterilized milking equipment. It also supplied these rural farmers with sufficient technical know-how to meet the quality and production needs of the processors.

> Many dairy farmers . . . were subsistence farmers who lived in small rural villages and worked on large collective farms . . . In many cases, small dairy farmers purchased their cows with financing assistance from the processors; generally, the processors dictate the terms of the loans, including the interest rate and the payback period. The Sanlu Company provided dairy cows and technical advice free to small dairy farmers who paid off their loans with milk. This was seen as a very competitive strategy by large processing firms and government agencies as small farmers can produce at relatively low cost: they often can utilize self-produced feeds that are gathered with unpaid family labour.[58]

At the same time, it contributed to the industrialized end of processing by centralizing collection for delivery to the mega-processor's processing plant. And since each station was contractually tied to a single processor, it allowed processors to dictate uniform pricing and quality standards, a critical factor in maintaining the uniformity of supply that facilitates large-scale, industrial processing.[59]

All in all, the Sanlu model worked because it was able to accommodate the needs of both the pre-industrialized producers of raw milk and the highly industrialized processors of that milk:

> This method seemed to work well by enabling local farmers to increase their income, through raising and milking cows, and local governments consequently increase tax revenues from the dairy farmers. Ms. Tian [Tian Wenhua, the founder, president, and general manager of the Sanlu Group] touted that the Sanlu model completely revolutionized the milk industry, benefiting both local farmers and governments while at the same time dramatically reducing production costs for processors.[60]

B. Competition and innovation

As noted above, China's dairy industry has been highly competitive.[61] And it was this more than anything that drove the developments that

---

[58] Xiu and Klein, 'Melamine in Milk Products', 466; see also Liu, 'Profits above Law', 380, 381; Gale and Hu, 'Supply Chain Issues', pp. 5–6.
[59] Xiu and Klein, 'Melamine in Milk Products', 466; Fuller et al., *Rapid Rise*, p. 20.
[60] Liu, 'Profits above Law', 379–80. See also Xiu and Klein, 'Melamine in Milk Products', 466.
[61] Xiu and Klein, 'Melamine in Milk Products', 467; Liu, 'Profits above Law', 375–80; Gale and Hu, 'Supply Chain Issues', pp. 3–4. Cf. Fuller et al., *Rapid Rise*, p. 31.

culminated in melamine adulteration. In this sense, melamine adulteration simply represents a particular product innovation that was inspired by market competition.[62]

The price squeeze resulting from this hyper-competitive environment became particularly bad in around 2005:

> In 2005, Big 6 milk processors made substantial investments in upgrading processing equipment, either through foreign investors or subsidies from local governments. The increased milk processing capacity made the firms desperate to find additional milk supplies. While the big milk processors clearly knew that the real solution to inadequate supply was to maintain large scale dairy farms of their own, none of them wanted to incur the cost of doing so for fear of being undercut by other firms . . .
>
> Sanlu could no longer leverage a monopoly over dairy farmers and milk stations that had supplied Sanlu for about a decade. Because the contractual relationships between Sanlu and raw milk providers were not strictly enforced, the suppliers frequently switched to other processing firms that promised higher prices and less rigid quality checks. The competition for milk supplies was so furious that big processors knowingly collected substandard raw milk.[63]

The Sanlu model itself was the product of this competition – as we saw above, it was, in fact, a highly innovative solution to the industrial discontinuities besetting China's milk production industry.[64] But, as we saw, the Sanlu model did not reduce production costs by improving productive efficiency. Rather, its real innovation was to allow the processor to exert market pressures on upstream producers to reduce their production costs, by using their fading but still significant monopsonistic power over the production chain effectively to dictate what the price of raw milk would be.[65] By the mid-point of the first decade of the 2000s, milk prices were right at, and occasionally even dipping beneath, production costs:

> With no control over price, quality inspection and other conditions of sale, reduction of average costs has been the principal way that the small farmers could maintain or increase profits. As milk supply increased about 150% from 2003 to 2006, farm price of milk decreased and milk

---

[62] See also Gong Qing, 'Investigation Report on the Chaotic Raw Milk Market in Hebei', *Caijing*, 21 September 2008.

[63] Liu, 'Profits above Law', 381. See also ibid., 375; Xiu and Klein, 'Melamine in Milk Products', 466.

[64] Gale and Hu, 'Supply Chain Issues', pp. 2–7; Liu, 'Profits above Law', 380.

[65] Gale and Hu, 'Supply Chain Issues', pp. 7–10; Liu, 'Profits above Law', 380–1.

producers were faced with a major cost-price squeeze. Costs of key inputs, including feed, electricity and gasoline, rose with the commodity boom in 2007–2008, causing major financial losses to the small dairy farmers.[66]

As noted above, competitive pressures in the dairy industry became particularly acute in 2005. Within a year, Chinese farmers would discover how to adulterate raw milk with melamine to increase its apparent protein content, as a way to reduce production costs as demanded by a price-competitive market.

The small-scale rural family farm has little capacity for technological upgrading, and the social-welfare function of dairy farming discouraged agglomeration into larger farms that could promote more efficient economies of scale. This left protein adulteration as one of the few ways in which farmers could continue to reduce production costs so as to compete in an already efficient, price-competitive market.[67] Chinese farmers had long been experimenting with 'protein additives' – additives that increase apparent protein content – not simply for milk, but for livestock feed and other protein-based food products (such as, as we saw above, wheat gluten).[68] Processors were aware of this, of course, and were themselves constantly improving their testing routines so as to better detect such additives.

Originally, farmers spiked protein content by using actual protein additives (similar to the way in which American pet-food manufacturers increase the protein content of pet food today). And this was the type of adulteration that testing was principally designed to detect.[69] Indeed, at the dawn of 2008, it seemed that the processing companies were winning the adulteration-detection race.[70] Sanlu in particular took considerable corporate pride in the quality and thoroughness of its product safety testing. In September 2007, China Central Television (CCTV) celebrated the company's stringent quality control procedures.[71] Some fifteen months later, in January 2008, Sanlu received a 'National Award of Science and Technology Progress' for 'Innovative Infant Formula Research and other Related Techniques'.[72]

---

[66] Xiu and Klein, 'Melamine in Milk Products', 466. See also Gale and Hu, 'Supply Chain Issues', pp. 7–10.

[67] Gale and Hu, 'Supply Chain Issues', p. 11.   [68] Tam and Yang, 'Food Safety'.

[69] Fairclough, 'Tainting of Milk'.   [70] Liu, 'Profits above Law', 380–1.

[71] 'CCTV Investigative Report'.

[72] Shumei Chen, 'Sham or Shame: Rethinking the China's Milk Powder Scandal from a Legal Perspective', *Journal of Risk Research*, 12 (2009): 725–47, 726.

From the supply side, all this triggered a search for cheap ways of increasing protein count, and hence increasing productivity, without actually adding easily detectable, alternative forms of protein. This was the genius of melamine, which, as we saw, increased protein count simply by increasing the amount of nitrogen in the milk:

> Two dairy farmers from Hebei province ... said additives have long helped farmers fool dairy-company tests for protein, fat content and freshness ... One of them, who has raised dairy cows for 20 years and is a farm-association leader, says salespeople for years would go from farm to farm in dairy-cow areas hawking 'protein powder' for use as an additive. It would often be delivered in unmarked brown paper bags weighing 25 kilograms, or about 55 pounds, and costing 300 yuan to 400 yuan, or $44 to $60, he says.
>
> About two years ago [i.e., in 2006], farmers and Chinese authorities say, some manufacturers offered a new version of protein powder that they said could still fool dairies that had caught on to other protein additives. It contained melamine, but wasn't labeled as such. 'Everyone just called it protein powder,' says the second farmer. 'Nowhere did it say it was melamine,' he says. 'People never thought about it and never thought they needed to know more details.'[73]

We should not let our moral revulsion to the consequences of this innovation blind us to its sophistication. Chinese rural communities were the first in the world to discover that melamine could be used to increase the protein count of raw milk.[74] Indeed, the ultimate adulteration process that emerged in China was quite technologically advanced:

> Researchers say the adulteration was nothing short of a wholesale re-engineering of milk ... 'Adulteration used to be simple. What they did was very high-tech,' says Chen [Chen Junshi, a risk assessment specialist at China's Center for Disease Control and Prevention]. Researchers have since learned that the emulsifier used to suspend melamine – a compound that resists going into solution – also boosted apparent milk-fat content ... Chen says a dean of a school of food science told him that it would take a university team 3 months to develop this kind of concoction.[75]

There is a tendency among those who work out of the perspective of the orthodox competition model to treat innovation as an unqualified good (cf. Jessop, Ch. 5, p. 117), treating it as if it were something that should be

---

[73] Fairclough, 'Tainting of Milk'. See also Barboza and Barrionuevo, 'Filler in Animal Feed'.
[74] Xiu and Klein, 'Melamine in Milk Products', 467, 468; Xin and Stone, 'Chinese Probe', 1310–11.
[75] Xin and Stone, 'Chinese Probe', 1310–11.

pursued simply for its own sake. Many may therefore be uncomfortable with characterizing melamine milk adulteration as an 'innovation'. After all, if innovation is a good thing per se, and melamine contamination was clearly bad, then such adulteration is not properly characterized as an innovation.

But, as has been well demonstrated, most recently by Louis Kaplow and Steven Shavell, the orthodox model tells us that markets are and should be concerned only with efficiency.[76] Everything else is – in Robert Bork's words – a 'non-sequitur' from the perspective of competition regulation.[77] A market works by simply looking around and finding who produces what at the least cost. It does not concern itself with issues of how these lower costs are obtained, or with what their social costs might be with regard to, for example, wages, distribution, or more generally to fairness.[78] This is not to imply that such issues are not important. They are relevant, but the critical point is that they are relevant for other aspects of regulation – what some call 'social regulation' – just not for market regulation (including competition regulation). A market's contribution to human society lies in its ability to improve that society's (efficient) use of resources. From such a perspective, any discovery that improves some aspect of that efficiency is a good regardless of whatever other social effects it may have, because to the extent that these other effects do not impact efficiency, they are simply 'non sequiturs' from the perspective of the market itself.

All this, of course, begs the question of what goes into the cost, and many would argue that market concerns can be made to parallel social concerns by promoting a more accurate costing of production, by reducing market externalities. A market externality is simply a cost of production that is not borne by either the seller or the purchaser. Pollution, for example, clearly has economic costs, in the form of less productive workers (due to more health problems) and less productive agricultural yield, for example. But these are costs that are for the most part not completely borne by the producer or buyer of the product causing the pollution, and so its costing of production will not take these costs into account. The standard solution that the orthodox model advances for this kind of

---

[76] Louis Kaplow and Steven Shavell, *Fairness versus Welfare* (Cambridge, MA: Harvard University Press, 2002).

[77] Robert H. Bork, *The Antitrust Paradox*, 2nd edn (New York: Free Press, 1993), p. 428: 'A different line of attack comes from those who observe, quite correctly, that people value things other than consumer welfare, and therefore, quite incorrectly, that antitrust ought not to be confined to advancing that goal. As non sequiturs go, that one is world class.'

[78] See also Coase, 'Problem of Social Cost'.

problem is to develop institutions that can help internalize into the producer's cost of production the cost of these externalities.[79] (This is the justification, for example, for class-action litigation.)

By definition, markets do not take externalities into account in rewarding or punishing products. Each efficiency it promotes is simply an efficiency *with regard to those resources that the market is able to price*. In fact, Harold Demesetz has really advanced a persuasive argument that market externalities can themselves often be a product and a reflection of a particular market's pursuit of efficiency.[80] And this means that markets similarly do not consider whatever external costs a particular innovation has in deciding whether or not to reward that innovation. Markets will reward any innovation that results in a more efficient use of resources as those resources are priced by the market.

Seen in this light, the disastrous health effects of melamine milk adulteration was, from the perspective of China's market for raw milk, an externality. Economists often talk about costs to health as externalities: pollution is perhaps the classic example economists use to explain an externality, and its cost lies primarily in its cost to health. The 'external' nature of the health cost of melamine adulteration is particularly apparent in one farmer's claim that 'Everyone just called [the adulterative additive] protein powder . . . Nowhere did it say it was melamine . . . People never thought about it and never thought they needed to know more details.'[81]

Externalities are an inevitable feature of markets. No market anywhere is inclusive enough to take all costs of production into account in its pricing mechanisms. The market for raw milk in China is no different in this regard. And from the perspective of that market (again, a critical qualifier), melamine milk adulteration appears no different from any other innovation that lowered production costs.[82]

IV.   Melamine milk adulteration and the limits of the orthodox model

Thus, from a (neoliberal) economic perspective, China's melamine milk adulteration tragedy was not a problem of politics and was not a problem

---

[79] See generally ibid.

[80] Harold Demesetz, 'The Problem of Social Cost: What Problem? A Critique of the Reasoning of A. C. Pigou and R. H. Coase', *Review of Law and Economics*, 7 (2011): 1–13.

[81] Fairclough, 'Tainting of Milk'. See also Barboza and Barrionuevo, 'Filler in Animal Feed'.

[82] See also Liu, 'Profits above Law', 375–6.

of compromised markets. It was a problem of markets themselves. Of course, it is well recognized, even in the most neoliberal of discourses, that markets can and inevitably will produce social costs in addition to social welfare – externalities are an example of this. And orthodox competition theory also offers a solution to this problem. As described above, it argues that these social costs are properly addressed using other aspects of the regulatory system.[83] This allows market competition to optimize the market's wealth generation. Clearly, an inegalitarian market that produces more overall, whose larger product is then redistributed through an external public law system, leaves society better off than an egalitarian market that produces less overall, regardless of how egalitarian its market distribution is.

In the case of melamine milk adulteration, that other system would have been food safety regulation. China has long had serious problems with its food safety regulatory system, but, at least since the early 2000s, China has also put considerable effort into improving it.[84] And as noted above, by the end of 2007 it appeared to be winning in the battle against raw milk adulteration. Why did the system fail?

A.   The regulatory environment for milk safety in China

By the time of the tragedy, China's regulation of its raw milk supply was generally along the lines advocated by the orthodox model. Food safety regulation was separated from the market and carried out by dedicated government regulators. This included, most importantly in the context of raw milk production, that of the Administration of Quality Supervision, Inspection and Quarantine (AQSIQ), a central-level administrative agency. But other centralized agencies, such as the State Food and Drug Administration, and the ministries of health, agriculture, commerce, and industry, also administer certain different aspects of this regime.[85] But vertical and horizontal fragmentation of the regulatory authority in China's food safety regulation has therefore been a problem.[86] In the context of melamine milk adulteration, this fragmentation allowed the Shijiazhuang municipal government to ignore central regulations in order to facilitate (and perhaps even order) Sanlu's attempted cover-up of the adulteration.

---

[83] Kaplow and Shavell, *Fairness versus Welfare*. In the context of Asia, see also Lawrence S. Liu, 'In Fairness We Trust? Why Fostering Competition Law and Policy Ain't Easy in Asia', unpublished paper dated 19 October 2004.
[84] Tam and Yang, 'Food Safety'.   [85] Ibid., 12–16.   [86] Ibid., 12–16.

But there is much more to China's regulatory fragmentation than local protectionism. In fact, China's raw milk market was and is a regulator's nightmare. As discussed above, China's raw milk comes overwhelmingly from over 100,000 small-scale, family farms operating primarily in impoverished and highly underdeveloped areas of the country. Milk from these farms is collected by locally and privately owned small milk collection stations, of which, as has been noted, there were some 20,000 at the time of the crisis. Such a non-industrialized industrial structure is going to be highly resistant to national or centralized regulatory schemes. Production is simply too diffuse, and the local environment in which production takes place too opaque, for the centralized regulation (either public or private) characteristic of industrial modernity, particularly in a country the size of China.[87]

On the other hand, however, as we also saw, the downstream sector of the dairy industry is industrialized. And this makes *decentralized* regulation problematic as well.[88] The raw milk being produced is not being consumed locally, and so the social costs of local shirking on milk testing are externalized to other parts of the country. At the same time, many of these localities are also heavily dependent on the income produced by raw milk sales, and they therefore are not going to be too interested in restraining those sales any more than is absolutely necessary.[89] China's bifurcated dairy industry thus presents regulators with a devil's choice: the upstream end is too decentralized to allow for centralized regulation; but its centralized downstream industrial processors are not conducive to decentralized regulation, either.

The structural problems facing regulators in China were recognized well before the melamine milk crisis. As noted in a report on China's food safety regime published by the UN Resident Co-ordinator in China six months prior to the discovery of the crisis,

> The fact that about 80% of Chinese food producers and processors are small and medium sized enterprises makes both enforcement by regulators and compliance by the industry particularly challenging. In addition, the implications of closing businesses that do not meet standards are significant considering the large number of workers employed in by these enterprises.[90]

---

[87] Xiu and Klein, 'Melamine in Milk Products', 467; Xin and Stone, 'Chinese Probe', 1311; United Nations, 'Occasional Paper', p. 18; Drew Thompson and Hu Ying, 'Food Safety in China: New Strategies', *Global Health Governance*, 1 (issue 2) (2007): 4–5, www.ghgj.org/Thompson_and_Ying.htm.
[88] Tam and Yang, 'Food Safety', 14–15.   [89] Tam and Yang, 'Food Safety', 17.
[90] United Nations, 'Occasional Paper', p. 18.

China's regulatory dilemma in this regard is well evinced both in the history of the evolution of that regulatory regime and in the industrial topology of the melamine crisis itself. Prior to the mid 1990s, China's dairy production was primarily localized. The large national mega-processors had yet to emerge, and local milk producers served primarily local consumers, as well as those in more distant cities. The regulation of food safety was similarly localized, carried out via an extensive network of locally administered supply and marketing co-operatives (*gongxiaoshe*). During this time, the combination of local marketing and local regulation was generally sufficient to ensure that the food being produced was safe.[91] But the industrialization of milk processing disrupted this scheme. The emergence of mega-processors meant that raw milk production was no longer directed primarily at local markets. As we analysed above, milk safety became a concern of remote consumer markets, which the localized regulatory regime was structurally unable to address and was uninterested in addressing.[92]

The structural nature of this regulatory problem is well evinced in the industrial topology of the crisis. China's downstream dairy manufacturing is not *completely* industrialized. Fifty per cent of milk processing is still done by locally owned and locally administered processors serving primarily local and regional markets, as it was prior to the 1990s. The dairy products manufactured by these smaller regional processors were overwhelmingly found to be free of melamine.[93]

(A number of studies have suggested that melamine contamination was also occasioned by numerous exceptions in China's national milk quality inspection that reflected China's leadership's greater concern with economic growth over health and safety. These exceptions are indeed problematic, and have contributed to other milk adulteration crises in China. But as far as melamine contamination is concerned, they do not seem to have played much of a role. The market effectiveness of mela-mine contamination lay precisely in its sophisticated ability to escape detection by existing tests for milk quality, not in its ability to trigger

---

[91] Yang and Tam, 'Food Safety', 22. In an earlier draft of this article, presented at the workshop on 'Regulatory Compliance in China: The Lessons of Regulatory Effectiveness', held at the Georgetown Law Center, 2–5 November 2004 (on file with the author), Yang and Tam state that '[t]the state exercised close supervision over the *gongxiaoshe* as well as the producers and therefore maintained reasonable level of product quality.'

[92] Yang and Tam, 'Food Safety', 22.

[93] Xiu and Klein, 'Melamine in Milk Products', 466. See also Yang and Tam, 'Food Safety', 17 ('In most cases, fake and substandard products are not sold around the places where they are made. Instead, they are transported to other localities').

exceptions from quality testing.[94] In fact, no national food safety programme in any country appears to have routinely screened dairy products for melamine prior to autumn 2008.[95])

B. The regulatory presumptions of competition theory and their application to China

China's regulatory model generally conformed to that advanced by orthodox competition law theory. Regulation was indeed separated from the market, and for the most part from polities (at least as far as the melamine tragedy was concerned), and the market was thus allowed to pursue its competitive efficiencies without the regulatory imposition of non-economic considerations. But in China, in the context of the melamine tragedy, this model failed to work as predicted. As we shall see, this is because this model is founded on a number of presumptions about the nature of the regulatory environment that, while justified in the context of advanced industrial economies, become problematic when applied to less industrialized and more peripheral economic regions like that of China's rural raw milk producers (see also Dowdle, Ch. 1, pp. 24–33; cf. Jessop, Ch. 5).

Ultimately, the orthodox competition regulation presumes the presence of what we might call a monocratic (i.e., nationally coherent) socio-economic regulatory space (cf. Dowdle, Ch. 13, p. 307). This is the kind of social regulatory space found in the North Atlantic economies whose experiences are the principal referents from which orthodox competition theory is compiled. It is the kind of national space that is produced by industrialization, and in particular by the later stage of industrialization that has been variously termed 'managerial capitalism' or 'Fordism'.[96] It is characterized by a high degree of rationality and

---

[94] Xin and Stone, 'Chinese Probe', 1311.

[95] See Xiu and Klein, 'Melamine in Milk Products', 468 ('Although it has long been known that trace amounts of melamine occur in some food products (due to its use in certain industrial applications), the melamine scandal in China revealed that most countries throughout the world had no (or inadequate) tolerance standards for melamine in food products').

[96] Fernand Braudel, *Civilization and Capitalism, 15th–18th Century. Volume 3, The Perspective of the World*, trans. Siân Reynolds (Berkeley: University of California Press, 1992), pp. 365–8, 600–1. See also Michael W. Dowdle, 'Public Accountability in Alien Terrain: Exploring for Constitutional Accountability in the People's Republic of China', in Michael W. Dowdle (ed.), *Public Accountability: Designs, Dilemmas and Experiences* (Cambridge University Press, 2006), pp. 332–44.

homogeneity. This uniformity and homogeneity makes both society and markets more transparent and more inclusive. It allows national regulators and remote citizens to see, understand, and participate in markets and political spaces, no matter how removed they might be from their particular social environment or geographic locale.[97]

These features are critical to the effectiveness of the orthodox model of market regulation. As noted above, that model demands the segregation of market regulation – including competition regulation – from social regulation. But such a model only works if social regulation – the regulation that takes care of market externalities – can be centralized. Centralization is critical for allowing the localized cost of externalities to link up with the remote markets that create them.

Such centralization becomes increasingly difficult the less industrialized the national regulatory space is.[98] The less industrialized the national socio-economic space, the more fragmented that space will tend to be.[99] Social and economic fragmentation increases the administrative costs of centralization.[100] At the same time, however, social and market fragmentation increases the prevalence of externalities, because market fragmentation is synonymous with market exclusion. And the more a market excludes, the more opportunity there is for externalities.[101]

But, in such environments, *decentralization* of the social regulation will also be problematic, as we saw in the case of China. The more fragmented the national markets, the more likely it is that different geographies will have different governmental concerns and interests

---

[97] Dowdle, 'Public Accountability', pp. 332–44; Michael J. Piore and Charles F. Sabel, *The Second Industrial Divide: Possibilities for Prosperity* (New York: Basic Books, 1984), pp. 49–65.

[98] Cf. James Scott, *Seeing Like a State: How Certain Schemes to Improve the Human Condition Have Failed* (New Haven: Yale University Press, 1998).

[99] Eric Sean Williams, *The End of Society? Defining and Tracing the Development of Fragmentation through the Modern and into the Post-modern Era* (Ann Arbor: UMI Dissertation Publishing, 2011). See also Arslan Razmi, *Integration, Informalization, and Income Inequality in Developing Countries: Some General Equilibrium Explorations in Light of Accumulating Evidence*, Department Working Paper Series 39 (Amhurst, MA: University of Massachusetts at Amhurst Economics, 2007), available at http://scholarworks.umass.edu/econ_workingpaper/39.

[100] Charles F. Sabel, 'Learning by Monitoring: The Institutions of Economic Development', in Neil Smelser and Richard Swedberg (eds.), *The Handbook of Economic Sociology* (Princeton University Press and Russell Sage Foundation, 1994), pp. 137–65.

[101] Cf. Pan A. Yotopoulos and Sagrario L. Floro, 'Income Distribution, Transaction Costs and Market Fragmentation in Informal Credit Markets', *Cambridge Journal of Economics*, 16 (1992): 303–26.

and correspondingly less incentive to comport with a centralized regulatory framework. And, at the same time, the centre will have greater difficulty monitoring local compliance because of lack of socio-economic homogeneity across regions.[102]

As we saw, this is exactly what caused the regulatory failure that led to melamine milk adulteration in China. China tried to adopt a modern regulatory structure to regulate food safety. This involved allowing the markets to do what markets do, and trying to account for externalities, in the form of less safe food, by assigning them to other centralized regulatory regimes that operated outside the market. The problem was that China's national socio-economic space was simply too non-industrial and otherwise too fragmented to support effective centralized regulation.

And with regulation itself effectively decentralized, this encourages localities to put their own economic interests above national needs.[103] Moreover, the fragmented nature of China's regulatory system encouraged them to do so. Without a centralized social regulatory apparatus, externalities from remote regions cannot be linked back to their markets of origin. The only way that a locality can protect itself from foreign externalities is to isolate itself as much as possible from these markets. At the same time, China's decentralized economy also has limited capacity to redistribute wealth across regions.[104] Protectionism can thus be seen as a rational response, particularly on the part of poorer, more peripheral regions, to such problems of redistribution.[105]

For this reason, one significant fragmentation fault line is that which divides the poorer, production-oriented and export-oriented regions from the wealthier, consumption-oriented regions (cf. Dowdle, Ch. 1, p. 25).[106] We noted above that rural milk producing regions generally did not directly consume the milk they produced. These regions being at the upstream end of an increasingly industrialized agricultural production chain and being generally poor, their industry tends to be oriented towards export to more urban regions.[107] This is a universal characteristic of the periphery; it is not unique to China.[108]

---

[102] Cf. Scott, *Seeing Like a State*.   [103] See, e.g., Tam and Yang, 'Food Safety', 17.

[104] John Knight and Li Shi, 'Fiscal Decentralization: Incentives, Redistribution and Reform in China', *Oxford Development Studies*, 27 (1999): 5–32, 30.

[105] See, e.g., Sun Zidou, 'Causes of Trade Wars over Farm Products, Their Harmful Effects, and Suggested Solutions', *Chinese Economy*, 26 (1993): 95–104.

[106] Cf. Tam and Yang, 'Food Safety', 21–5.   [107] Ibid., 17.

[108] See generally Braudel, *Civilization and Capitalism, Volume 3*, pp. 21–44.

At the same time, one of the effects of price competition is to assign the surplus value of production to the consumer. This means that under normal (price-sensitive) market dynamics, export-oriented regions do not actually gain significant benefits from increases in productivity, since they end up exporting to other regions the added surplus value such increases produce. Recall, along these lines, that even as the national dairy industry was booming, rural producers were not moving up the value chain, and by around 2005 were actually facing a greater economic squeeze than before. This, too, further limits the utility of the orthodox model to peripheral economies.

C.   The peripheral limits of competition

Nor is this situation at all unique to China. It is in fact typical of more peripheral economies. The more peripheral national economies of Asia are often economically fragmented in regulatory terms in ways similar to China's. As in China, these economies are primarily export- and production-oriented, and they tend to be dominated by product-chain relationships with more industrialized downstream industries located outside their region.[109] They are more volatile, and less susceptible to centralization and centralized regulation.[110]

The ubiquity of regulatory fragmentation found in peripheral Asian economies suggests strongly that the orthodox competition law model that dominates global competition law discourse will often be dysfunctional in peripheral economies (see also Dowdle, Ch. 1, pp. 29–32; cf. Jessop, Ch. 5, p. 120). Because these regulatory spaces resist centralized regulation they have difficulty addressing the externalities caused when competition law focuses purely on promoting market efficiency. Regulating such markets cannot simply be about promoting economic efficiency while leaving social costs to other parts of the (centralized) regulatory system, because the centralized regulatory system will simply be unable to regulate these concerns effectively. Indeed, Tony Prosser's recent study, *The Limits of Competition Law*, reminds us that even in advanced industrial countries like that of the United Kingdom,

---

[109] See Bob Jessop and Ngai-Ling Sum, *Beyond the Regulation Approach: Putting Capitalist Economies in their Place* (Cheltenham: Edward Elgar, 2006), pp. 152–96; see also Frederic C. Deyo, Richard F. Doner, and Eric Hershberg (eds.), *Economic Governance and the Challenge of Flexibility in East Asia* (Lanham, MD: Rowman & Littlefield, 2001).

[110] See also Dowdle, 'Public Accountability', pp. 332–44.

it is sometimes necessary to temper a market's pursuit of efficiency
with pursuit of distributional fairness, because externalized regulation is
simply not able to address adequately the social implications that stem
from that market's otherwise unequal distributional tendencies.[111]

Finally, because of the weaknesses of the central regulatory system,
the more localized markets of the periphery are also more likely to have
complex social-regulatory functionalities than their counterparts in
more core economies (cf. Prosser, Ch. 10, pp. 255–8). As was the case
with the family milk farm in China, peripheral markets can be important
sources of individual social security independent of their capacity to
stimulate aggregate wealth creation.[112] This is well demonstrated in John
Gillespie's contribution to this volume (Ch. 8). It is also demonstrated
in recent work by Frederic Deyo, sometimes working with others,
comparing labour reproduction in peripheral versus core economic
environments in Asia.[113] Deyo found that in more peripheral regions,
rural agricultural markets provided an important source of security to
the migrant industrial labour being employed, with very little security,
by factories in outside regions. During the Asian economic crisis of the
late 1990s, the security these rural family farms could provide to laid-off
workers played a critical role in Thailand's efforts to weather the early
years of the crisis.[114]

For all these reasons, there is good reason to suspect that the orthodox
competition model, with its presumptions of an effective, centralized
socio-regulatory system administering a coherent, national socio-
economic regulatory space – one that is more consumption oriented
than production oriented – will often be dysfunctional when applied
to peripheral economic environments. These environments are more
likely to be export oriented, and thus will not benefit from the orthodox
theory's emphasis on promoting consumer surplus over producer surplus. They are more likely to be fragmented, and their markets more
likely to bear significant social functionalities independent of aggregate
wealth generation, and thus be unable to support the segregation of market

---

[111] Tony Prosser, *The Limits of Competition Law: Markets and Public Services* (Oxford
University Press, 2005).

[112] Cf. Polanyi, *The Great Transformation*.

[113] See, e.g., Frederic C. Deyo, 'Reforming Labor, Belaboring Reform: Structural Adjustment
in Thailand and East Asia', in Yoichiro Sato (ed.), *Growth and Governance in Asia*
(Honolulu: Asia-Pacific Center for Security Studies, 2004), pp. 97–114.

[114] See also Pasuk Phongpaichit and Chris Baker, *Thailand's Crisis* (Singapore: Singapore
Institute of Southeast Asian Studies, 2000), pp. 35–82.

regulation, with its unstated dependence on the existence of an effective centralized system of social regulation. In sum, competition regulation in the periphery should not be derived from competition regulatory norms that emerged out of core advanced industrial economies.[115]

---

[115] For example, one proposed solution to some of the problems addressed in this chapter, particularly those associated with production chain squeeze, has been cartelization. See Gale and Hu, 'Supply Chain Issues', p. 12–13; Thompson and Hu, 'Food Safety in China', p. 14. Cf. Mats Bergman, 'Antitrust, Marketing Cooperatives, and Market Power', *European Journal of Law and Economics*, 4 (1997): 73–92. See also Aravind R. Ganesh, 'The Right to Food and Buyer Power', *German Law Journal*, 11 (2010): 1190–243; Jeffrey Henderson, 'Global Production Networks, Competition, Regulation and Poverty Reduction: Policy Implications', University of Manchester, Centre on Regulation and Competition Working Paper Series no. 115, 2005. Cf. Jeffrey R. Fear, *Cartels and Competition: Neither Markets nor Hierarchies*, Working Papers Collection 07-011 (Cambridge, MA: Harvard Business School, 2006).

10

Competition law and the role of the state in East Asia

TONY PROSSER

I. Introduction: the public interest in competition law

Competition law and policy present us with a fascinating and often paradoxical mix of the apparently universal and the highly contingent. In much of the literature the goals of consumer welfare and efficiency maximization are apparently applicable to any market economy; 'there is only one economy'.[1] Yet this universality is a mirage. It is undermined by the divergences in different types of market economy revealed by the varieties of capitalism literature.[2] Perhaps even more so, it is undermined by the various intellectual bases for designing competition law: one would expect radically different systems to be inspired by, for example, ordoliberalism and the Chicago School. Conversely, at first sight institutional arrangements would appear to be highly contingent, containing major variations in, for example, the degree of distancing of key institutions from direct government intervention, and the possibility of bypassing public authorities through private enforcement (cf. Gillespie, Ch. 8). Yet this diversity is concealed by an extraordinary degree of convergence of doctrine, economic ideology (see Sum, Ch. 4), and prescribed institutional form (see Maher, Ch. 3). This appearance of unity has been brought about primarily through the use of legal transplants in the development of new national competition laws outside Europe. In earlier times the dominant transplant model tended to be that of the United States, but this has been overshadowed more recently by the success of a transplant model drawn from the competition law of the European Union (EU).

---

[1] Dani Rodrik, *One Economics, Many Recipes: Globalization, Institutions, and Economic Growth* (Princeton University Press, 2007).

[2] See Peter A. Hall and David Soskice, (eds.), *Varieties of Capitalism: The Institutional Foundations of Comparative Advantage* (Oxford University Press, 2001), and the considerable body of literature it has spawned.

Of course, the use of legal transplants has been the subject of major debate on the extent to which legal rules can be applied independently of the general social or cultural context into which they are imported. For example, in his leading work on transplants, Alan Watson has consistently emphasized the autonomy of law from a social and cultural context.[3] Thus,

> legal rules move easily and are accepted into the system without too great difficulty. This is so even when the rules come from a different kind of system ... [U]sually legal rules are not particularly devised for the particular society in which they now operate and ... this is not a matter for great concern.[4]

By contrast, Pierre Legrand has emphasized that the meaning of legal rules is given not by their form of words but by the general cultural meanings in which they operate.[5] As a result,

> At best, what can be displaced from one jurisdiction to another is, literally, a meaningless form of words. To claim more is to claim too much. In any meaningful sense of the term, 'legal transplants', therefore, cannot happen. No rule in the borrowing jurisdiction can have any significance as regards the rule in the jurisdiction from which it is borrowed.[6]

More fruitful middle ground has been established by Roger Cotterrell in attempting to classify different types of community which might shape responsiveness to transplants.[7] In this, one could for example contrast traditional communities with more instrumental ones associated with economic liberalization. Similarly, a 'community of belief' associated with Marxist-Leninist ideology may also be resistant to such instrumental forms of law. However, such resistance may be contingent and may be overcome by, for example, the need to attract direct investment from overseas. (See also Gillespie, Ch. 8, pp. 185–91.)

There is, however, a further complication facing the use of legal transplants in the competition law context; this is that there is no single

---

[3] Alan Watson, *Legal Transplants: An Approach to Comparative Law* (Edinburgh: Scottish Academic Press, 1974).

[4] Watson, *Legal Transplants*, p. 96.

[5] Pierre Legrand, 'What Legal Transplants?', in David Nelken and Johannes Feest (eds.), *Adapting Legal Cultures* (Oxford: Hart, 2001), pp. 55–70.

[6] Legrand, 'What Legal Transplants?', p. 63.

[7] Roger Cotterrell, 'Is There a Logic of Legal Transplants?' in Nelken and Feest, *Adapting Legal Cultures*, pp. 71–92.

model of competition law which can be transplanted.[8] Imelda Maher has pointed to two very different ideal types of competition law: 'There is a fundamental tension within competition law that is linked to opposing theoretical bases. One emphasizes its roots in private law and the other takes a more constitutional orientation.'[9] The first approach to competition law sees it as a means of protecting private autonomy and efficiency through preserving freedom of contract; the latter associates it with broader constraints on concentration of economic power for reasons of public interest and of pluralism.

On the first approach, competition law is likely to have little to say about actions of the state in economic management. It may assume that maximizing private autonomy simply requires minimizing the state's role; the state is to be 'rolled back' through political actions rather than made subject to a competition law essentially concerned with private economic relations. Any remaining regulation will be the task of political controls falling outside the realm of competition law (see also Dowdle, Ch. 1, pp. 29–31). The state may indeed benefit either from complete exclusion from the application of the law or from extensive exemptions. A competition law which is conceived as private law will simply not be seen as relevant to state activities.

On the second, constitutionally oriented, approach, we should expect to see a more nuanced understanding of state economic management and greater collaboration between competition law and other public law means for accountability. Competition law will recognize that there must be a balancing of, on the one hand, private autonomy and efficiency, and, on the other, the legitimate concerns of public policy (see also Dowdle, Ch. 9, pp. 217–18). As a result, it will require reasoned justifications for the balance between competition and other values, and will assess the proportionality of the outcome. This will require both private and public law techniques to be used, and competition law spans the theoretical divide between the two; it is both private and public law. It will also be embedded in a wider public law regime, including regulatory bodies

[8] David Gerber, *Global Competition: Law, Markets and Globalization* (Oxford University Press, 2010), pp. 262–9.

[9] Imelda Maher, 'Regulating Competition', in Christine Parker, Colin Scott, Nicola Lacey, and John Braithwaite (eds.), *Regulating Law* (Oxford University Press, 2004), pp. 186–206, at p. 189 (footnote omitted). See also Tony Prosser, 'Regulatory Agencies, Regulatory Legitimacy and European Private Law', in Fabrizio Cafaggi and Horatia Muir Watt (eds.), *Making European Private Law: Governance Design* (Cheltenham: Edward Elgar, 2008), pp. 235–53.

operating through law, and with an important role for the courts through judicial review or appeal. Investigations into the transplant of competition laws into Asian economies have neglected the latter, public law dimension, despite the fundamental importance of public enterprises and of state economic management in these economies. This reflects the relatively undeveloped nature of public law in the nations to be examined. By contrast, in western Europe competition law can be seen, in addition to its private law role, as forming part of a broader public law regime which imposes constraints on the operation of the state itself.

In the next section of this chapter I shall show how complex the relationships between public law and the state will be even in the relatively liberal economies of the EU, and at how many different levels competition law has to be adjusted to accommodate a special role for the state in some form. The third section provides preliminary mapping of the ways in which this accommodation has been addressed in some Asian economies, covering some nations whose competition laws have been based on west European models (Singapore, Hong Kong, Taiwan, and South Korea) and those in which marketization has yet fully to penetrate economic society (China and Vietnam). In the fourth and final section, I shall speculate on what this tells us about the relationship between the state and competition law, and shall suggest ways of taking the debate forward.

II.   Competition law and the state in western Europe

I have shown elsewhere that there are often conflicts between competition policy and other governmental goals (generally, but not exclusively, redistributive goals)[10] (see also Jessop, Ch. 5). In the pristine world of traditional economic thinking, it may be possible to separate the two and see non-competition policies as limited to external interventions through the tax and social security systems, but in practice things are not so simple and the areas of policy are inextricably intertwined (see also Dowdle, Ch. 1, pp. 29–31).[11] This goes some way to explaining the extent and variety of means by which the rigours of competition law may be shaped or relaxed by different forms of politics. Here I shall examine some of the most important examples in western European economies.

---

[10] Tony Prosser, *The Limits of Competition Law: Markets and Public Services* (Oxford University Press, 2005), chs. 1, 2.
[11] Ibid., pp. 18, 26.

First, the key institutions of competition policy may themselves be part of the central state and subject to direct political influence. The most striking example of this would be the competition law system of the United Kingdom prior to the Competition Act 1998.[12] Not only did this system have only a very limited application to public services and nationalized industries, it placed the principal responsibility for decision-making in the hands of ministers and made that decision-making highly discretionary. As one authoritative writer put it, '[t]he Secretary of State for Trade and Industry is the sun around which British competition policy orbits.'[13] Second, the tests the minister applied were not even competition-based, but rather concerned the question of whether restrictions on competition were contrary to 'the public interest'. The latter concept was almost completely undefined. On this model, competition law and in particular its enforcement were essentially matters of politics, and, although there was a role for independent institutions in the form of the Office of Fair Trading and the Monopolies and Mergers Commission, this was usually an advisory one, with the ultimate decision remaining firmly in the hands of the Secretary of State and including scope for political criteria in decision-making.

The Competition Act 1998 and the Enterprise Act 2002[14] replaced this model with a different one, in which the Office of Fair Trading and the Competition Commission were given substantial independence and substantial powers of final decision, subject to appeal to an independent 'competition court' in the form of the Competition Appeal Tribunal. The Secretary of State retained only residual responsibilities; for example for mergers affecting national security and mergers affecting media plurality. It should be noted, though, that following the banking crisis of 2007–8 a further public interest area of 'the stability of the UK financial system' was rapidly added.[15] The new system also permits private enforcement before the Competition Appeal Tribunal. It would thus seem to represent a major relocation of competition law outside politics and into a system of independent regulatory agencies reflecting closely that of the EU (and perhaps the global approach more generally; see Maher, Ch. 3). However,

---

[12] Competition Act 1998, 1998 Chapter 41.

[13] Stephen Wilks, *In the Public Interest: Competition Policy and the Monopolies and Mergers Commission* (Manchester University Press, 1999), p. 150.

[14] Enterprise Act 2002. 2002 Chapter 40.

[15] Enterprise Act 2002 (Specification of Additional Section 58 Consideration) Order 2008. 2008 No. 2645.

even after these reforms, the UK system does permit special considerations to be taken into account in several ways where matters of public
policy conflict with the law's pursuit of purely competitive markets.[16]

Subordination of economic competition to public policy may take
place, both in the United Kingdom and the EU, through limiting the
scope of application of competition law. Thus it will not apply to 'matters
which are intrinsically prerogatives of the state, services such as national
education and compulsory basic insurance schemes, and a number of
activities conducted by organizations performing largely social functions,
which are not meant to engage in industrial or commercial activity'.[17]
This may exclude certain types of activity which form part of the central
prerogatives of the state; for example, in *Belgium* v. *Humbel* the European
Court of Justice held that courses provided under a national education
system were not 'services provided for remuneration' and thus are not
subject to competition law as the state was 'not seeking to engage in
gainful activity but is fulfilling its duties towards its own population in
the social, cultural and educational fields'.[18] Similarly, the Court has held
that competition law may not apply to the provision of non-economic
regulatory activities such as air safety and anti-pollution surveillance.[19]

More commonly, the decision whether competition law applies or not
will be determined not by the nature of the activity but by the economic
environment in which it is undertaken and the reason why the good or
service is being provided. It is quite clear that ownership is irrelevant to
the scope of competition law, which applies to publicly owned enterprises
just as it applies to private ones. This was not the case with the old UK
competition law, where the nationalized industries benefited from extensive exemptions, in law and in fact, from the application of competition
law.[20] As we shall see below, the question of the extent to which

---

[16] While further reform is now being planned which seeks to replace these multiple
authorities with a single-tier Competition and Markets Authority, this will not affect
the major theme of this article. See Department for Business, Innovation & Skills, *Growth,
Competition and the Competition Regime: Government Response to Consultation*
(London: Department for Business, Innovation and Skills, March 2012).

[17] Commission of the European Communities, *Green Paper on Services of General Interest*,
COM(2003) 270 final (21 May 2003), para. 45, available at http://eur-lex.europa.eu/
LexUriServ/site/en/com/2003/com2003_0270en01.pdf.

[18] *Belgium* v. *Humbel* (Case 263/86), [1988] ECR 5365.

[19] *SAT Fluggesellschaft mbH* v. *European Org. for the Safety of Air Navigation (Eurocontrol)*,
[1994] ECR I-43 [1994]; *Diego Cali and Figli Srl* v. *Servizi Ecologici Porto di Genova SpA
(SEPG)*, [1997] ECR I-1547.

[20] Prosser, *Limits of Competition Law*, p. 43.

competition law is applied to public enterprises has been an important and difficult one in the context of Asian economies (see, e.g., Zheng, Ch. 7, pp. 148–50, describing China); however, the answer of EU law to this question is quite clear; public ownership is irrelevant to the application of the competition rules and no exemptions from them based directly on state ownership exist. Similarly, state aids fall within the EC rules on competition, regardless of whether they are paid to a public or private enterprise. However, in EU competition law what is important is whether the entity in question is engaged in economic activity and so treated as an undertaking. This has been held not to cover organizations on the basis of social solidarity, in particular social security schemes where membership was compulsory and where benefits were provided independently of contributions.[21] The boundary between economic organizations and those with an exclusively social function may be a narrow one; for example, the UK Competition Appeal Tribunal decided in the *Bettercare* case that a health trust purchasing services was acting as an undertaking engaged in economic activities as it was participating in markets (albeit highly regulated ones), using business methods of contracting; the social purpose of the purchasing was irrelevant.[22] By contrast, the European Court of Justice held that the purchase of goods for a health service based on principles of social solidarity did not constitute economic activity due to the fact that these purchases were being made in the context of the provision of free public health services that would not be resold in the market.[23]

The effect of these decisions is to give considerable discretion to a member state on the question of whether it brings a public service, notably health care, within the scope of competition law. If it chooses to operate a service predominantly on the basis of 'social solidarity', as an 'inherently uncommercial act of involuntary subsidization of one social group by another',[24] decisions of the bodies comprising it will not be covered by competition law. If, however, the state chooses to introduce competition into the provision of the service by, for example, contracting

---

[21] See, e.g., *Poucet and Pistre* v. *Assurances Générales de France and Others* (joined cases C-2159/91 and 1260/91), [1993] ECR I-637.

[22] *BetterCare Group Limited* v. *Director General of Fair Trading*, [2002] CAT 7.

[23] *Federación Española de Empresas de Tecnología Sanitaria (FENIN)* v. *Commission of the European Communities* (Case C-205/03), [2006] ECR I-6295. See also *British United Provident Association Ltd (BUPA) and Others* v. *Commission* (Case T-289/03), [2008] ECR II-81.

[24] *Sodemare and Others* v. *Regione Lombardia* (Case C-70/95), [1997] ECR I-3395, Attorney General's Opinion para. 29.

out services to competing suppliers or by creating a competitive internal market, EU competition law will apply as these bodies will be classed as undertakings. It would seem clear that the English health service now falls within competition law as a result of continuing reforms to increase competition in that service.[25] The difficulty lies in the fact that many, perhaps most, systems are founded on a mix of market and social-solidarity-based provisions, and the point at which they will fall within the competition rules will be difficult to establish.

Finally, the promotion of economic competition may be subordinated to matters of public policy through the internalization of public policy and public service concerns within competition law itself. Clearly the pre-reform UK system of competition law discussed above achieved this through the role of the public interest test. The EU Mergers Regulation also permits public interest considerations to be taken into account when a potential merger has effects in relation to public security, media plurality and quality, or other 'legitimate interests' of the member state.[26]

However, it is in relation to the general application of competition law outside mergers that the scope for public interest considerations to be applied by government has been most fully debated. The most important provision is Article 106(3) of the Treaty on the Functioning of the European Union (TFEU),[27] which provides that the competition rules are applicable to

> [u]ndertakings entrusted with the operation of services of general economic interest ... insofar as the application of such rules does not obstruct the performance, in law or in fact, of the particular tasks assigned to them. The development of trade must not be affected to such an extent as would be contrary to the interests of the Union.

This was supplemented by the Treaty of Amsterdam in 1997, requiring that the member states and the Union 'shall take care that such services [of general economic interest] operate on the basis of principles and conditions which enable them to fulfil their missions'.[28] In 2009, the

---

[25] See Nina Boeger and Tony Prosser, 'United Kingdom', in Markus Krajewski, Ulla Neergaard, and Johan van de Gronden (eds.), *The Changing Legal Framework for Services of General Interest in Europe: Between Competition and Solidarity* (Nijmegen: T.M.C. Asser, 2009), pp. 357–82.

[26] Council Regulation (EC) No. 139/2004 of 20 January 2004 on the control of concentrations between undertakings, [2004] OJ L24, 1–22, Art. 21(4).

[27] Treaty on the Functioning of the European Union (Consolidated Versions) (hereinafter TFEU), [2008] OJ C 115/1–12.

[28] Treaty of Amsterdam amending the Treaty on European Union, [1997] OJ C 340/1, Art. 16; TFEU, Art. 7d.

Lisbon Treaty further amended the TFEU and a Protocol was added on Services of General Interest.[29]

The meaning of 'services of general economic interest' and the added scope this provision gives to member states for the implementation of public service goals which would otherwise conflict with competition law are complex questions and have been much debated.[30] What is significant to note for the purposes of this chapter is that it has been left to each member state to determine which particular activities fall under this exception, subject to review by the EU courts on the basis of manifest error. However, a proportionality test is then applied to the action taken to ensure that an exception to the competition rules is indeed necessary to permit successful operation of the services of general economic interest.

EU competition law is thus applied to the state in ways very different from an open-ended public interest test which would give a national government freedom in determining when and where competition rules apply. However, there is still a recognition that some state action may require exemption from those rules. Returning to the two different theoretical bases for competition law referred to in the opening section of this chapter, competition law in the EU is applied to public services in a way which makes it more like public law than private law. It does not simply require that individual autonomy and economic efficiency are protected through free markets; rather it makes an assessment of the role of the state and applies to it familiar public law tools. Thus it will ask whether competition law is applicable at all, thereby accepting that in some areas public forms of control and accountability are more appropriate than competition, for example where the governing principle is social solidarity in service provision rather than the operation of competitive markets. If competition law is in principle applicable, but the state has attempted to limit its application in pursuit of a public purpose, the proportionality requirement means that governments must provide fully reasoned justifications for action infringing the rules, and these justifications are subject to examination by authorities other than the state itself in the form of the European Commission and the EU courts.

---

[29] Treaty of Lisbon, Protocol on Services of General Interest, [2007] OJ C 306/158; TFEU, Art. 14. See also Dragana Damjanovic and Bruno de Witte, 'Welfare Integration through EU Law: The Overall Picture in the Light of the Lisbon Treaty', in Ulla Neergaard, Ruth Nielsen, and Lynn Roseberry, (eds.), *Integrating Welfare Functions into EU Law - From Rome to Lisbon*, (Copenhagen: DJØF Publishing, 2009), pp. 53–94.

[30] See also Prosser, *Limits of Competition Law*, chs. 6–7.

In effect, competition law limits the role of the state to one of articulating definable, targeted, and proportionate exemptions from competition rules, rather than permitting it to locate public activities outside the reach of those rules entirely. This is most apparent in the important state aids case of *Altmark*, where the European Court of Justice stipulated demanding conditions requiring transparency in the provision of financial compensation for the delivery of services of general economic interest.[31]

This public law role of competition law forms part of a wider public law regime. Within the United Kingdom, appeal to the Competition Appeal Tribunal has permitted wide-ranging examination of the decisions of the competition authorities, supplemented by judicial review. At EU level, apart from the examination of national action by the Commission, the Commission itself is subject to far-reaching judicial review by the EU courts. Moreover, the role of the general competition authorities will be supplemented by a range of other regulatory agencies. This is especially the case at the national level, where the creation of a network of independent national regulatory authorities has been a central theme of the liberalization of public utilities. In the United Kingdom, regulatory agencies are given 'concurrent powers' to apply competition law restrictions in their own sectors. The development of agencies is also increasing at the EU level, where, despite restrictions on the ability of the Commission to delegate powers to agencies, in the areas of public utility services and of financial services a wider range of powers has now been given to new regulatory bodies.[32]

Returning to the theme of legal transplants, one important question is the extent to which transplants of competition law from western Europe to East Asia carry with them this public law dimension. Do the competition regimes permit independent assessment of the proportionality of exemptions of competition law? Are they part of a wider regime of public law institutions which complement each other's decisions and permit scrutiny of them? Or do they simply import a private law vision of competition law, which leaves the role of the state untouched and is concerned only with private relationships? I shall return to this point in

---

[31] *Altmark Trans GmbH and Regierungspräsidium Magdeburg* v. *Nahverkehrsgesellschaft Altmark GmbH* (Case C-280/00), [2003] ECR I-7747.

[32] Leigh Hancher and Saskia Lavrijssen, 'Networks on Track: From European Regulatory Networks to European Regulatory "Network" Agencies', *Legal Issues of European Integration*, 36 (2009): 23–55, at 36; Eilis Ferran, 'Understanding the New Institutional Architecture of EU Financial Market Supervision', University of Cambridge Faculty of Law Working Paper 29/2011, 2011.

my conclusion after considering the different ways in which a number of Asian competition law systems have treated the activities of the state.

III.   Competition law and the state in selected Asian economies[33]

As shown in the earlier chapters in this volume on Japan, China, and Vietnam, legal transplants have played a central role in the competition law of many Asian economies. While the US model had some early influence, that of the EU has recently become especially influential (directly or through UK law), sometimes applied in almost a literal fashion. The use of rules and principles imported into a radically different environment should provide opportunities for fascinating and revealing research as the systems bed down, a point to which I shall return in the next section of this chapter.

The jurisdictions to be studied fall into three groups: those strongly influenced by recent UK practice and law (Singapore and Hong Kong); those with older competition laws based on a mixture of US and EU law (Taiwan and South Korea); and those with economies which are not fully marketized and which have a major state sector and a distinctive competition law structure reflecting this (China and Vietnam).

A.   Jurisdictions adopting the UK model: Singapore and Hong Kong

I shall examine first of all two Asian jurisdictions which have adopted the model adopted by the United Kingdom after the reforms commenced by the Competition Act 1998. These are Singapore and Hong Kong. In one sense these legislative transplants appear to have been largely successful, in that the effect of the transplanted law has been largely along the lines intended: the construction of a regulatory regime for competition that, in

---

[33] For an introduction to the use of competition law in Asian economies see Mark Furse, *Antitrust Law in China, Korea and Vietnam* (Oxford University Press, 2009). I have benefited from the papers which form the basis of the other chapters of this book, and from the Global Competition Law and Economics Series Conference, 'Competition Law and the State', organized by University College London and the University of Hong Kong, Hong Kong, 18–19 March 2011 (papers are available at www.ucl.ac.uk/laws/global-competition/hongkong-2011/secure/index.shtml). I also refer to two useful Ph.D. theses generously referred to me by my colleague Brenda Sufrin: Corinne Li-Anne Chew, 'A Singaporean Competition Law', unpublished Ph.D. thesis, King's College London, 2006; Hua Su, 'Competition Law and Policy in a Transitional China: Transplantation and Localisation', unpublished Ph.D. thesis, Queen Mary, University of London, 2008.

relation to private enterprise, resembles that of the Anglo-European West. Even here, however, there need to be substantial caveats. First, the Hong Kong legislation faced difficulties in passing the legislature before it was enacted in June 2012. The second caveat is that both Singapore and Hong Kong have quite atypical economies; both resemble city states with considerable domestic and regulatory autonomy, and both host very advanced and modernized economies driven by a highly globalized trading base. Third, and most importantly for this chapter, there are significant differences from the UK and European models in both the degree of independence of the competition authorities and the treatment of public enterprise.

1. Singapore

Singapore has traditionally had a major reliance on state enterprises in the form of statutory boards and government-linked corporations with a state shareholding. These appear to have been run efficiently and within the framework of a market economy.[34]

Singapore's Competition Act,[35] enacted in 2004 and revised in 2006, is modelled directly on the UK Competition Act 1998, which of course is itself directly based on what are now Arts. 101–102 of the TFEU. It contains prohibitions of anti-competitive agreements and abuse of a dominant position. The Singapore law adopts a broad definition of an undertaking covered by the competition rules which is wide enough to include the activities of state-owned companies; the definition is in fact itself derived directly from EU case law rather than the UK statute.[36] Also drawing on the TFEU and adopting its provisions which are also contained in UK law, the Act contains a limited exception for undertakings entrusted with the operation of services of economic interest; it includes a further exclusion of agreements and conduct made or engaged in to comply with a legal requirement.[37] There is a further exclusion which comes into operation where the Minister of Trade and Industry makes an order excluding agreements or conduct on the ground that there are 'exceptional and compelling reasons of public policy' for doing so.[38] This is also based directly on the UK law.

---

[34] Chew, 'Singaporean Competition Law', pp. 26–32.
[35] Competition Act (Chapter 50b) (originally Act 46 of 2004; revised 2006).
[36] Chew, 'Singaporean Competition Law', p. 117. Cf. Competition Act (Singapore), s. 2(1).
[37] Competition Act (Singapore), sch. 3, para. 2(1)–(2).   [38] Ibid., sch. 3, para. 4.

There are, however, two potentially important differences between the Singapore Act and the UK model. First, section 33(4) of the Act provides that the Act's prohibitions do not apply to agreements, activities, or conduct on the part of the government or any statutory body, or any person acting on their behalf. Statutory bodies may be brought into the scope of the Act by ministerial order. This exclusion has been interpreted narrowly by the Competition Commission Singapore: it was decided, for example, that a government-owned ticketing company accused of abuse of dominance did not act on behalf of the government or a statutory body, and so was in breach of the Act when it imposed exclusive purchasing obligations on a statutory body.[39] Second, in the United Kingdom the major utility regulators in the fields of electronic communications, energy, rail, and water (and, soon, health care) possess 'concurrent powers' to apply the Act's prohibitions within their sectors. Thus the UK statute attempts to create a coherent body of law which applies to public utilities as it does to other enterprises. In the case of Singapore, the prohibitions simply do not apply where 'other written law, or code of practice issued under any written law, relating to competition gives another regulatory authority jurisdiction in the matter'.[40] Today, this exception is limited to the regulation of the post, water, bus and rail transport, cargo depots, and some banking activities covered by other regulators.[41] This is, however, less important than would appear, as the regulators in these sectors have developed their own competition codes similar in effect to the provisions of the Competition Act. Similarly, the Act's prohibition of anti-competitive mergers does not apply to these regulated industries.[42]

Enforcement of the Singapore legislation is carried out by the Competition Commission Singapore with an appeal to a Competition Appeal Board, again similar to the UK regime. Private enforcement is possible in the Singapore courts following a decision by the Commission that there

---

[39] See Competition Commission Singapore, 'Notice of Infringement Decision: Abuse of a Dominant Position by SISTIC.com Pte Ltd', s. 4(2) (4 June 2010). See generally Yena Lim, 'Competition Law and State Regulation: Setting the Stage and Focus on State-owned Companies', paper delivered at the Global Competition Law and Economics Series Conference, 'Competition Law and the State', Hong Kong, 19–21 March 2011.

[40] Competition Act (Singapore), sch., 3, para. 5. See generally Chew, 'Singaporean Competition Law', pp. 118–20, 305–6.

[41] Chew, 'Singaporean Competition Law', pp. 118–20, 305–6. See also Competition Act (Singapore), sch. 3, para. 5.

[42] Competition Act (Singapore), s. 54 and sch. 4.

has been an infringement of a statutory prohibition.[43] The Singapore Act, however, gives wide powers of general direction to the relevant minister, the Minister of Trade and Industry. Such general directions may relate to the Commission's policy on the performance of its functions and the discharge of its duties, although the directions may not be inconsistent with the provisions of the Competition Act itself.[44] No such provision appears in the UK Competition Act, previous powers of ministerial direction having been repealed by the Enterprise Act 2002. Indeed, the Singapore provisions are more similar to those that applied to the former UK nationalized industries than to today's independent competition authorities. The Commission is appointed at the minister's discretion, and appointments may be revoked by the minister at any time 'if he considers such revocation necessary in the interest of the effective or economical performance of the functions of the Commission under this Act or in the public interest'.[45] Once again, this is in marked contrast to the position in the United Kingdom, where, although appointments to the Office of Fair Trading are made by the Secretary of State following the Nolan procedures (requiring open advertisement, transparent interviewing, and oversight by an external assessor), members may only be removed on the ground of incapacity or misbehaviour, thereby preventing dismissal on the grounds of policy differences with the minister.[46]

Overall, then, the special exemptions for the government and statutory bodies and for regulated sectors have had a relatively limited effect, and do not provide a blanket exclusion for publicly owned companies. The major difference from the United Kingdom in the Singapore competition legislation is the relative lack of formal independence of the enforcement machinery. One way to conceive this lack of regulatory independence is as a means of ensuring that compelling state policies are adequately reflected in the competition law regime. We shall see that this is broadly consistent with what we find in the other Asian jurisdictions examined below. And, as will be discussed later, such compromising of regulatory independence may represent a distinctly Asian way of ensuring that the regulatory pursuit of competition does not become absolute, but is always conducted within a larger regulatory environment that recognizes the existence of valid but competing state interests. The question then arises of how transparently the balancing process between competition and

---

[43] Ibid., s. 86(1).   [44] Ibid., s. 8.
[45] Ibid., sch. 1, para. 5.   [46] Enterprise Act 2002, sch. 2, para. 3(2).

other policies takes place. Otherwise the legislation is virtually a direct transplant from the United Kingdom, and in principle can potentially be applied to the activities of public bodies.

2. Hong Kong

After an initial reluctance to adopt a competition law and reliance instead on the open nature of its economy, the Hong Kong government introduced a Competition Bill into the Legislative Council in July 2010. It faced significant opposition, but passed into law – the Competition Ordinance[47] – on 13 June 2012. The Ordinance is even more closely based on the UK Competition Act than is the case of the Singapore legislation. It prohibits conduct which prevents, restricts, or distorts competition in Hong Kong taking the form of anti-competitive agreements or abuse of a dominant position, and prohibits mergers that substantially lessen competition (although initially only in relation to the telecommunications industry). In principle, it applies to undertakings generally, irrespective of ownership, as in the United Kingdom. There are limited exemptions, notably, as is the case in EU and UK law, for agreements or conduct on the part of undertakings entrusted with the operation of services of general economic interest or undertaken to comply with legal requirements. There is also an exemption where action is based on exceptional and compelling reasons of public policy, but only on the basis of an order made by the Chief Executive indicating where this exemption will apply, an exemption which is also similar to the position in UK law.[48] However, there is an exemption for 'all statutory bodies', although this is specified as not including companies, and statutory bodies may be brought within the scope of the legislation by order of the Chief Executive in Council.[49] Such an order may, however, only be made in limited circumstances, in particular, only where the statutory body is engaging in an economic activity in direct competition with another undertaking, and an order cannot be made in relation to bodies directly related to the provision of an essential public service or the implementation of public policy.[50] The power to apply the legislation to statutory bodies is thus considerably more limited than in Singapore. This is of considerable potential importance, given the existence of more

---

[47] Competition Ordinance (Hong Kong), Ordinance No. 14 of 2012.
[48] Competition Act 1998 (UK), sch. 3, para. 7.
[49] Competition Ordinance (Hong Kong), s. 3.   [50] Ibid., s. 5(2).

than five hundred such bodies in Hong Kong exercising regulatory and economic functions.[51]

Enforcement is through a Competition Commission and a Competition Tribunal. The latter has a greater power than its UK counterpart (the Competition Appeal Tribunal), as it has sole power to decide on breaches of the prohibitions rather than being limited to hearing appeals. In the original version of the Bill private enforcement was to be possible, either as a follow-on action after a finding of breach of the law by the authorities, or on a stand-alone basis without the need for such a finding. However, after criticisms that stand-alone actions could be used by large companies to harass SMEs, amendments to the Bill in early 2012 limited private enforcement to follow-on actions.[52]

The Tribunal 'consists of the judges of the Court of First Instance . . . by virtue of their appointments as such judges'.[53] It 'has the same jurisdiction to grant remedies and reliefs, equitable or legal, as the Court of First Instance',[54] with appeal directly to the Court of Appeal[55] (part of the High Court, which sits at the middle tier of Hong Kong's three-tiered judicial system). Thus there is more independent enforcement of the legislation than is the case in Singapore.

As in the case of Singapore, the Hong Kong provisions are directly shaped by its highly marketized and globalized economy and by the influence of the UK legal tradition. This does not, however, explain why the Bill has faced a substantial degree of opposition in the Legislative Council, both from large enterprises and SMEs.[56] Such opposition explains, for example, the absence of a general merger regime from the legislation. It appears to have been based, publicly at least, on opposition in principle on the grounds that the law would infringe 'economic liberty', but also from extensive lobbying from large companies fearing the effects of the law on them, and from SMEs fearing that it would be used to harass them by larger competitors. Effective lobbying is facilitated by the heavy representation of business in the Legislative Council. By contrast, consumer interest is weak and lacks representation in the political process, but it remains to be seen to what extent implementation

---

[51] Mark Williams, 'Hong Kong's Competition Bill: Lobbying, Opposition, Politics', paper delivered at the Global Competition Law and Economics Series Conference, 'Competition Law and the State', Hong Kong, 19–21 March 2011.

[52] Competition Ordinance (Hong Kong), s. 110(1).   [53] Ibid., s. 135(1).

[54] Ibid., s. 142(2).   [55] Ibid., s. 154(1).

[56] See generally Williams, 'Hong Kong's Competition Bill', from which this paragraph draws heavily.

will gain political support. Anyway, there is limited scope for its application to statutory bodies and this may be of considerable importance. While Hong Kong's Competition Ordinance does strongly reflect the provisions of UK law, the context in which it operates is radically different.

In contrast to Singapore, the enforcement machinery for competition law in the Hong Kong Ordinance is relatively independent. This may reflect the effect of UK legal tradition, and also the great degree of scepticism that exists both in Hong Kong society as a whole and the Hong Kong business community regarding the Hong Kong government's capacity to insulate its regulation of the economy from mainland political pressures.

B. Nations adopting other Western models: Taiwan and South Korea

The next two nations for examination, while possessing developed competition law systems, have not been influenced by UK experience in the same way. Both Taiwan and South Korea have competition law systems which derive from an accretional layering of European (particularly German ordoliberal) and US (largely neoliberal) influences. In these cases also, we can see some tempering of competition concerns in relation to public bodies similar to that noted in the two jurisdictions discussed above. In Taiwan, this tempering comes about both from a rejection of regulatory independence (as in Singapore) and from the possibility of internalizing public interest concerns into competition decision-making. In South Korea, it comes about primarily by partly insulating a portion of the economy from the reach of the competition regime, namely that portion occupied by South Korea's distinctive *chaebol* conglomerates.

1.   Taiwan

The competition law regime in Taiwan is derived primarily from the US model, although its basic principles are compatible with those of the United Kingdom and the EU as well. Like US antitrust law, Taiwan's Fair Trade Act,[57] initially promulgated in 1991, applies to 'enterprises' rather than to 'undertakings'. These are defined as including companies, sole proprietorships and partnerships, trade associations, and 'any other person or organization engaging in transactions through the provision of goods and services'.[58] This appears to be wide enough to include state-owned enterprises. The Act prohibits concerted action between enterprises,

---

[57] Fair Trade Act (Gongping Jiaoyi Fa) (Taiwan) (1991).   [58] Ibid., Art. 2.

unless it meets certain requirements discussed below. The legislation also prohibits various forms of abuse of market power by a monopolistic enterprise, and there is a system of merger control.[59] The Act has been amended recently to increase penalties substantially and to establish a leniency programme for whistle-blowers.

There is, however, an exemption from the application of the Act where another law governs competition, provided that the latter does not conflict with the legislative purposes of the Fair Trade Act.[60] Furse notes that

> [t]his does not create a general exemption from [the Act], which has general application to all economic sectors, although the requirements at various parts of [the Act] to balance the public interest against any competitive harms may mean that various industries, such as those relating to sensitive national interests, are not constrained by the oper-ation of [the Act].[61]

Thus the law allows conflicting public interest considerations to penetrate the competition regime, so long as they are expressed in legislation. Guidance issued by the Fair Trade Commission noted that the Act does not apply to public law actions taken by the executive branch of government, but suggested that it was applicable to executive government provision of products or services which have market value or charge fees.[62] Furse also notes that the legislation applies to some, but not all, emanations of the state and that its application is not always consistent, with the Act having been applied in part to a state bookshop but not a government-owned printing unit, for example.[63]

As the above quotation suggests, the Taiwan legislation does go some way to accommodate public interest considerations by internalizing them within the decision-making process rather than in exemptions from the legislation itself. For example, Article 1 of the Act provides that its purpose is 'maintaining trading order, protecting consumers' interests, ensuring fair competition, and promoting economic stability and prosperity'. It has been suggested that this has permitted decisions to reflect mercantilist logic, or the protection of employee welfare, or social

---

[59] Fair Trade Act (Taiwan), Arts. 11–13; see also Furse, *Antitrust Law*, pp. 177–97.
[60] Fair Trade Act (Taiwan), Art. 46.   [61] Furse, *Antitrust Law*, p. 140.
[62] See Fair Trade Commission (Taiwan), 'Criteria for Applying the Fair Trade Act to Private Law Acts by the Executive Government Entities', 6 April 1995, available at www.ftc.gov. tw/internet/english/doc/docDetail.aspx?uid=743&docid=10251.
[63] Furse, *Antitrust Law*, p. 140.

customs, or the maintenance of employment.[64] Unlike in the case of US legislation, the prohibition on concerted actions between enterprises does not apply where action falling within a set of specified categories is 'beneficial to the economy as a whole and is in the public interest', and approval has been given by the Fair Trade Commission.[65] However, the categories are relatively narrow and do not amount to an overarching public interest test. The greater apparent concern with recognizing competing aspects of the public interest (compared with the laws of Singapore or Hong Kong) may have to do with the earlier drafting of the law. The Taiwan legislation was passed in 1991 (its drafting dating to the early 1980s), before the more undiluted neoliberalism of the 'Washington Consensus' would come to be seen as the global norm (cf. Sum, Ch. 4, pp. 81–4).

The existence of the power of the authorities to consent to some types of concerted action makes the nature of the administrative institutions particularly important. The main one is the Fair Trade Commission. This is set up as part of the government under the administration of the Executive Cabinet rather than as an independent regulatory agency. The chair of the Commission holds the rank of cabinet minister; appointments are made by the president on the recommendation of the premier.[66] This structuring of the Fair Trade Commission as part of the government rather than as an independent agency may reflect a greater concern for the need to ensure that competing matters of public interest are given due consideration in the administration of the competition regime. However, in practice, according to one assessment, the Commission 'has made substantial progress in promoting competition policies to the general population and effectively enforcing the new law, despite initial scepticism that it would be unable to operate'.[67]

2. South Korea

In the case of South Korea, competition law exists within a broader constitutional framework. Article 119 of the South Korean Constitution

---

[64] Mark Williams, *Competition Policy and Law in China, Hong Kong and Taiwan* (Cambridge University Press, 2005), pp. 384–5, cited in Furse, *Antitrust Law*, p. 136.

[65] Fair Trade Act (Taiwan), Art. 14(1). For detailed discussion, see Furse, *Antitrust Law*, pp. 148–52.

[66] Furse, *Antitrust Law*, pp. 137–40.

[67] Mark Williams, 'Competition Policy: One Theory, Three Systems', *China Perspectives*, 51 (2004): 51–63, 55.

states that the economic order is based on respect for the freedom and creative initiative of enterprises and individuals in economic affairs, while also setting out the power of the state to regulate economic affairs within the framework of a free and fair market.[68] As a reflection of this, South Korea's competition law has historically been more similar to that of the EU, particularly that of Germany, although it may now be gravitating closer to the more neoliberal model of the United States.[69] The Monopoly Regulation and Fair Trade Act 1980,[70] which has been extensively amended, prohibits horizontal agreements in the form of 'improper cartels' and 'unfair business practices', as well as 'abuse of market dominance' and some unfair trade practices not linked to dominance. There is also a system of merger control. More like the American system, the legislation applies to 'enterprisers', defined as 'a person who operates a manufacturing business, a service business, or any other business'; it also includes officers or others acting as their agents. This is treated as covering all sectors, including government entities operating in commercial areas.[71]

Particular industrial sectors can be removed from the scope of the Act by legislation, and there is a general exemption for conduct carried out in accordance with any other legislation; an example would be the specific legislation regulating competition in the telecommunications field.[72] Exemptions from the Act's prohibition of horizontal agreements can be granted by the Fair Trade Commission, the national body responsible for administering the competition law, on broader grounds than under Article 101 of the TFEU, including industry rationalization and industrial restructuring. Such exemptions have rarely been granted and have been refused even in some cases involving direct government initiatives.[73] There thus seems only to be limited scope in practice for internalizing broader public interest considerations.

As noted above, South Korea's competition regime is administered by the Fair Trade Commission. The Commission is headed by a chair and vice-chair appointed by the president on the basis of recommendations made by the prime minister. The legislation states that the holders of

[68] See also Furse, *Antitrust Law*, p. 215.
[69] Gerber, *Global Competition*, pp. 221–2.
[70] Monopoly Regulation and Fair Trade Act [Dokcheom gyuje mit gongjeong georae beomnyul] (South Korea), Act No. 3320 (as amended).
[71] Monopoly Regulation and Fair Trade Act (South Korea), Art. 2(1).
[72] Ibid., Art. 58.
[73] Furse, *Antitrust Law*, pp. 226–7.

these two posts are considered to be 'political appointees', making the Commission more like an entity of government than an independent regulatory body. On the other hand, the Act also states that the Commission is established 'for the purpose of independently promoting the objectives of this Act'.[74] The remaining members are appointed on the recommendation of the chair. Regardless of the formal position, the Commission has shown considerable independence in promoting competition policy.[75] There is also some provision for private enforcement and for damages.

However, the legislation does not tell us the complete story about the actual operation of competition policy in South Korea; this will depend on the interpretation adopted of the scope of the legislation and of the degree of independence shown by the Commission. A particular form of industrial conglomerate, known as *chaebol*, has historically played a central role in the development of the South Korean economy, resembling the role that the similarly structured *keiretsu* have played in postwar Japan's economic development (cf. Vande Walle, Ch. 6, p. 140). These *chaebol* have been deliberately fostered by the South Korean government since the 1960s as part of South Korea's drive towards a globally competitive economy. Their existence thus results in a high degree of economic concentration that nevertheless operates with government support. The Act has special provisions relating to *chaebol*, for example prohibiting 'undue internal dealings', limiting intra-group transactions and imposing ceilings on shareholdings. However, these have been circumvented and, on a number of occasions, relaxed.[76] There has historically been political pressure towards informally immunizing *chaebol*, at least partially, from the operations of the existing competition regime, although this has been weakening more recently.[77]

The *chaebol* bring us to what is sometimes regarded as the most well-known, distinguishing element of Asian competition policy – the use of protected economic conglomerates to promote economic development and international economic competitiveness. Because of their express

---

[74] Monopoly Regulation and Fair Trade Act 1980 (South Korea), Arts. 37(3), 35(1). See Furse, *Antitrust Law*, pp. 217–18.

[75] Gerber, *Global Competition*, p. 221.

[76] See Ohseung Kwon, 'Retrospect and Prospect on Korean Competition Law', *Journal of Korean Law*, 4 (2005): 1–28, 20–8.

[77] Gerber, *Global Competition*, p. 222.

role in promoting international competitiveness, these conglomerates are generally portrayed as alternative – if perhaps flawed – pathways to promoting competition. But they can also be seen in a different light, one more relevant to the focus of this chapter. They are intended to promote not only competitiveness, but also industrial upgrading independent of present levels of competitiveness (cf. Dowdle, Ch. 1, pp. 27–9). And in this sense, they, too, work to further a 'public interest' which, as we saw in the context of Europe and the United Kingdom, may be seen as lying outside, and perhaps even in contradiction to, the direct reach of classical competition law. Indeed, this kind of Asian conglomerate is associated with other social policy concerns in addition to industrial upgrading that similarly lie outside, and may be contrary to, those of competition law, such as macroeconomic stabilization, and providing social and economic stability and social welfare protection for the workforce (cf. Dowdle, Ch. 1, pp. 30–2, 34).

C.   Countries that are incompletely marketized: China and Vietnam

The final two states to be discussed have economic contexts which depart radically from those examined so far. They are different in two respects. First, both are in the process of transition from reliance on state planning. Second, both are more 'peripheral' in the context of Asian capitalism; they are more upstream and less developed. These two conditions make their economies significantly less marketized and less completely penetrated by the dynamic of free market exchange compared with the countries examined earlier. They have embraced Anglo-European forms of competition regulation with distinct ambivalence, and with a pronounced concern for the need to balance the promotion of economic competition with competing state concerns. Both have chosen to do this primarily by isolating significant areas of their economies, notably the state-run sector, from their competition law regimes.

1.   China

Although the Chinese economy and political system are still organized on very divergent models from more westernized Asian systems, there has been some influence from UK and EU competition frameworks in recent reforms. Of course, the Chinese economy remains to a considerable degree politically controlled. Key features include a large number of state-run enterprises (contributing an estimated one-third of GDP) and strong regional protectionism[78] (see generally Zheng, Ch. 7, pp. 146–51).

In 2007 China enacted an Antimonopoly Law, which entered into force in 2008.[79] As with EU law, it contains prohibitions on some types of anti-competitive agreement and on abuse of dominance. But the law also sets out a much wider range of policy objectives than do the competition laws of the United Kingdom and the EU. According to Article 1,

> This Law is enacted for the purpose of preventing and restraining mon-opolistic conducts, protecting fair competition in the market, enhancing economic efficiency, safeguarding the interests of consumers and social public interest, [and] promoting the healthy development of the socialist market economy.[80]

As Furse points out, there is no mechanism for reconciling conflicts between this 'bewildering array of objectives, some of which may con-flict'[81] (cf. Zheng, Ch. 7, pp. 160–3).

Reflecting the wide range of objectives expressed to underlie the Law, the key competition law institutions – the Antimonopoly Committee and the Antimonopoly Law Enforcement Agency – are under direct state control. The former is an 'advisory and co-ordinating organ' under the control of the State Council (China's executive branch) and with close links to other ministerial and executive bodies, including the Ministry of Commerce. Its head is one of China's vice-premiers. The Antimonopoly Law Enforcement Agency shares its management and support staff with other ministries and departments.[82] There is, however, some provision for private enforcement, although at the time of writing the Chinese courts have been extremely reluctant to accept private litigation in this area.[83]

There has been considerable debate about the applicability of the Anti-monopoly Law to state enterprises[84] (see also Zheng, Ch. 7, pp. 159–60). There is no explicit exclusion of such enterprises, as the law is stated simply to be 'applicable to monopolistic conduct in economic activities'. Chapter 5 of that law, on 'Abuse of Administrative Powers to Eliminate

---

[78] For a detailed analysis of the sectoral and temporal relationships between liberalization and regulation see Roselyn Hsueh, *China's Regulatory State: A New Strategy for Global-ization* (Ithaca: Cornell University Press, 2011).

[79] Antimonopoly Law of the People's Republic of China [Fanlongduan Fa] (effective 2008).

[80] Ibid., Art. 1.   [81] Furse, *Antitrust Law*, p. 69.   [82] Ibid., pp. 70–2.

[83] Ibid., pp. 118–20.

[84] Xueguo Wen, 'Market Dominance by China's Public Utility Enterprises', *Antitrust Law Journal*, 75 (2008): 151–71.

or Restrict Competition', is directly addressed to the state sector.[85] However, the Act also provides that in the case of 'industries controlled by the state-owned economy' the state 'regulates and controls their business operations and the prices of their commodities and services so as to safeguard the interests of consumers and promote technical progress'.[86]

The result appears to be that, at least in the case of the public utility services which combine the role of business operators and industry administrators, the final determination of whether there has been a breach of the Antimonopoly Law on the part of these state sector enterprises is itself an administrative question that is to be determined by the state entity running the enterprise. In this sense, 'the abuse of privileged market status of [public utility enterprises] is woven into the system reform [of these enterprises] and administrative monopoly in China'[87] (see also Zheng, Ch. 7, pp. 156–7). In addition to the Antimonopoly Law, China's Anti-Unfair Competition Law of 1993 also prohibits public utility enterprises from some types of abuse of a dominant position, but the penalty is an administrative one, at most a small fine.[88] There are also wide public interest exceptions to the prohibition on monopoly agreements.[89]

What all this suggests is that, in China, the influence of public policies that might compete with the promotion of economic competition is particularly strong, not only in comparison with Anglo-European models, but even in comparison with the other Asian countries examined above. And, in this sense, there are interesting parallels between China's maintenance of a distinctly state-controlled sector of its economy and the state-supported maintenance of economically dominant conglomerates associated with Japan and South Korea. In both cases, the alternative capitalisms represented by such practices are intended, at least in part, to serve social and developmental public policy interests that are seen as existing in tension with neoliberal models of economic competition. In the case of China, the state economic sector is theoretically justified by its alleged superiority in addressing the non-economic concerns of

---

[85] Antimonopoly Law (China), Arts. 32–37. See also Su, 'Competition Law', pp. 97–101.
[86] Antimonopoly Law (China), Arts. 2, 7. See also Furse, *Antitrust Law*, pp. 13, 73–4.
[87] Wen, 'Market Dominance', p. 155. See also Antimonopoly Law (China), Art. 51, which gives final determination of violations by administrative bodies or others acting under law or administrative regulation to the supervising authority.
[88] Anti-unfair Competition Law of the People's Republic of China [Fanbu Zhengdang Jingzheng Fa], Art. 6. See also Wen, 'Market Dominance', 166.
[89] Antimonopoly Law (China), Art. 15. See generally Furse, *Antitrust Law*, pp. 83–5.

employment stability and worker welfare (see also Zheng, Ch. 7, pp. 153–6). It is also portrayed as a superior economic device for promoting industrial transformation. Whether such claims are themselves justified in practice, or even whether they honestly represent the true economic thinking of China's political class, is of course an open question. But in its theoretical affinity with Japan and South Korea's distinctive use of economic conglomerates, China's continued reliance on a state-run economic sector could be seen as representing a more extreme manifestation of a distinctly Asian way of integrating possibly non-economic, public interests into its competition law framework.

2.   Vietnam

A little can be added here about Vietnam, which is in some ways analogous to China as a transitional economy, although without China's rapid industrialization and entry to global markets. Here a Law on Competition was passed in 2004 and came into effect in 2005. The Law prohibits some types of anti-competitive agreement, abuse of dominance, and mergers resulting in market shares of over 50 per cent, subject to exceptions. But, as in the case of China, it also requires that the promotion of economic competition is conditioned by other considerations. Article 4(2) of the Law provides that competition

> must be undertaken on the principles of honesty; non-infringement of the interests of the State, the public interest, and the lawful rights and interests of enterprises and consumers; and compliance with the provisions of this Law.

The Law explicitly applies to 'enterprises conducting business in State monopoly industries and sectors' and to the public utility sectors, although in the latter case it does not apply where there is regulation by other laws.[90] The Law also makes it clear, however, that in the state-monopolized sectors the administration retains the role of setting, selling, or purchasing prices and also retains control of public utility enterprises, thereby effectively exempting them. But enterprises in these sectors will be subject to the general requirements of the competition laws where they undertake activities outside the sectors.[91] A further provision of the Law is directed at state management agencies, setting out a number of prohibitions on anticompetitive activities on their part, notably forbidding them to force an

---

[90] Competition Law [Luật Cuộc thi] (Vietnam) (effective 2005), Art. 2(1).
[91] Ibid., Art. 15. See generally Furse, *Antitrust Law,* pp. 307, 328.

enterprise, organization, or individual to purchase or sell goods or services from an enterprise appointed by the agency. This does not, however, apply to goods and services belonging to a state monopoly.[92] The enforcement machinery as a whole under the Law is characterized by a lack of independence, and some decisions, notably those relating to exemptions, may be taken only by the relevant minister or by the Prime Minister.[93]

The overall effect of the Vietnamese law is thus to confirm the conclusions drawn from the study of China: the administration retains the central role in the regulation of the state-monopolized sectors and there is no independent enforcement machinery for the law. The law may, however, be applied to areas where liberalization has taken place. Once more, the protection of the state sector from the full scope of competition law chimes in with a more general Asian approach to the protection of public interests other than neoliberal competitive markets.

IV.   A structure for analysis of competition law and the state in Asian economies

Competition law transplants in Asia come from a variety of UK and EU models. However, with the possible exception of Hong Kong, all the Asian systems examined above display distinctive structural sensitivities which allow public interest and public policy concerns significantly to penetrate and influence the competition law regime. In Singapore, Taiwan, China, and Vietnam, for example, this is reflected in the fact that the competition agency is not independent but is embedded in government. In Taiwan it is also reflected in legal space for a distinctive combination of the neoliberal US antitrust model with devices for protecting public policy concerns. In South Korea, China, and Vietnam it is reflected in the practice of isolating significant economic sectors from the reach of competition law – the *chaebol* in the case of South Korea, and the state-run sector in the cases of China and Vietnam.

It follows that, as David Gerber has shown in Chapter 2, while the transplants themselves superficially suggest significant convergence with US–UK–EU models, this is misleading. Even where the basic structures seem similar, there is no reason to suppose that the application of competition law to the state and its public bodies will be the same in each of the systems. Given that most Asian competition laws have only recently been

---

[92] Competition Law (Vietnam), Art.6.
[93] Ibid., Arts 7, 25. See generally Furse, *Antitrust Law*, pp. 28, 308–10.

enacted, and that many of their key provisions remain highly ambiguous, there is certainly plenty of scope for further blurring of market and state in the actual application of the laws. Indeed, the country-specific chapters in this volume all show very vividly how, even where Asian competition frameworks seem convergent with Western models in terms of legislative and bureaucratic structure, considerable divergence often lurks just below the surface.

This leads initially to the banal but essential point that much more empirical work is needed on what happens in practice. It is important that this work be carried out with sensitivity to the cultures of each of the countries being examined: the worst possible basis for such work would be to assume that all market economies are essentially the same ('there is only one economy') and that Western practices will and should inevitably and necessarily be replicated in what are in fact radically different economies described here. The standard institutional economics approach linked with neoliberalism, which assumes that markets are much the same everywhere, simply will not work.

A.   Legal transplants

By itself, however, empirical work is not enough. It needs to be accompanied by theoretical and conceptual work that can take us beyond the institutional economics approach. On the basis of the discussion above, there are a number of strands of theoretical work which might be particularly helpful here. The first is that of legal transplants, referred to at the beginning of this chapter. (See also Vande Walle, Ch. 6, pp. 136–43; Gillespie, Ch. 8, pp. 191–4; Gerber, Ch. 2, pp. 40, 55–6.) As we have seen, in the countries discussed there has been an attempt to transplant Western legal rules and concepts into Asian economies; sometimes the transplant has been remarkably explicit and literal. The experience here supports neither the view associated with Alan Watson that rules may be applied in a way that is largely independent of social context, nor the alternative view of transplants as inherently impossible because they inevitable fall foul of the overriding social context. The view expressed by Cotterrell is much more appealing, attempting as it does the classification of different types of community which might shape varying degrees of responsiveness to transplants[94] (see also Gillespie, Ch. 8).

---

[94] Cotterrell, 'Is there a Logic?', pp. 80–90.

Some confirmation of Cotterrell's approach is given in the country case studies above. For example, the cases of Singapore and Hong Kong suggest that competition law transplants may be more successful where the economy and society are more anglicized (a point to which I shall return in my discussion of 'stateless societies' below), globalized, open, and industrially advanced. In the more internally distinctive but still globally exposed downstream economies of Taiwan and South Korea, the regulatory characteristics of the transplanted model are more likely to be compromised by embedding it in the larger, domestic political system rather than allowing it to operate independently. In more fragmented upstream economies which lack the strong regulatory capacities of more advanced states, or in which regulation takes a radically different form from that of the West,[95] the transplants may be more likely to apply differently to different economic sectors, as the other studies in this volume on China (Zheng, Ch. 7) and Vietnam (Gillespie, Ch. 8) appear to confirm. The same will be true, of course, in economies which are transitional and thus less completely marketized. (For further elaboration on this point, see Dowdle, Ch. 13.)

B.   The concept of the state

This brings us to the role of the state. The framework set out by Cotterrell is highly relevant to the whole of competition law in Asian economies, in particular because it allows us to begin unpacking how 'the state' (which is itself a distinctive 'community' of sorts) affects the larger competition regime in ways outside the formal competition law framework. It is in the public sphere that we are likely to see particularly strong variations between Western and Asian experience, between different regions (e.g., core and periphery), and between individual states. In particular, we shall need to examine in detail the relational structure of institutional interactions, for example relations between state enterprises and the core administration.[96]

We also need to consider in more detail the concept of the state. An obvious contrast is between the Marxist-Leninist concept of the state and the liberal model associated with Western competition law. In addition, analysis of different state traditions in Europe may provide a fruitful starting point for analysis. A seminal example is the work of Kenneth Dyson, which provides an essential corrective to any assumption in the

[95] See generally Hsueh, *China's Regulatory State.*
[96] See e.g. Yeung, Chapter 11 in this volume.

institutional economics approach that all states in capitalist economies are pretty much the same.[97] Dyson focuses on the role of the state both as market maker and regulator, and as an overarching source of legitimacy. He makes a basic distinction between 'state societies' and 'stateless societies'. For example,

> 'State' societies exemplify strongly non-economic, non-utilitarian attitudes towards political relations, which attitudes deny that the public interest is simply the sum of public interests; ... a stress on the unitary character of the 'public power'; a moralistic view of politics which involves strongly collectivist and regulatory attitudes, a notion of the inherent responsibilities of the executive power and an active conception of the administrator's role.[98]

By contrast,

> 'stateless societies' are characterized by the strength of pluralism ... an instrumental view of government and a pragmatic conception of politics, both of which are associated with a passive notion of a neutral, anonymous, detached and private administrative role.[99]

State societies include France and Germany, while paradigmatically stateless societies would include the United Kingdom and the United States. Note that Dyson's distinction is to be distinguished from the sociological question of whether a state is 'strong' or 'weak'; the distinction between state and stateless societies concerns the *role and concept* of the state, while that between strong and weak states concerns that state's *capacity*.

In state societies, the idea of the state is associated with affirmative provision of what Dowdle in this volume (Ch. 1, p. 30) refers to as 'citizenship goods', via 'services of general economic interest'.[100] By contrast, in stateless societies, the idea of the state is associated with more pluralistic, contingent, and indirect provision of 'the public interest' (as contrasted with the more materialist 'general economic interest') and it is society, rather than the state, that is supposed to provide the more concrete and material resources necessary for participation in the construction of that interest (which is how the stateless society conceptualizes citizenship). This analysis is useful in helping us to distinguish, within the context of competition law, between different approaches to the role of the state in providing public services (see also Dowdle, Ch. 1,

---

[97] Kenneth Dyson, *The State Tradition in Western Europe* (Colchester: ECPR Press, 2009).
[98] Ibid., pp. 51–2.   [99] Ibid., p. 52.   [100] Ibid., p. xiv.

pp. 30–2), and in particular between those of the United Kingdom and the United States, on the one hand, and those of the EU, on the other.

In contrast to the stateless societies of the United Kingdom and the United States, the competition law of the state societies of continental Europe have been strongly influenced by German ordoliberalism.[101] Ordoliberalism proceeds from the principle that the state precedes society and not the other way round.[102] The result is an 'economic constitution' which

> turned the core idea of classic liberalism – that the economy should be divorced from law and politics – on its head by arguing that the characteristics and effectiveness of the economy *depended* on its relationship to the political and legal systems. The ordoliberals recognized that fundamental political choices created the basic structures of an economic system.[103]

This economic constitutionalism requires a strong state to protect the economy, though it also constrains that state by limiting discretionary (or 'political') interventions in that economy (a concern still reflected, for example, in German calls in 1997 for EU competition law to be restructured around an independent cartel office). It does not presume a fundamental or necessary bifurcation between the state and the market, and does not see the role of the state as a merely residual one limited to the correction of market failures. Clearly this suggests a more complex and ambiguous role for the state in relation to competition and the market than that which typically informs neoliberal approaches to competition law.

Once more, the case studies above suggest a significant correlation between whether a society is a state society or a stateless society and particular characteristics of the competition law regimes. Hong Kong and Singaporean society, being initially founded on greenfield sites that subsequently experienced over a century of British colonial development, are – following the United Kingdom – likely to be much more stateless in their political and social orientation. And it is here that competition transplants have reflected UK models. The societies of Taiwan, South Korea, China, and Vietnam, by contrast, are much more oriented towards the 'state', and there competition transplants have tended to be more contingent.

---

[101] For an analysis of ordoliberalism, see David J. Gerber, *Law and Competition in Twentieth Century Europe: Protecting Prometheus* (Oxford: Clarendon Press, 1998), pp. 232–65.
[102] Dyson, *The State Tradition in Western Europe*, p. xiii.
[103] Gerber, *Law and Competition*, p. 246 (emphasis in original).

In addition to the research agendas suggested by Cotterrell in the context of legal transplants, Dyson's work gives us two additional research directions in analysing Asian states and competition law. The first is to examine how the role of the state is conceived; is it merely a corrective for markets, or is it considered to have a major role both in market creation and in the assertion against the market of key values such as citizenship? In relation to this, both local cultural conditions and the effects of past or present economic planning and largely state-controlled economic sectors will be important (see also Gerber, Ch. 2, pp. 47–9, 51–2). The second is to assess the capacities of different forms of competition law to respond to these differing roles and conceptions of the state. For example, the older, pre-1998 UK model based on the promotion of a nebulous 'public interest' might seem to have offered the greatest scope for the incorporation of state interests into the competition law framework. However, its very vagueness made it both inadequate as a statement of public interest values and incompatible with key economic values of calculability and predictability. In any event, it appears to have been supplanted by the European approach centred on the concept of 'services of general economic interest', which – in Europe at least – has required a clearer definition and justification of the state's public service goals and thus resulted in a more normatively defined vision of the state. Whether this is possible in the Asian economies discussed here remains to be investigated through more detailed study of their actual conditions.

V.   Conclusion: which competition law?

This brings me to my final theoretical issue, which relates to the point made at the beginning of this chapter that there is no single model of competition law which can be transplanted. I suggested that, following Maher, there are two useful ideal types of competition law which can be used to contrast different systems. The first, derived from private law, sees competition law as a means of protecting private autonomy and efficiency through preserving freedom of contract. The second, derived from public law, sees it as part of broader constraints on concentration of economic power for reasons of public interest and of democracy. But the Asian systems described in this chapter fit neither model.

The first model, which seeks to protect private autonomy and efficiency through freedom of contract, may be relevant to the more marketized systems such as those of Singapore and Hong Kong, but significant limitations exist even there to the applicability of this model. Thus, in the former case, the lack of independence of the enforcement machinery and, in the latter, the significant limitations to the applicability of the legislation result in the absence of qualities of predictability and calculability normally associated with advanced private-law-based systems. And, clearly, values of private autonomy and freedom of contract will have an even lesser role in the transitional systems such as China and Vietnam.

The second, public law, model is even less apparent. We saw that EU law has fashioned a sophisticated approach to assessing the application of competition law to the state services where it may be in conflict with other values such as public service. This operates through the competition authorities and the courts requiring reasoned justifications for qualifications to competition law and requiring that these be justified through a proportionality test. In the Asian systems examined here, there is clearly an acknowledgement that competition law values may conflict with other public policy values; indeed, this is a pervasive characteristic of all the systems studied. However, there is no suggestion of a machinery of public law for achieving the balancing of objectives in a reasoned and transparent way. Exemptions from the application of competition law are broad brush and vague, with little characterization of the relevant values and of how they are to be balanced; this will be left to the political process.

Part of the reason for this is that, unlike in the EU, competition law is not embedded in a broader public law regime. Thus, in the systems discussed, provision for judicial review is weak, reflecting a more authoritarian view of the state rather than a state tradition of public service as seen in continental Europe. Even in the case of Hong Kong, which has the most independent administration of competition law of all the cases discussed, public law and judicial review remain weak as a means of challenging government.[104] The same is true in the other regimes discussed, because of the history both of authoritarian forms of government and of a Marxist-Leninist ideology deeply suspicious of sources of power independent of the Party. Of course, weakness of judicial review is not a universal characteristic of Asian governance; one could contrast, for example, the recent, more activist role adopted by the Supreme Court

---

[104] For an example in a different context see *Clean Air Foundation Ltd.* v. *The Government of the HKSAR*, HCAL No.35 of 2007, unreported (26 July 2007), discussed in Rohan Price and John Kong Shan Ho, 'Air Pollution in Hong Kong: The Failure of Government and Judicial Review', *Public Law*, Issue 2 (2012): 179–97.

of Taiwan.[105] However, the history of the nations examined here has not encouraged the development of independent and effective review. Similarly, although there are other regulatory agencies in many of the cases discussed above, there seems to be little acceptance of a regime of independent bodies able to undertake arm's-length scrutiny of the relationship between public and private power.[106]

This lack of embedding of competition law in a broader public law framework may lead to major tensions. It suggests that a private law vision of competition law is the most likely to be developed in the states described here, but that this will work alongside a highly developed and interventionist state subject to minimal legal scrutiny. (See, e.g., Vande Walle, Ch. 6, discussing Japan; but see also Zheng, Ch. 7, discussing China. For an effort to reconcile these different approaches within a single regulatory model see Dowdle, Ch. 13.) Three possible ways of resolving the tensions may arise. The first, and least likely, is the development of new and independent public law institutions to fill the gap through permitting independent and transparent balancing of private and public interests. The second is that competition law takes a predominantly private law form and governs a distinct private sphere, autonomous from political intervention. All the examples described above suggest that this is extremely unlikely. The third, and most probable outcome, is the continued coexistence of a competition law largely transplanted from Western models with a substantial role for the state conceived as operating outside the competition law system through broad exemptions for public entities and through state influence of enforcement institutions which lack independence. This solution may limit the achievement of values of predictability and transparency normally associated with well-functioning systems of competition law, but is the only likely way forward. (See also Dowdle, Ch. 13. Cf. Jessop, Ch. 5, p. 118.)

Returning to the point I made at the outset of this chapter, the mixture of the universal and the contingent is highly characteristic of competition law. Although the use of legal transplants may suggest the universal, I have been at pains to emphasize the highly contingent nature of the relations between public and private. This contingency is evident even in

---

[105] Chien-Chih Lin, 'The Birth and Rebirth of the Judicial Review in Taiwan – Its Establishment, Empowerment, and Evolvement', *National Taiwan University Law Review*, 7 (2012): 167–222.

[106] For the very different role of regulation in China, see Hsueh, *China's Regulatory State*.

the systems of the West which are now largely uniform (at least formally); it will be even more so in the much more diverse systems of Asia. This means that further study must be highly sensitive to divergences in history and culture in relation to the meanings both of competition law and of the state, and this will require further empirical work. However, empirical work alone will not be enough, and there needs also to be further conceptual analysis of the relationship between competition law, public law, and the state. I hope that I have suggested some fruitful directions for such future analysis.

PART V

Into the future: Asian capitalism and competition regulation as dynamic systems

11

Globalizing competition in Asia: an evolutionary perspective

HENRY WAI-CHUNG YEUNG

I. Introduction

The emergence of highly competitive business firms from the three Asian newly industrialized economies (NIEs) of Singapore, South Korea, and Taiwan in the global economy during the last three decades has been nothing short of phenomenal. From their often-humble origin of small-scale and low-tech establishments, these Asian NIE firms have grown strategically as major market leaders today in respective industries and sectors. In 2009, over 70 per cent of the world's 100 million annual shipment of computer notebooks were produced by four Taiwanese firms (Quanta being the largest); two of the world's largest semiconductor foundry manufacturers are Taiwanese (TSMC and UMC); two of the top ten largest electronics manufacturing service (EMS) providers come from Taiwan and Singapore (Hon Hai and Venture); two-thirds of the world's US$20 billion offshore oil rigs orders are held in the books of two Singaporean marine engineering firms (Keppel Corp and SembCorp Industries); and Acer from Taiwan, Singapore Airlines, and Samsung and Hyundai from South Korea have become household brand names in the new millennium.

Moreover, compared with their modest origins, these leading Asian NIE firms are now succeeding not because of their competitiveness *domestically*. Rather, they have become competitive as integral parts of production networks that are becoming increasingly *globalized*.[1] While much social science literature has been written on globalization and its impact in the Asia–Pacific region, we know relatively little about how business firms from developing and NIE countries in Asia are being

---

[1] UNCTAD, *World Investment Report 2006: FDI from Developing and Transition Economies: Implications for Development* (New York: United Nations, 2006); UNCTAD, *World Investment Report 2009: Transnational Corporations, Agricultural Production and Development* (New York: United Nations, 2009).

articulated into global production networks.[2] This relative lack of understanding of the competitive dynamics and evolutionary emergence of
Asian NIE firms within this increasingly transnationally disaggregated
production space reflects a general underestimation of the critical
importance of transnational *firm-to-firm* co-operation as a key driver of
globalization processes.

All this has important implications for our understanding of the
nature and dynamics of economic competition in NIEs. More traditional
approaches to economic competition see such competition in terms of a
single ideal type. This ideal type is modelled on how competition seemed
to operate in the distinctly national economic spaces of twentieth-century
North Atlantic industrialization (i.e. Fordism). A study of recent evolutionary developments in the place and role of the firm in the so-called
'developmental states' of Asia shows that the nature and dynamics of
economic space are much more contingent and dynamic than can be
captured by this perspective. And, if this is the case, the roles and dynamics
of competition within these spaces are also more contingent and dynamic
than is generally acknowledged (see also Jessop, Ch. 5).

To understand how Asian NIE firms compete successfully in the
global economy, I argue that we need to go beyond the domestic- and
state-centric view of developmental state theory by developing a theoretical perspective that accounts for the complex and changing firm–state
relations in Asia. In section 2, I address the need to re-focus the developmental state debate away from an emphasis on the role of the state and
instead on to an emphasis on the role of the firm independent of the
state. This is because, as shown in section 3, evolutions in the nature of
industrial production, and in particular the disaggregation of that production into global production networks, severely constrains the state's
capacity to structure a domestic firm's economic competitiveness on its
own, and this in turn gives local firms much greater autonomy in
structuring their entry and place in global markets. Section 4 theorizes

---

[2] Cf. Helmut Schütte (ed.), *The Global Competitiveness of the Asian Firm* (New York:
St. Martin's Press, 1994); John A. Mathews, *Dragon Multinational: A New Model for
Global Growth* (Oxford University Press, 2002); Arnoud DeMeyer, Peter Williamson,
Frank-Jürgen Richter, and Pamela C. M. Mar (eds.), *Global Future: The Next Challenge
for Asian Business* (Singapore: John Wiley & Sons (Asia), 2005); Henry Wai-chung Yeung,
'From Followers to Market Leaders: Asian Electronics Firms in the Global Economy', *Asia
Pacific Viewpoint*, 48 (2007): 1–25; Henry Wai-chung Yeung, 'Regional Development and
the Competitive Dynamics of Global Production Networks: An East Asian Perspective',
Regional Studies, 43 (2009): 325–51.

this evolutionary development, showing how this development is best described in terms of NIE firms disembedding themselves from the developmental state and re-embedding themselves in global production networks that revolve around global leading firms rather than around state bureaucracies. In the conclusion I shall explore some of the implications this has for our understanding of competition and its regulation.

II. 'Bringing the firm back in'

While the rise of these Asian NIE firms during the past two decades has been extraordinary, many pundits have attributed the competitive success of these firms and their home economies to the relentless efforts of the so-called developmental state. They argue that state initiatives such as an active industrial policy and financial support have enabled these 'national champions' to venture into and compete successfully in the global economy. Although this contemporary thought on the central role of the state in economic development has a very long intellectual pedigree, dating back to the mercantilist period at the dawn of modern capitalism, Hugo Radice notes that

> the *locus classicus* of the modern DS [developmental state] concept was undoubtedly East Asia ... At the heart of the DS thesis is the relationship between the state and the business sector, especially with regard to the direction and funding of industrial investment.[3]

This *statist approach* to the globalization of Asian firms and their home economies, however, has unfortunately ignored the complex and dynamic evolutionary nature of firm–state relations within the changing context of economic globalization. In this chapter I explain how the global competitive emergence of Asian NIE firms cannot be simply read off from and explained by their embeddedness in the developmental state. Since the 1990s, I argue, these Asian firms have strategically disembedded from state apparatus and successfully re-embedded themselves in *global production networks*. This shift in the strategic partnership of Asian NIE firms from firm–state to firm–firm networks has profound implications for our understanding of the present and future trajectories of competition in what this volume is calling 'Asian capitalism', in that it presages the demise of the *traditional* vision of the

---

[3] Hugo Radice, 'The Developmental State under Global Neoliberalism', *Third World Quarterly*, 29 (2008): 1153–74, 1153–4.

developmental state as the primary planner of economic development in Asia (see also Deyo, Ch. 12; cf. Jessop, Ch. 5, pp. 118–19).

Along these lines, we need to revisit the firm–state debate in order to situate the competitive dynamics of economic globalization. This brief section points to the changing historical specificity in which the embeddedness of Asian firms in their home states should be understood. The embedded firm–state relations in Asia should be recognized as being a historical construct rather than a permanent fixture, and therefore as being subject to competitive change and adjustments in an era of accelerated globalization. The next section proceeds with a theoretically informed analysis of the competitive dynamics of globalization, through which Asian NIE firms have emerged to become key drivers of their regional economies. Beginning with a critical deconstruction of Peter Evans's concept of 'embedded autonomy',[4] this section draws upon important insights from different theoretical literature in order to analyse the strategic disembedding and re-embedding processes of Asian NIE firms.

III.   Dynamics of competitive change and adjustments

As alluded to in the introduction to this chapter, capitalist national firms are indeed important in general and should be *more* important in the study of the changing position of these Asian NIEs in the global economy today.[5] However, we are immediately confronted with the thorny empirical issue of exactly who is the key director in the globalization of these Asian NIEs and how this direction works. Is it still the developmental state itself, working through its 'national firms' – that is, private or state-linked firms that originated from and are controlled by national actors selected and controlled by the NIE state itself? Or is it something different?

To answer these questions this chapter draws on two emerging and interrelated research frontiers that call for more theoretical attention to trans-local actors and processes, evolutionary dynamics of change, and

---

[4] Peter Evans, *Embedded Autonomy: States and Industrial Transformation* (Princeton University Press, 1995).

[5] Henry Wai-chung Yeung, 'Remaking Economic Geography: Insights from East Asia', *Economic Geography*, 83 (2007): 339–48; Henry Wai-chung Yeung, 'The Rise of East Asia: An Emerging Challenge to the Study of International Political Economy', in Mark Blyth (ed.), *Routledge Handbook of International Political Economy* (Routledge, 2009), pp. 201–15.

institutional contexts. The first is that of global production networks.[6] This literature showcases the critical importance, within East Asian regional and national economies, of firms decoupling from the state and *strategically recoupling* with other firms into global production networks. These disembedding and re-embedding processes cannot be fully understood, however, without paying simultaneous attention to their evolutionary dynamics and institutional contexts. This in turn calls for the second strand of emerging theoretical literature that informs this chapter, that which deals with issues of path dependency, lock-in effects, and dynamics of change in the context of evolutionary economic geography[7] (see also Dowdle, Ch. 1, relating this to regulatory capacities). As we shall see, these evolutionary trajectories are particularly relevant for analysing the changing dynamics of firm–state relations in East Asia.

Chalmers Johnson's original articulation of the developmental state focused on the role played by a particular state institution in Japan, the Ministry of International Trade and Industry (MITI).[8] Subsequent

---

[6] Peter Dicken, Philip Kelly, Kris Olds, and Henry Wai-chung Yeung, 'Chains and Networks, Territories and Scales: Towards an Analytical Framework for the Global Economy', *Global Networks*, 1 (2001): 89–112; Jeffrey Henderson, Peter Dicken, Martin Hess, Neil Coe, and Henry Wai-chung Yeung, 'Global Production Networks and the Analysis of Economic Development', *Review of International Political Economy*, 9 (2002): 436–64; Neil Coe, Martin Hess, Henry Wai-chung Yeung, Peter Dicken, and Jeffrey Henderson, '"Globalizing" Regional Development: A Global Production Networks Perspective', *Transactions of the Institute of British Geographers*, New Series, 29 (2004): 468–84; Neil Coe, Neil, Martin Hess, and Peter Dicken (eds.), theme issue on 'Global Production Networks: Debates and Challenges', *Journal of Economic Geography*, 8 (2008): 267–440; Martin Hess and Henry Wai-chung Yeung (eds.), *Environment and Planning A*, theme issue on 'Global Production Networks', 38 (2006): 1193–305; Henry Wai-chung Yeung, 'Rethinking Relational Economic Geography'. *Transactions of the Institute of British Geographers*, New Series, 30 (2005): 37–51; Yeung, 'Regional Development'.

[7] Ron A. Boschma and Koen Frenken, 'Why is Economic Geography Not an Evolutionary Science? Towards an Evolutionary Economic Geography', *Journal of Economic Geography*, 6 (2006): 273–302; Ron Martin and Peter Sunley, 'Path Dependence and Regional Economic Evolution', *Journal of Economic Geography*, 6 (2006): 395–437; Ron Martin and Peter Sunley, 'Complexity Thinking and Evolutionary Economic Geography', *Journal of Economic Geography*, 7 (2007): 573–601; Ron A. Boschma and Ron Martin, 'Constructing an Evolutionary Economic Geography', *Journal of Economic Geography*, 7 (2007): 537–48; Pernilla S. Rafiqui, 'Evolving Economic Landscapes: Why New Institutional Economics Matters for Economic Geography', *Journal of Economic Geography*, 9 (2009): 329–53. Cf. Danny MacKinnon, Andrew Cumbers, Andy Pike, Kean Birch, and Robert McMaster, 'Evolution in Economic Geography: Institutions, Political Economy, and Adaptation', *Economic Geography*, 85 (2009): 129–50.

[8] Chalmers Johnson, *MITI and the Japanese Economic Miracle: The Growth of Industrial Policy, 1925–1975* (Stanford University Press, 1982).

proponents of the developmental state have focused somewhat more attention on the special role of the firm. For example, Alice Amsden, highly cognisant of the shop-floor level operationalization of state industrialization policies, has noted:

> The translation of high growth rates of output into high growth rates of productivity depends on what happens *inside the unit of production*. Closing the loop between growth and productivity, therefore, involves an analytical shift, a change in the center of gravity from the state to the other key institution of industrialization, the firm.[9]

But even where the firm is sometimes counted and independently analysed, however, the Asian developmental state is still seen primarily as a product of the policy regimes of the state rather than of the competitive dynamics of the market. Developmental-state theory's excessive pre-occupation with *state* initiatives and *state* capacities has locked it into a conceptual path dependency that cannot perceive possible sources of agency outside state policymakers.

As many have noted, however, this focus can no longer account for the dynamic articulation of the Asian NIE firms into the global economy. To Kanishka Jayasuriya, this statist view of East Asian development 'now shows all the hallmarks of a degenerating research programme that is no longer capable of setting out an interesting or relevant agenda'.[10] He thus laments that

> developmental state theorists, because they understand 'policy capacity' as a set of fixed institutional endowments or attributes, are unable to grasp how these capacities change in response to broader changes in the constellation of social and economic interests. What we require is a more constitutive conception of the state and policy capacity that recognises that the state is not an 'entity', but a complex and constituted set of relationships between frameworks of political authority and the international political economy, domestic social forces, and the broader ideational notions of authority or stateness.[11]

Similarly, Sean O'Riain argues for understanding the constitutive role that firms play, via processes of globalization, in state-driven development, because 'under the globalization project, transnational firms, networks and

---

[9] Alice H. Amsden, *Asia's Next Giant: South Korea and Late Industrialization* (Oxford University Press), p. 112 (emphasis in original).

[10] Kanishka Jayasuriya, 'Beyond Institutional Fetishism: From the Developmental to the Regulatory State', *New Political Economy*, 10 (2005): 381–7, 386.

[11] Ibid., 383.

flows of money, information, and resources have deeply penetrated the most successful localities and nations – the global is no longer a context for developmental strategies but rather a constitutive element of them'.[12]

More specifically, at least in the Asian context, there has been in the developmental state literature a curious neglect of the theoretical and empirical possibility that these Asian firms might be growing out of and beyond the reach of the traditional developmental state. As Mark Beeson recently noted, 'the relative long-term decline of the state may be inevitable and not a bad thing'.[13] This evolutionary change in firm–state relations from one of structural dependence in the early phase of industrialization and economic development to increasing autonomy and decoupling in recent decades arises primarily through the growing participation of these Asian NIE firms in networks of global production. Here, the economic advantages of disaggregating and decentralizing production processes across states (see Dowdle, Ch. 1, pp. 17–19) compel firms to reposition themselves, not just internally within their domestic economies, but more importantly externally, with other firms engaged in these increasingly transnational production processes.

The shift from firm–state partnerships to firm–firm networks has profound implications for our understanding of the present and future trajectories of regional economies in East Asia. While the delocalization of production has not completely reduced industrial policymaking to a futility 'tantamount to watering one's own garden in a world where the plants can relocate' to use Linda Weiss's evocative depiction[14] (for a study that seems to refute Weiss's view, see Deyo, Ch. 12), it does call into question the continued role of the developmental state as the *primary* shaper of economic evolution in Asian economies today. This strategic embedding of Asian NIE firms in different global production networks can be seen as a spontaneous competitive adaptation that is charting new paths of economic growth and evolution that operate outside the strategic visions of state industrial policymakers.

---

[12] Sean O'Riain, *The Politics of High-Tech Growth: Developmental Network States in the Global Economy* (Cambridge University Press, 2004), p. 27.

[13] Mark Beeson, 'Politics and Markets in East Asia: Is the Developmental State Compatible with Globalization?', in Richard Stubbs and Geoffrey R. D. Underhill (eds.), *Political Economy and the Changing Global Order*, 3rd edn (Oxford University Press, 2006), pp. 443–53, at p. 451.

[14] Linda Weiss, 'Is the State being "Transformed" by Globalisation?', in Linda Weiss (ed.), *States in the Global Economy: Bringing Domestic Institutions Back In* (Cambridge University Press, 2003), pp. 293–317, at p. 296.

Three caveats should be put in place before proceeding further. First, this shift in firm–state relations does not denounce the value of developmental state theory in explaining many other facets of East Asian societies, such as political change and social welfare programmes. (In this volume, see Jessop, Ch. 5, pp. 107, 109–10; Prosser, Ch. 10; Deyo, Ch. 12.) Indeed, Richard Stubbs recently concluded his critical review of the developmental state literature with a caution:

> the concept of the DS [developmental state] still has currency although its existence and value continue to be hotly contested. Much depends on how the DS is defined. The narrower the definition the easier it is to pronounce the death of the DS. The broader the definition the more aspects of the original construction can be located in contemporary societies around East Asia.[15]

Second, even in the economic realm, the developmental state continues to function effectively in certain areas such as promoting new industries (e.g., biomedical and environmental technologies sectors) and steering restructuring of the domestic economies (e.g., the 2008 global financial crisis). Third, this paper is not about economic growth per se, but the key actor(s) implicated in this competitive growth dynamic – leading national firms – and their global articulations that go well beyond their domestic operations.

IV. Reconceptualizing firm interdependencies: from 'embedded autonomy' within the state to 'strategic re-embeddedness' outside the state

In his comparative institutional analysis of industrial transformation in Brazil, India, and South Korea, Peter Evans argues that 'embedded autonomy' is a necessary condition for the efficacy of the developmental state to carry out its developmental roles as either 'midwife' or 'husbandry' of domestic industries.[16] To him, the state must enjoy some independence and autonomy from the domestic elites, particularly those in business and industries, in order for it to avoid rent-seeking behaviour by these elites and to exercise its capacity for promoting economic development. This insulation of the state from economic actors and

---

[15] Richard Stubbs, 'What Ever Happened to the East Asian Developmental State? The Unfolding Debate', *Pacific Review*, 22 (2009): 1–22, 17.

[16] See generally Evans, *Embedded Autonomy*.

other interest groups, however, needs to be grounded in an embedded relationship between the autonomous state and domestic business elite, because the former plans its industrial policies in consultation with the latter and implements such policies with the co-operation of the intended recipients. He further argues that the developmental state secures internal coherence through developing an effective and rule-following bureaucracy:

> Unless loyalty to the rest of the state apparatus takes some kind of precedence over ties with other social groups, the state will not function. The kind of coherent, cohesive bureaucracy that is postulated in the Weberian hypothesis must have a certain degree of autonomy vis-à-vis society.[17]

The success of industrial transformation is therefore a question of both the autonomy and the capacity of state institutions.

As noted earlier, however, this Weberian-inspired 'embedded autonomy' conception of the developmental state can be quite problematic, as it does not really explain the dynamics of bureaucratic rationality, nor does it consider the evolutionary relationships between the developmental state and business firms in the context of changing competition through globalization processes. What will happen to state–firm relations if economic actors in these Asian NIEs 'grow up' over time and become much less dependent on their developmental state 'parents'? Do they eventually 'grow out of the plan', to paraphrase Barry Naughton's 1995 book title,[18] and strike out for a new life on their own in the global economy? What does this evolutionary change leave us with when it comes to understanding the international political economy of Asian NIEs? With the exception of Evans, the first-wave studies of the developmental state have not dealt with these questions because they were focusing mostly on the nurturing or even directive role of the developmental state.

To understand the dynamic relationship between the developmental state and its leading firms, we need to look elsewhere for a dynamic evolutionary view of institutional change that posits structural change vis-à-vis path dependence in state–firm relations. Here, we enter the

---

[17] Evans, *Embedded Autonomy*, p. 41; see also Linda Weiss, *The Myth of the Powerless State: Governing the Economy in a Global Era* (Cambridge: Polity Press, 1998); Linda Weiss (ed.), *States in the Global Economy: Bringing Domestic Institutions Back In* (Cambridge University Press, 2003).

[18] Barry Naughton, *Growing Out of the Plan: Chinese Economic Reform, 1978–1993* (Cambridge University Press, 1995).

realm of evolutionary economic geography.[19] As noted by Boschma and Martin, 'the basic concern of evolutionary economic geography is with the processes by which the economic landscape – the spatial organization of economic production, distribution and consumption – is transformed over time'.[20] Here, we can discern some useful conceptual toolkits to rethink the state–firm relations in a more dynamic selection environment that is associated with economic globalization.

Martin and Sunley argue that an evolutionary approach in economic geography 'raises the question whether the evolution of networks and connections can be analysed in terms of changes in underlying generative rules'.[21] In the context of state–firm relations in the Asian NIEs, one major change in these *generative rules* is the increasing globalization of production activity and thus a concomitant evolutionary process of globalizing networks, from an endogenous regional construct measured in terms of relational assets and knowledge repertories to global articulation and external competition. This evolutionary perspective raises several questions: Is the developmental state increasingly being replaced by more global developmental-institutional articulations? Are state-centric institutions becoming less important for firm dynamics and growth in today's globalizing world economy?

Seen in this light, Evans's conception of the developmental state as preconditioned on relations of embedded autonomy with society and economy is problematic. Conceptually, it tends to lock the state and the multitude of other actors, particularly firms and business groups, into a recursive mode of mutual dependence that does not allow for new and competitive forces to work themselves out of these lock-in relations. Admitting this major weakness of his 'embedded autonomy' framework, Evans himself points out:

> Unfortunately, while a comparative institutional approach may have facilitated uncovering these contradictory political dynamics, they were certainly not predicted in my initial discussion of state–society relations. My version of the comparative institutional approach offered some ideas about how states might affect industrial transformation but had relatively

---

[19] Boschma and Frenken, 'Economic Geography'; Martin and Sunley, 'Path Dependence'; Boschma and Martin, 'Constructing an Evolutionary Economic Geography'; Rafiqui, 'Evolving Economic Landscapes'.

[20] Boschma and Martin, 'Constructing an Evolutionary Economic Geography', 539 (emphasis omitted).

[21] Martin and Sunley, 'Path Dependence', 593.

little to say about how this transformation would change the basis of subsequent state involvement.[22]

Put in the context of the Asian NIEs, a strict conception of embedded autonomy may well explain the *initial* origin of certain state-initiated projects of industrialization during the 1960s and the 1970s.[23] But it cannot adequately account for the more recent dynamics by which key actors have emerged from these projects and industries during the past two decades. Not only have these actors grown out of the state plan, but their successful articulation into global production networks has rendered state planning in such areas as industrial policies and national champions increasingly ineffective and unacceptable, if not outright wrong.[24] As is forcefully argued by Mark Beeson,

> once the development state has effectively done its job and 'caught up' with established industrial economies at the leading edge of production and knowledge, it is far from clear that state planners are any wiser about the course of future technological development than the private sector. In other words, there are limits to what states can do, specific circumstances in which planning development seems to be effective, and a danger of entrenching a counterproductive institutional inertia where the relationships between political and economic elites are inadequately monitored and transparent, or where they linger on past their expiry dates.[25]

But at the same time as such 'institutional inertia' threatens the continued growth of Asian NIE firms today, what comes to their rescue is the even more complex organization of the global economy, in the form of global production networks. Three decades of successful policy interventions by the developmental state in these Asian NIEs have now produced a whole army of leading, national-champion firms that can compete on their own feet in the global economy. Graduating from their earlier dependence on the developmental state for capital and technologies, these Asian NIE firms have taken on a more direct role in steering the development of their respective industries and sectors, a role previously occupied by the developmental state. This evolutionary change in 'role play' between leading firms and the developmental state does not

---

[22] Evans, *Embedded Autonomy*, p. 225.
[23] Cf. Meredith Woo-Cumings (ed.), *The Developmental State* (Ithaca, NY: Cornell University Press, 1999); J. Megan Greene, *The Origins of the Developmental State in Taiwan: Science Policy and the Quest for Modernization* (Cambridge, MA: Harvard University Press, 2008).
[24] Weiss, 'Is the State Being "Transformed"?', p. 296.
[25] Beeson, 'Politics and Markets', p. 451.

take place naturally or in an institutional vacuum. More importantly, it is firmly grounded in a process of new path creation that entails a shift of strategic partnership from state–firm to firm–firm relations in these Asian NIEs.

These new strategic partnerships represent a form of strategic coupling. Strategic coupling describes a process in which, through co-ordinating, mediation, and the arbitrage of strategic interests in pursuit of shared interests and common strategic objectives, initially independent economic actors develop shared interdependencies binding them to one another. In the context of the Asian NIEs working in the global economy, this binding links local firms with global counterparts in the global economy. These trans-local and transnational linkages can be both material (e.g., involving reciprocal and interdependent flows in goods and capital) and non-material (e.g., involving reciprocal and interdependent flows in information, intelligence, and practices).

This strategic coupling process exhibits three distinctive attributes. First, it is strategic because the process does not happen without active intervention and intentional action on the part of the participants. As argued by people like John Mathews, Ivo Zander, and myself, such strategizing is most useful and profitable in a market condition of disequilibrium, because such a condition allows for the arbitraging of different opportunities.[26] This view of strategizing concurs with the Schumpeterian concept of entrepreneurship, which postulates the function of the entrepreneur as someone serving as a disruptive and dynamic force in an economy that has reached a static equilibrium.[27] Second, strategic coupling is contingent and subject to change. A typical strategic coupling involves an ongoing series of temporary coalitions among an ever-changing population of actors and institutions.[28] Third, its

---

[26] John A. Mathews, *Strategizing, Disequilibrium and Profit* (Stanford University Press, 2006); John A. Mathews and Ivo Zander, 'The International Entrepreneurial Dynamics of Accelerated Internationalisation', *Journal of International Business Studies*, 38 (2007): 387–403; Henry Wai-chung Yeung, *Entrepreneurship and the Internationalisation of Asian Firms: An Institutional Perspective* (Cheltenham: Edward Elgar, 2002); Henry Wai-chung Yeung, 'Transnationalizing Entrepreneurship: A Critical Agenda for Economic Geography', *Progress in Human Geography*, 33 (2009): 210–35.

[27] Joseph A. Schumpeter, *The Theory of Economic Development: An Inquiry into Profits, Capital, Credit, Interest and the Business Cycle*, trans. Redvers Opie (Cambridge, MA: Harvard University Press, 1962 [1934]), p. 66.

[28] Michael Taylor, 'The Small Firm as a Temporary Coalition', *Entrepreneurship and Regional Development*, 11 (1999): 1–19; Michael Taylor and Bjorn T. Asheim, 'The Concept of the Firm in Economic Geography', *Economic Geography*, 77 (2001): 315–28.

processes transcend territorial boundaries and geographical scales, as actors from different sites (firms, states, regions, and localities) converge and then re-converge at different nodes in the network, their practices radiating out to diverse geographies at both the most global and the highly local levels (see also Gillespie, Ch. 8, pp. 187–8, 192–3, identifying this phenomenon in the context of Vietnamese business networks).

In general, there are two mutually constitutive dimensions to this dynamic process of strategic coupling. The first dimension refers to the *disembedding* of leading firms from the developmental state over time in response to the changing selection environment. The second dimension points to the *re-embedding* of these firms in global production networks orchestrated by lead firms from advanced industrialized economies. These two dimensions are really two sides of the same coin: the growing disembedding of firms from home states necessitates the re-embedding of these economic actors in another organizational platform such as global production networks.

Starting with the late 1980s, this disembedding of lead firms from the developmental state began to take place in all three Asian NIEs. In South Korea, perhaps the strongest form of the developmental state among the three NIEs in guiding national champions, leading *chaebol* groups have embarked on a massive globalization drive since the early 1990s, partly facilitated by the financial liberalization implemented by the first civilian government under Kim Young-Sam. This disembedding was a product both of the *chaebol* groups and of a state whose power and control over these *chaebol* was waning in the wake of democratization and liberalization.

This shift of the developmental state from a 'midwifery' or even 'husbandry' role to one of 'nursing' can also be witnessed in Taiwan and Singapore. Leading firms in both these countries began to dis-embed themselves from the developmental state apparatus even before they did so in South Korea – in the late 1980s. In Taiwan, the developmental state was never as powerful and effective in governing the market and growing national champions as in South Korea.[29] Indeed, as Megan Greene

---

[29] Amsden, *Asia's Next Giant*; Robert Wade, *Governing the Market: Economic Theory and the Role of Government in East Asian Industrialization* (Princeton University Press, 1990). See also Yongping Wu, *Political Explanation of Economic Growth: State Survival, Bureaucratic Politics, and Private Enterprises in the Making of Taiwan's Economy, 1950–1985* (Cambridge, MA: Harvard University Asia Center, 2005); Greene, *Origins of the Developmental State*.

shows, the political leadership in Taiwan had never shown more than 'a halfhearted commitment to promoting an industrial science policy'. She notes:

> A coherent science policy evolved only haltingly and as the result of a complex interaction among eager technocrats, academicians, and foreign advisers and a shortsighted political leadership. At no time was it a direct result of top-down policy originating from the political leadership.[30]

In Singapore, the developmental state had chosen to work with foreign capital since its inception and therefore produced a class of domestic private firms that were not dependent on – and might sometimes even be alienated by – the state's direction. Initially, the state deliberately intervened in the domestic economy to an even greater extent than in South Korea and Taiwan, by establishing a wide range of state-owned enterprises (SOEs), such as Singapore Airlines, Keppel, and Sembcorp, that today operate at the forefront of the global economy. Beginning in the late 1980s, however, Singapore's developmental state embarked on a difficult process of corporatizing and privatizing these SOEs. However, Singapore lacked the local private entrepreneurs and capitalists who could take over these gigantic SOEs and thus had to rely on foreign capital – which of course brought with it greater foreign control, which in turn triggered the first wave of disembedding national firms from the state.[31] This was also the time when Singapore underwent what Gary Rodan terms a 'second industrial revolution', upgrading its industries and economic competitiveness through carefully managed wage increase and labour policies.[32]

In all three of Asia's NIEs, this re-embedding process required local firms to go beyond their domestic economies and to participate directly in globalization.[33] The success of this re-embedding process was due to

---

[30] Greene, *Origins of the Developmental State in Taiwan*, p. 3.

[31] Henry Wai-chung Yeung, 'Strategic Governance and Economic Diplomacy in China: The Political Economy of Government-Linked Companies from Singapore', *East Asia: An International Quarterly*, 21 (2004): 40–64, 47, Table 1.

[32] Garry Rodan, *The Political Economy of Singapore's Industrialization: National State and International Capital* (Basingstoke: Palgrave Macmillan, 1989). See also Henry Wai-chung Yeung, 'Institutional Capacity and Singapore's Developmental State: Managing Economic (In)Security in the Global Economy', in Helen E. S. Nesadurai (ed.), *Globalisation and Economic Security in East Asia: Governance and Institutions* (London: Routledge, 2005), pp. 85–106.

[33] Yeung, *Entrepreneurship*; Henry Wai-chung Yeung, *Chinese Capitalism in a Global Era: Towards Hybrid Capitalism* (London: Routledge 2004).

two recent evolutions in the world economy: the emergence of distinctly transnational professional communities, and the vertical disaggregation of industrial production.

The critical role that communities and social capital play in economic development is now well recognized. One such community that has emerged relatively recently is the transnational community of elite professionals and businesspersons who shuttle constantly around the globe.[34] As described by David Levy, present-day global production networks

> exist within the 'transnational space' that is constituted and structured by transnational elites, institutions, and ideologies ... Within this space, transnational communities emerge with economic systems, relations of power, and institutional forms that are distinct from, though interacting with, national or region-bound forms.[35]

This space has transformed the dynamics of international knowledge formation, changing the one-way process often described as a 'brain drain' – the tendency of highly trained professionals in NIE economies to leave those economies and relocate in more advanced economies – into a two-way process of brain circulation, in which these elite professionals are constantly moving between the NIE economies and the more established industrial economies of the North Atlantic. Through their constant movements, these technologists and entrepreneurs have formed a transnational community of informal brain networks characterized by certain common social identity and, sometimes, nationalistic sentiments (see also Gillespie, Ch. 8, pp. 187–8).

Another condition that has been critical for the re-embedding process is the transnational disaggregation of industrial organization (see also Dowdle, Ch. 1, pp. 17–19; for an investigation into how this affects competition, see Dowdle, Ch. 9). As noted by Anne Saxenian, 'The deepening social division of labor in the industry creates opportunities for innovation in formerly peripheral regions [i.e., the present-day NIEs] – opportunities that did not exist in an era of highly integrated producers

---

[34] AnnaLee Saxenian, *The New Argonauts: Regional Advantage in a Global Economy* (Cambridge, MA: Harvard University Press, 2006); AnnaLee Saxenian and Charles F. Sabel, 'Venture Capital in the "Periphery": The New Argonauts, Global Search, and Local Institution Building', *Economic Geography*, 84 (2008): 379–94; Yeung, 'Transnationalizing Entrepreneurship'.

[35] David L. Levy, 'Political Contestation in Global Production Networks', *Academy of Management Review*, 33 (2008): 943–63, 953.

[before the 1980s].'[36] In many industries, such as global electronics and information and communication technology, this ever growing competitive demand for vertical specialization by both brand name firms and their equipment manufacturers has resulted in a vertical disaggregation of processes of production. Production processes that once occurred entirely in-house are now increasingly spread throughout a geographically dispersed network of specialized firms.[37] As Boy Lüthje has observed,

> Through their continuing acquisitions CM [contract manufacturing] companies act as transnational network builders, assembling a variety of plants with different manufacturing practices in specific national and global markets. Contract manufacturing, therefore, can be characterized as a mode of integrating, coordinating, and regulating diverging economic, social, and cultural conditions in global production systems.[38]

Such integration allows global lead firms to take advantage of the comparative advantages many NIE firms enjoy in human capital, production flexibility, and cost competitiveness. This, in turn, allows these Asian NIE firms to embed themselves in the strategic imperatives of global lead firms and their transnational production networks rather than in national industrial planning schemes.[39]

V. Conclusion

This recent reinterpretation of the developmental state in East Asia demonstrates the continuing vitality of the developmental state debate, and is no less ferocious in comparison with the 'first wave' of the debate

---

[36] AnnaLee Saxenian, 'Transnational Communities and the Evolution of Global Production Networks: The Cases of Taiwan, China and India', *Industry and Innovation*, 9 (2002): 183–202, 184–5.

[37] John H. Dunning and Sarianna M. Lundan, *Multinational Enterprises and the Global Economy*, 2nd edn (Cheltenham: Edward Elgar, 2008).

[38] Boy Lüthje, 'Electronics Contract Manufacturing: Global Production and the International Division of Labor in the Age of the Internet', *Industry and Innovation*, 9 (2002): 227–47, 228.

[39] See also Thomas R. Leinbach and John T. Bowen Jr, 'Air Cargo Services and the Electronics Industry in Southeast Asia', *Journal of Economic Geography*, 4 (2004): 1–24; John T. Bowen Jr, 'Global Production Networks, the Developmental State and the Articulation of Asia Pacific Economies in the Commercial Aircraft Industry', *Asia Pacific Viewpoint*, 48 (2007): 312–29; John T. Bowen Jr, and Thomas R. Leinbach, 'Competitive Advantage in Global Production Networks: Air Freight Services and the Electronics Industry in Southeast Asia', *Economic Geography*, 82 (2006): 147–66; Henry Wai-chung Yeung, 'Industrial Clusters and Production Networks in Southeast Asia: A Global Production Networks Approach', in Ikuo Kuroiwa and Mun Heng Toh (eds.), *Production Networks and Industrial Clusters: Integrating Economies in Southeast Asia* (Singapore: Institute of Southeast Asian Studies, 2008), pp. 83–120.

that flourished during the late 1980s and early 1990s. For the most part, these 'second wave' studies are not challenging the basic tenets of the canonical studies in the 'first wave' theories of the developmental state. Rather, they are developing a more dynamic and transnational conception of state–firm relations that takes into account the changing context of economic developments in the global economy and the rise of new forms of economic interdependences beyond the state–firm nexus.

This chapter shows how evolutions in the drivers of globalization are causing a disembedding and re-embedding of Asian NIE firms that are themselves charting a possibly new pathway of development in these NIEs. It shifts our analytical attention away from a state-centric view of industrial transformation in the Asian NIEs that has been the focus of the earlier debates over the developmental state. Michael Hobday is quite right to claim that

> The activities and strategies of firms in engaging with international production networks cannot be properly accounted for within theories of the developmental state, as latecomer firm behaviour tends to be treated (usually implicitly) as an automatic response to policy and economic circumstances, rather than as a shaping influence in its own right.[40]

In comparison with the 'bringing the state back in' approach that has tended to dominate the comparative institutional analysis (ICA) literature over the past several decades,[41] this chapter's firm-specific and bottom-up analysis of changes in the structure and dynamics of Asian NIEs provides a clearer picture of the evolutionary trajectories inherent in the ever-changing nature of both Asian and global competitiveness. It gives us a new perspective on the nature of firm–state relations in an era of intensified transnational interdependences in industrial production. Instead of reducing this relationship to a single ideal type, it shows that it is much more historically contingent and evolutionarily dynamic than has traditionally been recognized (cf. Jessop, Ch. 5). This calls for a 'bringing the *firm* back in', and correspondingly, for bringing the dynamic growth of Asian NIE firms to the forefront of comparative institutional analysis.

This has important implications for our understanding of the nature of economic competition in Asia. Like the earlier development-state

---

[40] Michael Hobday, 'The Electronics Industries of the Asia-Pacific: Exploiting International Production Networks for Economic Development', *Asian-Pacific Economic Literature*, 15 (2001): 13–29, 25.

[41] For a critique of this approach see Yeung, 'Rise of East Asia'.

literature's focus on the state, our understanding of the dynamics of economic competition (and its regulation) has focused on industrial and regulatory ideal types drawn from *national* economic markets. Our discussion above shows that, at least in the context of NIEs, this vision is flawed. Insofar as both the NIE and its firms are concerned, global competitiveness is not about markets, but about networks. Networks can contain aspects of both market and non-market (bureaucratic) ordering, but at the same time can be independent of both.[42] This makes the structure and dynamics of global competition (and competitiveness) much more contingent and nuanced than can be captured by a single, market-based archetype (cf. Dowdle, Ch. 13). Firms that are 'competitive' in the context of a network, or that are contributing to the market competitiveness of the network, might not be competitive from the perspective of market competition, and vice versa (see also Jessop, Ch. 5). At least as far as both Asian NIEs and their firms are concerned, global competitiveness is no longer (if it ever was) simply domestic competitiveness writ large.

---

[42] Oliver E. Williamson, 'Comparative Economic Organization: The Analysis of Discrete Structural Alternatives', *Administrative Science Quarterly*, 36 (1991): 269–96; Walter W. Powell, 'Neither Market nor Hierarchy: Network Forms of Organization', *Research in Organizational Behavior*, 12 (1990): 295–336.

Addressing the development deficit of competition policy: the role of economic networks

FREDERIC C. DEYO

I. Introduction: competition and development

The 'development space' for diversification and upgrading policies in developing countries is being shrunk behind the rhetorical commitment to universal liberalization and privatization. The rules being written into multilateral (e.g. WTO free trade) ... agreements actively prevent developing countries from pursuing the kinds of industrial and technology policies adopted by the newly developed countries of East Asia aimed at accelerating the 'internal' articulation of the economy ... [and] limits ... their rise up the value chain.[1]

The neoliberal economic reform project, encouraged and supported by international financial institutions (IFIs), core-country governments, the European Union, and the OECD, and institutionalized most forcefully by the World Trade Organization (WTO), promotes a model of economic order based on market relations and impersonal transactions among parties oriented predominantly to price. While it is universally recognized that such a model is unrealizable in the actually existing world of economic relations and transactions, as so forcefully argued in Karl Polanyi's classical discussion of the 'fictive' nature of the 'commodification' of labour, land, and money[2] (see also Jessop,

This chapter is adapted from Frederic C. Deyo, 'Small Enterprises, Supplier Networks, and Industrial Parks: Creating High-Skill Developmental Labor Systems', in *Reforming Asian Labor Systems: Economic Tensions and Worker Dissent* (Ithaca, NY: Cornell University Press, 2012). Copyright 2012 Cornell University, and used by permission of the publisher, Cornell University Press.

[1] Robert Wade, 'The WTO and the Shrinking of Development Space', in J. Timmons Roberts and Amy Bellone Hite (eds.), *The Globalization and Development Reader* (Malden, MA: Blackwell Publishing, 2007), pp. 277–94, at pp. 277–8.
[2] Karl Polanyi, 'The Self-Regulating Market and the Fictitious Commodities: Labor, Land, and Money', in Polanyi, *The Great Transformation: The Political and Economic Origins of Our Time* (Boston, MA: Beacon Press 2001 [1944]), pp. 71–80.

Ch. 5), it remains to be said that the neoliberal project, especially during its dramatic, market-fundamentalist phase during the 1980s and 1990s, pushed governments both to 'deregulate' their economies and at the same time to liberate market forces by reducing the influence of those non-state institutional and social distortions of price-making in domestic and international markets (Sum, Ch. 4).

These various neoliberal, market-oriented reforms have ironically sought to enhance domestic market competition through the creation of *re-regulatory* policies and regulatory agencies, including most prominently competition law regimes, mandated to institutionalize and enhance the workings of markets themselves, thus creating a contradiction between regulatory 'roll-back' – the defining goal of neoliberalism – and a renewed 'roll-out' of new regulatory policy.[3] At the same time, trade unionism, worker protection, and pro-worker legislation have been politically marginalized and constrained insofar as they impede the functioning and flexibility of labour markets. Internationally, the reform project has, in large measure through IFI pressures and the enforcement mechanisms of the WTO, pushed for the opening of domestic markets to foreign trade and investment.[4]

These various market-oriented reforms, including what we might term neoliberal 'competition policy' (pro-market competition reforms, including, but not limited to, reforms in domestic competition law legislation), have also confronted opposing socio-economic agendas and goals whose partial eclipse during the 1980s and early 1990s, particularly in debt-burdened countries subject to IMF conditionalities and externally imposed debt regimes,[5] have eventuated in a 'softening' and broadening of the reform project to embrace new compensating protections for workers, communities, firms, and economic sectors.

And if socio-political considerations have encouraged a rethinking of market reform and competition policy (sometimes referenced as a shift from the old 'Washington Consensus' to the new 'augmented'

---

[3] Michael Moran, 'The Rise of the Regulatory State in Britain', *Parliamentary Affairs*, 54 (2001): 19–34; David Levi-Faur and Jacint Jordana, 'The Rise of Regulatory Capitalism: The Global Diffusion of a New Order', *Annals of the American Academy of Political and Social Science*, 598 (2005): 200–17.

[4] Jamie Peck and Adam Tickell, 'Neoliberalizing Space', *Antipode*, 24 (2002): 380–404.

[5] Phillip McMichael, *Development and Social Change: A Global Perspective*, 4th edn (Thousand Oaks, CA: Pine Forge Press, 2008).

Washington Consensus[6]), a further, though related, set of debates has addressed its implications for long-term national economic growth, as suggested by Robert Wade in the quotation that opens this chapter. Here the concern shifts from social equity, economic compensation, and political stability to more narrowly construed economic development outcomes. And it is here that debates regarding the 'development deficit' of competition policy, and more specifically its outcomes for the 'competitiveness' of domestically operating firms, present themselves (see also Jessop, Ch. 5, pp. 105–10).

Market reform advocates view the question of development through the lens of efficiency. Economies and particular economic sectors grow and successfully compete through accruals to their flexibility and efficiency in adapting to market volatility, shifting human and financial resources from lower to higher value-added activities, and responding to new opportunities presented by technological change (cf. Dowdle, Ch. 1, pp. 21–9). Efficiency thus envisioned enhances competitiveness through cost reduction, responsiveness to change, and market flexibility. Domestic deregulation, along with external economic liberalization, by enhancing competitive pressures on local firms ensures that previously protected or less efficient firms either shut down or respond to new pressures through enhanced efficiencies. And these positive outcomes are in turn enhanced by competition policies that ensure that economic deregulation by the state gives way to a greater reliance on free-functioning 'markets', and not simply to alternative *private* forms of market regulation and control, as in cases of market dominance or cartelization.

Developmental critics of pro-market competition policy point to several problems with such an approach to economic growth. First, they note the problematic tension between policies of deregulation that seek to enhance the functioning of markets, on the one hand, and the need, on the other, for robust new regulatory regimes, including domestic and international competition policy itself, as well as the elaboration of a variety of political measures with which those regimes are often associated, to ensure that markets do in fact function as intended. Second, they note that the focus on market-led growth attends largely to considerations of 'static' efficiencies as firms and economic sectors respond and react, within given market

---

[6] See, e.g., Mark Breeson, 'South-East Asia and the International Financial Institutions', in Garry Rodan, Kevin Hewison, and Richard Robison (eds.), *The Political Economy of South-East Asia: Markets, Power and Contestation*, 3rd edn (Oxford University Press, 2006), pp. 240–57.

niches, to immediate competitive pressures. These responses typically emphasize cost containment and flexible adaptation to market pressures in lieu of longer-term efforts to restructure, redeploy, and develop new capabilities, organizational structures, and human resources in order to achieve longer-term 'dynamic' efficiencies, despite the fact that such efforts may eventuate in short-term inefficiencies (see also Dowdle, Ch. 1, pp. 27–9). A case in point is the often criticized South Korean programme of industrial deepening in heavy and chemical industries during the 1970s and early 1980s, a programme that produced glaring short-term inefficiencies and that defied market rationality at the time, but that laid the groundwork for a structural shift into new technologies and world competitive activities (e.g. steel production, transportation equipment, etc.) that later propelled this economy into the ranks of the 'developed' world as signalled by South Korea's 1996 entry into the OECD club of rich countries.

A third, but less often noted development deficit relates to the incompatibility of neoliberal pro-market policy with the nurturing of economic networks among both firms and workers which may function to enhance sectoral 'competitiveness' in international markets through exclusionary interfirm networks, technical co-operation, professional and interpersonal networking, and other forms of collaboration that would seem in principle to be at odds with the market-focused prescriptions of competition policy (see also Jessop, Ch. 5, pp. 108, 116–17).

II. Networks and developmental labour systems

Bob Jessop's discussion of the role of social policy in reform-era industrial development policy provides an excellent starting point for our discussion of networks and development.[7] Of particular importance is his discussion of the 'competition state', which, he argues, seeks to

> secure economic growth within its borders and/or to secure competitive advantages for capitals based in its borders ... by promoting the economic and extra-economic conditions that are currently deemed vital for success in competition with economic actors and spaces located in other states.[8]

Social policy and social institutions, he argues, constitute particularly important supply-side conditions for the competitive success of firms and working populations. And in the context of the emerging 'knowledge-based economy', with its increased reliance on intellectual labour, the role of the competition state focuses on the mobilization and

---

[7] Bob Jessop, *The Future of the Capitalist State* (Cambridge: Polity Press, 2002).
[8] Ibid., p. 96.

expansion of 'soft social resources', such as knowledge, social capital, inter-firm collaboration, R & D networking, and increased capacities for technology transfer, collective learning, and entrepreneurship. Insofar as the competition state seeks *proactively* to advance those innovative capacities essential for sectoral upgrading into higher value-added niches in global production networks and world markets, Jessop argues, it subsumes more and more domains of social life into the discursive and policy space of the market economy itself.

This chapter focuses on one such domain of social life – the socio-economic networks that help to organize and regulate much of economic activity – as well as on the ways in which states use these networks, both organizational and interpersonal, to encourage economic competitiveness and development, thus providing a partial response to Robert Wade's concern as quoted (at the beginning of this chapter) relating to the impact of trade liberalization agreements on development policy. More specifically, I examine the ways in which such networks may sometimes encourage the emergence of 'developmental labour systems', those institutional arrangements that encourage and foster among workers the job involvement and self-direction, training and skill acquisition, and technical collaboration essential to industrial upgrading. Such developmental labour systems are sometimes found in the upper tiers of organized industrial supply chains. More often, they occur within agglomerated, science-based industrial parks.

An important question arises in this regard. If developmental labour systems have traditionally been associated with job security, internal labour markets, and a variety of morale-enhancing employment protections, as in large Japanese companies, how can they be generated and sustained in the context of labour market deregulation, flexibilization, and contingency? This question applies with special force to the matter of worker training, as the use of contingent and contractual work has made worker development and training – a critical component of industrial upgrading – increasingly problematic. In South Korea, for example, increasingly prevalent fixed-duration contracts among skilled and technical workers, and the growth of 'non-regular' work for many others, has so foreshortened the time horizon for returns to training, and so increased the risks of the poaching of already trained workers by other firms, that an important institutional foundation for that country's industrial training system has been threatened. (An example of this problem is to be found in the experience of Toyota's Thailand assembly plant, where strong reliance on contingent labour has discouraged plant-level training.[9]) In this context, a new set of institutional incentives is required, incentives that reside less in the institutional structures of firms themselves, and more in broader, encompassing institutional supports that transcend firms.

In principle at least, those networks can provide important opportunities for information sharing, technical collaboration, professional development, reputation building, and job networking.[10] Indeed, AnnaLee Saxenian points in this regard to the sometimes *positive* role of high levels of job turnover, especially among skilled and technical workers, in augmenting the communication of new ideas and technologies among firms.[11] And as contingent employment has gradually displaced regular employment even among skilled and technical workers, occupational and professional networks and associations have become ever more important to increasingly mobile employees in negotiating their own career paths.

Governments, at both national and local levels, can play an important facilitative role in encouraging these socio-economic networks. Particularly important in this regard are technology transfer requirements, agreements under which international companies undertake to provide training for in-house or supply-chain technical staff, and institutional encouragement of collaborative R & D in product development and technology upgrading. These networks may perhaps most directly be encouraged in technology-based industrial parks, where information sharing, collaborative production and research, technical conferences and seminars, and other activities both benefit participating firms[12] and

---

[9] Richard Doner, personal communication, 15 June 2012.

[10] Martin Kenny, 'Lessons from the Development of Silicon Valley and its Entrepreneurial Support Network for Japan', in Shahid Yusuf, Kaoru Nabeshima, and Shoichi Yamashita (eds.), *Growing Industrial Clusters in Asia: Serendipity and Science* (Washington, DC: World Bank Publications, 2008), pp. 39–66, at p. 58.

[11] See, e.g., AnnaLee Saxenian, *Regional Advantage: Culture and Competition in Silicon Valley and Route 128* (Cambridge, MA: Harvard University Press, 1994). See also AnnaLee Saxenian and Jinn-Yuh Hsu, 'The Silicon Valley–Hsinchu Connection: Technical Communities and Industrial Upgrading', *Industrial and Corporate Change*, 10 (2001): 893–920. A similar dynamic has been found operating among less technically skilled workers, specifically janitorial workers in Silicon Valley, see Alan Hyde, 'A Closer Look at the Emerging Employment Law of Silicon Valley's High-Velocity Labour Market', in Joanne Conaghan, Richard Michael Fischl, and Karl Klare (eds.), *Labour Law in an Era of Globalization: Transformative Practices and Possibilities* (Oxford University Press, 2004), pp. 233–52.

[12] Richard Appelbaum, 'Big Suppliers in Greater China', in Hung Ho-fung (ed.), *China and the Transformation of Global Capitalism* (Baltimore: Johns Hopkins University Press, 2009), pp. 65–85, at p. 77. See also Sam Ock Park, 'ICT Clusters and Industrial

encourage professional networking and entrepreneurial ventures among skilled, technical, and professional workers.

The following discussion centres first on the emergence and promotion of supplier networks linking small- and medium-sized firms to larger downstream firms, then on the creation and functioning of industrial parks, and finally on the developmental labour systems varyingly associated with these two patterns of inter-firm networking. I illustrate the discussion by reference to the somewhat differing experiences of industrial development in Taiwan, South Korea, the Chinese mainland, and Thailand. These countries are selected to examine the developmental and labour outcomes of reform in the very different economic and political contexts of these four jurisdictions.

Insofar as supplier development programmes have traditionally embraced a variety of import replacement, domestic content, technology transfer, and trade protection policies that are increasingly prohibited under ever tighter restrictions on 'market distorting' trade and technology policies, the 'development space' for targeted industrial and supply chain policies has shrunk. This constraint forces governments to 'quietly (push) ahead to encourage new activities in ways that by-pass or go under-the-radar of the international agreements'.[13] One such approach is increased emphasis on collaborative inter-firm relations, as illustrated by developmental supply chains.

Henry Yeung (Ch. 11) provides a useful starting point in his discussion of the ways in which Asian firms have increasingly embedded themselves in global production networks, and conversely, the tendency for transnational companies to insert themselves into local industrial districts. I follow Yeung's lead here in addressing the developmental implications of this embedding process, noting the importance of the *way* in which such embedding occurs, on the one hand, and the state policies, on the other hand, that may encourage negative or positive developmental outcomes. In this regard, Michael Dowdle (Ch. 1, p. 18) points to the tendency for vertically integrated supply chains to consign labour-intensive, cost-based production to more local firms in less developed economies, while confining higher-value, technology-intensive and innovative activities to downstream, and often international, firms operating in advanced industrialized

Restructuring in the Republic of Korea', in Shahid Yusuf, Kaoru Nabeshima, and Shoichi Yamashita (eds.), *Growing Industrial Clusters in Asia: Serendipity and Science* (Washington, DC: World Bank Publications), pp. 195–216, at pp. 196, 200.

[13] Wade, 'WTO and the Shrinking of Development Space', p. 290.

economies. Further, foreign manufacturing companies, especially those with headquarters in Japan, tend to encourage their own home-country suppliers to follow them to offshore production sites, thus pre-empting high-value supplier niches which foreign firms in more developing economies might otherwise occupy. These anti-developmental outcomes are further reinforced by the labour outcomes with which they are associated. Upstream supplier firms, operating as they do in hyper-competitive market segments, employ cheap, low-skilled labour for much of their production operations, and, from the standpoint of downstream customers, are readily replaceable by other firms. Further, the growing volatility of international markets forces on them the need to flexibilize their workforces, to reduce worker benefits, and to employ large numbers of casual, part-time, and other 'irregular' workers.

In many industries, buyer firms are under little direct pressure to cultivate developmentally dynamic local supply chains. This applies both to cost-driven industries such as wearing apparel, and to high-technology industries such as electronics. The Philippines illustrates both of these. In the context of the declining garment industry, Rene Ofreneo notes the lack of backward linkage to local textile or supplier firms as many garment factories rely overwhelmingly on imported materials.[14] In the case of electronics, rapid growth has been associated less with the augmentation of local technical skills than with a predominant reliance on semi-skilled labour within both assembly plants and the local supply firms serving those plants. Lacking government support, these two major national industries have failed to spur national industrial upgrading through a nurturing of dynamic, skill- and technology-intensive domestic supply chains.

In some cases, of course, sectoral technologies and markets have encouraged the emergence of dynamic supply chains even in the absence of government incentives. In the car industry, for example, major assemblers often depend critically on the innovative and engineering capabilities of their upper-tier suppliers. To take an example from Thailand: Aapico, a domestic joint-venture firm with investors from Malaysia and Singapore, is a dynamic, technologically advanced producer of car assembly jigs and other car parts for regional assemblers.[15] The success of this company derives in large measure from the variety of co-operative

---

[14] Rene Ofreneo, 'Development Choices for Philippine Textiles and Garments in the Post-MFA Era', *Journal of Contemporary Asia*, 39 (2009): 543–61, 544.

[15] This paragraph draws from Frederic Deyo and Richard F. Doner, 'Dynamic Flexibility and Sectoral Governance in the Thai Auto Industry: The Enclave Problem', in Frederic C. Deyo,

networks and linkages it has developed with assemblers and other suppliers. These networks encourage engineering collaboration, joint production agreements, sectoral representation before the Ministry of Industry, and co-operative training programmes. The advantages these networks present from the standpoints of skill development, recruitment, R & D, and technology learning are viewed by management as critical for the success of this small company in achieving ISO certification in areas demanded by assemblers.

While this particular Thai case highlights the importance of sectoral or technological factors in shaping domestic supply chains, generally the growth of car assembly operations both in Thailand and in many other developing countries has not always had such positive developmental outcomes. This is due in part to the excessive dependence of Thailand's car industry on foreign suppliers, and its vulnerability to global financial turbulence (as witnessed during the late 1990s financial crisis, when many Thai car suppliers collapsed or were purchased by foreign companies).[16] But where such states have been able to encourage dynamic supply chains among domestic or locally sited firms, particularly in developmentally important or design-intensive sectors (such as cars), sector-specific market and technology policies on the part of downstream firms have been influenced by state policies. In South Korea, for example, the state created new incentives for major companies to develop the capabilities of supplier firms under a 'shared growth' programme linking large and small firms.[17] Such policies work to encourage downstream companies to cultivate domestic suppliers that co-engineer parts and components, assume important R & D functions, and learn to respond quickly to shifts in markets and technology.

Setting aside the importance of early government support for the spectacular growth of the South Korean car industry, even the relatively more ineffectual development role of the Thai government in promoting the car industry in Thailand illustrates the importance of such policy. Unlike South Korea, Thailand's car industry, as noted above, is heavily dependent on Japanese and other foreign companies for capital, technology, access to export markets, and, most importantly, supply chain co-ordination by

Richard F. Doner, and Eric Hershberg (eds.), *Economic Governance and the Challenge of Flexibility in East Asia* (Lanham, MD: Rowman & Littlefield, 2001), pp. 107–35.

[16] Richard Doner, *The Politics of Uneven Development: Thailand's Economic Growth in Comparative Perspective* (Cambridge University Press, 2009).

[17] 'Big Businesses Come Up with "Shared Growth" Plans', *Korea Herald*, 6 March 2011.

major assemblers such as Toyota and Honda. As part of their investment licensing agreement with the Thai Board of Investment, these
international companies until recently have been committed, under
domestic content regulation, to using domestic suppliers for their local
assembly operations. These linkages were initially promoted under the
Board of Investments Unit for Industrial Linkage Development
(BUILD) programme, established in 1991. As the inadequacies of this
programme were subsequently realized – in practice, Japanese companies
directed much of their first-tier outsourcing to Japanese supplier transplants
in Thailand rather than to local Thai firms – and as domestic content
legislation increasingly ran into difficulties with market liberalization
requirements, a follow-up National Supplier Development Programme
was launched in 1994, followed in 1995 by a sectoral multi-agency Master
Plan for the Development of Supportive Industries.[18] Perhaps in response to
the limited success of these programmes, the Thai Office of Small and
Medium Enterprises has more recently begun focusing on the supply side
of these linkages. In 2010, it announced a programme that provided
increased assistance to domestic SMEs in their efforts to export to regional
buyers, in many cases as suppliers, thus taking advantage of new opportunities presented by ASEAN regional trade liberalization.[19]

   While these various policy efforts achieved only mixed results, their
encouragement of training, R & D, technology transfer, and technical co-
operation suggests the importance not only of economic considerations
in SME policy, but also of growing appreciation of the close relationship
between the economic and social dimensions of economic policy, as seen
also in an increased emphasis on human resource development in Thai
industrial policy.[20] In this sense, the emergence and promotion of inter-
firm relations and networks comprise only one element of a more general
turn to the social dimensions of development. This turn is even more
dramatically evidenced in the promotion of high-tech industrial parks.

III.   Industrial clusters and high-tech industrial parks

During the 1970s and 1980s, East Asia's high-tech industrial parks
comprised an important instrument of industrial upgrading as 'developmental states' sought to build on the successes of early labour-intensive

---

[18] Doner, *Politics of Uneven Development*, p. 121.
[19] 'B100m Budget to Help SMEs Enter Asean', *Bangkok Post*, 3 May 2010.
[20] Doner, *Politics of Uneven Development*, pp. 125, 251.

export-oriented industrialization. These parks functioned not only to encourage economically dynamic networks of firms, but also to encourage professional networks among skilled and technical workers that further propelled developmental upgrading.

Taiwan's high-tech industrial zones, including most famously the Hsinchu Science Industrial Park, were an important early precursor. At the Hsinchu park, as described by Lin Chien-ju, an ensemble of large electronics firms and small high-tech suppliers, together facing high levels of worker turnover among both operators and engineers, were supported in part by government programmes that addressed a broad range of shared problems relating to all phases of production. These included an Employment Services Centre that provided both job placement and assistance with training and R & D activities. As well, special tax incentives were introduced to allow companies to use stock bonuses to attract and retain engineers, and an Industrial Technology Research Institute was established to encourage professional collaboration and networking among engineers and technical workers and to foster technology transfer from foreign companies.[21] (It should be noted, on the other hand, that the role of government in cluster development varies greatly across industrial sectors, even within the same park. Tain-Jy Chen, for example, finds that government played a critical role in the development of the integrated circuits industries in Taiwan's Hsinchu Science Park, but a less important role in other clusters in that same park.[22])

The Hsinchu park, established in 1980, was followed in 2001 by the creation of a second science park, the Southern Taiwan Science Park.[23] While this second park also endeavoured to address the collective requirements of technology-intensive companies, the imprint of neoliberal reform is to be seen in the ways in which those requirements were met. First, firms in the new park relied more extensively on contract labour than did their Hsinchu counterparts. Second, the new park was largely administered and controlled by local government, rather than by the national government as in the case of Hsinchu, thus modelling the administrative decentralization that is a hallmark of neoliberal

---

[21] Lin Chien-ju, 'Institutions, Local Politics, and Firm Strategies: Two Labor Systems in Taiwan', Ph.D. dissertation, Department of Sociology, Binghamton University, 2010.

[22] Tain-Jy Chen, 'The Emergence of Hsinchu Science Park as an IT Cluster', in Shahid Yusuf, Kaoru Nabeshima, and Shoichi Yamashita (eds.), *Growing Industrial Clusters in Asia: Serendipity and Science* (Washington DC: World Bank Publications, 2008), pp. 67–90, at p. 67.

[23] This discussion is based heavily on Lin, 'Institutions'.

reform. And third, private temporary placement companies, rather than government employment agencies, played the major role in managing both labour markets and training in the context of the more fluid labour markets in this more recently established park. In these and other ways, the newer park constructed its labour regime in a way more reflective of new currents of economic thinking. In both cases, it should be added, technical networks and recruitment were greatly assisted by the several technological institutes and colleges whose local presence had itself influenced the initial decisions to establish the parks.

Although Taiwan sets a high bar in establishing high-tech industrial parks, other countries pursued a similar approach during those early years of high-growth industrialization. In South Korea, the Daedeok Science Town, located in Daejeon, hosts 232 research and education institutes (eighteen of them government supported), including three major technology universities that produce large numbers of technical and engineering graduates, many at Ph.D. level. This science zone, first established in 1973 to spearhead research, is now a major locus of innovation and product development in such areas as telecommunications, biotechnology, and atomic energy. Collectively, the many research institutes in this park provide an important venue for professional collaboration, mutual learning, job placement, and joint research/production ventures among locally established high-tech firms, many quite small. Similarly, in 1980 Singapore established the Singapore Science Park. That park houses more than 350 transnational and local firms and institutions, comprising more than 9,000 researchers, engineers, and support staff. On its website it presents itself as a 'campus environment set within lush landscapes, ... an epitomy [sic] of complete work-play business lifestyle with its extensive range of business support services as well as recreational and lifestyle amenities'.[24]

More recently, the Chinese government has established the Zhongguancun Science Park, sometimes dubbed 'China's Silicon Valley'. This park benefits from the research activities and science training of nearby Peking (Beijing) University and Tsinghua (Qinghua) University, two of China's premier universities, to provide research workers and to support and promote technology transfer and development for industrial exports.[25] Following the Singapore model, this park provides a broad

---

[24] Singapore Science Park website, available at www.sciencepark.com.sg/introduction.html.
[25] Cong Cao, 'Zhongguancun and China's High-Tech Parks in Transition: Growing Pains or Premature Senility?', *Asian Survey*, 44 (2004): 647–68.

range of community, employment, housing, training, and other facilities to support the activities of the many small private firms that
populate the park and its immediate surroundings. Chinese policy has
to this point focused on technology transfer and adaptation, rather
than more fundamental innovation. This may be seen in China's
National Patent Development Strategy for 2011–20, which places less
emphasis on 'inventions' than on more mundane 'utility-model'
patents applicable to the operations of manufacturing suppliers.[26]
For this reason, much effort has gone into attracting such international IT firms as IBM, Microsoft, HP, Oracle, Cisco, Lucent Bell
Labs, and Sumitomo to collaborate with and utilize local suppliers that
have located themselves in this park.

If China's strong emphases on low- and medium-technology industrial
clusters of firms that collaborate, subcontract, share logistics, and pool
resources helps to reduce production costs,[27] they also provide the sorts
of mobility networks, job referrals, and contacts that technical and skilled
workers enjoy in high-tech parks in Taiwan, South Korea, and elsewhere.[28] While these networks do not as often eventuate in the dramatic
developmental outcomes of their counterparts in those industrially more
advanced countries, they nonetheless play an important role in lubricat-
ing the labour markets on which cluster firms rely.[29]

Given the important role of East Asian governments in thus
attending to the socio-institutional requisites of industrial advance
through support for high-tech industrial districts and parks, as well
as for the housing, recreational, and other community requirements of
workers in these parks, it is clear that Jessop's argument about
the importance of mobilizing and expanding 'soft social resources'
applies with special force to the cases thus far examined in this
chapter.[30]

[26] 'When Innovation, Too, Is Made in China', *New York Times*, 2 January 2011, B3.
[27] 'Developer Pushes China Cluster Mode,' *Bangkok Post*, 19 March 2001, available at www.
bangkokpost.com/business/economics/227473/developer-pushes-china-cluster-model.
[28] Shahid Yusuf, 'Can Clusters be Made to Order?', in Shahid Yusuf, Kaoru Nabeshima, and
Shoichi Yamashita (eds.), *Growing Industrial Clusters in Asia: Serendipity and Science*
(Washington, DC: World Bank Publications, 2008), pp. 1–37, at p. 3.
[29] Steven Casper, 'How Do Technology Clusters Emerge and Become Sustainable? Social
Network Formation and Inter-firm Mobility within the San Diego Biotechnology Cluster', *Research Policy*, 36 (2007): 438–55.
[30] Jessop, *Future of the Capitalist State*, p. 96.

IV.   Industrial parks in the lesser dragons

Asia's second-tier industrializers – Indonesia, Malaysia, and Thailand – have sought to emulate the industrial successes of South Korea and Taiwan, although with more mixed results. In Thailand, the Thaksin government sought, with only partial success (due to political opposition), to promote industrial clusters as part of an attempted return to industry policy and sector-specific development planning.[31] In part, that effort built on the earlier experience of the Industrial Estate Authority in establishing the Hi-Tech Industrial Estate north of Bangkok. This estate provides a range of housing, educational, health, and other services for resident firms and workers. But while the estate was initially intended to promote export-oriented, environmentally 'clean', high-technology industries, it has in practice offered mid-level technical and general training, along with placement of local employees in standard production work. As in the case of China, there is strong reliance in this estate on foreign firms in securing the technology, training, and high-level technical workforce needed for local operations.

While the Hi-Tech Industrial Estate does contribute to ongoing efforts to shift Thailand's export manufacturing base into higher-value-added products, there is little effort to promote the cutting-edge technological innovation found in the science parks of South Korea or Taiwan. In part in response to the disappointing outcomes of this earlier venture, Thailand's National Science and Technology Development Agency opened the Thailand Science Park in 2002, seeking more explicitly to support technology-intensive businesses through R & D collaboration with researchers at nearby universities, including the Asian Institute of Technology and four other national research institutes. This park seeks to give the government a more forceful role in encouraging private firms to engage in greater research and development activities.[32] Whether, given Thailand's political and institutional weakness, this park will achieve its stated goals is uncertain.

While high-tech industrial parks play a key developmental role in industrially advanced countries, other countries that possess weaker technological, educational, and industrial infrastructures and that are more dependent on foreign capital for their industrial development rely

---

[31] Doner, *Politics of Uneven Development*, p. 232.

[32] 'Technology Agency Hopes to Boost R & D by Expanding Thailand Science Park', *Nation*, 12 May 2009.

largely on the developmental possibilities residing in supply chains. For a country like Thailand, it is perhaps helpful to set aside a restricted focus on Schumpeterian *innovation*, and to take more seriously the continuing developmental potential afforded by technology transfer and incremental improvement, as lesser economies attempt upward mobility in international production networks and world markets.[33] If South Korea, Taiwan, and Singapore are to assume full status in the 'core' of the world economy by capturing the economic rents of foundational innovation, they must institutionalize new innovative capacities that go beyond the learning and adaptation of technologies invented elsewhere.[34] Less demanding are the requirements of upward mobility facing China, Thailand, or the Philippines, where technology transfer and adaptation, rather than innovation, offer continuing possibilities for economic advance within the middle ranks of the world economy.[35] In this lesser context, the developmental promotion of domestic supplier networks, as discussed earlier, assumes relatively greater importance. As noted by Richard Doner, different levels of development require different institutional tasks and capabilities corresponding to different levels of difficulty.[36]

V.   Creating high-skill developmental labour systems

While high-tech industrial parks and clusters take to an entirely new level the sorts of economic network sometimes found in vertical supply chains, they are associated as well with the emergence of economic networks among skilled and technical workers. As in the case of inter-firm networks, these latter professional networks tend to carve out exclusionary zones of mobility and opportunity that compromise the functioning of flexible labour markets. In this sense, they offer a prime example of developmental initiatives that contradict the principal tenets of

---

[33] Richard Doner suggests that this distinction may be too stark, that innovation may only comprise a late culmination of earlier steps beginning with reverse engineering and other initiatives best understood as incremental adaptations. This said, however, the distinction does point to very real cross-national and sectoral differences in technological and learning capacities. Personal communication, 15 June 2012.

[34] Manuel Castells, *The Information Age: Society, Economy and Culture*, 2nd edn, vol. 1: *The Rise of the Network* Society (Malden, MA: Blackwell Publishing, 2000), p. 124. Also Chen, 'Emergence of Hsinchu Science Park', p. 78.

[35] For discussion of this difference see Jeffrey Sachs, 'A New Map of the World', *Economist*, 22 June 2000: 81–3.

[36] Doner, *Politics of Uneven Development*, p. 4.

competition policy, albeit in this instance in labour markets rather than product markets.

Competition policy, as traditionally considered, focuses primarily on product markets. To the extent that it attends to services, it emphasizes final consumption. Rarely does it explicitly engage labour markets. But having said this, it is clear that pro-market competition policy has in fact powerfully, if less directly, informed labour market policy, as IFIs, corporations, and national governments have persisted in pushing for labour market deregulation and flexibility. Indeed, it can be argued that labour market reform has comprised a more coherent and successful aspect of competition policy than parallel efforts to reduce impediments to market competition in product markets themselves. And it is in this context that economic networks have played so important a role in addressing the developmental deficits of pro-market reform policies.

From the standpoint of labour, this may be seen in three important areas: labour market functioning, training, and the encouragement of entrepreneurship. First, as noted earlier, inter-firm and professional/technical networks provide modalities for job search, reputation building, and career development that are often compromised by growing labour market contingency and flexibility. Second, the provision and promotion of training, a critical function of industrial labour systems from the standpoint of both employers and workers, has become increasingly important and problematic in the context of organizational de-verticalization, growing economic turbulence, market segmentation, new technologies favouring small dynamic firms, and the growth of contingent and contractual work across all skill groups, including professionals. The state's role in creating or facilitating the development of dynamic supply chains and industrial parks can play an important role in this regard. Third, and as important, are the entrepreneurial incentives and opportunities that network-promotion policies create for workers. It was noted that worker entrepreneurialism is important for the efficient functioning of flexible labour markets, for the success of training initiatives, and for the livelihood security of workers and their families. Of particular interest here are opportunities for technical and engineering workers to start new businesses, in some cases as spin-off firms supported or sponsored by their former employers.[37] Such spin-offs occur most often in large, well-established clusters with nearby research institutions.[38]

[37] Kenny, 'Lessons', p. 49; Chen, 'Emergence of Hsinchu Science Park', p. 82.
[38] Yusuf, 'Can Clusters be Made to Order?', p. 7.

VI.   Conclusion: competition, competitiveness, and economic networks

Insofar as networked inter-firm relations and professional networks supplant or circumvent price-driven market transactions with particularistic ties rooted in personal and social considerations and long-term trust, they comprise exclusionary bonds that close the transactional spaces and opportunities otherwise available to non-networked economic agents. These exclusionary social bonds and networks stand in a problematic relationship to the substance and intent of competition policy, both domestic and international. But, having said this, it must also be noted that official encouragement of these networks has found an accepted place within the neoliberal project. It may thus be argued that network-based competitive strategies and supportive state policies have found a relatively secure perch within, rather than at the margins of or outside, the neoliberal project, despite their inconsistency with market competition and competition policy.

This paradox may be explained in several ways. First, their emphasis on supply-side synergies and dynamic labour markets ensures that they operate outside the market to which competition policy normally attends (cf. Jessop, Ch. 5, pp. 106–7). It is in this sense that they function 'beneath the radar'. Second, these networks are often the product of indirect and often very modest state interventions, interventions that are seen as promoting development by indirectly focusing on social policy rather than directly focusing on industrial policymaking. Third, these networks tend to be organized at local, rather than national levels, thus supporting a primary thrust of reform policy: the decentralization and localization of government activities. Alvin So and others have noted in this regard the developmental role of local, rather than national, government in China during recent years.[39] And, fourth, they are seen as being the product less of state policy than of social structural dynamics, particularly in the case of the largely informal (and invisible) social relations that comprise the 'glue' of inter-firm networks, thus conforming to the mandate for state deregulation.

Thus, while it might appear that state policies that promote competition-inhibiting inter-firm networks would seem to defy major tenets of

---

[39] Alvin So, 'Rethinking the Chinese Development Miracle', in Hung Ho-fung (ed.), *China and the Transformation of Global Capitalism* (Baltimore: Johns Hopkins University Press, 2009), pp. 50–63.

neo-liberal market reform, such policies are unlikely to be drawn into the policy debates surrounding competition policy, and indeed have garnered financial and advisory encouragement from the World Bank, the Asia Development Bank, and other IFIs in Asia and beyond. In this way, they are not conceptualized as alternatives to the forms of socio-economic ordering recommended by the neoliberal model. In the next and concluding chapter in this volume (Ch. 13), Dowdle explores further what all this might mean for the evolution of 'global competition law'.

Whither Asia? Whither capitalism? Whither global competition law?

MICHAEL W. DOWDLE

I. Introduction

The subject of this volume is a story twice told. It is, in both accounts, a story of competition. It is first a story of competition law, which regulates competition between firms in the context of the marketplace. But today's orthodox understanding of competition law itself is but spoils derived from a larger competition, a competition among different kinds of capitalism. And it was out of this larger competition that Asian capitalism was also born.

This volume began as an exploration of how the marketplace competition of competition law was regulated under a purported Asian capitalism – whether, in this context at least, Asian capitalism did indeed represent something different, normatively or descriptively, from the North Atlantic capitalisms described by David Soskice and Peter Hall (and others) in their discussion of 'varieties of capitalism'. Here, I shall argue, what the chapters in this volume collectively show is that there is indeed an Asian approach to competition regulation, one that derives from an Asian capitalism, but that is distinguished, not as an alternative model to the orthodox model, but as a unique melding of a diversity of regulatory models.

In other words, and following up on the concluding observations made by Bob Jessop in Chapter 5 (pp. 117–20), what makes Asian capitalist regulation of competition distinct is its pluralist, meta-regulatory character. This is distinctly 'Asian' in the sense that, as Barry Hooker and others have famously shown, Asia, more than anywhere else, has long experience with legal pluralism – at least in the harder, systemic form that we are talking about here.[1] This correspondence is not coincidental.

---

[1] M. B. Hooker, *Legal Pluralism: An Introduction to Colonial and Neo-colonial Laws* (Oxford: Clarendon, 1975). See also Michael W. Dowdle, 'Asian Regionalism and Law: The Continuing Contribution of "Legal Pluralism"', in Mark Beeson and Richard Stubbs (eds.), *Routledge Handbook of Asian Regionalism* (London: Routledge, 2012), pp. 226–35.

Asian pluralism in competition regulation derives from the same global dynamics that five hundred years earlier gave rise to Asian legal pluralism. Moreover, as we shall also see, these dynamics – which used to be primarily Asian in location – are increasingly colonizing the global stage, including the North Atlantic economies that had long been insulated from them. This being the case, Asia's distinctly pluralist way of regulating competition may have something important to tell us about a possible future of competition regulation that goes in a different direction from that presently envisioned by 'global competition law'.

II.   Core versus peripheral regulatory ordering in the Asian (and world) regulation of competition

As described in Chapter 1, the issue of an Asian capitalism has two dimensions: an external dimension and an internal dimension. The external dimension seeks to identify Asian capitalism by contrasting it with other varieties of capitalism. This involves identifying and categorizing norms and structures that impart a systematic coherence to Asian capitalism, such as production networks or the prevalence of the 'developmental state' model of competition regulation. The internal component looks at the internal architecture of that capitalism, how and why different actors and regions take different functions – as between the upstream versus the downstream ends of production chains, for example – and how this diversity of functions nevertheless coheres into a single conceptual capitalism.

Let's look at the internal component first. What might this have to tell us about Asian regulation of competition? As noted in Chapter 1, the geography that we have defined as 'Asia' in the context of Asian capitalism evinces a clear, and clearly contiguous, core–periphery gradient (Dowdle, Ch. 1, pp. 16–19). The chapters of this volume show that this gradient can also be observed in the region's regulation of competition, and in ways largely consistent with the hypotheses developed in the first chapter. Chapters by both John Gillespie (Ch. 8) and myself (Ch. 9) show that the peripheral markets examined by them did indeed exhibit social functionalities that are significantly more complex than those presumed by the orthodox model. They also have a distinctly wider range of social functionalities; and were also significantly more fragmented.

All this would indeed suggest that the orthodox model of competition would be problematic when applied to more peripheral economies. This hypothesis is supported in particular by the analysis in Chapter 9 of the role that neoliberal market competition played in China's melamine milk adulteration crisis of 2008. But further support comes from Frederic Deyo's study of Asian industrial parks in the context of Asia's evolving, what we might call 'post-development', state in Chapter 12. One of the findings of Deyo's study is that the post-industrial industrial park model that worked so well in promoting competitive factor endowments in Taiwan and South Korea was not so effective when transplanted to China and Thailand. In these more peripheral regions, industrial parks ended up focusing more on simply attracting elite foreign firms by offering relative conveniences rather than by offering unique, geography-specific resources. While this latter strategy may be effective in promoting (perhaps temporarily) economic growth in the static sense, it does not appear to promote dynamic capacity for local economic *development* in the way in which Taiwan and South Korea are able to. In this sense, Deyo's study provides additional demonstration that competitive institutions and strategies that work for core regions will not necessarily work in the same way when transferred to peripheral regions, even when both regions belong to a single 'Asian capitalism'.

But whether or not Asia is distinct in all this is difficult to say. There are very few studies of what markets and market competition tend to look like in more peripheral geographies even in the context of the North Atlantic economies. The orthodox, neoliberal model is a model that has been derived exclusively from the experiences of core economies. But one suspects, in fact, that the experiences described herein of the peripheral economies' encounters with an orthodox model of competition law are probably not much different from those of peripheral economies in other parts of the world, including those that are embedded in the North Atlantic *économie-monde(s)*, although some of the discussion in Chapter 9 suggests that they might be aggravated in Asian capitalism by its more pronounced use of production chains (cf. Dowdle, Ch. 9, pp. 218–27). But, in the main, the peripheral economic dynamics that trigger market complexity and fragmentation have also been identified in Europe and Latin America.[2]

---

[2] This observation is further supported by Herman Schwartz, 'Dependency or Institutions? Economic Geography, Causal Mechanisms, and Logic in the Understanding of Development', *Studies in Comparative International Development*, 42 (2007): 115–35; Fernand Braudel, *Civilization and Capitalism, 15th–18th Century. Volume 3, The Perspective of the World*, trans. Siân Reynolds (Berkeley: University of California Press, 1992), p. 39; Johann Heinrich von Thünen, *Von Thunen's Isolated State: An English Edition of Der Isolierte Staat*, ed. Peter Hall, trans. Carla M. Wartenberg (Oxford: Pergamon, 1966 [1826]).

Following on from Schumpeter's observation regarding the special role of 'core firms' in defining an economy's capacities,[3] one suspects that in the context both of varieties of capitalism and of the varieties of *économie-monde* that form around them, it is primarily in the cores of these economies that the distinguishing structural differences are found, and not so much in their peripheries.

Our lack of study devoted to peripheral economic dynamics is one of the more glaring omissions in our efforts to develop a global competition law. Such few studies as do exist tend to treat peripheral divergences from the global model as simple regulatory or economic failings. The standard analytic template in this regard is simply to identify deviations and bemoan them as obviously contributing to the underdevelopment of the locale under examination.[4] Even our rather cursory exploration of this issue in this volume suggests that this template is grossly oversimplified. As theorized in Chapter 1 and demonstrated in Chapter 9, peripheral economies clearly have a distinct set of capitalist logics at play: their markets often have different internal structures and a different (and more diverse) set of social functionalities. A 'global competition law' that fails to take this into account is not going to be global at all.

III.   The global dimension of Asian competition regulation

Therefore, as far as a distinctly Asian approach to competition deriving from a distinctly Asian capitalism is concerned, it is likely to reside in the other dimension of a purported Asian capitalism, the more global dimension that distinguishes Asian capitalism as a system from other varieties of capitalist systems.

A.   The complexity of the task

At first blush, however, the chapters to this volume do not seem to support such a project. When we speak of an Asian capitalism or an Asian way of regulating competition, we generally have in mind some conceptual framework with unifying features that both delineate its boundaries and distinguish it from the coherent versions of North Atlantic capitalisms

---

[3] Joseph A. Schumpeter, *Capitalism, Socialism, and Democracy*, 3rd edn (New York: Harper & Row, 1975), pp. 84–5.

[4] See, e.g., World Bank, *Doing Business* (Washington, DC: The World Bank and International Finance Corporation, 2004–). See also IFC and World Bank, 'Doing Business: Measuring Business Regulation', available at www.doingbusiness.org/.

described by Hall and Soskice (cf. Sum, Ch. 4). In the context of Asia, we see this to some extent in the disaggregation of production into transnational production chains and production networks (e.g., Yeung, Ch. 11). But, as far as competition law is concerned, it is harder to find something fitting this description.

Prior to the 1990s, we might have talked about the 'developmental state' as a distinctly Asian approach to competition. But over the past two decades, most, if not all, Asian countries have made significant commitments to bring more North Atlantic modes of regulating competition into their positive regulatory frameworks.[5] Each of the three countries presented in the country-specific chapters to this volume – Japan, China, and Vietnam – have over the course of the last ten years adopted legal frameworks for regulating competition that come directly from the North Atlantic model. In the light of this, it seems hard to talk any more about a distinctly 'Asian alternative' to the orthodox model.

And at the same time, we have also seen that North Atlantic competition regulatory regimes are themselves much more complex and diversified than the orthodox model itself portrays (Jessop, Ch. 5; cf. Sum, Ch. 4). This diversity and complexity lies in the many exceptions, both contemporary and historical, that North Atlantic economies make to their competition regimes, but which do not generally show up in the global competition law discourse – exceptions for public goods and services; exceptions for certain industries, exceptions to promote innovation, exceptions that protect the labour force, and so on (see, e.g., Dowdle, Ch. 1, pp. 28, 31; Prosser, Ch. 10, pp. 231–8). In fact, as quoted in Chapter 1, Joseph Schumpeter has argued that, so great are these exceptions, they swallow up the rule as far as the core firms that actually shape and structure the economy are concerned.[6] So, while there does not appear to be a particular, distinguishing feature of Asian regulation of competition, at the same time the particular regulatory models commonly attributed to North Atlantic modes of regulating competition seems itself to be more speculative than real.

---

[5] See also David J. Gerber, *Global Competition: Law, Markets and Globalization* (Oxford University Press, 2010), pp. 205–35; R. Ian McEwin, *Competition Law in Southeast Asia* (Cambridge University Press, forthcoming).

[6] Schumpeter, *Capitalism, Socialism, and Democracy*, pp. 84–5. See also James Crotty, 'Core Industries, Coercive Competition and the Structural Contradiction of Global Neoliberalism', in Nicholas Phelps and Philip Raines (eds.), *The New Competition for Inward Investment: Companies, Institutions and Territorial Development* (Cheltenham: Edward Elgar, 2003), pp. 9–38.

B.   Asian capitalism and legal pluralism

In sum, we have not found in Asian capitalism a distinct, alternative regulatory *model* for ordering and regulating competition in the way in which we originally framed the pursuit. But these chapters nevertheless do collectively evince a distinct, and distinctly Asian, *approach* to regulating competition, an approach itself that derives from a similarly distinctive aspect of Asian capitalism. Moreover, this is an approach that corresponds to a particularly Asian form of regulation that has long been identified in other contexts as what M. B. Hooker famously referred to as 'legal pluralism'. Asian competition regulation is distinctly 'pluralist' in comparison with its North Atlantic counterpart.

What is legal pluralism in this context? This term has a fair diversity of meaning nowadays, but not all of them are consistent with what Hooker was trying to identify in the context of Southeast Asian law. For Hooker, legal pluralism was not simply the presence of a diversity of 'soft law' legal institutions. Hooker's legal pluralism was a distinctly constitutional phenomenon, not simply a sociological phenomenon. It is a vision of legal pluralism that takes, consciously or unconsciously, the monocratic conceptual framework for law articulated by Hans Kelsen and H. L. A. Hart as its starting point. Both Kelsen and Hart, following Max Weber, saw municipal law as being monocratic, in the sense of having a single conceptual point of origin from which the rest of the legal system was rationally extracted. Kelsen famously located this point of origin in what he variously called the Grundnorm or the constitution, depending on whether he was conceptualizing it epistemically or temporally.[7] Hart located it in his 'rule of recognition', and identified it as being sociological in character. Hooker claims that what distinguished Southeast Asian legal systems was that they were frequently not monocratic in this sense, they were polycratic – in the sense of containing multiple points of epistemic or constitutional sourcing.[8] This is what he meant by 'legal pluralism'.[9]

---

[7] Hans Kelsen, *Pure Theory of Law*, trans. Max Knight (Berkeley: University of California Press, 1967 [1934]), pp. 205–8 (on the Grundnorm), 221–4 (on the constitution). See also H. L. A. Hart, *The Concept of Law*, 2nd edn (Oxford: Clarendon Press, 1994 [1961]).

[8] See generally Hooker, *Legal Pluralism*. Hooker also identified a legal pluralism operating in certain African legal systems.

[9] John Griffiths, in his germinal article on legal pluralism, referred to Hooker's legal pluralism being a 'weak' form of legal pluralism, as contrasted with a 'strong' form that does not distinguish between state and non-state forms of 'law' in its determination of plurality. John Griffiths, 'What Is Legal Pluralism?', *Journal of Legal Pluralism and Unofficial Law*, 24 (1987): 1–55, 5.

But what does this mean in the context of competition regulation? Notice, to begin with, the 'capitalisms' to which the various works on capitalism refer are also monocratic. Each state has one particular variety of capitalism. The correspondence between the state's monocratic variety of capitalism and its monocratic national legal system is not mere coincidence. Hall and Soskice identify a particular variety of capitalism in a state's legal regulation of corporate governance. To the extent that a state's law is monocratic, its regulation of corporate governance will be monocratic; and that means that that state's particular variety of capitalism will also be monocratic.

And, of course, if a state's particular variety of capitalism is monocratic, so, too, is the way in which that capitalism regulates competition. This is plainly evident in the conceptual hegemony of what we are referring to as the orthodox model of competition regulation (see especially Sum, Ch. 4). That model is not conceptualized as coexisting in national regulatory space with other models of competition regulation. Of course, as we discussed in Chapter 1 (p. 31), a state often removes particular aspects of its economy from the reach of that model – such as labour (see, e.g., Deyo, Ch. 12) and public services (see, e.g., Prosser, Ch. 10, pp. 231–8). But these removals are conceptualized as exceptions, not as alternative forms of competition regulation stemming from alternative forms of capitalist ordering. In Kelsenian terms, we could say that, in its North Atlantic guise, competition regulation functions as the Grundnorm of a state's 'economic constitution', aka its variety of capitalism.

By contrast, what this volume suggests is that just as Asian legal systems are distinctly 'pluralist' – in the sense of being polycratic rather than monocratic – so, too, is Asian capitalism's regulation of competition.

Of course, as is described particularly well by Bob Jessop in Chapter 5, in reality all national economies actually comprise a diversity of capitalisms, just as all national environments actually comprise a diversity of legal 'systems' in the soft-law sense of the term.[10] But, as noted above, North Atlantic models of competition regulation do not conceptualize this diversity in terms of being polycratic. Rather, they conceptualize it as consisting of exceptions to a nevertheless monocratic framework. What distinguishes Asian modes of competition regulation in this regard is the willingness to conceptualize this diversity in distinctly polycratic terms.

---

[10] Griffiths, 'What Is Legal Pluralism?', 11. See also Sally Merry, 'Legal Pluralism', *Law and Society Review*, 22 (1988): 869–96.

Perhaps the clearest example of this is found in China's Antimonopoly Law (Zheng, Ch. 7). Here the law itself expressly recognizes two different capitalist models operating simultaneously in the Chinese economy. These are what are sometimes called the 'private economy' – arguably a variant of CME capitalism, given that law's gravitation towards the German as opposed to the US competition law – and the state-run economy, of the sort that is sometimes referred to as 'state capitalism', and the Antimonoply Law applies a differently conceptualized mode of competition regulation to each (see also Prosser, Ch. 10, pp. 249–52).

A different example of this can be seen in John Gillespie's study of competition regulation in Vietnam. Within the context of Vietnam's national economy, Gillespie identifies three distinct varieties of capital-ism, each corresponding to a different social-class identity. This parallels even more closely Hooker's particular description of legal pluralism, in which the different legal 'systems' often attached to different ethnic or economic classes of the population. In contrast to China, however, the diversity of capitalisms found in Vietnam, which corresponds to the different 'networks' that are the subjects of Gillespie's case studies, are not codified or recognized in Vietnam's positive Competition Law. But they are nevertheless socially articulated, not as exceptions to the state law, but as stemming from alterative sources of ordering. Moreover, the party-state seems to accept this distinctly polycratic arrangement by balancing these different capitalisms against one another rather than by simply distinguishing them as particular exceptions to a single normative model.

In this sense, both China's and Vietnam's regulatory treatment of competition lies much more along the lines of that particular kind of meta-regulation that Andrew Dunsire has famously termed 'collibration'.[11] Collibration is a style of meta-regulation that regulates, not directly through the establishment of a comprehensive system of legal norms applied directly and uniformly across the whole of the regulated society, but indirectly, by constantly arbitraging between different regulatory systems that overlap within the target regulatory space. As a very simple example of this, imagine a new type of contract dispute brought before a court. It is a new kind of dispute, so there are no established rules under contract law for its resolution. In such a circumstance, one way in which

---

[11] Andrew Dunsire, *Manipulating Social Tensions: Collibration as an Alternative Mode of Government Intervention*, MPIFG Discussion Paper 93/7 (Cologne: Max-Plank-Institut für Gesellschaftsforschung, 1993).

the court could regulate this new development is simply through the articulation of a new or more refined principle of contract law.[12] Alternatively, the court might focus instead on the question of whether this dispute actually lies in contract, as opposed to, say, tort or some aspect of public law.[13] This would be more in the form of collibrative regulation – regulating by arbitraging between different regulatory systems, rather than by interpreting and applying the rules internal to a particular system.

To some extent, North Atlantic economies also do this in the context of competition law, most clearly by arbitraging disputes between competition law and public law. As Tony Prosser has demonstrated, the public law system can be seen as an alternative economic system to the private economic system governed by competition law.[14] And as both he and Imelda Maher showed in their respective contributions to this volume, regulatory bodies in Europe in particular have often arbitraged between the public and private spheres in developing their overall regulation of competition (see, e.g., Prosser, Ch. 10, pp. 231–8). But the various capitalism literatures are concerned solely with what we might call private capitalisms, capitalisms formally driven by pursuit of and expectation of private gain. The orthodox model of competition regulation similarly sees competition regulation as only having meaning in the context of private markets (Dowdle, Ch. 1, pp. 21–4). The public–private arbitration explored by Prosser and Maher is therefore not conceptualized as an arbitration between different 'capitalisms' or between different modes of 'competition law', the varieties of capitalism and the competition law literatures' understanding of these terms.

Simon Vande Walle's study of the ongoing evolution of competition regulation in Japan can be seen as similarly articulating a distinctively pluralist, collibrational view of competition regulation. But, here, the collibration is inter-temporal rather than continuous. More like the North Atlantic economies, Japan has tended to adhere to a single mode of competition regulation, at least formally (see generally Vande Walle, Ch. 6). For the most part, it has not applied differently theorized competition-regulatory models to different sectors operating simultaneously within the economy. But whereas North Atlantic competition

---

[12] See, e.g., Ronald Dworkin, *Law's Empire* (Cambridge, MA: Belknap Press, 1986).
[13] See, e.g., *O'Reilly* v. *Mackman*, [1983] 2 AC 237.
[14] Tony Prosser, *The Limits of Competition Law: Markets and Public Services* (Oxford University Press, 2005), pp. 20–4, 35–8.

regulatory regimes seem particularly entrenched in their national space[15] (as is consistent with their constitutional character – recall that entrenchment is a distinguishing feature of constitutionalism[16]), Japan has consistently oscillated between the North Atlantic and its own indigenous regulatory models in response to changes in its economic condition. Such oscillation is consistent with a collibrative style of regulation, and could in this sense mark Japan's approach to competition regulation as having a distinctly pluralist character to it as well.

Tony Prosser's chapter, 'Competition law and the role of the state in East Asia', gives further support for this distinctly pluralist approach to competition regulation. We noted above that in North Atlantic economies, the capitalist regime and its particular manifestation of competition take on a constitutional quality. In global competition law, we see this reflected in the orthodox model's preference – if not insistence – that competition law be administered by an independent regulatory agency that is able to operate above everyday politics, a form of entrenchment consistent with the distinctive entrenchment characteristic of constitutions.[17] In Asia, however, this is not the case. As described by Prosser, Asian governments have been significantly more inclined to link competition regulation to everyday politics, rather than to try to isolate it from that politics. Even under the more authoritarian regimes of East and Southeast Asia, everyday 'politics' is a distinctly pluralist and collibrative regulatory regime compared with the technocratic forms of regulation advocated by the orthodox model (in the form, for example, of 'independent' competition authorities).[18]

Some might argue that the real reason why many East and Southeast Asian countries prefer to condition the competition regime on politics, either formally or informally, is because they have no intention of adhering to that regime in the first place. Indeed, the same criticism is likely to be levelled against Asia's pluralist model as a whole. What we are calling 'legal pluralism', one might argue, is really just legal fraud. It is a condition in which the state wants to appear to be promoting market perfecting competition, perhaps in order to attract outside investors,

---

[15] See generally Gerber, *Global Competition*.
[16] Bruce A. Ackerman, *We the People, Vol. 1: Foundations* (Cambridge, MA: Harvard University Press, 1991), pp. 3–34.
[17] Ibid., pp. 3–34.
[18] Cf. Bronwen Morgan, *Social Citizenship in the Shadow of Competition: The Bureaucratic Politics of Regulatory Justification* (Aldershot: Ashgate, 2003).

perhaps in order to appear to be serving the public good of its own populace. While in fact, due possibly to an affinity for corruption or for other self-serving or protectionist reasons, it has no real intention of doing so. In this case, 'pluralism' is simply another name for a political state doing whatever it wants to at any particular point in time.

It is common for people to have difficulty in taking seriously practices and perspectives that deviate from their own presumptions. It is very easy, and perhaps comforting, to look at a regulatory system that deviates from our own expectations and simply attribute those deviations to ignorance or bad faith. But, as I have argued elsewhere, and as evinced in the interpretive strategy known as the 'principle of charity' (which argues that 'we make maximum sense of the words and thoughts of others when we interpret in a way that optimises agreement'[19]), it is not a good strategy for making sense out of social behaviour – especially in cases such as this, where the chapters in this book offer little support for any such scepticism.[20] With the possible exception, ironically enough, of post-war Japan, whose competition law was dictated to it by its US occupiers, Asia's competition laws have generally been the product of significant deliberation. China spent over ten years on the development of its Antimonopoly Law. Vietnam spent five years in the drafting of its Competition Law. And even Japan's subsequent oscillations have taken place against a background of considerable deliberation and debate. The energy devoted to these issued by the participants in the development of these competition laws (and oscillations) clearly suggests that they believed that these laws were going to mean something important.

Similarly, the distinctly political character of competition regulation described by Prosser is overt and acknowledged, and even described in positive law. It is not hidden or disguised. This is not the way one goes about perpetuating legislative fraud. The policymakers and politicians described in these chapters who are involved in the distinctive 'politics' that shape Asian competition regulation are described as doing so openly, through argument over public justification, something that is

---

[19] Donald Davidson, *Inquiries into Truth and Interpretation* (Oxford: Clarendon, 1984), p. 197.

[20] For an application of the principle of charity to comparative law, see Michael W. Dowdle, 'Of Parliaments, Pragmatism, and the Dynamics of Constitutional Development: The Curious Case of China', *New York University School of Law Journal of International Law and Politics*, 35 (2002): 1–200, 77–87; Michael W. Dowdle, 'Constitutional Listening', *Chicago-Kent Law Review*, 88 (2012): 115–56.

far removed from dynamics of 'political capitalism' described by Max Weber (Jessop, Ch. 5, pp. 112–13).

Finally, the correspondence between Asia's pluralist approach to competition regulation and its pluralist legal systems is not coincidental. Both seem to have been born out of and to reflect the same larger environmental dynamic. Asia's legal pluralism was a product of a pre-modern Southeast Asia's uniquely globalized *économie-monde*. Since the thirteenth century, Southeast Asia has sat at the heart of what was probably the world's most globalized trade network, a network driven by a distinctly 'global' demand for Southeast Asian spices. With each succeeding century, new civilizations would come to Southeast Asia to try to tie into or otherwise gain control of that network: Indian civilization in the twelfth century, Arab-Muslim civilization in the fifteenth century, European civilization in the late sixteenth century, and Chinese civilization since an indeterminate time. As each civilization established itself, it brought its culture, including its legal culture. But since their principal interest in establishing themselves was trade, not simple conquest of land for land's sake, none felt particularly threatened by – much less the need to overcome and eliminate through cultural, religious, or legal confrontation – the practices and accoutrements of the civilizations that were there before them. (It probably helped, in this regard, that the Muslim civilization that entered and colonized the regions from around the fourteenth to the seventeenth centuries was itself distinctly pluralist in its treatment of other cultures.) Instead of supplanting earlier laws, the laws of the new trading colonizers were simply laid down on top of these earlier laws, serving to maintain the prior cultural expectation of the people of the colonizing civilization without worrying about or disrupting the prior cultural expectations of the people who were there before them. Legal pluralism was the result of this unique process of continual cultural overlayering.[21]

So, too, might we say about present-day Asian capitalism. At the more elite and more internationalized levels of Asia's economy, IFI conditionalities, the development community, and American soft power are transplanting LME capitalism into social spaces that are sympathetic to its visions (see also Gillespie, Ch. 8, pp. 186–91). At the same time, at the level of the higher-end productive economy, a different, Japanese form of capitalism, once centred on disaggregated

---

[21] See generally M. B. Hooker, *A Concise Legal History of South-East Asia* (Oxford: Clarendon, 1978). See also Dowdle, 'Asian Regionalism and Law', pp. 226–32.

forms of production, is being transplanted through production chains and now production networks (Yeung, Ch. 11; cf. Deyo, Ch. 12). These transplanted forms of capitalism generally do not reach the lower ends of the economy, however, and so there often remains there other, more traditional, forms of capitalism, such as relational capitalism, production-oriented capitalism, even state-socialist capitalism (Gillespie, Ch. 8, pp. 183–5; see also Dowdle, Ch. 9, pp. 218–27). It is the coexistence of this socially layered arrangement of capitalisms that give Asian approaches to competition law its distinctly pluralistic character, just as it was the coexistence of socially layered legal expectations that gave Southeast Asian law its distinctly pluralist character.

C.   But why not pluralism? Explaining North Atlantic divergence

But how should we regard Asian capitalism's distinctly pluralist approach to competition? Some, following perhaps the perspective of Robert Bork, would dismiss this approach as simply a 'non sequitur' with regard to what competition is really about.[22] Asia's pluralist approach to competition regulation, they would say, is not really about competition in the traditional sense of pursuing an efficiently functioning market that maximizes social welfare. It may be about politically driven distribution; it may be about protecting producers; it may even be about protecting workers or promoting political-economic stability. But this is simply not what competition and competition law is meant to do.[23] Asian 'competition' is to competition what headcheese is to cheese – a usable food to be sure, but not really cheese.

But aren't we really looking at this question from the wrong direction? We have been describing Asian capitalism by comparing and contrasting it with what I have been calling the 'orthodox' North Atlantic model. In this way, we treat the North Atlantic model as ordinary, and Asian competition as extraordinary, as the 'constitutive other'. But as the chapters that comprise Part I of this book show, in many ways it is global competition law that is problematic. The actual dynamics, inputs, and effects of competition and its regulation in a sociological sense are significantly more complex that the 'orthodox model' gives them credit for being. As suggested by Prosser (Ch. 10), Jessop (Ch. 5), and

---

[22] Robert H. Bork, *The Antitrust Paradox*, 2nd edn (New York: Free Press, 1993), p. 428.
[23] See Lawrence S. Liu, 'In Fairness We Trust? Why Fostering Competition Law and Policy Ain't Easy in Asia', unpublished paper, 19 October 2004.

Joseph Schumpeter before them,[24] hidden behind the unified theoretical and doctrinal front of that model lurks a complexity whose exceptions may be so great as to swallow the orthodoxy.

From this perspective, it would be the pluralist model of Asia, not the monocratic model of northern Europe, that seems to be more consistent with the actual reality of competition, even as that phenomenon is practised in North Atlantic capitalisms. And this argues that it is the vision of competition advanced by the North Atlantic capitalisms that need justification more than that of Asia. In other words, perhaps the real question we should be asking is not so much 'why is the Asian model the way it is?', but 'why is the orthodox model the way it is?'.

The orthodox model that defines global competition law was itself the product of competition. That model derives directly from US antitrust law, which began to take shape in the latter part of the nineteenth century.[25] Throughout the North Atlantic economies, industrialization converted firms into large accumulators and repositories of surplus value. The universal question of industrialization was what to do with the value that was being collected in these firms: how to 'regulate' it and how to distribute it. Different populations and classes within society laid claim to that value. Initially these included primarily workers – because, they said, it derived from their labour; investors – because, they said, that value derived from their investment; and the state – because, it said, that value derived from the larger socio-political environment that it provided.

On the European continent, two possible solutions to this problem emerged. Perhaps the first was that advocated by Karl Marx; it argued that surplus value should be distributed to the workers whose labour created such value.[26] The solution that actually found implementation, however, was that of German corporatism, in which firms were permitted to remain autonomous, but nevertheless were engaged as agents of the state, being allowed to keep some of the surplus value while apportioning the rest in accordance with state policies (under this system, workers' claims to surplus value had to be advanced through the state, and so worker mobilization took the form of

---

[24] Schumpeter, *Capitalism, Socialism, and Democracy*, pp. 84–5.

[25] See generally Stephen Skowronek, *Building a New American State: The Expansion of National Administrative Capacities, 1877–1920* (Cambridge University Press, 1982).

[26] See, of course, Karl Marx and Friedrich Engels, *The Communist Manifesto* (New York: Penguin, 1967 [1848]).

political parties rather than private economic associations). In order to further promote this arrangement, the state also encouraged participating firms to organize into cartels and otherwise to engage in monopolistic practices, thus increasing the amount of surplus value that the firm could collect.[27]

The United States rejected both these options. The Smithian leaning of the general American polity caused them to be highly distrustful of cartels and monopolies, which they referred to as 'trusts'. They feared that the aggregated corporate power that would be created by corporatist cartelization would allow these cartels to overwhelm the democratic system of the American state and reduce the United States to a corporate oligarchy.[28] But, at the same time, America's long-standing vision of itself as a distinctly classless society made it ideologically hostile to Marx's socialist solution. The possible development of a distinct political identity among industrial workers was seen as being as much a threat to American democracy as was cartelization.[29]

The American solution, therefore, was to invent (or discover) a new social class, that of the consumer,[30] and direct surplus value to that class via regulatory pursuit of an idealized model of competition (cf. Jessop, Ch. 5, pp. 99, 102–3). There was justification for this: the archetypical American was not an industrialist or an industrial worker. But all Americans – including those who were industrialists or industrial workers – were consumers, and so this solution was seen as being as distinctly supportive of American democracy. It was out of this American solution that American antitrust law was born.[31]

For the next half century, the American and continental models would operate largely in ignorance of one another.[32] The German model would spread to several other countries on the European continent, particularly those in central Europe. It would also spread to Asia, most notably Japan,

---

[27] See generally Carl Landauer, *Corporate State Ideologies: Historical Roots and Philosophical Origins* (Berkeley: Institute of International Studies, University of California, Berkeley, 1983), pp. 59–92.

[28] Skowronek, *Building a New American State.*

[29] See generally Eric Foner, 'Why Is There No Socialism in the United States?', *History Workshop Journal*, 17 (1984): 57–80.

[30] See, e.g., Walter Lippmann, *Drift and Mastery: An Attempt to Diagnose the Current Unrest* (New York: Prentice Hall, 1961 [1914]), pp. 54–5.

[31] Michael J. Sandel, *Democracy's Discontent: America in Search of a Public Philosophy* (Cambridge, MA: Belknap Press, 1996), pp. 231–49.

[32] Gerber, *Global Competition*, pp. 19–38.

whose *zaibatsu* system of industrial organization was directly inspired by German corporatism. But this mutual lack of interest ended with the ending of the Second World War. Many American policymakers and scholars attributed the descent of Germany and Japan into authoritarianism to that model. The way they saw it, that authoritarianism was a natural evolutionary consequence of the huge power concentrations that had been created by the corporatist state's creation of, and later dependence on, industrial cartels. In order to prevent a re-emergence of authoritarianism in Germany or Japan, who at the time were suspected of being culturally predisposed to authoritarianism and militarism, the victorious allies, led by the Americans, sought to reconstruct both German and Japanese industrialization along American lines, imposing on both these post-war polities a competition legislation derived from the American model.[33]

Of course, both Japan (as Simon Vande Walle explains in Ch. 6) and Germany embraced this new competition regime with pronounced ambivalence, and in actual practice their industrial systems continued to operate more along corporatist than American lines.[34] But even with this, the normative extension of the American antitrust system to Europe and to Japan led many American policymakers, economists, and jurists to begin to see the American antitrust law framework more as a kind of scientific principle rather than as a political choice.

The transformation of American antitrust law into a global framework for competition law was further catalysed by a number of subsequent developments. The first was that of the cold war. The Soviet Union emerged out of the Second World War to challenge, both politically and ideologically, the global power of the United States and Europe. Part of the Soviet challenge issued from its ideological embrace of Marx's worker-centred solution to the issue of distribution of the surplus of industrialization. Regardless of whether this accurately described the actual workings of Soviet industry, many, even in North Atlantic economies, found the Soviet worker-centred ideology attractive vis-à-vis what they saw as the corporate-centred industrial system of the Americans.[35]

---

[33] John Owen Haley, *Antitrust in Germany and Japan: The First Fifty Years, 1947–1998* (Seattle: University of Washington Press, 2001), pp. 14–24.

[34] Ibid., pp. 46–8, 62.

[35] See, e.g., John Maynard Keynes, 'A Short View Of Russia', in *The Collected Writings of John Maynard Keynes* (London: Macmillan, 1971 [1925]), Vol. 9, pp. 253–71. See also Mark Mazower, *Dark Continent: Europe's Twentieth Century* (Harmondsworth: Penguin Books, 1999), pp. 17–27.

The American system of industrial organization, including the particular role that 'competition' played in that organization, was thus mobilized in the service of geo-political competition.[36] Economic competition became intimately and theoretically linked with other defining features that were argued by Americans to distinguish the superiority of their political-economic system from that of the Soviets, such as democracy and the protection of political and civil rights.[37] Even more than was the case with the extension of the American antitrust system to other advanced industrial capitalist economies of a now friendly Germany and Japan in the aftermath of the Second World War, competition with the socialist system of the Soviet Union encouraged Americans to see and theorize their industrial system in truly absolutist terms – as the right and best system for any country, for any economy, developed or not, looking to join the progress of history.[38]

A second development that catalysed the transformation of the American system from a political choice into a global principle was the oil shock of the early 1970s and the ensuing economic recession it triggered in the North Atlantic economies. As noted above, through the 1950s and 1960s, Europe remained intellectually ambivalent with regard to the American system. Cartels and de facto cartelization continued to be seen as significant and valid regulatory tools in effectuating the regulation of capitalism and ensuring the appropriate distribution of the surplus value it generated. But the prolonged economic recession of the 1970s triggered by the oil shock itself prompted a crisis of European regulatory confidence, and increasing numbers of Europeans saw the American model of competition regulation as part of their ticket back to renewed economic growth and security.[39] Europe now much more fully embraced the American model (at least on a policy level), and this was seen as further

---

[36] Cf. Robert M. Collins, *More: The Politics of Economic Growth in Postwar America* (Oxford University Press, 2000), pp. 45–51.

[37] See, e.g., Milton Friedman, *Capitalism and Freedom* (University of Chicago Press, 1962); F. A. Hayek, *The Road to Serfdom* (University of Chicago Press, 1994 [1944]).

[38] Cf. Dan W. Puchniak, 'Besprechungsaufsatz/Review Essay: A Skeptic's Guide to Miwa and Ramseyer's *The Fable of the Keiretsu*', *Journal of Japanese Law*, 24 (2007): 273–90, 276 ('no match made in heaven produces more bliss than economists who meet leftist scholars who they can blame for [a] debacle'). See, e.g., Francis Fukuyama, *The End of History and the Last Man* (New York: Free Press, 1992).

[39] Giandomenico Majone, 'The Rise of the Regulatory State in Europe', in Robert Baldwin, Colin Scott, and Christopher Hood (eds.), *A Reader on Regulation* (Oxford University Press, 1998), pp. 193–213.

confirming that model's legitimacy as a universal principle of global economic progress.

Many interpreted the collapse of the Soviet socialist system in both the Soviet Union and eastern Europe as further confirming the universality of the American system.[40] As described above, the United States had framed its competition with the Soviet Union in part as a competition between economic systems, and the fall of the Eastern bloc therefore seemed to confirm the universal superiority of the American LME economic system.

Support for that perspective was given an even greater boost less than a decade later with the onset of the Asian economic crisis in 1997. Beginning in the 1970s, and picking up steam into the 1980s and early 1990s, some scholars and economists in the United States began suggesting that the dramatic economic growth and development of Japan had taken place within an industrial system that did not conform to the tenets of the American model. Through the 1980s and into the 1990s, Taiwan and South Korea followed Japan into advanced industrialization and, again, followed similar paths that seemed to contradict the tenets of the American model. Into the 1990s, similar contrarian trajectories were being found through the now rapidly developing states of East and Southeast Asia. In sum, a fair number of North Atlantic observers began to see the rise of Asia as evidence that the American LME variety of capitalism, including its particular model of competition regulation, was not a universal principle after all, and possibly that embedded in the Asian rise was an alternative model of capitalism, such as the 'developmental state', was better than that of the United States in promoting development.[41] By the mid 1990s, the Asian-inspired developmental-state variety of capitalism had become a compelling intellectual challenger to the American model. To many, particularly in the United States, the Asian economic crisis in 1997 discredited this model and, with that, the American model – now known as 'the Washington consensus' – seemed to stand

---

[40] See, e.g., Fukuyama, *End of History*.

[41] See, e.g., Chalmers A. Johnson, *Japan, Who Governs? The Rise of the Developmental State* (New York: W. W. Norton, 1995); Peter Evans, *Embedded Autonomy: States and Industrial Transformation* (Princeton University Press, 1995); Charles F. Sabel, 'Learning by Monitoring: The Institutions of Economic Development', in Neil Smelser and Richard Swedberg (eds.), *The Handbook of Economic Sociology* (Princeton University Press and Russell Sage Foundation, 1994), pp. 137–65.

uncontested as a universal principle of modern economic development and performance[42] (see also Sum, Ch. 4, pp. 83–4).

(Many have similarly used the prolonged economic stagnation of Japan's 'lost decade' of the 1990s to promote the North Atlantic orthodoxy. But, as described by Simon Vande Walle in Chapter 6, and also according to other studies,[43] Japan's subsequent neoliberal reform of its 'developmental state' in the early 1990s does not seem to have triggered any end to the stagnation. In this sense, the neoliberal 'regulatory state' model cannot claim to have been any more successful at restoring Japan to economic growth than the developmental state model.)

What all this shows is that over the years, and through its association with American geopolitical posturing, the American way of structuring capitalism and competition has developed a strong symbolic meaning and significance in addition to those of its actual effects on a particular economy. This also explains why the competition law scholars and practitioners who come out of this tradition are so pronouncedly homogeneous in their theoretical interpretations of what it is that law does and why it is important – and, correspondingly, their dismissive attitude to alternative interpretations that come from outside the neoliberal perspective of micro-economics. Competition breeds solidarity.[44] The orthodoxy of the orthodox competition model is an orthodoxy that has emerged out of six decades of *geopolitical* competition. It is as much, if not more so, a political phenomenon as an economic phenomenon. And this is why it is able to persist despite its weak correlation with how the capitalism it purports to regulate is actually structured (cf. Jessop, Ch. 5).

IV.   Whither global competition law?

What all this means, ironically, is that if we really like our competition law pure and uncontaminated by extraneous 'non sequitur' concerns, it is the messy, complex, and pluralist Asian model, not the simple,

---

[42] Robert Gilpin, *Global Political Economy: Understanding the International Economic Order* (Princeton University Press, 2001), pp. 329–30. See, e.g., Jeffrey A. Frankel, 'The Asian Model, the Miracle, the Crisis and the Fund', in Paul Krugman (ed.), *Currency Crises* (University of Chicago Press, 2000), pp. 327–38.

[43] See, e.g., Dan W. Puchniak, 'The Japanization of American Corporate Governance? Evidence of the Never-Ending History for Corporate Law', *Asian-Pacific Law and Policy Journal*, 9 (2007): 7–70, 60–9.

[44] Cf. Laurence Iannaccone, 'Why Strict Churches Are Strong', *American Journal of Sociology*, 99 (1994): 1180–211; Carl Schmitt, *The Concept of the Political*, trans. George Schwab (University of Chicago Press, 1996 [1927]), pp. 26–7.

homogenized, orthodox model of the North Atlantic, that should be the principal focus of our attentions. This is particularly true as far as our interest in the possible trajectories of a global competition law are concerned.

As presently conceptualized, global competition law is simply domestic competition law writ large. It is a point of domestic evolutionary confluence which will spontaneously transform these domestic norms into global norms. But, in fact, the global capitalist environment is not simply a larger variant of national capitalism. It has its own distinct structure, its own distinct dynamics. And it is still quite unclear what 'competition' looks like under this new form of capitalism. But, almost certainly, it will not look like a national competition law writ large.

As described in particular by Henry Yeung in Chapter 11, at the global level, the boundaries on which the orthodox model of competition relies to visibilize competition – the boundaries that delineate firms, the boundaries that delineate both product and consumer markets, and the boundaries that delineate the reach of public and private regulatory environments – become quite blurred. Firms are no longer geographically specific sites of production and marketing, but interdependent task specialization components in a larger transnational complex of production and marketing. For many, their profits are realized less through market competition, and more through what are effectively bureaucratic forms of distribution as constructed through a web of long-term contracting.[45] Markets are not insular, they interact, and what is competition-promoting from the perspective of one market can be anti-competitive from the perspective of another.[46] Relatedly, dynamics of market domination may come more from monopsonies than from monopolies, since these global networks tend to engage each other in product competition (which is innately monopolistic in its product pricing structures) rather than price competition.[47] At the same time, however, monopsonies often work to benefit consumers, particularly

---

[45] Cf. Oliver E. Williamson, *The Economic Institutions of Capitalism* (New York: Free Press, 1985).

[46] Aravind R. Ganesh, 'The Right to Food and Buyer Power', *German Law Journal*, 11 (2010): 1190–243.

[47] See, e.g., Jeffrey Henderson, 'Global Production Networks, Competition, Regulation and Poverty Reduction: Policy Implications', University of Manchester, Centre on Regulation and Competition Working Paper Series 115, 2005; see also Ganesh, 'Right to Food', pp. 1194–7.

when they take the form of import cartels, and are therefore permitted under global competition law. But they can and often do so at considerable cost to the population in lesser-developed, exporting countries – costs to which global competition law, with its defining focus on placing consumer welfare over producer welfare, is epistemically blind (as is explored in Chapter 1).

Ironically, the orthodox model was itself a response to problems in regulating competition that arose out of a similar shift in the scale of capitalism. Prior to industrial exploitation of mass production, capitalism was primarily local.[48] In the United States, its regulation, including its competition regulation, could adequately be handled through the practices and doctrines set out by the common law. But industrialization changed all that. It made both markets and production national rather than local. And in the process it constructed a kind of capitalism that escaped the reach of the common law's local orientation. The orthodox competition model was the model that replaced the common law model. It was a model that was specifically suited to addressing the distinctive problems that arose in a national industrial capitalism that did not arise in a more local and craft-based capitalism.[49]

And now, a new scope of capitalism is emerging – one whose global reach transcends the regulatory reach of the state, just as the national reach of capitalisms of (Fordist) industrialization transcended the local reach of the common law. It differs from more Fordist, state-centric forms of capitalism in ways that are fundamental and critical to competition regulation. Unlike the national capitalisms of the industrial era, this global capitalism is not a homogenizing or levelling force. It exploits rather than contests local comparative advantages in production and marketing, exploiting and promoting one country's comparative advantage in cheap labour, while at the same exploiting and promoting some other country's comparative advantage in design-based marketing. In the process, it constructs a diversity of markets, markets that in the former are driven by cost competition and are less responsive to local demand, and in the latter are driven by product competition and are more responsive to local demands.[50]

But, at the same time, even under this new global capitalism, the nation-state remains the primary forum for the structuring of inter-firm

---

[48] Braudel, *Perspective of the World*, pp. 287–9.
[49] See generally Skowronek, *Building a New American State*.
[50] Frederic C. Deyo, Richard F. Doner, and Eric Hershberg (eds.), *Economic Governance and the Challenge of Flexibility in East Asia* (Lanham, MD: Rowman & Littlefield), 2001.

competition. What global capitalism does is take over the Schumpeterian structuring of inter-firm co-operation (what he called 'correspective competition'), by taking advantage of differences in national constructions of competition (e.g., price-based vs product-based; production-based vs consumer-based) (see generally Jessop, Ch. 5). The global regulatory environment of this new global capitalism is in this sense distinctly and inevitably variegated. Here, the monocratic regulatory homogeneity of the orthodox model described by Ngai-ling Sum in Chapter 4 becomes dysfunctional (see also Dowdle, Ch. 9).[51] The regulation of global capitalism will have to operate through and with this diversity of national regulatory systems, rather than compressing them all into a single, monocratic regulatory 'constitution'.

And, as we saw above, this is the realm of legal pluralism. It is the realm of collibration. And this returns us to Asian capitalism, and its distinctly pluralistic, collibrative way of regulating competition.

Let us return, along these lines, to the chapter by Frederic Deyo. One of the common critiques of the developmental state has been that even if state management of capitalism does promote development during its earlier stages, such management will ultimately result in the state being captured by the firms and interests that benefit from its initial strategy. They will then use that capture to prevent the state from adopting and exploiting new economic activities, thereby causing the state's economy to become increasingly less efficient and to stagnate.[52]

Both Deyo's chapter and the preceding chapter by Henry Yeung show that, in fact, this has not been the case, particularly as far as the economies of Taiwan and South Korea are concerned. They show that the developmental state can evolve, and that it can evolve out from under the state's strategic direction. As Yeung's production networks render state direction of the economy increasingly irrelevant, so, too, do they render a firm's capacity to capture that aspect of developmental state governance irrelevant. And, as Deyo shows, whatever capture such states may have experienced, it has not prevented these formerly 'developmental states' from developing new regulatory systems that are innovatively well suited to this new form of capitalism by retreating from state guidance of developmental

---

[51] Cf. Sabel, 'Learning by Monitoring'; Williamson, *Economic Institutions of Capitalism*.

[52] See, e.g., Paola Bongini, Stijn Claessens, and Giovanni Ferri, 'The Political Economy of Distress in East Asian Financial Institutions', *Journal of Financial Services Research*, 19 (2001): 5–25; David C. Kang, 'Bad Loans to Good Friends: Money Politics and the Developmental State in South Korea', *International Organization*, 56 (2002): 177–207.

strategies and instead focusing on the development of high-value, geographically grounded factors endowments (i.e., the 'competition state', as per Bob Jessop[53]).

The reason why this particular critique of the developmental state does not hold up is precisely because the critique presumes a monocratic economic political economy, one in which there is only one legality, only one capitalism, and correspondingly only one set of rules for the regulation of competition and for the regulation of the regulation of competition. Under such conditions, winning the competition for control over the regulatory state itself allows a firm to solidify its monopoly status as far as both market competition and political competition are concerned. Hence stagnation. But under conditions of capitalist and legal pluralism, such capturing of a state's constitutional-regulatory system does not necessarily give one a political or economic monopoly, because there are in fact other, parallel constitutional systems at play. The state can continue to regulate autonomously simply by arbitraging among its diversity of constitutions and diversity of capitalist forms and environments – that is, via pluralist collibration. The ability of the state to respond to the new capitalism described by Yeung, contrary to the prediction of standard political economics, in the way that Deyo describes provides at least some evidence that Asian capitalism's distinctively pluralist and collibrative styles of regulating competition could indeed be markedly well-suited for regulating the kind of competition that is being engendered by global capitalism. And, for this reason, it might itself make a better platform from which to evolve a truly global competition law.

And, in fact, Deyo also provides some evidence that this is indeed becoming the case. Deyo first notes that these new forms of regulation sit in conceptual tension with the orthodox model of competition:

> Insofar as networked inter-firm relations and professional networks supplant or circumvent price-driven market transactions with particularistic ties rooted in personal and social considerations and long-term trust, they comprise exclusionary bonds that close the transactional spaces and opportunities otherwise available to non-networked economic agents. These exclusionary social bonds and networks stand in a problematic relationship to the substance and intent of competition policy. (Deyo, Ch. 12, p. 299)

Nevertheless, the global competition community appears largely to have accepted them. As he concludes, these new regulatory arrangements have

---

[53] Bob Jessop, *The Future of the Capitalist State* (Cambridge University Press, 2002).

garnered financial and advisory encouragement from the World Bank, the Asia Development Bank, and other IFIs in Asia and beyond. In this way, they are not conceptualized as alternatives to the forms of socio-economic ordering recommended by the neoliberal model. (Deyo, Ch. 12, p. 300)

Here we have a description of what looks suspiciously like the emergence of a pluralist global competition law. One that is in some aspects neoliberal, but in other aspects not. It is an emergent, pluralist legal regime: one that, according to Deyo at least, seems to be taking at least some inspiration from the pluralism of Asian capitalism's distinctive way of regulating competition.

As many have noted, globalization is disaggregating the historical unity of the state. States are increasingly becoming collections of cultures, legalities, and capitalisms, rather than monocratic expressions of a single culture, a single legality, or even a single capitalism, even at the formal level.[54] (Southeast) Asia's history may be becoming our future. And with it so, too, its distinct pluralisms with regard to the regulation of competition. (Along these same lines, in private conversation with the author in March 2012, Professor Walter Stoffel of the Department of International Law and Company Law at the University of Fribourg and former president of the Swiss Competition Commission, suggested that deliberations within the International Competition Network (see Maher, Ch. 3, pp. 57–8) seem to be evolving in this direction as well.)

V.   Conclusion

But at the same time, however, Asian capitalism is not really Asian. Many of the defining features that today identify it as an alternative to North Atlantic varieties of capitalism – the developmental state, and the use of cartel-like conglomerates and national champions – were themselves originally imported from Europe in the nineteenth century. Asian capitalism, LME capitalism, and CME capitalism, are not really divergent alternatives. They are simply strands in an ongoing historical

---

[54] See Kanishka Jayasuriya, 'Globalization and the Changing Architecture of the State: The Regulatory State and the Politics of Negative Coordination', *Journal of European Public Policy* 8 (2001): 102–23; Colin Scott, 'Regulation in the Age of Governance: The Rise of the Post Regulatory State', in Jacint Jordana and David Levi-Faur (eds.), *The Politics of Regulation: Institutions and Regulatory Reforms for the Age of Governance* (Cheltenham: Edward Elgar, 2004), pp. 145–74.

evolutionary 'discourse' about the nature and possibilities (and possible pitfalls) of capitalism writ large. Each variety is continually evolving, evolving in response to each another, and evolving in ways that are and have to be epistemically and ideologically unbounded over the long run. And it is in their discursive agglomeration, not in any single one's survival as the fittest, that the possibilities of our future will remain unbounded. Our ability to negotiate our own future does not lie in making the proper choice between the Asian model of competition regulation and its more orthodox counterpart. Ultimately, it lies in the fruits of their discourse.

BIBLIOGRAPHY

I. Books, chapters in books, articles, and papers

Abegaz, Berhanu. 2005. 'The Diversified Business Group as an Innovative Organisational Model for Large State-Enterprise Reform in China and Vietnam'. *International Journal of Entrepreneurship and Innovation Management* 5: 379–400.

Ackerman, Bruce A. 1991. *We the People, Volume 1: Foundations.* Harvard University Press.

ADB (Asian Development Bank). 2006. 'Competition Law Toolkit: Overview of Competition Law Practices'. Dated 31 October. Available at www2.adb.org/Documents/Others/OGC-Toolkits/Competition-Law/complaw020000.asp (accessed 12 June 2012).

2007. 'Competition Law Toolkit', dated 17 January. Available at www2.adb.org/Documents/Others/OGC-Toolkits/Competition-Law/default.asp (accessed 12 June 2012).

ADB and Christine Veloso Lao. 2006. *Report and Proceedings from the Competition Law and Policy Roundtable, 16–17 May 2006, New Delhi, India.* Manila: Asian Development Bank.

ADBI (Asian Development Bank Institute). Undated. '3rd AEGC Workshop: Costs and Benefits of Competition Policy, Law and Regulatory Bodies'. Available at www.adbi.org/event/3070.3rd.aegc.workshop/ (accessed 12 June 2012).

'Administration of Quality Inspection and Supervision [AQSIQ]: Mengniu, Yili, Guangming Liquid Milk Removed from Chinese Famous Brands Product [Hijian Zongju: Chexiao Mengniu, Yili, Guangming Yetainai Zhongguo Mingpai Chanpin Chenghao]'. 2008. CCTV.com, 22 September. Available at http://news.cctv.com/china/20080922/101235.shtml (accessed 26 June 2012).

Aizenman, Joshua, and Brian Pinto (eds.). 2005. *Managing Economic Volatility and Crises: A Practitioner's Guide.* Cambridge University Press.

Akerlof, George A., and Rachel E. Kranton. 2010. *Identity Economics: How Our Identities Shape Our Work, Wages, and Well-Being.* Princeton University Press.

Altman, Jon, and Sally Ward (eds.). 2002. *Competition and Consumer Issues for Indigenous Australians: A Report to the Australian Competition and*

Consumer Commission. Canberra: Australian Competition and Consumer Commission.

Altvater, Elmar. 1994. 'Operationsfeld Weltmarkt oder: Die Transformation des souveränen Nationalstaats in den nationalen Wettbewerbsstaat'. *Prokla: Zeitschrift für Kritische Wissenschaft*, 24: 517–47.

Amato, Giuliano. 1997. *Antitrust and the Bounds of Power: The Dilemma of Liberal Democracy in the History of the Market*. Oxford: Hart Publishing.

Amsden, Alice H. 1989. *Asia's Next Giant: South Korea and Late Industrialization*. Oxford University Press.

Anandarajah, Kala, and Dominique Lombardi. 2010. 'China's First Public Anti-cartel Action under the Anti-Monopoly Law', *Mondaq*, 11 June 2010. Available at www.mondaq.com/article.asp?articleid=102700 (accessed 14 June 2012).

Anderlini, Jamil, and Peter Smith. 2008. 'Officials Knew of Tainted Baby Milk', *Financial Times*, 16 September. Available at www.ft.com/intl/cms/s/0/ d75a0d08-8388-11dd-907e-000077b07658.html#axzz1yxlmjBc3 (accessed 27 June 2012).

Anderson, Philip A., and Michael L. Tushman. 1991. 'Managing Through Cycles of Technological Change'. *Research Technology Management* 34 (3): 26–31.

Ando, Mitsuyo, and Fukunari Kimura. 2005. 'The Formation of International Production and Distribution Networks in East Asia'. In Takatoshi Ito and Andrew K. Rose (eds.), *International Trade in East Asia*. University of Chicago Press, pp. 177–216.

'The Antimonopoly Law's Bumpy Journey of Twenty-One Years [Fanlongduan Fa 21 Nian Fengyu Licheng]'. 2008. *Zhongguo Jingji Shibao [China Economic Times]*, 29 July 2008. Available at www.competitionlaw.cn/show.aspx? id=3984&cid=13 (accessed 14 June 2012).

'Antimonopoly Law One Year On: Multinational Corporations Involved in Sixty-Nine Percent of Cases [Fanlongduan Fa Shishi Yinian: Kuaguo Gongsi Canyu Anjia Zhan 69%]'. 2009. Franchise Attorneys: Texu Kingying Lushi, 17 November. Available at www.fclaw.com.cn/Details.asp?id=13994 (accessed 14 June 2012).

Appelbaum, Richard. 2009. 'Big Suppliers in Greater China'. In Hung Ho-fung (ed.), *China and the Transformation of Global Capitalism*. Baltimore: Johns Hopkins University Press, pp. 65–85.

Arezki, Rabah, and Markus Brückner. 2011. 'Food Prices and Political Instability'. IMF Institute: IMF Working Paper, WP-11-62 (March 2011). Available at www.imf.org/external/pubs/ft/wp/2011/wp1162.pdf (accessed 15 July 2012).

Averitt, Neil W., and Robert H. Lande. 1997. 'Consumer Sovereignty: A Unified Theory of Antitrust and Consumer Protection Law'. *Antitrust Law Journal* 65: 713–56.

Ayres, Ian, and John Braithwaite. 1992. *Responsive Regulation: Transcending the Deregulation Debate*. Oxford University Press.

'B100m Budget to Help SMEs Enter Asean.' 2010. *Bangkok Post*, 3 May. Available at www.bdo-thaitax.com/bdo/in-the-news/2170 (accessed 19 June 2012).

Bandurski, David. 2008. 'Press Controls Feed China's Food Problem'. *Wall Street Journal Asia*, 7 October. Available at http://online.wsj.com/article/SB12233 2462058208791.html (accessed 27 June 2012).

Banerjee Abhijit V., and Esther Duflo. 2011. *Poor Economics: A Radical Rethinking of the Way to Fight Global Poverty*. New York: Public Affairs.

Barboza, David. 2009. 'Former Executive Pleads Guilty in China Milk Scandal'. *New York Times*, 1 January, A10.

Barboza, David, and Alexei Barrionuevo. 2007. 'Filler in Animal Feed Is Open Secret in China'. *New York Times*, 30 April. Available at www.nytimes.com/2007/04/30/business/worldbusiness/30food.html?pagewanted=all (accessed 16 June 2012).

Beaton-Wells, Caron, and Ariel Ezrachi (eds.). 2011. *Criminalising Cartels: Critical Studies of an International Regulatory Movement*. Oxford: Hart Publishing.

Beeman, Michael L. 2002. *Public Policy and Economic Competition in Japan: Change and Continuity in Antimonopoly Policy, 1973-1995*. London: Routledge.

Beeson, Mark. 2006. 'Politics and Markets in East Asia: Is the Developmental State Compatible with Globalization?'. In Richard Stubbs and Geoffrey R. D. Underhill (eds.), *Political Economy and the Changing Global Order*, 3rd edn. Oxford University Press, pp. 443-53.

Beresford, Melanie. 2010. 'The Development of Commercial Regulation in Vietnam's Market Economy'. In John Gillespie and Albert Chen (eds.), *Legal Reforms in China and Vietnam*. London: Routledge, pp. 254-68.

Berger, Peter L. and Thomas Luckmann. 1967. *The Social Construction of Reality*. Garden City, NJ: Anchor Books.

Bergman, Mats. 1997. 'Antitrust, Marketing Cooperatives, and Market Power'. *European Journal of Law and Economics* 4: 73-92.

'Big Businesses Come Up with 'Shared Growth' Plans'. 2011. *Korea Herald*, 6 March. Available at http://view.koreaherald.com/kh/view.php?ud=20110306000284&cpv=0 (accessed 19 June 2012).

Bisson, T. A. 1976. *Zaibatsu Dissolution in Japan*. Westport, CT: Greenwood Press.

Black, William K. 2005. 'When Fragile Becomes Friable: Endemic Control Fraud as a Cause of Economic Stagnation and Collapse', paper presented at the IDEAS Conference, New Delhi, 19-20 December. Available at www.pragoti.in/node/2976 (accessed 7 July 2012).

   2009. 'How the Servant Became the Predator: Finance's Five Fatal Flaws'. Next New Deal: The Blog of the Roosevelt Institute. Available at www.nextnewdeal.net/how-servant-became-predator-finances-five-fatal-flaws (accessed 7 July 2012).

Boeger, Nina, and Tony Prosser. 2009. 'United Kingdom'. In Markus Krajewski, Ulla Neergaard, and Johan van de Gronden (eds.), *The Changing Legal*

Framework for Services of General Interest in Europe: Between Competition and Solidarity. Nijmegen: T.M.C. Asser Press, pp. 357–82.

Bongini, Paola, Stijn Claessens, and Giovanni Ferri. 2001. 'The Political Economy of Distress in East Asian Financial Institutions'. *Journal of Financial Services Research* 19: 5–25.

Bork, Robert. H. 1993. *The Antitrust Paradox*, 2nd edn. New York: Free Press.

Boschma, Ron A., and Koen Frenken. 2006. 'Why Is Economic Geography Not an Evolutionary Science? Towards an Evolutionary Economic Geography'. *Journal of Economic Geography* 6: 273–302.

Boschma, Ron A., and Ron Martin. 2007. 'Constructing an Evolutionary Economic Geography'. *Journal of Economic Geography* 7: 537–48.

Bowen, John T., Jr. 2007. 'Global Production Networks, The Developmental State and the Articulation of Asia Pacific Economies in the Commercial Aircraft Industry'. *Asia Pacific Viewpoint* 48: 312–29.

Bowen, John T., Jr, and Thomas R. Leinbach. 2006. 'Competitive Advantage in Global Production Networks: Air Freight Services and the Electronics Industry in Southeast Asia'. *Economic Geography* 82: 147–66.

Boyer, Robert. 1996. 'State and Market: A New Engagement for the Twenty-first Century?' In Robert Boyer and Daniel Drache (eds.), *States against Markets: The Limits of Globalization*. London: Routledge, pp. 84–114.

Boyer, Robert, and Yves Saillard (eds.). 2002. *Régulation Theory: State of the Art*, trans. Carolyn Shread. London: Routledge.

Bradley, David. 2008. 'Melamine in Milk'. Sciencebase: Science News and Views, 17 September. Available at www.sciencebase.com/science-blog/melamine-in-milk.html (accessed 26 June 2012).

Braithwaite, John. 2002. *Restorative Justice and Responsive Regulation*. Oxford University Press.

Braithwaite, John, and Peter Drahos. 2000. *Global Business Regulation*. Cambridge University Press.

Branigan, Tania. 2008. 'China Milk Scandal Company "Asked Government to Help in Cover-Up"'. *Guardian*, 1 October. Available at www.guardian.co.uk/world/2008/oct/01/china.milk (accessed 27 June 2012).

Bratsis, Peter. 2003. 'The Construction of Corruption, or Rules of Separation and Illusions of Purity in Bourgeois Societies'. *Social Text* 21(4): 9–33.

Braudel, Fernand. 1992. *Civilization and Capitalism, 15th–18th Century. Volume 3, The Perspective of the World*, trans. Siân Reynolds. Berkeley: University of California Press.

Breeson, Mark. 2006. 'South-East Asia and the International Financial Institutions'. In Garry Rodan, Kevin Hewison, and Richard Robison (eds.), *The Political Economy of South-East Asia: Markets, Power and Contestation*, 3rd edn. Oxford University Press, pp. 240–57.

Brenchley, Fred. 2003. *Allan Fels: A Portrait of Power*. Sydney: Wiley.

Breslin, Shaun. 2004. *Capitalism with Chinese Characteristics: The Public, the Private and the International*, Working Paper 104. Perth: Murdoch University Asia Research Centre. Available at http://dspace.cigilibrary.org/jspui/ bitstream/123456789/12979/1/Capitalism%20with%20Chinese%20Characteristics%20the%20Public%20the%20Private%20and%20the%20International. pdf (accessed 17 June 2012).

Brittan, Leon, and Karel Van Miert. 1996. 'Towards an International Framework of Competition Rules'. *International Business Lawyer* 24: 454–7.

Brooks, Donald H., and Simon J. Evenett (eds.). 2005. *Competition Policy and Development in Asia*. New York: Palgrave Macmillan.

Bryan, Dick, and Michael Rafferty. 2006. *Capitalism with Derivatives: A Political Economy of Financial Derivatives, Capital and Class*. Basingstoke: Palgrave Macmillan.

Bryson, Bill. 2003. *A Short History of Nearly Everything*. New York: Broadway Books.

Buckley, Peter J., Jeremy Clegg, and Chengqi Wang. 2007. 'Is the Relationship between Inward FDI and Spillover Effects Linear? An Empirical Examination of the Case of China'. *Journal of International Business Studies* 38: 447–559.

Bukharin, Nikolai I. 1972 [1915]. *Imperialism and the World Economy*. London: Merlin Press.

Buxbaum, Richard M. 1993. 'Is "Network" a Legal Concept?'. *Journal of Institutional and Theoretical Economics* 149: 698–705.

Cao, Cong. 2004. 'Zhongguancun and China's High-Tech Parks in Transition: Growing Pains or Premature Senility?' *Asian Survey* 44: 647–68.

Carney, Michael, Eric Gedajlovic, and Xiaohua Yang. 2009. 'Varieties of Asian Capitalism: Toward an Institutional Theory of Asian Enterprise'. *Asia Pacific Journal of Management* 26: 361–80.

Carney, Michael, Eric Gedajlovic, and Xiaohua Yang (eds.). 2009. Special Issue: Varieties of Asian Capitalism: Indigenization and Internationalization, *Asia Pacific Journal of Management* 26 (3): 361–609.

Casper, Steven. 2007. 'How Do Technology Clusters Emerge and Become Sustainable? Social Network Formation and Inter-firm Mobility within the San Diego Biotechnology Cluster'. *Research Policy* 36: 438–55.

Castells, Manuel. 2000. *The Information Age: Society, Economy and Culture*, 2nd edn, Volume 1: The Rise of the Network Society. Malden, MA: Blackwell Publishing.

'Catalog of Prices Controlled by the National Development and Planning Commission and Other Central Government Agencies [Guojia Jiwei he Guowuyuan Youguan Bumen Dingjia Mulu]' (China). 2001, 4 July. Available at www.ndrc. gov.cn/zcfb/zcfbl/zcfbl2003pro/t20050707_27540.htm (accessed 15 July 2012).

'CCTV in Focus Interview: Ocean Shippers Discover "Negative Rates" [Yangshi Jiaodian Fangtan: Hayun Jingxian "Fuyunjia"]'. 2006. Sohu.com, 22 September. Available at http://news.sohu.com/20060922/n245477144.shtml (accessed 14 June 2012).

'CCTV Investigative Report of Sanlu Milk Powder: Thousands of Tests before Leaving Factory [CCTV Ceng Shenru Diaocha Sanlu Naifen: Jing Qianxiang Jiance Cai Chu Chang]'. 2008. Cnfol.com, 12 September. Available at http://news.cnfol.com/080912/101,1603,4759687,00.shtml (accessed 27 June 2012).

Cernat, Lucian. 2005. 'Eager to Ink but Ready to Act? RTA Proliferation and International Cooperation on Competition Policy'. In Philippe Brusick, Ana María Alverez, and Lucian Cernat (eds.), *Competition Provisions in Regional Trade Agreements: How to Assure Development Gains*. New York: United Nations Publications, pp. 1–34.

Cerny, Philip G. 1990. *The Changing Architecture of Politics: Structure, Agency and the Future of the State*. London: Sage Publications.

    1997. 'Paradoxes of the Competition State: The Dynamics of Globalization'. *Government and Opposition* 32: 251–274.

Chapman, William. 1991. *Inventing Japan: The Making of a Postwar Civilization*. New York: Simon & Schuster.

Chen, Shumei. 2009. 'Sham or Shame: Rethinking China's Milk Powder Scandal from a Legal Perspective'. *Journal of Risk Research* 12: 725–47.

Chen, Tain-Jy. 2008. 'The Emergence of Hsinchu Science Park as an IT Cluster'. In Shahid Yusuf, Kaoru Nabeshima, and Shoichi Yamashita (eds.), *Growing Industrial Clusters in Asia: Serendipity and Science*. Washington, DC: World Bank Publications, pp. 67–90.

Cheshier, Scott. 2010. 'The New Class in Vietnam'. Ph.D. dissertation, School of Business and Management, Queen Mary, University of London. Available at https://qmro.qmul.ac.uk/jspui/bitstream/123456789/443/1/CHESIERNewClass2010.pdf (accessed 8 November 2012).

Cheshier, Scott, and Jonathan Pincus. 2010. 'Minsky au Vietnam: State Corporations, Financial Instability and Industrialisation'. In Daniela Tavasci and Jan Toporowski (eds.), *Minsky, Crisis and Development*. Basingstoke: Palgrave Macmillan, pp. 188–206.

Cheung, Gordon C. K. 2012. 'The Significance of the Overseas Chinese in East Asia'. In Mark Beeson and Richard Stubbs (eds.), *Routledge Handbook of Asian Regionalism*. London: Routledge, pp. 77–89.

Chiang, Yi-Chein, Tung Liang Liao, and Yu-Ling Liu. 2008. 'Performance and Investments in China from Industrial Perspectives: Evidence from Taiwan Firms'. *Review of Pacific Basin Financial Markets and Policies* 11: 331–46.

'China Closes Thousands of Milk Collection Stations'. 2009. *China Daily*, 3 June. Available at www.chinadaily.com.cn/business/2009–06/03/content_8038447.htm (accessed 27 June 2012).

'China to Destroy 10,000 Tons of Tainted Baby Formula'. 2008. Xinhua News Agency, 16 September. Available at www.china.org.cn/health/2008–09/16/content_16464641.htm (accessed 27 June 2012).

'China Seizes 22 Companies with Contaminated Baby Milk Powder'. 2008. Xinhua News Agency, 16 September. Available at http://news.xinhuanet.com/english/2008-09/17/content_10046949.htm (accessed 27 June 2012).

'China's Airline Companies Form Price Coalition: Air Ticket Prices Increase [Guonei Hangkong Gongsi Dacheng Jiage Tongmeng; Jipiao Jiage Pubian Shangsheng]'. 2005. *Beijing Xiandai Shangbao* [Beijing Modern Business Journal], 4 April. Available at http://finance.sina.com.cn/chanjing/b/20050404/07401484238.shtml (accessed 14 June 2012).

'China's Big Four Airlines Jointly Set Prices to Increase Profits [Zhongguo Si Da Hangkong Lianshou Zhiding Piaojia Yi Tisheng Lirun]'. 2010. Xiamen Huoyun Wang [Logistics Website of the City of Xiamen], 15 March. Available at www.xmwuliu.net/WuLiuXinWen/20100315/89748.html (accessed 14 June 2012).

Clarke, Donald C. 2003. 'Economic Development and the Rights Hypothesis: The China Problem'. *American Journal of Comparative Law* 51: 89–111.

——— 2007. 'Legislating for a Market Economy'. *China Quarterly* 191: 567–85.

——— 2011. 'Nothing but Wind: The Past and Future of Comparative Corporate Governance'. *American Journal of Comparative Law* 59: 75–110.

Cling, Jean-Pierre, Nguyễn Thị Thu Huyền, Nguyễn Hữu Chí, Phan T. Ngọc Trâm, Mireille Razafindrakoto, and François Roubaud. 2010. *The Informal Sector in Vietnam: A Focus on Hanoi and Ho Chi Minh City*. Hanoi: The Gioi.

Coase, Ronald H. 1960. 'The Problem of Social Cost'. *Journal of Law and Economics* 3: 1–44.

Coe, Neil, Martin Hess, and Peter Dicken (eds.). 2008. Theme Issue on Global Production Networks: Debates and Challenges. *Journal of Economic Geography* 8: 267–440.

Coe, Neil, Martin Hess, Henry Wai-chung Yeung, Peter Dicken, and Jeffrey Henderson. 2004. '"Globalizing" Regional Development: A Global Production Networks Perspective'. *Transactions of the Institute of British Geographers*, New Series 29: 468–84.

Collins, Hugh. 2009. 'The Weakest Link: Legal Implications of the Network Architecture of Supply Chains'. In Marc Amstutz and Gunther Teubner (eds.), *Networks: Legal Issues of Multilateral Co-operation*. Oxford: Hart Publishing, pp. 187–210.

Collins, Robert M. 2000. *More: The Politics of Economic Growth in Postwar America*. Oxford University Press.

Commission of the European Communities. 2003. Green Paper on Services of General Interest, COM (2003) 270 final. 21 May. Available at http://eur-lex.europa.eu/LexUriServ/site/en/com/2003/com2003_0270en01.pdf (accessed 20 June 2012).

Competition Commission Singapore. 2010. 'Notice of Infringement Decision: Abuse of a Dominant Position by SISTIC.com Pte Ltd'. 4 June 2010 (Case

no. CCS 600/008/07). Non-confidential version available at www.ccs.gov.sg/
content/dam/ccs/PDFs/Public_register_and_consultation/Public_register/
Abuse_of_Dominance/SISTIC%20Infringement%20Decision%20(Non-
confidential%20version).pdf (accessed 20 June 2012).

Cooke, Bill, and Sadhvi Dar. 2008. 'Introduction: The New Development Management'. In Sadhvi Dar and Bill Cooke (eds.), *The New Development Management: Critiquing the Dual Modernization*. London: Zed Books, pp. 1–14.

Cotterrell, Roger. 2001. 'Is There a Logic of Legal Transplants?' In David Nelken
and Johannes Feest (eds.), *Adapting Legal Cultures*. Oxford: Hart Publishing,
pp. 71–92.

Craig, David, and Doug Porter. 2006. *Development beyond Neoliberalism? Governance, Poverty Reduction and Political Economy*. London: Routledge.

Crotty, James. 2003. 'Core Industries, Coercive Competition and the Structural
Contradiction of Global Neoliberalism'. In Nicholas Phelps and Philip Raines
(eds.), *The New Competition for Inward Investment: Companies, Institutions
and Territorial Development*. Cheltenham: Edward Elgar, pp. 9–38.

Crouch, Colin. 2004. *Post-Democracy*. Cambridge: Polity Press.

Cseres, K. J. 2007. 'The Controversies of the Consumer Welfare Standard'. *Competition Law Review* 3: 121–73.

Dale, Gareth. 2010. *Karl Polanyi: The Limits of the Market*. Cambridge: Polity
Press.

Damjanovic, Dragana, and Bruno de Witte. 2009. 'Welfare Integration through EU
Law: The Overall Picture in the Light of the Lisbon Treaty'. In Ulla Neergaard,
Ruth Nielsen, and Lynn Roseberry (eds.), *Integrating Welfare Functions into
EU Law – From Rome to Lisbon*. Copenhagen: DJØF Publishing, pp. 53–94.

Dang, Phong, and Melanie Beresford. 1998. *Authority Relations and Economic
Decision-Making in Vietnam: An Historical Perspective*. Copenhagen: NIAS
Publications.

Davidson, Donald. 1984. *Inquiries into Truth and Interpretation*. Oxford: Clarendon Press.

Davies, William. 2010. 'Economics and the "Nonsense" of Law: The Case of the
Chicago Antitrust Revolution'. *Economy and Society* 39: 64–83.

Davis, Kenneth Culp, and Richard J. Pierce, Jr. 1994. *Administrative Law Treatise*,
3rd edn., 2 vols. Boston, MA: Little, Brown.

Dean, Mitchell. 1999. *Governmentality: Power and Rule in Modern Society*. Thousand Oaks, CA: Sage.

Demesetz, Harold. 2011. 'The Problem of Social Cost: What Problem? A Critique
of the Reasoning of A. C. Pigou and R. H. Coase'. *Review of Law and
Economics* 7: 1–13.

DeMeyer, Arnoud, Peter Williamson, Frank-Jürgen Richter, and Pamela
C. M. Mar (eds.). 2005. *Global Future: The Next Challenge for Asian
Business*. Singapore: John Wiley & Sons (Asia).

Deng, Guosheng, and Scott Kennedy. 2010. 'Big Business and Industry Association Lobbying in China: The Paradox of Contrasting Styles'. *China Journal* 63: 101–25.

Department for Business, Innovation and Skills (United Kingdom). 2012. *Growth, Competition and the Competition Regime: Government Response to Consultation.* London: Department for Business, Innovation and Skills, March 2012. Available at www.bis.gov.uk/assets/biscore/consumer-issues/docs/g/12-512-growth-and-competition-regime-government-response.pdf (accessed 20 June 2012).

'Developer Pushes China Cluster Model'. 2001. *Bangkok Post,* 19 March. Available at www.bangkokpost.com/business/economics/227473/developer-pushes-china-cluster-model (accessed 19 June 2012).

Deyo, Frederic C. 2004. 'Reforming Labor, Belaboring Reform: Structural Adjustment in Thailand and East Asia'. In Yoichiro Sato (ed.), *Growth and Governance in Asia.* Honolulu: Asia-Pacific Center for Security Studies, pp. 97–114.

Deyo, Frederic C., and Richard F. Doner. 2001. 'Dynamic Flexibility and Sectoral Governance in the Thai Auto Industry: The Enclave Problem'. In Frederic C. Deyo, Richard F. Doner, and Eric Hershberg (eds.), *Economic Governance and the Challenge of Flexibility in East Asia.* Lanham, MD: Rowman & Littlefield, pp. 107–36.

Deyo, Frederic C., Richard F. Doner, and Eric Hershberg (eds.). 2001. *Economic Governance and the Challenge of Flexibility in East Asia.* Lanham, MD: Rowman & Littlefield.

Dezalay, Yves, and Bryant G. Garth. 2002. *The Internationalization of Palace Wars: Lawyers, Economists, and the Contest to Transform Latin American States.* University of Chicago Press.

Dick, Andrew R. 1993. 'Japanese Antitrust: Reconciling Theory and Evidence'. *Contemporary Policy Issues* 11: 50–61.

Dicken, Peter, Philip Kelly, Kris Olds, and Henry Wai-chung Yeung. 2001. 'Chains and Networks, Territories and Scales: Towards an Analytical Framework for the Global Economy'. *Global Networks* 1: 89–112.

Dickson, Bruce J. 2003. *Red Capitalists in China: The Party, Private Entrepreneurs, and Prospects for Political Change.* Cambridge University Press.

DiMaggio, Paul. 1997. 'Culture and Cognition: An Interdisciplinary Review'. *Annual Review of Sociology* 23: 263–87.

Dobson, William D. 2006. 'Drivers of Change in China's Dairy Industry – Implications for the U.S. and World Dairy Industries'. Babcock Institute Discussion Paper 2006-4. Madison, WI: Babcock Institute for International Dairy Research and Development, University of Wisconsin-Madison. Available at http://babcock.wisc.edu/node/465 (accessed 17 June 2012).

Doner, Richard. 2009. *The Politics of Uneven Development: Thailand's Economic Growth in Comparative Perspective.* Cambridge University Press.

Dowdle, Michael W. 2002. 'Of Parliaments, Pragmatism, and the Dynamics of Constitutional Development: The Curious Case of China'. *New York University School of Law Journal of International Law and Politics* 35: 1–200.

2006. 'Public Accountability in Alien Terrain: Exploring for Constitutional Accountability in the People's Republic of China'. In Michael W. Dowdle (ed.), *Public Accountability: Designs, Dilemmas and Experiences*. Cambridge University Press, pp. 329–57.

2012. 'Asian Regionalism and Law: The Continuing Contribution of "Legal Pluralism"'. In Mark Beeson and Richard Stubbs (eds.), *Routledge Handbook of Asian Regionalism*. London: Routledge, pp. 226–35.

2012. 'Constitutional Listening'. *Chicago-Kent Law Review* 88: 115–56.

Downs, Erica S. 2008. 'Business Interest Groups in Chinese Politics: The Case of the Oil Companies'. In Cheng Li (ed.), *China's Changing Political Landscape: Prospects for Democracy*. Washington, DC: Brookings Institution Press, pp. 121–41.

'Drafting of Antimonopoly Law Accelerates after Ten Years in the Making. Foreign Companies Rebut Monopoly Charges [Fanlongduan Fa Yunniang 10 Nian Jiasu Chutai. Waiqi Fanbo Longduan]'. 2004. *Beijing Qingnian Bao* [Beijing Youth Daily], 28 May. Available at http://hyconference.edu.cn/chinese/law/574907.htm (accessed 14 June 2012).

Drexl, Josef. 2004. 'International Competition Policy after Cancun: Placing a Singapore Issue on the WTO Development Agenda'. *World Competition* 27: 419–57.

Dunning, John H., and Sarianna M. Lundan. 2008. *Multinational Enterprises and the Global Economy*, 2nd edn. Cheltenham: Edward Elgar.

Dunsire, Andrew. 1993. *Manipulating Social Tensions: Collibration as an Alternative Mode of Government Intervention. MPIFG Discussion Paper 93/7*. Cologne: Max-Plank-Institut für Gesellschaftsforschung.

1996. 'Tipping the Balance: Autopoiesis and Governance'. *Administration and Society* 28: 299–334.

Dworkin, Ronald. 1986. *Law's Empire*. Cambridge, MA: Belknap Press.

Dyson, Kenneth. 2009. *The State Tradition in Western Europe*. Colchester: ECPR Press.

Ehlermann, Claus-Dieter. 1995. 'Reflections on a European Cartel Office'. *Common Market Law Review* 32: 471–86.

Elhauge, Einer, and Damien Géradin. 2007. *Global Competition Law and Economics*. Oxford: Hart Publishing.

Elkins, Zachary, and Beth Simmons. 2005. 'On Waves, Clusters and Diffusion: A Conceptual Framework'. *Annals of the American Academy of Political and Social Science* 598: 33–51.

Emch, Eric M. 2004. '"Portfolio effects" in Merger Analysis: Differences between EU and US Practice and Recommendations for the Future'. *Antitrust Bulletin* 49: 55–100.

European Commission. 2012. 'Mergers: Commission Blocks Proposed Merger between Deutsche Börse and NYSE Euronext', press release, 1 February. Available at http://europa.eu/rapid/pressReleasesAction.do?reference=IP/12/94.

Evans, Peter. 1995. *Embedded Autonomy: States and Industrial Transformation.* Princeton University Press.

Facey, Brian A., and Dany H. Assaf. 2002. 'Monopolization and Abuse of Dominance in Canada, the United States, and the European Union: A Survey'. *Antitrust Law Journal* 70: 513–91.

Fair Trade Commission (Gongping Jiaoyi Weiyuanwei) (Taiwan). 1995. 'Criteria for Applying the Fair Trade Act to Private Law Acts by the Executive Government Entities'. 6 April. English translation available at www.ftc.gov.tw/internet/english/doc/docDetail.aspx?uid=743&docid=10251 (accessed 20 June 2012).

Fairclough, Gordon. 2008. 'Tainting of Milk is Open Secret in China'. *Wall Street Journal*, 3 November. Available at http://online.wsj.com/article/SB122567367498791713.html (accessed 27 June 2012).

FAO (Food and Agriculture Organization of the United Nations). 2006. *Food Outlook: Global Market Analysis No. 2.* December. Available at ftp://ftp.fao.org/docrep/fao/009/j8126e/j8126e00.pdf (accessed 27 June 2012).

Farmer, Susan Beth. 2009. 'The Evolution of Chinese Merger Notification Guidelines: A Work in Progress Integrating Global Consensus and Domestic Imperatives'. *Tulane Journal of International and Comparative Law* 18: 1–92.

FDA (Food and Drug Administration) (United States). 2007. 'Consumer Update: Contaminant Found in Second Pet Food Ingredient'. 23 April. Available at www.fda.gov/ForConsumers/ConsumerUpdates/ucm048190.htm (accessed 27 June 2012).

—— 2007. 'Detention without Physical Examination of All Vegetable Protein Products from China for Animal or Human Food Use Due to the Presence of Melamine and/or Melamine Analogs'. Important Alert 99-29, 2 May. Available at www.accessdata.fda.gov/cms_ia/importalert_267.html (accessed 27 June 2012).

—— 2007 'Joint Update: FDA/USDA Trace Adulterated Animal Feed to Poultry'. Press release, 30 April. Available at www.fda.gov/NewsEvents/Newsroom/PressAnnouncements/2007/ucm108902.htm (accessed 26 June 2012).

—— 2007. 'Pet Food Recall: Frequently Asked Questions'. 2 April. Available at http://web.archive.org/web/20070407113721/www.fda.gov/cvm/Menu-FoodRecallFAQ.htm (accessed 27 June 2012).

Fear, Jeffrey R. 2006. *Cartels and Competition: Neither Markets Nor Hierarchies.* HBS (Harvard Business School) Working Papers Collection, Working Paper 07-011. Available at www.hbs.edu/research/pdf/07–011.pdf (accessed 28 June 2012).

Ferran, Eilis. 2011. 'Understanding the New Institutional Architecture of EU Financial Market Supervision'. University of Cambridge Faculty of Law Working Paper 29/2011.

Fforde, Adam. 2007. *Vietnamese State Industry and the Political Economy of Commercial Renaissance: Dragon's Tooth or Curate's Egg?* Oxford: Chandos Publishing.

Fingleton, John. 2011. 'Competition Agencies and Global Markets: The Challenges Ahead'. In Paul Lugard (ed.), *The International Competition Network at Ten: Origins, Accomplishments and Aspirations.* Cambridge: Intersentia, pp. 173–204.

First, Harry. 2000. 'Antitrust in Japan: The Original Intent'. *Pacific Rim Law and Policy Journal* 9: 1–71.

2001. 'The Vitamins Case: Cartel Prosecutions and the Coming of International Competition Law'. *Antitrust Law Journal* 68: 711–29.

FitzGerald, Gerald, and David McFadden. 2011. 'Filling a Gap in Irish Competition Law Enforcement: The Need for a Civil Fines Sanction'. Competition Authority, Dublin, 9 June. Available at www.tca.ie/EN/Promoting-Competition/Presentations–Papers/The-need-for-civil-fines.aspx (accessed 12 June 2012).

'Five Airline Companies Suspected for Colluding to Raise Prices; Scheme Approved by General Administration of Civil Aviation [Wu Da Hangkong Gongsi Yi Gongmou Zhangjia; Fangan Huo Minhangju Renke]'. 2009. *Guangzhou Ribao* (Guangzhou Daily), 22 April. Available at http://finance.jrj.com.cn/2009/04/2209124197055.shtml (accessed 14 June 2012).

'Five High Speed Rail Systems are Suffering Losses because of Lack of Passengers [Zhongguo 5 tiao yiyunying gaotie kuisun yanzhong shang zuoludi shi zhuyin]'. 2011. Yahoo News (Chinese edition), 25 June. Available at http://news.cn.yahoo.com/ypen/20110625/434652.html (accessed 17 June 2012)

Foner, Eric. 1984. 'Why Is There no Socialism in the United States?'. *History Workshop Journal* 17: 57–80.

'Four General Contractors: 'No More Bid-rigging' [Zenekon yon sha 'dangō to ketsubetsu']'. 2005. *Asahi Shimbun*, 29 December.

'Fourteen Shipping Companies Operating in Sino-Japan Shipping Routes Form Self-Discipline Coalition [14 Jia Riben Hangxie Chuandong Zucheng Yunjia Zilü Lianmeng]'. 2009. Tianjin Ocean Network, 30 July. Available at www.dolphin-gp.com/cn/content.php?id=1248417093 (accessed 15 June 2012).

Fox, Eleanor M., and Abel M. Mateus (eds.). 2011. *Economic Development: The Critical Role of Competition Law and Policy.* Cheltenham: Edward Elgar.

Frankel, Jeffrey A. 2000. 'The Asian Model, the Miracle, the Crisis and the Fund'. In Paul Krugman (ed.), *Currency Crises.* University of Chicago Press, pp. 327–38.

Freyer, Tony A. 2006. *Antitrust and Global Capitalism, 1930–2004.* Cambridge University Press.

Friedman, Milton. 1962. *Capitalism and Freedom*. University of Chicago Press.

Fritz, Verena, and Alina Rocha Menocal. 2007. 'Developmental States in the New Millennium: Concepts and Challenges for a New Aid Agenda'. *Development Policy Review* 25: 531–52.

Fukuyama, Francis. 1992. *The End of History and the Last Man*. New York: Free Press.

Fuller, Frank H., Jikun Huang, Hengyun Ma, and Scott Rozelle. 2005. 'The Rapid Rise of China's Dairy Sector: Factors behind the Growth in Demand and Supply'. Working Paper 05-WP 394, Iowa State University Center for Agricultural and Rural Development, May.

Furse, Mark. 2009. *Antitrust Law in China, Korea and Vietnam*. Oxford University Press.

Gainsborough, Martin. 2009. 'The (Neglected) Statist Bias and the Developmental State: The Case of Singapore and Vietnam'. *Third World Quarterly* 30: 1317–28.

2010. *Vietnam: Rethinking the State*. London: Zed Books.

Gal, Michal S. 2003. *Competition Policy for Small Market Economies*. Harvard University Press.

Galbraith, John Kenneth. 1978. *The New Industrial State* 3rd rev. edn Boston, MA: Houghton Mifflin.

Galbreath, Carolyn. 2010. 'Criminalization of Cartel Offences in Ireland: Implications for International Cartels', paper presented at American Bar Association, Section for Antitrust Law Spring Meeting, San Francisco, April 2010. Available at www.tca.ie/EN/Promoting-Competition/Speeches – Presentations/ Criminalisation-of-Cartel-Offences-in-Ireland – Carolyn-Galbreath.aspx? page=1&year=2010 (accessed 11 June 2012).

Gale, Fred, and Dinghuan Hu. 2009. 'Supply Chain Issues in China's Milk Adulteration Incident', paper presented at the International Association of Agricultural Economists' 2009 Conference, Beijing, China, 16–22 August. Available at http://ageconsearch.umn.edu/bitstream/51613/2/China%20Dairy%20industry %20IAAE%20_June2009.pdf (accessed 17 June 2012).

Ganesh, Aravind R. 2010. 'The Right to Food and Buyer Power'. *German Law Journal* 11: 1190–243.

Géradin, Damien, Marc Reysen, and David Henry. 2010. 'Extraterritoriality, Comity and Cooperation in EC Competition Law'. In Andrew T. Guzman (ed.), *Cooperation, Comity, and Competition Policy*. Oxford University Press, pp. 21–44.

Gerber, David J. 1998. *Law and Competition in Twentieth Century Europe: Protecting Prometheus*. Oxford: Clarendon Press.

1998. 'System Dynamics: Toward a Language of Comparative Law'. *American Journal of Comparative Law* 46: 719–37.

2004. 'Constructing Competition Law in China: The Potential Value of European and U.S. Experience'. *Washington University Global Studies Law Review* 3: 315–31.

2008. 'Economics, Law and Institutions: The Shaping of Chinese Competition Law'. *Journal of Law and Policy* 26: 271–99.

2010. 'Convergence in the Treatment of Dominant Firm Conduct: The United States, the European Union, and the Institutional Embeddedness of Economics'. *Antitrust Law Journal* 76: 951–73.

2010. *Global Competition: Law, Markets and Globalization*. Oxford University Press.

Gerlach, Michael L. 1997. *Alliance Capitalism: The Social Organization of Japanese Business*. Berkeley: University of California Press.

Gibson, James L. 2008. 'Group Identities and Theories of Justice: An Experimental Investigation into the Justice and Injustice of Land Squatting in South Africa'. *Journal of Politics* 70: 700–16.

Gillespie, John. 2009. 'Testing the Limits to the "Rule of Law": Commercial Regulation in Vietnam'. *Journal of Comparative Asian Development* 12: 245–72.

2011. 'Exploring the Role of Legitimacy and Identity in Framing Responses to Legal Globalization in a Transforming Socialist Asia'. *Wisconsin International Law Journal*: 534–608.

Gilpin, Robert. 2001. *Global Political Economy: Understanding the International Economic Order*. Princeton University Press.

Gilson, Ronald J., and Curtis J. Milhaupt. 2011. 'Economically Benevolent Dictators: Lessons for Developing Democracies'. *American Journal of Comparative Law* 59: 227–88.

Global Competition Review. 2012. *Ratings Enforcement 2012*. London: Law Business Research. Available at www.globalcompetitionreview.com/surveys/survey/516/Rating-Enforcement/ (accessed 11 June 2012).

Gong Qing. 2008. 'Investigation Report on the Chaotic Raw Milk Market in Hebei [Diaocha Hebei Naiyuan Luanxiang]'. *Caijing*, 21 September.

Graham, Cosmo, and Fiona Smith (eds.). 2004. *Competition, Regulation and the New Economy*. Oxford: Hart Publishing.

Granovetter, Mark. 2005. 'The Impact of Social Structure on Economic Outcomes'. *Journal of Economic Perspectives* 19: 33–50.

Great Britain. Board of Trade. 1976. *Survey of International Cartels and Internal Cartels, 1944, 1946*, 2 vols. London: Central Library, Department of Industry.

Greene, J. Megan. 2008. *The Origins of the Developmental State in Taiwan: Science Policy and the Quest for Modernization*. Harvard University Press.

Griffin, Joseph P. 1999. 'Extraterritoriality in US and EU Antitrust Enforcement'. *Antitrust Law Journal* 67: 159–99.

Griffiths, John. 1987. 'What Is Legal Pluralism'. *Journal of Legal Pluralism and Unofficial Law* 24: 1–55.

Guan, Na, Qingfeng Fan, Jie Ding, Yiming Zhao, Jingqiao Lu, Yi Ai, Guobin Xu, Sainan Zhu, Chen Yao, Lina Jiang, Jing Miao, Han Zhang, Dan Zhao,

Xiaoyu Liu, and Yong Yao. 2009. 'Melamine-Contaminated Powdered Formula and Urolithiasis in Young Children'. *New England Journal of Medicine* 360: 1067–74.

Ha, Hannah, John Hickin, and Gerry O'Brien. 2010. 'China Steps Up Antitrust Capacity Building – Cartels a Focus', *Mondaq*, 20 July. Available at www.mondaq.com/article.asp?articleid=105788 (accessed 14 June 2012).

Haley, John O. 1992. *Authority without Power: Law and the Japanese Paradox*. Oxford University Press.

2001. *Antitrust in Germany and Japan: The First Fifty Years, 1947–1998*. Seattle: University of Washington Press.

2004. 'Competition Policy for East Asia'. *Washington University Global Studies Law Review* 3: 277–84.

Hall, Clare, Colin Scott, and Christopher Hood. 1999. *Telecommunications Regulation: Culture, Chaos and Interdependence inside the Regulatory Process*. London: Routledge.

Hall, Peter A., and David Soskice. 2001. 'An Introduction to Varieties of Capitalism'. In Peter A. Hall and David Soskice (eds.), *Varieties of Capitalism: The Institutional Foundations of Comparative Advantage*. Oxford University Press, pp. 1–70.

(eds.). 2001. *Varieties of Capitalism: The Institutional Foundations of Comparative Advantage*. Oxford University Press.

Hancher, Leigh, and Saskia Lavrijssen. 2009. 'Networks on Track: From European Regulatory Networks to European Regulatory 'Network' Agencies'. *Legal Issues of European Integration* 36: 23–55.

Hart, H. L. A. 1994 [1961]. *The Concept of Law*, 2nd edn. Oxford: Clarendon Press.

Hau, Anthony Kai-ching, Tze Hoi Kwan, and Philip Kam-tao Li. 2009. 'Melamine Toxicity and the Kidney'. *Journal of the American Society of Nephrology* 20: 245–50.

Hayashi, Shūya. 2009. 'The Goals of Japanese Competition Law'. In Josef Drexl, Laurence Idot, and Joël Monéger (eds.), *Economic Theory and Competition Law*. Cheltenham: Edward Elgar, pp. 45–69.

Hayek, F. A. 1945. 'The Use of Knowledge in Society'. *American Economic Review* 35: 519–30.

1948. *Individualism and Economic Order*. University of Chicago Press.

1994 [1944]. *The Road to Serfdom*. University of Chicago Press.

Hearn, Adrian H. In press. *The Politics of Trust: China's Relations with Cuba and Mexico*. Durham NC: Duke University Press.

Heilmann, Sebastian. 2006. 'Regulatory Innovation by Leninist Means: Communist Party Supervision in China's Financial Industry'. *China Quarterly* 181: 1–21.

Henderson, Jeffrey. 2005. 'Global Production Networks, Competition, Regulation and Poverty Reduction: Policy Implications'. Working Paper Series 115, University of Manchester, Centre on Regulation and Competition. Available at www.competition-regulation.org.uk/conferences/mcr05/henderson.pdf (accessed 12 July 2012).

Henderson, Jeffrey, Peter Dicken, Martin Hess, Neil Coe, and Henry Wai-chung Yeung. 2002. 'Global Production Networks and the Analysis of Economic Development'. *Review of International Political Economy* 9: 436–64.

Hess, Martin, and Henry Wai-chung Yeung (eds.). 2006. *Environment and Planning A*, theme issue on 'Global Production Networks', 38: 1193–305.

Hirsch, Joachim. 1995. *Der nationale Wettbewerbsstaat*. Berlin: Edition ID-Archiv.

Hirschman, Albert. 1977. *The Passions and the Interests*. Princeton University Press.

Hobday, Michael. 2001. 'The Electronics Industries of the Asia-Pacific: Exploiting International Production Networks for Economic Development'. *Asian-Pacific Economic Literature* 15: 13–29.

Hooker, M. B. 1975. *Legal Pluralism: An Introduction to Colonial and Neo-Colonial Laws*. Oxford: Clarendon Press.

1978. *A Concise Legal History of South-East Asia*. Oxford: Clarendon Press.

Horverak, Qyvind. 1988. 'Marx's View of Competition and Price Determination'. *History of Political Economy* 20: 275–98.

Hsueh, Roselyn. 2011. *China's Regulatory State: A New Strategy for Globalization*. Ithaca, NY: Cornell University Press.

Huang, Yasheng. 1996. *Inflation and Investment Controls in China: The Political Economy of Central–Local Relations during the Reform Era*. Cambridge University Press.

2008. *Capitalism with Chinese Characteristics: Entrepreneurship and the State*. New York: Cambridge University Press.

Huang, Yong. 2008. 'Pursuing the Second Best: The History, Momentum, and Remaining Issues of China's Anti-Monopoly Law'. *Antitrust Law Journal* 75: 117–31

Hyde, Alan. 2004. 'A Closer Look at the Emerging Employment Law of Silicon Valley's High-Velocity Labour Market'. In Joanne Conaghan, Richard Michael Fischl, and Karl Klare (eds.), *Labour Law in an Era of Globalization: Transformative Practices and Possibilities*. Oxford University Press, pp. 233–52.

Iannaccone, Laurence. 1994. 'Why Strict Churches Are Strong'. *American Journal of Sociology* 99: 1180–211.

IFC (International Finance Corporation) and World Bank. Undated. 'Doing Business: Measuring Business Regulation'. Available at www.doingbusiness.org/ (accessed 15 July 2012).

Inglehart, Ronald. 1981. 'Post-materialism in an Environment of Insecurity'. *American Political Science Review* 75: 880–900.

1997. *Modernization and Postmodernization: Cultural, Economic and Political Change in 43 Societies*. Princeton University Press.

Inglehart, Ronald, and Daphna Oyserman. 2004. 'Individualism, Autonomy and Self-Expression: The Human Development Syndrome'. In Henk Vinken, Joseph Soeters, and Peter Ester (eds.), *Comparing Cultures, Dimensions of Culture in a Comparative Perspective*. Leiden: Brill, pp. 79–96.

International Competition Network, Competition Policy Implementation Working Group. 2008. 'Report on Agency Effectiveness'. Seventh Annual Conference of the ICN, Kyoto, 14–16 April. Available at www.internatio-nalcompetitionnetwork.org/library.aspx?search=&group=13&type=0&work-shop=0 (accessed 11 June 2012).

——— 2009. 'Report on the Agency Effectiveness Project, Second Phase: Effectiveness of Decisions'. Eighth Annual Conference of the ICN, Zurich, 3–5 June. Available at www.internationalcompetitionnetwork.org/library.aspx?search=&group=13&type=0&workshop=0 (accessed 11 June 2012).

Iyori, Hiroshi, and Akinori Uesugi. 1994. *The Antimonopoly Laws and Policies of Japan*. New York: Federal Legal Publications.

Jacobs, Andrew. 2008. 'Chinese Release Increased Numbers in Tainted Milk Scandal'. *New York Times*, 2 December. Available at www.nytimes.com/2008/12/03/world/asia/03milk.html (accessed 27 June 2012).

Janow, Merit E., and James F. Rill. 2011. 'The Origins of the ICN'. In Paul Lugard (ed.), *The International Competition Network at Ten: Origins, Accomplishments and Aspirations*. Cambridge: Intersentia, pp. 21–38.

Japan Chamber of Commerce and Industry (Nippon shōkō kaigisho). 2004. 'Views Concerning the 'Outline of Proposed Amendments to the Antimonopoly Act' ['Dokusenkinshihō kaisei (an) no gaiyō' ni tai suru iken]', 25 June. Available at www.jcci.or.jp/nissyo/iken/040625dokkinhou.htm (accessed 13 June 2012).

Jayasuriya, Kanishka. 1999. 'Introduction: A Framework for the Analysis of Legal Institutions in East Asia'. In Kanishka Jayasuriya (ed.), *Law, Capitalism and Power in Asia: The Rule of Law and Legal Institutions*. London: Routledge, pp. 1–27.

——— 2001. 'Globalization and the Changing Architecture of the State: The Regulatory State and the Politics of Negative Coordination'. *Journal of European Public Policy* 8: 102–23.

——— 2005. 'Beyond Institutional Fetishism: From the Developmental to the Regulatory State'. *New Political Economy* 10: 381–7.

Jessop, Bob. 1998. 'The Rise of Governance and the Risks of Failure: The Case of Economic Development'. *International Social Science Journal* 155: 29–46.

——— 2001. 'Regulationist and Autopoieticist Reflections on Polanyi's Account of Market Economics and the Market Society'. *New Political Economy* 6: 213–32.

——— 2002. *The Future of the Capitalist State*. Cambridge: Polity Press.

——— 2007. 'Knowledge as a Fictitious Commodity: Insights and Limits of a Polanyian Analysis'. In Ayse Buğra and Kaan Ağartan (eds.), *Reading Karl*

Polanyi for the 21st Century: Market Economy as a Political Project. Basing-stoke: Palgrave Macmillan, pp. 115–34.

2011. 'The Continuing Ecological Dominance of Neoliberalism in the Crisis'. In Alfredo Saad-Filho and Galip L. Yalman (eds.), *Economic Transitions to Neoliberalism in Middle-Income Countries: Policy Dilemmas, Economic Crises, Forms of Resistance.* London: Routledge, pp. 24–38.

2011. 'Metagovernance'. In Mark Bevir (ed.), *The SAGE Handbook of Govern-ance.* London: Sage, pp. 106–23.

Jessop, Bob, and Ngai-Ling Sum. 2006. *Beyond the Regulation Approach: Putting Capitalist Economies in their Place.* Cheltenham: Edward Elgar.

2006. 'Towards a Cultural International Political Economy: Post-Structuralism and the Italian School'. In Marieke de Goede (ed.), *International Political Economy and Poststructural Politics.* Basingstoke: Palgrave Macmillan, pp. 157–76.

JFTC (Japan Fair Trade Commission). 1991. 'Guidelines Concerning Distribution Systems and Business Practices under the Antimonopoly Act [Ryūtsū tor-ihiki kankō ni kan suru dokusenkinshihōjō no shishin]', 11 July. Translated into English and available at www.jftc.go.jp/en/legislation_guidelines/ama/pdf/distribution.pdf (accessed 13 June 2012).

2001. 'Concerning the Treatment of the Resale System for Copyrighted Works [Chosakubutsu saihan seido no toriatsukai ni tsuite]', 23 March. Available at www.jftc.go.jp/sosiki/chosakuken.pdf (accessed 13 June 2012).

2010. 'Annual Report 2010 [Heisei 22 nendo kōsei torihiki iinkai nenji hōkoku]'. Available at www.jftc.go.jp/info/nenpou/h22/index.html (accessed 13 June 2012).

Continually updated. 'Concerning the Publication of the Enterprises to which the Leniency System has been Applied [Kachōkin genmen seido no tekiyō jigyōsha no kōhyō ni tsuite]'. Available at www.jftc.go.jp/dk/genmen/kou-hyou.html (accessed 13 June 1012).

Jia Hepeng. 2004. 'Country Fighting against Monopolies'. ChinaDaily.com.cn, 5 December. Available at www.chinadaily.com.cn/english/doc/2004–12/05/content_397413.htm (accessed 14 June 2012).

Johnson, Chalmers A. 1982. *MITI and the Japanese Miracle: The Growth of Industrial Policy, 1925–1975.* Stanford University Press.

1995. *Japan, Who Governs? The Rise of the Developmental State.* New York: W. W. Norton.

Kagan, Robert A. 2000. 'Introduction: Comparing National Styles of Regulation in Japan and the United States'. *Law and Policy* 22: 225–44.

2001. *Adversarial Legalism: The American Way of Law.* Cambridge, MA: Harvard University Press.

Kahn, Joel S., and Francesco Formosa. 2002. 'The Problem of "Crony Capitalism": Modernity and the Encounter with the Perverse'. *Thesis Eleven* 69: 47–66.

Kanazawa, Yoshio. 1963. 'The Regulation of Corporate Enterprise: The Law of Unfair Competition and the Control of Monopoly Power'. In Arthur Taylor von Mehren (ed.), *Law in Japan. The Legal Order in a Changing Society*. Harvard University Press, pp. 480–506.

Kang, David C. 2002. 'Bad Loans to Good Friends: Money Politics and the Developmental State in South Korea'. *International Organization* 56: 177–207.

Kaplow, Louis, and Steven Shavell. 2002. *Fairness versus Welfare*. Cambridge, MA: Harvard University Press.

Karlsson, Charlie, and Jan Larsson. 1990. 'Product and Price Competition in a Regional Context'. *Papers in Regional Science* 69: 83–99.

Kelsen, Hans. 1967 [1960]. *Pure Theory of Law*, 2nd edn, trans. Max Knight. Berkeley: University of California Press.

Kennedy, Scott. 2005. *The Business of Lobbying in China*. Boston, MA: Harvard University Press.

Kenny, Martin. 2008. 'Lessons from the Development of Silicon Valley and its Entrepreneurial Support Network for Japan'. In Shahid Yusuf, Kaoru Nabeshima, and Shoichi Yamashita (eds.), *Growing Industrial Clusters in Asia: Serendipity and Science*. Washington, DC: World Bank Publications, pp. 39–66.

Keynes, John Maynard. 1971 [1925]. 'A Short View Of Russia'. *The Collected Writings of John Maynard Keynes*. London: Macmillan, vol. 9, pp. 253–71.

Kim, Annette Miae. 2008. *Learning To Be Capitalists: Entrepreneurs in Vietnam's Transition Economy*. Oxford University Press.

King, Desmond S., and Jeremy Waldron. 1988. 'Citizenship, Social Citizenship and the Defence of Welfare Provision'. *British Journal of Political Science* 18: 415–43.

King, Lawrence Peter, and Ivan Szelényi. 2004. *Theories of the New Class: Intellectuals and Power*. Minneapolis: University of Minnesota Press.

Knight, John, and Li Shi. 1999. 'Fiscal Decentralization: Incentives, Redistribution and Reform in China'. *Oxford Development Studies* 27: 5–32.

Koizumi, Junichirō. 2001. 'Policy Speech by Prime Minister Junichirō Koizumi to the 151st Session of the Diet', 7 May. Provisional English translation available at www.mofa.go.jp/announce/pm/koizumi/speech0105.html (accessed 13 June 2012).

Kono, Takujiro. 2011. Presentation at the ICN Cartel Workshop 2011, Leniency Program of Japan Fair Trade Commission, 12 October. Available at http://ec.europa.eu/competition/information/icn_workshop_2011/presentations/mini_plenary_4b/takujiro_kono.ppt (accessed 13 June 2012).

Kooiman, Jan. 2003. *Governing as Governance*. London: Sage Publications.

Kovacic, William E. 2011. 'A Regulator's Perspective on Getting the Balance Right'. In R. Ian McEwin (ed.), *Intellectual Property, Competition Law and Economics in Asia*. Oxford: Hart Publishing, pp. 23–34.

Kovacic, William E., Hugh M. Hollman, and Patricia Grant. 2011. 'How Does Your Competition Agency Measure Up?'. *European Competition Journal* 7: 25–45.

Krugman, Paul. 1991. 'Increasing Returns and Economic Geography'. *Journal of Political Economy* 99: 483–99.

—— 1994. 'Competitiveness: A Dangerous Obsession'. *Foreign Affairs* 73(2): 28–44.

Krugman, Paul, and Anthony Venables. 1995. 'Globalization and the Inequality of Nations'. *Quarterly Journal of Economics* 110: 857–80.

Kuroiwa, Ikuo. 2005. 'Formation of Inter-country Production Networks in East Asia: Application of International Input-Output Analysis'. Paper presented at the 15th International Conference on Input–Output Techniques, Beijing, 27 June–1 July. Available at www.iioa.org/pdf/15th%20Conf/kuroiwa.pdf (accessed 17 June 2012).

Kwon, Ohseung. 2005. 'Retrospect and Prospect on Korean Competition Law'. *Journal of Korean Law* 4: 1–28.

Lam, Willy. 2008. 'Milk Scandal Sours China's "Soft Power"'. *Asia Times Online*, 10 October. Available at www.atimes.com/atimes/China/JJ10Ad02.html (accessed 27 June 2012).

Landauer, Carl. 1983. *Corporate State Ideologies: Historical Roots and Philosophical Origins*. Berkeley: Institute of International Studies, University of California, Berkeley.

Langman, Craig. 2009. 'Melamine, Powdered Milk, and Nephrolithiasis in Chinese Infants'. *New England Journal of Medicine* 360: 1139–41.

Larner, Wendy, and William Walters (eds.). 2006. *Global Governmentality: Governing International Spaces*. London: Routledge.

Laursen, Thomas, and Sandeep Mahajan. 2005. 'Volatility, Income Distribution, and Poverty'. In Joshua Aizenman and Brian Pinto (eds.), *Managing Economic Volatility and Crises: A Practitioner's Guide*. Cambridge University Press, pp. 101–35.

Leftwitch, Adrian. 1995. 'Bringing Politics Back In: Towards a Model of the Developmental State'. *Journal of Development Studies* 31: 400–27.

Legrand, Pierre. 2001. 'What Legal Transplants?'. In David Nelken and Johannes Feest (eds.), *Adapting Legal Cultures*. Oxford: Hart Publishing, pp. 55–70.

Leinbach, Thomas R., and John T. Bowen Jr. 2004. 'Air Cargo Services and the Electronics Industry in Southeast Asia'. *Journal of Economic Geography* 4: 1–24.

Lenin, Vladimir I. 2011 [1918]. *Imperialism: the Highest Stage of Capitalism*. Eastford, CT: Martino Publishing.

Le Thanh Vinh. 2010. 'Development Thinking and the Competition Law Enforcement in Vietnam [Tu duy phat trien va van de thuc thi Luat Canh tranh tai Viet Nam]'. *Tap chi Nghien cuu Lap phap* (Legislative Studies) 176 (15): 42–7.

Levi-Faur, David, and Jacint Jordana. 2005. 'The Rise of Regulatory Capitalism: The Global Diffusion of a New Order'. *Annals of the American Academy of Political and Social Science* 598: 200–17.

Levy, Brian, and Pablo T. Spiller. 1996. 'A Framework for Resolving the Regulatory Problem'. In Brian Levy and Pablo T. Spiller (eds.), *Regulations, Institutions and Commitment*. Cambridge University Press, pp. 1–35.

Levy, David L. 2008. 'Political Contestation in Global Production Networks'. *Academy of Management Review* 33: 943–63.

Leydesdorff, Loet, and Henry Etzkowitz (eds.). 1997. *Universities and the Global Knowledge Economy: A Triple Helix of University–Industry–Government Relations*. London: Thomson Learning.

Lim, Yena. 2011. 'Competition Law and State Regulation: Setting the Stage and Focus on State-owned Companies'. Paper delivered at Global Competition Law and Economics Series Conference, 'Competition Law and the State', Hong Kong, 19–21 March. Available at www.ucl.ac.uk/laws/global-competition/hongkong-2011/secure/docs/2_lim_paper.pdf (accessed 20 June 2012).

Lin, Chien-Chih. 2012. 'The Birth and Rebirth of the Judicial Review in Taiwan – Its Establishment, Empowerment, and Evolvement'. *National Taiwan University Law Review* 7: 167–222.

Lincoln, Edward J. 2001. *Arthritic Japan: The Slow Pace of Economic Reform*. Washington, DC: Brookings Institution Press.

Lippmann, Walter. 1961 [1914]. *Drift and Mastery: An Attempt to Diagnose the Current Unrest*. New York: Prentice Hall.

Litwinski, John A. 2001. 'Regulation of Labor Market Monopsony'. *Berkeley Journal of Employment and Labor Law* 22: 49–98.

Liu, Chenglin. 2009. 'Profits above the Law: China's Melamine Tainted Milk Incident'. *Mississippi Law Journal* 79: 371–417.

Liu, Jianhua. 2006. *China's New Market Order* [Zhongguo Shichang Xin Zhixu]. Beijing: Tsinghua University Press.

Liu, Lawrence S. 2004. 'In Fairness We Trust? – Why Fostering Competition Law and Policy Ain't Easy in Asia', unpublished paper dated 19 October. Available at http://ssrn.com/abstract=610822 (accessed 12 July 2012).

Lu, Ethel. 2009. 'Radical Shifts in China's Milk Market'. *China Today*, 14 January. Available at http://china.org.cn/business/news/2009–01/14/content_17105973.htm (accessed 17 June 2012).

Lüthje, Boy. 2002. 'Electronics Contract Manufacturing: Global Production and the International Division of Labor in the Age of the Internet'. *Industry and Innovation* 9: 227–47.

McCubbins, Mathew D., Roger G. Noll, and Barry R. Weingast. 1987. 'Administrative Procedures as Instruments of Political Control'. *Journal of Law, Economics, and Organization* 3: 243–77.

1989. 'Structure and Process, Politics and Policy: Administrative Arrangements and the Political Control of Agencies'. *Virginia Law Review* 75: 431–82.

McEwin, R. Ian. Forthcoming. *Competition Law in Southeast Asia*. Cambridge University Press.

McGregor, Richard. 2010. *The Party: The Secret World of China's Communist Rulers*. London: Allen Lane, pp. 70–103.

Machikita, Tomohiro, and Yasushi Ueki. 2010. 'Spatial Architecture of the Production Networks in South East Asia'. ERIA Discussion Paper Series, ERIA-DP-2010-01. Jakarta: Economic Research Institute for ASEAN and East Asia. Available at www.eria.org/pdf/DP-2010–01.pdf (accessed 17 June 2012).

MacKinnon, Danny, Andrew Cumbers, Andy Pike, Kean Birch, and Robert McMaster. 2009. 'Evolution in Economic Geography: Institutions, Political Economy, and Adaptation'. *Economic Geography* 85: 129–50.

McKinsey Global Institute. 2000. 'Why the Japanese Economy is Not Growing: Micro Barriers to Productivity Growth'. Available at www.mckinsey.com/~/media/McKinsey/dotcom/Insights%20and%20pubs/MGI/Research/Productivity%20Competitiveness%20and%20Growth/Why%20the%20Japanese%20economy%20is%20not%20growing/MGI_Why_the_Japanese_economy_is_not_growing_Report.ashx (accessed 13 June 2012).

Maclachlan, Patricia L. 2002. *Consumer Politics in Postwar Japan: The Institutional Boundaries of Citizen Activism*. New York: Columbia University Press.

McMichael, Phillip. 2008. *Development and Social Change: A Global Perspective*, 4th edn. Thousand Oaks, CA: Pine Forge Press.

Maher, Imelda. 1999. *Competition Law: Alignment and Reform*. Dublin: Round Hall Sweet & Maxwell.

——— 2002. 'Competition Law in the International Domain: Networks as a New Form of Governance'. *Journal of Law and Society* 29: 112–136

——— 2004. 'Regulating Competition'. In Christine Parker, Colin Scott, Nicola Lacey, and John Braithwaite (eds.), *Regulating Law*. Oxford University Press, pp. 187–206.

——— 2004. 'Regulatory Compliance and the Rule of Law: Evaluating the Performance of the Australian Competition and Consumer Commission'. In Michael Barker (ed.), *Appraising the Performance of Regulatory Agencies*. Canberra: Australian Institute of Administrative Law, pp. 208–27.

——— 2005. 'Networking Competition Authorities in the European Union: Diversity and Change'. In Claus-Dieter Ehlermann and Isabela Atanasiu (eds.), *European Competition Law Annual 2002: Constructing The EU Network Of Competition Authorities*. Oxford: Hart Publishing, pp. 223–36.

——— 2009. 'Functional and Normative Delegation to Non-majoritarian Institutions: The Case of the European Competition Network'. *Comparative European Politics* 7: 414–34.

——— 2012. 'Transnational Legal Authority in Competition Law and Governance: Territoriality, Commonality and Networks'. In Günther Handl, Joachim Zekoll, and Peer Zumbansen (eds.), *Beyond Territoriality: Transnational Legal Authority in an Age of Globalization*. Leiden: Brill Academic Publishers, pp. 414–38.

Maher, Imelda, and Anestis S. Papadopoulos. 2012. 'Competition Agency Net-works around the World'. In Ariel Ezrachi (ed.), *Research Handbook on International Competition Law*. Cheltenham: Edward Elgar, pp. 60–88.

Majone, Giandomenico. 1998. 'The Rise of the Regulatory State in Europe'. In Robert Baldwin, Colin Scott, and Christopher Hood (eds.), *A Reader on Regulation*. Oxford University Press, pp. 193–213.

Marshall, Alfred. 1922. *Principles of Economics*, 8th edn. New York: Macmillan.

Marshall, Ross, and Thomas B. Fischer. 2006. 'Regional Electricity Transmission Planning and SEA'. *Journal of Environmental Planning and Management* 49: 279–99.

Marshall, T. H. 1950. *Citizenship and Social Class, and Other Essays*. Cambridge University Press.

Martin, Ron, and Peter Sunley. 2006. 'Path Dependence and Regional Economic Evolution'. *Journal of Economic Geography* 6: 395–437.

  2007. 'Complexity Thinking and Evolutionary Economic Geography'. *Journal of Economic Geography* 7: 573–601.

Marx, Karl. 1963 [1883]. *Capital, Volume I: A Critique of Political Economy*. London: Lawrence & Wishart.

  1963 [1894]. *Capital, Volume III: The Process of Capitalist Production as a Whole*. London: Lawrence & Wishart.

Marx, Karl, and Friedrich Engels. 1967 [1848]. *The Communist Manifesto*. New York: Penguin.

Mashaw, Jerry. 2006. 'Accountability and Institutional Design: Some Thoughts on the Grammar of Governance'. In Michael W. Dowdle (ed.), *Public Account-ability: Designs, Dilemmas and Experiences*. Cambridge University Press, pp. 115–56.

Mathews, John A. 2002. *Dragon Multinational: A New Model for Global Growth*. Oxford University Press.

  2006. *Strategizing, Disequilibrium and Profit*. Stanford University Press.

Mathews, John A., and Ivo Zander. 2007. 'The International Entrepreneurial Dynamics of Accelerated Internationalisation'. *Journal of International Business Studies* 38: 387–403.

Matsushita, Mitsuo. 1990. *Introduction to Japanese Antimonopoly Law* (with John D. Davis). Tokyo: Yuhikaku.

  1993. *International Trade and Competition Law in Japan*. Oxford University Press.

  1997. 'The Antimonopoly Law of Japan'. In Edward M. Graham and J. David Richardson (eds.), *Global Competition Policy*. Washington, DC: Institute for International Economics, pp. 151–97.

  2010. 'Reforming the Enforcement of the Japanese Antimonopoly Law'. *Loyola University Chicago Law Journal* 41: 521–34.

Mazower, Mark. 1999. *Dark Continent: Europe's Twentieth Century*. London: Penguin Books.

Mazumdar, Surajit. 2008. 'Crony Capitalism: Caricature or Category?' MPRA (Munich Personal RePEc Archive) Paper No. 19626. February. Available at http://mpra.ub.uni-muenchen.de/19626/ (accessed 15 July 2012).

Megginson, William L. 2005. *The Financial Economics of Privatization*. Oxford University Press.

Mehra, Salil K., and Meng Yanbei. 2009. 'Against Antitrust Functionalism: Reconsidering China's Antimonopoly Law'. *Virginia Journal of International Law* 49: 379–429.

Merry, Sally. 1988. 'Legal Pluralism'. *Law and Society Review* 22: 869–96.

Meseguer, Covadonga. 2005. 'Policy Learning, Policy Diffusion and the Making of a New Order'. *Annals of the American Academy of Political and Social Science* 598: 67–82.

Meyler, Bernadette. 2006. 'Economic Emergency and the Rule of Law'. *DePaul Law Review* 56: 539–67.

Milhaupt, Curtis J., and Katharina Pistor. 2008. *Law and Capitalism: What Corporate Crises Reveal about Legal Systems and Economic Development Around the World*. University of Chicago Press.

Mill, John Stuart. 2004 [1848]. *Principles Of Political Economy: With Some Of Their Applications To Social Philosophy*, abridged and ed. Stephen Nathanson. Indianapolis: Hackett Publishing.

Miller, Peter, and Nikolas Rose. 2008. *Governing the Present: Administering Economic, Social and Personal Life*. Cambridge: Polity.

'Ministry of Commerce: No Discrimination Against Foreign Companies in Antimonopoly Merger Review [Shangwubu: Fanlongduan Shencha Wei Qishi Qaizi]'. 2010. *Morning Post*, 12 August 2010. Available at www.morning-post.com.cn/xwzx/jjxw /2010-08-12/66994.shtml (accessed 14 June 2012).

Ministry of Trade (Vietnam). 2009. 'Survey of the Community's Understanding about the Competition Law [KHẢO SÁT MỨC ĐỘ NHẬN THỨC CỦA CỘNG ĐỒNG ĐỐI VỚI LUẬT CẠNH TRANH]'. Unpublished report, Hanoi.

Mission on Japanese Combines. 1946. *Report of the Mission on Japanese Combines. . . . : A Report to the Department of State and the War Department*. Washington, DC: United States Government Printing Office.

Monti, Giorgio. 2004. 'Article 82 EC and New Economy Markets'. In Cosmo Graham and Fiona Smith (eds.), *Competition, Regulation and the New Economy*. Oxford: Hart Publishing, pp. 17–54.

Moorthy, K. Sridhar. 1988, 'Product and Price Competition in a Duopoly'. *Marketing Science* 7: 141–68.

Moran, Michael. 2001. 'The Rise of the Regulatory State in Britain'. *Parliamentary Affairs* 54: 19–34

Morck, Randall, Daniel Wolfenzon, and Bernard Yeung. 2005. 'Corporate Governance, Economic Entrenchment, and Growth'. *Journal of Economic Literature* 43: 655–720.

Morgan, Bronwen. 2003. *Social Citizenship in the Shadow of Competition: The Bureaucratic Politics of Regulatory Justification*. Aldershot: Ashgate.

Morikawa, Hidemasa. 1992. *Zaibatsu: The Rise and Fall of Family Enterprise Groups in Japan*. University of Tokyo Press.

'Most Liquid Milk in China Does Not Contain Melamine'. 2008. Xinhua News Agency, 18 September. Available at http://news.xinhuanet.com/english/2008–09/19/content_10076616.htm (accessed 27 June 2012).

Motta, Massimo, and Alexandre de Streel. 2006. 'Excessive Pricing and Price Squeeze under EU Law'. In Claus-Dieter Ehlermann and Isabela Atanasiu (eds.), *European Competition Law Annual 2003: What is an Abuse of a Dominant Position?* Oxford: Hart Publishing, pp. 91–125.

Murayama, Makoto. 2002. 'Private Enforcement of Antitrust Law in Japan'. In Clifford A. Jones and Mitsuo Matsushita (eds.), *Competition Policy in the Global Trading System: Perspectives from the EU, Japan and the USA*. Leiden: Kluwer Law International, pp. 243–54.

  2003. *The Japanese Antimonopoly Act/Nihon no Dokusen Kinshihō*. Tokyo: Shōji Hōmu.

Muris, Timothy J. 2005. 'Principles for a Successful Competition Agency'. *University of Chicago Law Review* 72: 165–87.

Nakasone, Yasuhiro. 2010. 'Japan Adrift in a Changing World'. *Japan Times*, 16 September.

National Bureau of Statistics of China (Zhonghua Renmin Gongheguo Guojia Tongjiju). 2007. 'People's Republic of China 2006 National Economic and Social Development Statistics [Zhonghua Renmin Gongheguo 2006 nian Guomin Jingji he Shehui Fazhan Tongji Gongbao]', 28 February. Available at www.stats.gov.cn/tjgb/ndtjgb/qgndtjgb/t20070228_402387821.htm (accessed 14 June 2012).

National Development and Reform Commission (Guojia Fazhan he Gaige Weiyuanhui) (China). 2009. 'Notice on Opinions Concerning Inhibiting Excess Capacity and Duplicate Construction in Certain Industries in Order to Guide Healthy Industrial Development [Guanyu Yizhi Bufen Hangye Channeng Guosheng he Chongfu Jianshe yindao Chanye Jiankang Fazhan de Ruogan Yijian]', 26 September. Available at www.sdpc.gov.cn/zcfb/zcfbqt/2010qt/t20100513_346554.htm (accessed 14 June 2012).

National Development and Reform Commission (Guojia Fazhan he Gaige Weiyuanhui) and Ministry of Commerce (Shangwu Bu) (China). 2007. 'Guidance Catalog on Foreign Investment [Waishang Touzi Chanye Zhidao Mulu]'. Available at www.sdpc.gov.cn/zcfb /zcfbl/2007ling/W020071107537750156652.pdf (accessed 14 June 2012).

Naughton, Barry. 1996. *Growing Out of the Plan: Chinese Economic Reform 1978–93*. Cambridge University Press.

  2007. *The Chinese Economy: Transitions and Growth*. Boston, MA: MIT Press.

2008. 'SASAC and rising corporate power'. *China Leadership Monitor* 24 (Spring): 1–9. Available at http://media.hoover.org/documents/CLM24BN. pdf (accessed 15 June 2012).

2010. 'China's Distinctive System: Can It Be a Model for Others?' *Journal of Contemporary China* 19: 437–60.

Nee, Victor. 2005. 'Organization Dynamics of Institutional Change: Politicized Capitalism in China'. In Victor Nee and Richard Swedberg (eds.), *The Economic Sociology of Capitalism*. Princeton University Press, pp. 53–74.

Nee, Victor, and Richard Swedberg (eds.). 2005. *The Economic Sociology of Capitalism*. Princeton University Press.

Neumann, Franz. 1942. *Behemoth: The Structure and Practice of National Socialism*. London: Gollancz.

Ng Tze-wei. 2008. 'Lawyers Warned to Shun Milk Suits'. *South China Morning Post*, 23 September, A2.

Nguyen Sa. 2007. 'Vietnamese Companies Join Forces to Regain Laptop Market Share'. VietNamNet Bridge, 1 October, original posting no longer available. Republished at http://duongcodon.blogspot.sg/2007/01/vietnamese-companies-join-forces-to.html (accessed 17 June 2012).

Nishimura, Nobufumi, and Fumio Sensui. 2006. 'The Enactment of the Original AMA and its Implications for the Current AMA [Genshi Dokusenkinshihō no Seitei Katei to Genkōhō he no shisa]'. Available at www.jftc.go.jp/cprc/english/cr-0206.pdf (accessed 13 June 2012).

2008. 'The Enactment of the Original AMA and its Implications for the Current AMA – the JFTC's Organization, Judicial System, Damages and Criminal System [Genshi Dokusenkinshihō no Seitei Katei to Genkōhō he no shisa – Kōtorii no Soshiki, Shihōseido, Songaibaishō, Keijiseido]'. Available at www. jftc.go.jp/cprc/english/cr-0408.pdf (accessed 13 June 2012), English summary available at www.jftc.go.jp/cprc/english/cr-0408abstract.pdf (accessed 13 June 2012).

Nolan, Peter. 1995. *China's Rise, Russia's Fall: Politics, Economics and Planning in the Transition from Stalinism*. New York: St. Martin's Press.

North, Douglass C. 1990. *Institutions, Institutional Change, and Economic Performance*. Cambridge University Press.

OECD. 1986. 'Science Technology Industry'. *STI Review* 1: 84–129.

2001. *Regulatory Reform in Ireland: Enhancing Market Openness Through Regulatory Reform*. Paris: OECD Publications. Available at www.oecd.org/dataoecd/30/57/2510988.pdf (accessed 12 June 2012).

2002. *China in the World Economy: The Domestic Policy Challenges*. Paris: OECD Publications.

2009. *China: Defining the Boundary Between the Market and the State*. Paris: OECD Publications.

Ofreneo, Rene. 2009. 'Development Choices for Philippine Textiles and Garments in the Post-MFA Era'. *Journal of Contemporary Asia* 39: 543–61.

Oi, Jean C. 1992. 'Fiscal Reform and the Economic Foundations of Local State Corporatism in China'. *World Politics* 45: 99–126.

Okun, Arthur. 1975. *Equality and Efficiency: The Big Tradeoff.* Washington, DC: Brookings Institution Press.

O'Riain, Sean. 2004. *The Politics of High-Tech Growth: Developmental Network States in the Global Economy.* Cambridge University Press.

Orru, Marco, Nicole Woolsey Biggart, and Gary G. Hamilton (eds.). 1996. *The Economic Organization of East Asian Capitalism.* London: Sage Publications.

O'Sullivan, Fran. 2008. 'Embassy Officials Slow to Call Toxic Alert'. *New Zealand Herald News*, 21 September. Available at www.nzherald.co.nz/nz/news/article.cfm?c_id=1&objectid=10533363 (accessed 27 June 2012).

Owen, Bruce M., Su Sun, and Wentong Zheng. 2008. 'China's Competition Policy Reforms: The Antimonopoly Law and Beyond'. *Antitrust Law Journal* 75: 231–68 .

Owens, Timothy J., Dawn T. Robinson, and Lynn Smith-Lovin. 2010. 'Three Faces of Identity'. *Annual Review of Sociology* 36: 477–99.

Palan, Ronen. 1998. 'The Emergence of an Offshore Economy'. *Futures* 30: 63–73.

Papadopoulos, Anestis S. 2010. *The International Dimension of EU Competition Law and Policy.* Cambridge University Press.

Parisi, Francesco. 2005. 'Positive, Normative and Functional Schools in Law and Economics'. In Jürgen G. Backhaus (ed.), *The Elgar Companion to Law and Economics*, 2nd edn. Cheltenham: Edward Elgar, pp. 58–73.

Park, Sam Ock. 2008. 'ICT Clusters and Industrial Restructuring in the Republic of Korea'. In Shahid Yusuf, Kaoru Nabeshima, and Shoichi Yamashita (eds.), *Growing Industrial Clusters in Asia: Serendipity and Science.* Washington, DC: World Bank Publications, pp. 195–216.

Parker, Christine, and Vibeke Lehmann Nielsen. 2010. 'Deterrence and the Impact of Calculative Thinking on Business Compliance with Competition and Consumer Regulation'. *Antitrust Bulletin* 56: 377–426.

Patel, Raj, and Philip McMichael. 2010. 'A Political Economy of the Food Riot'. *Review, A Journal of the Fernand Braudel Center* 12: 9–35.

Peck, Jamie. 2010. *Constructions of Neo-Liberal Reason.* Oxford University Press.

Peck, Jamie, and Adam Tickell. 2002. 'Neoliberalizing Space'. *Antipode* 24: 380–404.

Peerenboom, Randall P. 2007. *China Modernizes Threat to West: Model for the Rest?* Oxford University Press.

Pei, Minxin. 2006. *China's Trapped Transition: The Limits of Developmental Autocracy.* Cambridge, MA: Harvard University Press.

Peng, Yushang. 2004. 'Kinship Networks and Entrepreneurs in China's Transition Economy'. *American Journal of Sociology* 109: 1045–74.

Peritz, Rudolph J. R. 1996. *Competition Policy in America, 1888–1992: History, Rhetoric, Law*. Oxford University Press.

Peters, B. Guy. 1996. 'United States Competition Policy Institutions: Structural Constraints and Opportunities'. In G. Bruce Doern and Stephen Wilks (eds.), *Comparative Competition Policy*. Oxford: Clarendon Press, pp. 40–68.

Petit, Nicholas. 2005. 'The Proliferation of National Regulatory Authorities alongside Competition Authorities: A Source of Jurisdictional Confusion?'. In Damien Géradin, Rodolphe Muñoz, and Nicolas Petit (eds.), *Regulation through Agencies in the EU: A New Paradigm of European Governance*. Cheltenham: Edward Elgar, pp. 180–214.

Pham, Alice. 2005. 'The Development of Competition Law in Vietnam in the Face of Economic Reforms and Global Integration'. *Northwestern Journal of International Law and Business* 26: 547–64.

Phongpaichit, Pasuk and Chris Baker. 2000. *Thailand's Crisis*. Singapore: Singapore Institute of Southeast Asian Studies.

Piore, Michael J., and Charles F. Sabel. 1984. *The Second Industrial Divide: Possibilities for Prosperity*. New York: Basic Books.

Polanyi, Karl. 2001 [1944]. *The Great Transformation: The Political and Economic Origins of our Time*. Boston, MA: Beacon Press.

2001 [1944]. 'The Self-Regulating Market and the Fictitious Commodities: Labor, Land, and Money'. In *The Great Transformation: The Political and Economic Origins of Our Time*. Boston, MA: Beacon Press, pp. 71–80.

Pollack, Mark A. 1997. 'Delegation, Agency, and Agenda Setting in the European Community'. *International Organization* 51: 99–134.

Porter, Michael E. 1990. *The Competitive Advantage of Nations*. New York: Free Press.

Porter, Michael E., and Mariko Sakakibara. 2004. 'Competition in Japan'. *Journal of Economic Perspectives* 18: 27–50.

Posner, Richard A. 2007. *Economic Analysis of the Law*, 7th edn. New York: Aspen Publishers.

Pournara, Julia, and Costas D. Vainanidis. 1993. 'Greek Anti-trust Law: A Critical Appraisal'. *European Competition Law Review* 14: 226–230.

Powell, Walter W. 1990. 'Neither Market nor Hierarchy: Network Forms of Organization'. *Research in Organizational Behavior* 12: 295–336.

Price, Rohan, and John Kong Shan Ho. 2012. 'Air Pollution in Hong Kong: The Failure of Government and Judicial Review'. *Public Law* issue 2: 179–97.

Procassini, Andrew A. 1995. *Competitors in Alliance: Industry Associations, Global Rivalries, and Business-Government Relations*. Westport, CT: Quorum.

Prosser, Tony. 2005. *The Limits of Competition Law: Markets and Public Services*. Oxford University Press.

2008. 'Regulatory Agencies, Regulatory Legitimacy and European Private Law'. In Fabrizio Cafaggi and Horatia Muir Watt (eds.), *Making European Private Law: Governance Design*. Cheltenham: Edward Elgar, pp. 235–53.

Puchniak, Dan W. 2007. 'Besprechungsaufsatz/Review Essay: A Skeptic's Guide to Miwa and Ramseyer's *The Fable of the Keiretsu*'. *Journal of Japanese Law* 24: 273–90.

——— 2007. 'The Japanization of American Corporate Governance? Evidence of the Never-Ending History for Corporate Law'. *Asian-Pacific Law and Policy Journal* 9: 7–70.

Puchniak, Dan W., Harald Baum, and Michael Ewing-Chow (eds.). 2012. *The Derivative Action in Asia: A Comparative and Functional Approach*. Cambridge University Press.

Puschner, Birgit, Robert H. Poppenga, Linda J. Lowenstine, Michael S. Filigenzi, and Patricia A. Pesavento. 2007. 'Assessment of Melamine and Cyanuric Acid Toxicity in Cats'. *Journal of Veterinary Diagnostic Investigation*. 19: 616–24.

Qian, Yingyi, and Barry R. Weingast, 1996. *China's Transition to Markets: Market-Preserving Federalism, Chinese Style*. Stanford: Hoover Institute.

Qian, Yingyi, and Chenggang Xu. 1993. 'Why China's Economic Reforms Differ: The M-Form Hierarchy and Entry/Expansion of the Non-state Sector'. *Economics of Transition* 1: 135–70.

Radice, Hugo. 2008. 'The Developmental State under Global Neoliberalism'. *Third World Quarterly* 29: 1153–74.

Rafiqui, Pernilla S. 2009. 'Evolving Economic Landscapes: Why New Institutional Economics Matters for Economic Geography'. *Journal of Economic Geography* 9: 329–53.

Rama, Martin. 2008. *Making Difficult Choices: Vietnam in Transition. Commission on Growth and Development*, Working Paper 40. Washington: International Bank for Reconstruction and Development/The World Bank. Available at www.growthcommission.org/storage/cgdev/documents/gcwp040bilingual web.pdf (accessed 17 June 2012).

Ramstetter, Eric, and Phan Minh Ngoc. 2007. *Changes in Ownership and Producer Concentration after the Implementation of Vietnam's Enterprise Law*, Working Paper Series 2007-06.Kitakyushu: International Centre for the Study of East Asian Development. Available at http://file.icsead.or.jp/user04/760_210_20110623101822.pdf (accessed 17 June 2012).

Ramzy, Austin. 2008. 'China's Tainted Milk Scandal of 2008'. *Time Magazine*, 26 September. Available at www.time.com/time/world/article/0,8599,1844750,00.html (accessed 26 June 2012).

Razmi, Arslan. 2007. 'Integration, Informalization, and Income Inequality in Developing Countries: Some General Equilibrium Explorations in Light of Accumulating Evidence'. University of Massachusetts at Amhurst Economics Department Working Paper Series: Paper 39. Available at http://scholarworks.umass.edu/econ_workingpaper/39 (accessed 27 June 2012).

Rodan, Garry. 1989. *The Political Economy of Singapore's Industrialization: National State and International Capital*. Basingstoke: Palgrave Macmillan.

Rodrik, Dani. 2006. 'Goodbye Washington Consensus, Hello Washington Confusion? A Review of the World Bank's Economic Growth in the 1990s: Learning from a Decade of Reform'. *Journal of Economic Literature* 44: 973–87.

2007. *One Economics, Many Recipes: Globalization, Institutions, and Economic Growth*. Princeton University Press.

Roe, Mark J. 2000. 'Political Preconditions to Separating Ownership from Corporate Control'. *Stanford Law Review* 53: 539–606.

Rose, Carol M. 1996. 'Propter Honoris Respectum: Property as the Keystone Right?'. *Notre Dame Law Review* 71: 329–365.

Rosenthal, Douglas E., and Mitsuo Matsushita. 1997. 'Competition in Japan and the West: Can the Approaches Be Reconciled?'. In Edward M. Graham and J. David Richardson (eds.), *Global Competition Policy*. Washington, DC: Institute for International Economics, pp. 313–38.

Rubin, Edward L. 1990. 'The Concept of Law and the New Public Law Scholarship'. *Michigan Law Review* 89: 792–836.

Ruskola, Teemu. 2011. 'Where Is Asia? When Is Asia? Theorizing Comparative Law and International Law'. *UC Davis Law Review* 44: 879–96.

Sabel, Charles F. 1994. 'Learning by Monitoring: The Institutions of Economic Development'. In Neil Smelser and Richard Swedberg (eds.), *The Handbook of Economic Sociology* 1st ed. Princeton University Press and Russell Sage Foundation, pp. 137–65.

Sachs, Jeffrey. 2000. 'A New Map of the World'. *Economist*, 22 June, 81–3.

Said, Edward W. 1979. *Orientalism*. New York: Penguin Books.

Sandel, Michael J. 1996. *Democracy's Discontent: America in Search of a Public Philosophy*. Cambridge, MA: Belknap Press.

'Sanlu Liquid Milk Back on Chinese Market after Melamine Scandal'. 2008. Xinhua News Agency, 13 November. Available at http://news.xinhuanet.com/english/2008-11/13/content_10353146.htm (accessed 27 June 2012).

Saxenian, AnnaLee. 1994. *Regional Advantage: Culture and Competition in Silicon Valley and Route 128*. Boston, MA: Harvard University Press.

2002. 'Transnational Communities and the Evolution of Global Production Networks: The Cases of Taiwan, China and India'. *Industry and Innovation* 9: 183–202.

2006. *The New Argonauts: Regional Advantage in a Global Economy*. Boston, MA: Harvard University Press.

Saxenian, AnnaLee, and Jinn-Yuh Hsu. 2001. 'The Silicon Valley-Hsinchu Connection: Technical Communities and Industrial Upgrading'. *Industrial and Corporate Change* 10: 893–920.

Saxenian, AnnaLee, and Charles F. Sabel. 2008. 'Venture Capital in the "Periphery": The New Argonauts, Global Search, and Local Institution Building'. *Economic Geography* 84: 379–94.

SCAP (Supreme Command for the Allied Powers). 1945. 'Directive No. 244 on the Dissolution of Holding Companies' (6 November 1945). Repr. in T. A. Bisson, *Zaibatsu Dissolution in Japan*. Westport, CT: Greenwood Press, 1976, pp. 243–4.

Schaede, Ulrike. 2000. *Cooperative Capitalism: Self-Regulation, Trade Associations, and the Antimonopoly Law in Japan*. Oxford University Press.

Scheiber, Harry, and Laurent Mayali (eds.). 2007. *Emerging Concepts of Rights in Japanese Law*. Berkeley, CA: Robbins Religious and Civil Law Collection.

Schick, Suzaynn, and Stanton A. Glantz. 2005. 'Philip Morris Toxicological Experiments with Fresh Sidestream Smoke: More Toxic than Mainstream Smoke'. *Tobacco Control* 14: 396–404.

Schmitt, Carl. 1996 [1927]. *The Concept of the Political*, trans. George Schwab. University of Chicago Press.

Schumpeter, Joseph A. 1962 [1934]. *Theory of Economic Development: An Inquiry into Profits, Capital, Credit, Interest and the Business Cycle*, trans. Redvers Opie. Boston, MA: Harvard University Press.

    1975 [1943]. *Capitalism, Socialism, and Democracy*, 3rd edn. New York: Harper & Row.

Schütte, Helmut (ed.). 1994. *The Global Competitiveness of the Asian Firm*. New York: St. Martin's Press.

Schwartz, Bernard. 1996. 'Administrative Law'. In Alan Morrison (ed.), *Fundamentals of American Law*. Oxford University Press, pp. 129–50.

Schwartz, Herman. 2007. 'Dependency or Institutions? Economic Geography, Causal Mechanisms, and Logic in the Understanding of Development'. *Studies in Comparative International Development* 42: 115–35.

Scott, Allen J., and Michael Storper. 1992. 'Regional Development Reconsidered'. In Huib Ernst and Verena Meier (eds.), *Regional Development and Contemporary Industrial Response*. London: Belhaven, pp. 3–24.

Scott, Colin. 2000. 'Accountability in the Regulatory State'. *Journal of Legal Studies* 27: 38–60.

    2004. 'Regulation in the Age of Governance: The Rise of the Post Regulatory State'. In Jacint Jordana and David Levi-Faur (eds.), *The Politics of Regulation: Institutions and Regulatory Reforms for the Age of Governance*. Cheltenham: Edward Elgar, pp. 145–74.

    2006. 'Spontaneous Accountability'. In Michael Dowdle (ed.), *Public Accountability: Designs, Dilemmas and Experiences*. Cambridge University Press, pp. 174–91.

    2012. 'Regulating Everything: From Megaregulation to Metaregulation'. *Administration* 60: 57–85.

Scott, James. 1998. *Seeing Like a State: How Certain Schemes to Improve the Human Condition Have Failed*. New Haven: Yale University Press.

Seita, Alex Y., and Jirō Tamura. 1994. 'The Historical Background of Japan's Antimonopoly Law'. *University of Illinois Law Review* 1: 115–85.

Senior, Nassau William. 1939 [1836]. *An Outline of the Science of Political Economy*. New York: Farrar & Rinehart.

Sidak, J. Gregory, and David Teece. 2005. 'Favouring Dynamic Competition over Static Competition in Antitrust Law'. In R. Ian McEwin (ed.), *Intellectual Property, Competition Law and Economics in Asia*. Oxford: Hart Publishing, pp. 53–94.

Silbey, Susan S. 2005. 'After Legal Consciousness'. *Annual Review of Law and Social Science* 1: 323–68.

Sindzingre, Alice. 2010. 'The Concept of Neopatrimonialism: Divergences and Convergences with Development Economics'. Paper presented at the GIGA (German Institute of Global and Area Studies) workshop 'Neopatrimonialism in Various World Regions'. Hamburg, 23 August 2010. Available at www.giga-hamburg.de/content/fsp1/pdf/neopat/paper_neopat_workshop_sindzingre.pdf (accessed 12 July 2012).

Skowronek, Stephen. 1982. *Building a New American State: The Expansion of National Administrative Capacities, 1877–1920*. Cambridge University Press.

Slaughter, Anne-Marie. 2004. *A New World Order*. Princeton University Press.

Smith, Adam. 1976 [1776]. *An Inquiry into the Nature and Causes of the Wealth of Nations*, 2 vols. Oxford: Clarendon Press.

So, Alvin. 2009. 'Rethinking the Chinese Development Miracle'. In Hung Ho-fung (ed.), *China and the Transformation of Global Capitalism*. Baltimore: Johns Hopkins University Press, pp. 50–63.

Song, Bing. 1995. 'Competition Policy in a Transitional Economy: The Case of China'. *Stanford Journal of International Law* 31: 387–422.

Souty, François. 2011. 'From the Halls of Geneva to the Shores of the Low Countries: The Origins of the International Competition Network'. In Paul Lugard (ed.), *The International Competition Network at Ten: Origins, Accomplishments and Aspirations*. Cambridge: Intersentia, pp. 39–50.

'State Administration for Industry & Commerce [SAIC] Report: Multinational Giants Show Signs of Monopolizing China's Markets [Guojia Gongshang Zongju Baogao: Kuaguo Jutou Zai Hua Jian Xian Longduan Taishi]'. 2004. *Xinwen Chenbao* (News Morning Daily), 15 November. Available at http://news.xinhua net.com/fortune/2004-11/15/content_2221465.htm (accessed 14 June 2012).

'State Businesses from the Core of the Economy'. 2010. *Voice of Vietnam Online*, March 10. Available at http://english.vov.vn/Home/State-businesses-form-the-core-of-economy/20103/113374.vov (accessed 15 June 2012).

'State Economic & Trade Commission Abolishes Nine National Bureaus Including Domestic Distribution Bureau [Jingmaowei Chexiao Guojia Guonei Maoyi ju Deng Jiu Ge Guojia Ju]'. 2001. *Sina*, 19 February. Available at http://finance.sina.com.cn/g/37340.html (accessed 14 June 2012).

Steinmo, Sven, and Kathleen Thelen. 1992. 'Historical Institutionalism in Comparative Politics'. In Sven Steinmo, Kathleen Thelen, and Frank Longstreth (eds.), *Structuring Politics*. Cambridge University Press, pp. 1–32.

Stephan, Andreas. 2008. 'Survey of Public Attitudes to Price-Fixing and Cartel Enforcement in Britain'. *Competition Law Review* 5: 123–45.

———. 2011. '"The Battle for Hearts and Minds": The Role of the Media in Treating Cartels as Criminal'. In Caron Beaton-Wells and Ariel Ezrachi (eds.), *Criminalising Cartels: Critical Studies of an International Regulatory Movement*. Oxford: Hart Publishing, pp. 381–94.

———. 2011. 'How Dishonesty Killed the Cartel Offence'. *Criminal Law Review* 6: 446–55.

Stubbs, Richard. 2009. 'What Ever Happened to the East Asian Developmental State? The Unfolding Debate'. *Pacific Review* 22: 1–22.

Sum, Ngai-Ling. 2005. 'From Regulation Approach to Cultural Political Economy'. EU Framework 6 DEMLOGOS Project, Work Package 1. Available at http://demologos.ncl.ac.uk/wp/wp1/papers/cpe2.pdf.

———. 2009. 'The Production of Hegemonic Policy Discourses: "Competitiveness" as a Knowledge Brand and its (Re)Contextualizations'. *Critical Policy Studies* 3: 50–76.

Sum, Ngai-Ling, and Bob Jessop. 2013. *Towards a Cultural Political Economy*. Cheltenham: Edward Elgar.

Sun Zidou. 1993. 'Causes of Trade Wars over Farm Products, Their Harmful Effects, and Suggested Solutions'. *Chinese Economy* 26: 95–104.

Suzumura, Kōtaro. 1997. 'Formal and Informal Measures for Controlling Competition in Japan: Institutional Overview and Theoretical Evaluation'. In Edward M. Graham and J. David Richardson (eds.), *Global Competition Policy*. Washington, DC: Institute for International Economics, pp. 439–74.

Swedberg, Richard. 1998. *Max Weber and the Idea of Economic Sociology*. Princeton University Press.

Takigawa, Toshiaki, and Mark Williams (eds.). 2009. *Antitrust Bulletin* 54 (1), Symposium Part I: Asian Competition Laws.

Tam, Waikeung, and Dali Yang. 2005. 'Food Safety and the Development of Regulatory Institutions in China'. *Asian Perspectives* 29: 5–36.

Tan Duc and Thien Nhan. 2005. 'Competition Law: Concerns over Its Implementation [Luat Canh Tranh: Ban khoan Cau chuyen thuc hien]', 2 August. Available at http://vietbao.vn/Kinh-te/Luat-canh-tranh-ban-khoan-chuyen-thuc-hien/20474629/87/ (accessed 20 June 2012).

Taussig, Markus. 2009. *A Policy Discussion Paper: Business Strategy During Radical Economic Transition: Viet Nam's First Generation of Larger Private Manufacturers and a Decade of Intensifying Opportunities and Competition*. Hanoi: United Nations Development Programme Viet Nam. Available at www.undp.org.vn/digitalAssets/19/19020_Business_strategies_during_radical_economic_transition-final.pdf (accessed 8 November 2012).

Taylor, Marcus, and Susanne Soederberg. 2007. 'The King is Dead (Long Live the King?): From Wolfensohn to Wolfowitz at the World Bank'. In David Moore (ed.), *The World Bank: Development, Poverty, Hegemony*, Scottsville: University of KwaZulu-Natal Press, pp. 453–78.

Taylor, Michael. 1999. 'The Small Firm as a Temporary Coalition'. *Entrepreneurship and Regional Development* 11: 1–19.

Taylor, Michael, and Bjorn T. Asheim. 2001. 'The Concept of the Firm in Economic Geography'. *Economic Geography* 77: 315–28.

'Technology Agency Hopes To Boost R&D By Expanding Thailand Science Park'. 2009. *Nation*, 12 May. Available at www.nationmultimedia.com/2009/05/12/business/business_30102450.php (accessed 19 June 2012).

Teles, Steven M. 2008. *The Rise of the Conservative Legal Movement: The Battle for Control of Law*. Princeton University Press.

Teubner, Gunther. 2001. 'Legal Irritants: How Unifying Law Ends up in New Divergences'. In Peter A. Hall and David W. Soskice (eds.), *Varieties of Capitalism: The Institutional Foundations of Comparative Advantage*. Oxford University Press, pp. 417–41.

Thatcher, Mark, and Alex Stone Sweet. 2002. 'Theory and Practice of Delegation to Non-Majoritarian Institutions'. *West European Politics* 25: 1–22.

Thompson, Drew, and Hu Ying. 2007. 'Food Safety in China: New Strategies'. *Global Health Governance* 1 (issue 2): www.ghgj.org/Thompson_and_Ying.htm (accessed 28 June 2012).

Thünen, Johann Heinrich von. 1966 [1826]. *Von Thunen's Isolated State: An English Edition of Der Isolierte Staat*, ed. Peter Hall, trans. Carla M. Wartenberg. Oxford: Pergamon Press.

Trebilcock, Michael J., and Edward M. Iacobucci. 2002. 'Designing Competition Law Institutions'. *World Competition* 25: 361–94.

2010. 'Designing Competition Law Institutions: Values, Structure, and Mandate'. *Loyola University Chicago Law Journal* 41: 455–71.

'Twenty-Three of China's Largest Aluminum Electrode Manufacturers to Jointly Reduce Production by Ten Percent [Zhongguo 23 Jia Dianjielü Gugan Qiye Jiang Lianhe Jianchan 10%]'. 2005. 2 December. Available at http://news.xinhuanet.com/fortune/2005-12/02/content_3868498.htm (accessed 15 June 2012).

Tyler, Tom R. 2006. 'Psychological Perspectives on Legitimacy and Legitimating'. *Annual Review of Psychology* 57: 375–400.

Uesugi, Akinori. 2005. 'How Japan Is Tackling Enforcement Activities Against Cartels'. *George Mason Law Review* 13: 349–65.

UNCTAD (United Nations Conference on Trade and Development). 2004. Model Law on Competition: Substantive Possible Elements for a Competition Law, Commentaries and Alternative Approaches in Existing Legislations. United Nations Publications. Available at http://r0.unctad.org/en/subsites/cpolicy/docs/Modelaw04.pdf (accessed 11 June 2012).

2006. *World Investment Report 2006: FDI from Developing and Transition Economies: Implications for Development.* New York: United Nations.

2008. *Investment Policy Review: Viet Nam.* New York: United Nations Publications.

2009. *World Investment Report 2009: Transnational Corporations, Agricultural Production and Development.* New York: United Nations.

United Nations, Office of Resident Coordinator in China. 2008. 'Occasional Paper: Advancing Food Safety In China'. March. Available at www.un.org.cn/cms/p/resources/30/841/content.html (accessed 27 June 2012).

United States Department of Justice. 2011. 'Press Release: Justice Department Requires Deutsche Börse to Divest its Interest in Direct Edge in Order to Merge with NYSE Euronext'. 22 December. Available at www.justice.gov/atr/public/press_releases/2011/278537.htm.

Upham, Frank K. 1996. 'Privatized Regulation: Japanese Regulatory Style in Comparative Perspective'. *Fordham International Law Journal* 20: 396–511.

2009. 'From Demsetz to Deng: Speculations on the Source'. *New York University Journal of International Law and Politics* 41: 512–602.

Vande Walle, Simon. 2011. 'Private Enforcement of Antitrust Law in Japan: An Empirical Analysis'. *The Competition Law Review* 8: 7–28.

Veltz, Pierre. 1996. *Mondialisation, villes et territoires: l'économie d'archipel.* Paris: Presses Universitaires de France.

Voss, Hinrich. 2011. *The Determinants of Chinese Outward Direct Investment.* Cheltenham: Edward Elgar.

Wade, Robert. 1990. *Governing the Market: Economic Theory and the Role of Government in East Asian Industrialization.* Princeton University Press.

2007. 'The WTO and the Shrinking of Development Space'. In J. Timmons Roberts and Amy Bellone Hite (eds.), *The Globalization and Development Reader.* Malden, MA: Blackwell Publishing, pp. 277–94.

Wakui, Masako. 2008. *Antimonopoly Law – Competition Law and Policy in Japan.* Bury St Edmunds: abramis.

Waller, Spencer W. 2001. 'The Language of Law and the Language of Business'. *Case Western Law Review* 52: 283–338.

Wang, Xiaoye. 2008. 'Highlights of China's New Anti-Monopoly Law'. *Antitrust Law Journal* 75: 133–50.

Wanner, Thomas K. 2007. 'The Bank's Greenspeak and Sustainable Development'. In David Moore (ed.), *The World Bank: Development, Poverty, Hegemony.* Scottsville: University of KwaZulu-Natal Press, pp. 145–70.

Watson, Alan. 1974. *Legal Transplants: An Approach to Comparative Law.* Edinburgh: Scottish Academic Press.

Weber, Max. 1978 [1922]. *Economy and Society: An Outline of Interpretive Sociology,* 2 vols., ed. Guenther Roth and Claus Wittich, trans. Ephraim Fischoff et al. Berkeley: University of California Press.

Weiss, Linda. 1998. *The Myth of the Powerless State: Governing the Economy in a Global Era*. Cambridge: Polity Press.

2003. 'Is the State being "Transformed" by Globalisation?'. In Linda Weiss (ed.), *States in the Global Economy: Bringing Domestic Institutions Back In*. Cambridge University Press, pp. 293–317.

(ed.). 2003. *States in the Global Economy: Bringing Domestic Institutions Back In*. Cambridge University Press.

Wen, Xueguo. 2008. 'Market Dominance by China's Public Utility Enterprises'. *Antitrust Law Journal* 75: 151–71.

Wenzel, Michael. 2002. 'The Impact of Outcome Orientation and Justice Concerns on Tax Compliance: The Role of Taxpayer's Identity'. *Journal of Applied Psychology* 87: 629–45.

'When Innovation, Too, Is Made in China'. 2011. *New York Times*, 2 January, B3. Available at www.nytimes.com/2011/01/02/business/02unboxed.html (accessed 19 June 2012).

Whish, Richard. 2012. *Competition Law*, 7th edn. Oxford University Press.

Whitman, James Q. 2007. 'Consumerism versus Producerism: A Study in Comparative Law'. *Yale Law Journal* 117: 340–406.

Wilks, Stephen. 1999. *In the Public Interest: Competition Policy and the Monopolies and Mergers Commission*. Manchester University Press.

Wilks, Stephen, and Ian Bartle. 2002. 'The Unanticipated Consequences of Creating Independent Competition Agencies'. *West European Politics* 25: 148–72

Williams, Eric Sean. 2011. *The End of Society? Defining and Tracing the Development of Fragmentation through the Modern and into the Post-modern Era*. Ann Arbor: UMI Dissertation Publishing.

Williams, Mark. 2004. 'Competition Policy: One Theory, Three Systems'. *China Perspectives* 51: 51–63.

2005. *Competition Policy and Law in China, Hong Kong and Taiwan*. Cambridge University Press.

2011. 'Hong Kong's Competition Bill: Lobbying, Opposition, Politics'. Paper delivered at Global Competition Law and Economics Series Conference, 'Competition Law and the State', Hong Kong, 19–21 March 2011. Synopsis available at www.ucl.ac.uk/laws/global-competition/hongkong-2011/secure/docs/5_williams.pdf (accessed 20 June 2012).

Williamson, Oliver E. 1985. *The Economic Institutions of Capitalism*. New York: Free Press.

1991. 'Comparative Economic Organization: The Analysis of Discrete Structural Alternatives'. *Administrative Science Quarterly* 36: 269–96.

Wong, Christine P. W. 1992. 'Fiscal Reform and Local Industrialization: The Problematic Sequencing of Reform in Post-Mao China'. *Modern China* 18: 197–227.

Wong, Edward. 2008. 'Courts Compound Pains of China's Tainted Milk'. *New York Times*, 17 October, A1.

Woo-Cumings, Meredith (ed.). 1999. *The Developmental State*. Ithaca, NY: Cornell University Press.

Wood, B. Dan, and James E. Anderson. 1993. 'The Politics of U.S. Antitrust Regulation'. *American Journal of Political Science* 3: 1–39.

Wood, Ellen. 2002. *The Origin of Capitalism: A Longer View*, rev. edn. London: Verso.

World Bank. 1994. *China: Internal Market Development and Regulation*. Washington DC: World Bank Publications.

2004. *World Development Report 2005: A Better Investment Climate for Everyone*. Oxford University Press.

2004–. *Doing Business*. Washington, DC: World Bank and International Finance Corporation.

Wu, Yongping. 2005. *Political Explanation of Economic Growth: State Survival, Bureaucratic Politics, and Private Enterprises in the Making of Taiwan's Economy, 1950–1985*. Cambridge, MA: Harvard University Asia Center.

Wu, Zhenguo. 2008. 'Perspectives on the Chinese Antimonopoly Law'. *Antitrust Law Journal* 75: 73–116.

Xiao, Geng, Xiuke Yang, and Anna Janus. 2009. 'State-Owned Enterprises in China: Reform Dynamics and Impacts'. In Ross Garnaut, Ligang Song, and Wing Thye Woo (eds.), *China's New Place in a World in Crisis*. Canberra: ANU E-Press, pp. 155–78.

Xin, Hao, and Richard Stone. 2008. 'Tainted Milk Scandal: Chinese Probe Unmasks High-Tech Adulteration with Melamine'. *Science*, 28 November, 1310–11.

Xiu, Changbai, and K. K. Klein. 2010. 'Melamine in Milk Products in China: Examining the Factors that Led to Deliberate Use of the Contaminant'. *Food Policy* 35: 463–70.

Yang, Dali L. 2004. *Reshaping the Chinese Leviathan*. Stanford University Press.

Yeung, Henry Wai-chung. 2002. *Entrepreneurship and the Internationalisation of Asian Firms: An Institutional Perspective*. Cheltenham: Edward Elgar.

2004. *Chinese Capitalism in a Global Era: Towards Hybrid Capitalism*. London: Routledge.

2004. 'Strategic Governance and Economic Diplomacy in China: The Political Economy of Government-Linked Companies from Singapore'. *East Asia: An International Quarterly* 21: 40–64.

2005. 'Institutional Capacity and Singapore's Developmental State: Managing Economic (In)Security in the Global Economy'. In Helen E. S. Nesadurai (ed.), *Globalisation and Economic Security in East Asia: Governance and Institutions*. London: Routledge, pp. 85–106.

2005. 'Rethinking Relational Economic Geography'. *Transactions of the Institute of British Geographers*, New Series 30: 37–51.

2007. 'From Followers to Market Leaders: Asian Electronics Firms in the Global Economy'. *Asia Pacific Viewpoint* 48: 1–25.

2007. 'Remaking Economic Geography: Insights from East Asia'. *Economic Geography* 83: 339–48.

2008. 'Industrial Clusters and Production Networks in Southeast Asia: A Global Production Networks Approach'. In Ikuo Kuroiwa and Mun Heng Toh (eds.), *Production Networks and Industrial Clusters: Integrating Economies in Southeast Asia*. Singapore: Institute of Southeast Asian Studies, pp. 83–120.

2009. 'Regional Development and the Competitive Dynamics of Global Production Networks: An East Asian Perspective'. *Regional Studies* 43: 325–51.

2009. 'The Rise of East Asia: An Emerging Challenge to the Study of International Political Economy'. In Mark Blyth (ed.), *Routledge Handbook of International Political Economy*. London: Routledge, pp. 201–15.

2009. 'Transnationalizing Entrepreneurship: A Critical Agenda for Economic Geography'. *Progress in Human Geography* 33: 210–35.

Yoshino, Naoyuki, and Eisuke Sakakibara. 2002. 'The Current State of the Japanese Economy and Remedies'. *Asian Economic Papers* 1: 110–26.

Yotopoulos, Pan A., and Sagrario L. Floro. 1992. 'Income Distribution, Transaction Costs and Market Fragmentation in Informal Credit Markets'. *Cambridge Journal of Economics* 16: 303–26.

Yusuf, Shahid. 2008. 'Can Clusters be Made to Order?'. In Shahid Yusuf, Kaoru Nabeshima, and Shoichi Yamashita (eds.), *Growing Industrial Clusters in Asia: Serendipity and Science*. Washington, DC: World Bank Publications, pp. 1–37.

Zhang, Qing. 2005. 'A Chinese Yuppie in Beijing: Phonological Variation and the Construction of a New Professional Identity'. *Language in Society* 34: 431–66.

Zhang, Xianchu. 2007. 'Commentary on "Legislating for a Market Economy in China"'. *China Quarterly* 191: 586–9.

II. Legislation and international acts

China

Antimonopoly Law of the People's Republic of China [Zhonghua Renmin Gongheguo Fanlongduan Fa]. Effective 1 August 2008. Available at www.gov.cn/flfg/2007-08/30/content_732591.htm (accessed 13 June 2012). Unofficial

English translation available at https://www.amcham-china.org.cn/amcham/ upload/wysiwyg/20070906152846.pdf (accessed 14 June 2012).

Anti-Unfair Competition Law of the People's Republic of China [Zhonghua Renmin Gongheguo Fanbu Zhengdang Jingzheng Fa]. Effective 1 December 1993. Available at www.saic.gov.cn/fldyfbzdjz/. English translation available at http://en.chinacourt.org/public/detail.php?id=3306 (accessed 13 June 2012).

Price Law of the People's Republic of China [Zhonghua Renmin Gongheguo Jiage Fa]. Effective 1 May 1999. Available at www.gov.cn/banshi/2005-09/12/ content_69757.htm (accessed 13 June 2012).

Provisional Provisions on Prohibition of Monopoly Pricing [Zhizhi Jiage Longduan Xingwei Zhanxing Guiding]. National Development and Reform Commission [Guojia Fazhan he Gaige Weiyuanhui] Order No. 3 (18 June 2003). Available at www.jincao.com/fa/09/law09.47.htm (accessed 14 June 2012).

Provisions on Acquisitions of Domestic Enterprises by Foreign Investors [Guanyu Waiguo Touzizhe Binggou Jingnei Giye De Guiding]. Ministry of Commerce [Shangwu Bu] Order No. 10 (6 August 2006). English translation available at www.sipf.com.cn/en/lawsandregulations/linvestors/otherlaw-sandregu/10/6658.shtml (accessed 14 June 2012).

European Union

Council Regulation No 1/2003 of 16 December 2002 on the implementation of the rules on competition laid down in Articles 81 and 82 of the Treaty. *Official Journal of the European Union* 46 (2003): L 1 (4 January), L 1/1–L 1/25.

Council Regulation No 139/2004 of 20 January 2004 on the control of concentrations between undertakings (the EC Merger Regulation). *Official Journal of the European Union* 47 (2004): L 24 (29 January), L 24/1–L 24/22.

Treaty of Amsterdam amending the Treaty on European Union, the Treaties Establishing the European Communities and Certain Related Acts. 1997. *Official Journal of the European Union* 40 (1997): C 340 (10 November), C 340/1–C 340/144.

Treaty of Lisbon amending the Treaty on European Union and the Treaty establishing the European Community, Protocol on Services of General Interest. 2007. *Official Journal of the European Union* 50 (2007): C 306 (17 December), pp. C 306/158–C 306/159.

Treaty on the Functioning of the European Union (Consolidated Versions). 2008. *Official Journal of the European Union* 51 (2008): C 115 (9 May), C 115/1–C 115/12.

Hong Kong

Competition Ordinance (Hong Kong). 2012. Ordinance No. 14 of 2012. *Government of Hong Kong Special Administrative Region Gazette*, 22 June 2012, Legal Supplement No. 1, A1323–A1609.

Japan

Act Concerning the Adjustment of Retail Business Activities of Large-scale Retail Stores [Daikibo kouritenpo ni okeru kourigyō no jigyōkatsudō no chōsei ni kan suru hōritsu]. Law No. 109 of 1973 (repealed by Law No. 91 of 1998).

Act against Delay in Payment of Subcontract Proceeds, etc. to Subcontractors [Shitauke daikin shiharai chien nado bōshi hō]. Law No. 120 of 1956.

Act for the Elimination of Excessive Concentration of Economic Power [Kado keizai shūchū haijo hō]. Law No. 207 of 1947. Translated into English in T. A. Bisson, *Zaibatsu Dissolution in Japan* (Westwood, CT: Greenwood Press, 1976).

Act on the Measures by Large-Scale Retail Stores for Preservation of the Living Environment [Daikibo kouritenpo ricchi hō]. Law No. 91 of 1998.

Act to Partially Amend the Act on the Prohibition of Private Monopolization and Maintenance of Fair Trade [Shiteki dokusen no kinshi oyobi kōsei torihiki no kakuho ni kan suru hōritsu no ichibu wo kaisei suru hōritsu]. Law No. 259 of 1953.

Act to Partially Amend the Act on the Prohibition of Private Monopolization and Maintenance of Fair Trade [Shiteki dokusen no kinshi oyobi kōsei torihiki no kakuho ni kan suru hōritsu no ichibu wo kaisei suru hōritsu]. Law No. 63 of 1977.

Act to Partially Amend the Act on the Prohibition of Private Monopolization and Maintenance of Fair Trade [Shiteki dokusen no kinshi oyobi kōsei torihiki no kakuho ni kan suru hōritsu no ichibu wo kaisei suru hōritsu]. Law No. 51 of 2009.

Act on Prohibition of Private Monopolization and Maintenance of Fair Trade [Shiteki dokusen no kinshi oyobi kōsei torihiki no kakuho ni kan suru hōritsu]. Law No. 54 of 1947. Translated into English at www.jftc.go.jp/e-page/legislation (accessed 12 June 2012).

Export–Import Transactions Act [Yushutsunyū torihiki hō]. Law No. 299 of 1952.

Small and Medium Enterprises Organization Act [Chūshō kigyō dantai soshikihō]. Law No. 185 of 1957.

Special Measures Act for the Stabilization of Designated Medium and Smaller Enterprises [Tokutei chūshō kigyō no antei ni kan suru rinji sochi hō]. Law No. 294 of 1952. Repealed by Law No. 185 of 1957.

Trade Association Act [Jigyōsha dantai hō]. Law No. 191 of 1948. Repealed by Law No. 259 of 1953. Partly translated into English in Masako Wakui, *Antimonopoly Law – Competition Law and Policy in Japan* (Bury St Edmunds: abramis, 2008), p. 319.

South Korea

Monopoly Regulation and Fair Trade Act [Dokcheom gyuje mit gongjeong georae beomnyul]. Act No. 3320 (as amended). Promulgated on 31 December 1980;

last amended 26 August 2002. English translation available at http://subject.
wanfangdata.com.cn/Antimonopoly/images/%E9%9F%A9%E5%9B%BD
Monopoly%20Regulation%20and%20Fair%20Trade%20Act%EF%BC%88
UNPAN011494%EF%BC%89.pdf (accessed 20 June 2012).

Singapore

Competition Act (Chapter 50b). Originally enacted as Act 46 of 2004, revised in
2006.

South Africa

Competition Act. Act No. 89 of 1998. Amended by Competition Amendment Act,
Act No 35 of 1999, Competition Amendment Act, Act No. 15 of 2000, and
Competition Second Amendment Act, Act No. 39 of 2000.

Taiwan

Fair Trade Act [Gongping Jiaoyi Fa]. Promulgated on 4 February 1991; last
amended 23 November 2011. English translation available at http://law.
moj.gov.tw/Eng/LawClass/LawAll.aspx?PCode=J0150002 (accessed 20 June
2012).

United Kingdom

Competition Act 1998. 1998 Chapter 41 (as amended).
Enterprise Act 2002. 2002 Chapter 40 (as amended).
Enterprise Act 2002 (Specification of Additional Section 58 Consideration) Order
2008 (UK). 2008 No. 2645.

United Nations

International Covenant on Economic, Social and Cultural Rights. GA Res. 2200A
(XXI), at 49, UN GAOR, 21st Sess., Supp. No. 16, UN Doc. A/6316 (16
December 1966).
Universal Declaration of Human Rights. GA Res. 217A(u1), UN Doc. 810 (10
December 1948).

United States

Administrative Procedures Act. Pub. L. 79–404, 60 Stat. 237 (5 USC §551 et seq.).
Enacted 11 June 1946.

Clayton Antitrust Act of 1914. Pub. L. 63–212, 38 Stat. 730 (15 USC §§12–27, 29 USC §§ 52–53). Enacted 15 October 1914.

Sherman Antitrust Act. 26 Stat. 209 (15 USC §§ 1–7). Enacted 2 July 1890.

United States Code (USC). Title 15, Chapter 1 – Monopolies and Combinations in Restraint of Trade (15 USC §§ 1–38).

Vietnam

Circular No. 2 on the Management of Construction Projects [Những quản lý dự án Xây dựng]. Ministry of Construction [Bộ Xây dựng]. 29 January 1993.

Competition Law [Luật Cuộc thi] (Vietnam). No. 27/2004/QH11. Effective 1 July 2005. English translation available at www.wipo.int/clea/docs_new/pdf/en/vn/vn057en.pdf (accessed 15 June 2012).

Decision 146 on Developing a Household Economy [Phát triển một kinh tế hộ gia đình] (Vietnam). Council of Ministers [Hội đồng những bộ trưởng]. 26 November 1986.

Decree 88-1999-ND-CP of the Government Promulgating the Regulations on Tenders [Chính phủ công bố những sự điều chỉnh trên những sự đầu thầu]. Central Government [Chinh Phu]. 1 September 1999.

Law on Tendering [Luật trên việc bỏ thầu] (Vietnam). No. 61-2005-QH11. Effective 1 July 2006.

III. Cases and judicial opinions
Australia

McCabe *v.* British American Tobacco Australia Services Limited. [2002] VSC 73 (22 March 2002); No. 8121 of 2001.

European Union

A. Ahlstrom OY and others *v.* EC Commission (Cases 89/85, 104/85, 114/85, 116–117/85 & 125–129/85). [1988] ECR 5193.

Albany International BV *v.* Stichting Bedrijfspensioenfonds Textielindustrie (Case C-67/96). [1999] ECR I-5751.

Altmark Trans GmbH and Regierungspräsidium Magdeburg *v.* Nahverkehrsgesellschaft Altmark GmbH (Case C-280/00). [2003] ECR I-7747.

Belgium *v.* Humbel (Case 263/86). [1988] ECR 5365.

British United Provident Association Ltd (BUPA) and Others *v.* Commission (Case T-289/03). [2008] ECR II-81.

Diego Cali and Figli Srl *v.* Servizi Ecologici Porto di Genova SpA (SEPG) (Case C-343/95). [1997] ECR I-1547.

Federación Española de Empresas de Tecnología Sanitaria (FENIN) *v.* Commission of the European Communities (Case C-205/03). [2006] ECR I-6295.

Gencor/Lonrho (Case IV/M.619) (EU), Commission Decision of 24 April 1996 declaring a concentration to be incompatible with the common market and the functioning of the EEA Agreement. *Official Journal of the European Union* 40 (1997): L 11 (14 January), L 11/30–L 11/72.

General Electric/Honeywell (Case COMP/M.2220) (EU). Commission Decision of 3 July 2001 declaring a concentration to be incompatible with the common market and the EEA Agreement. *Official Journal of the European Union* 47 (2004): L 48 (18 February), L 48/1–L 48/85.

Imperial Chemical Industries Ltd. *v.* Commission of the European Communities (Case 48/69). [1972] ECR 619.

Poucet and Pistre *v.* Assurances Générales de France and Others (joined cases C-2159/91 and 1260/91). [1993] ECR I-637.

SAT Fluggesellschaft mbH *v.* European Org. for the Safety of Air Navigation (Eurocontrol) (Case C-364/92). [1994] ECR I-43.

Sodemare and Others *v.* Regione Lombardia (Case C-70/95). [1997] ECR I-3395.

Hong Kong

Clean Air Foundation Ltd *v.* The Government of the HKSAR (Hong Kong). HCAL No.35 of 2007, unreported (26 July 2007).

Japan

Japan *v.* Idemitsu Kōsan K.K. 28(2) Shinketsushū 299, 985 Hanrei Jihō 3, 8 (Tokyo H. Ct., 26 September 1980), aff'd in part and rev'd in part, 30 Shinketsushū 244, 1108 Hanrei Jihō 3 (Japan Sup. Ct., 24 February 1984). Translated in J. Mark Ramseyer, 'The Oil Cartel Criminal Cases: Translations and Postscript', in John O. Haley, (ed.), *Law and Society in Contemporary Japan: American Perspectives* (Dubuque, IA: Kendall/Hunt Pub. Co.), pp. 74–78.

Japan *v.* Toppan mūa et al. 840 Hanrei Taimuzu 81, 88 (Tokyo High Ct, 14 December 1993).

K. K. Asahi shimbunsha et al. *v.* JFTC. 2 Hanrei Jihō 8 (Tokyo High Ct, 9 March 1953).

Satō *v.* Sekiyu renmei. 43(11) Minshū 1340 (Yamagata District Ct., 31 March 1981), rev'd 43(11) Minshū 1539 (Sendai High Ct., 26 March 1985), rev'd sub nom. *Nihon sekiyu K.K., v. Satō*, 43(11) Minshū 1259 (Sup. Ct., 8 December 1989).

United Kingdom

BetterCare Group Limited *v.* Director General of Fair Trading. [2002] CAT 7.
O'Reilly *v.* Mackman. [1983] 2 AC 237

United States

F. Hoffmann-La Roche Ltd. *v.* Empagran SA. 542 US 155 (2004).
Rausch *v.* Gardner., 267 F. Supp. 4 (E.D. Wis. 1967).
United States *v.* Aluminium Company of America (Alcoa). 148 F.2d 416 (2d Cir.
    1945).

INDEX

CPSIA information can be obtained
at www.ICGtesting.com
Printed in the USA
LVHW042039290719
625737LV00017B/435